# THE
# DESERTS
## OF CALIFORNIA

ALSO BY OBI KAUFMANN

*The Coasts of California: A California Field Atlas* (2022)

*The Forests of California: A California Field Atlas* (2020)

*The State of Water:*
*Understanding California's Most Precious Resource* (2019)

*The California Field Atlas* (2017)

# THE
# DESERTS
## OF CALIFORNIA

### Written and Illustrated
### by Obi Kaufmann

Heyday
Berkeley, California

Library of Congress Cataloging-in-Publication Data

Names: Kaufmann, Obi, author.
Title: The deserts of California : a California field atlas / written and illustrated by Obi Kaufmann.
Description: Berkeley, California : Heyday, [2023] | Series: The California lands trilogy; 3 | Includes bibliographical references.
Identifiers: LCCN 2022059822 | ISBN 9781597146180
Subjects: LCSH: Deserts--California. | Arid regions biodiversity--California--Maps.
Classification: LCC QH105.C2 K364 2023 | DDC 577.54/09794--dc23/eng/20230111
LC record available at https://lccn.loc.gov/2022059822


Cover Art: Obi Kaufmann
Cover Design: Ashley Ingram
Interior Design/Typesetting: Obi Kaufmann and Ashley Ingram

Published by Heyday
P.O. Box 9145, Berkeley, California 94709
(510) 549-3564
heydaybooks.com

Printed in China by Imago

10 9 8 7 6 5 4 3 2 1

FSC
www.fsc.org
MIX
Paper from
responsible sources
FSC® C005748

for Alli

## *Ethical presumptions of* The Deserts of California

*The Deserts of California* presumes that hope, like healing, relies on time. If there is time, there is hope. Although every desert habitat type is threatened, very little of it is yet extinct. Despite the complexity of the threat, everywhere there is precedent for resurgence.

The body of the desert does not exist as an object. It exists, as does the human body, as living space within a continuum of injury and regeneration.

# CONTENTS

Introduction  xv

*Keys and measures*  xxvi

00.01 An Acknowledged Truth: *Land of the people*
00.02 Ages of the Earth: *A geologic history of California's deserts*
00.03 Reading the Maps: *A key to the map icons*
00.04 National, State, and Regional Land Management:
        *California Desert Conservation Area*
00.05 Quadrangle Designations: *USGS California land measurement systems*
00.06 Special Concern for the Threatened and Endangered:
        *Desert animal species conservation*

01. The Dire and the Sublime: *Exploring California desert physiography*  1

    01.01 From the Arid to the Alpine: *California's desert regions*
        01.01a A Plurality of Adaptation:
            *The ecological sections of California's deserts*
        01.01b A Landscape of Compromise:
            *Major land designations of California's deserts*
        01.01c A Trend of Transformation:
            *The climate regions of California's deserts*
    01.02 Of Survival and Sun: *Arid lands of the West*
        01.02a An Ocean of Sagebrush:
            *The Great Basin Desert of the West*
        01.02b An Expanse of Yucca:
            *The Mojave Desert of the West*
        01.02c An Empire of Cactus:
            *The Sonoran Desert of the West*
    01.03 Global Belts of Wind and Weather: *Atmospheric circulation*
    01.04 World Map: *Deserts and botanic realms of the world*
    01.05 Life in the Rain Shadow: *Of physiography and climate*
        01.05a A Disappearing Baseline:
            *Precipitation patterns in California*
        01.05b Considering Drought in the Desert:
            *The West's drying climate*
    01.06 Earth Profile: *Peaks and topography of the desert*
        01.06a Kingdom of the Bighorn:
            *Desert-mountain sheep populations*
        01.06b Earth Puzzle: *Desert bedrock, faults, and soil*

01.07 The Age of Giants and Ice: *Mapping California's Last Glacial Maximum*
 01.07a Ancient Mohavia: *Paleogene California*
 01.07b Regarding Megafaunal Fruit:
  *Pleistocene distribution of Joshua trees*
01.08 Indigenous Regimes of Reciprocity:
 *Human–shrub management theory*

02. Every Sacred Drop: *California desert water* 53

02.01 A Thirst on the Land:
 *Potential evapotranspiration and the water deficit*
02.02 The High and Low Deserts:
 *Hydrologic regions of the Mojave and Sonoran Deserts*
02.03 Of Aquifers, Floodplains, and Geohydrology:
 *Groundwater basin estimates*
02.04 The Miracle of a Spring: *Surface saturation dynamics*
02.05 An Impossible Fish: *Pupfish biogeography*
02.06 The Sweetness of the Bitter Water: *The Amargosa River*
02.07 Reserves and Reservoirs: *The Colorado River in California*
 02.07a Desperately Needed, Desperately Taxed:
  *The Colorado River Watershed*
02.08 The Desert's Underground Artery: *The Mojave River*
02.09 Of Birds, Brine, and Beauty: *Mono Lake*
02.10 Rivers on the Edge: *Five desert rivers in California*
02.11 Desiccation and Desertification:
 *Owens River, Owens Valley, and Owens Lake*
02.12 A History of Incessant Injury: *The Salton Sea Watershed*
 02.12a Saving the Sea, Saving Ourselves: *Salton Sea Restoration*
 02.12b A Four-Million-Year Pulse: *Lake Cahuilla*

03. The Living Network: *Desert plant habitats* 109

03.01 Modeling Desert Life: *Conceptual ecology*
03.02 Survival Techniques: *Desert plant adaptations*
 03.02a Spines, Thorns, and Barbs: *The mechanical defense line*
03.03 Plant Patterns on the Land:
 *Generalized vegetation of California's desert regions*
03.04 Plant Patterns at Elevation: *Biozones*
 03.04a One Staircase of the Living Desert:
  *Botanical biozones of San Jacinto's eastern slope*
 03.04b Another Staircase of the Living Desert:
  *Botanical biozones of the Mojave Desert Preserve*
03.05 Working Together: *Defining ecosections and plant alliances*

03.05a Ecological Subsections of the Deserts of
Southeastern California
03.05b Ecological Subsections of the Deserts of
Northeastern California
03.06 All in the Family: *Taxonomic families of representative desert plants*
03.07 Protected Pieces of the Whole:
*Ecological reserves in the northwestern Mojave Desert*
03.08 Poppies and People: *Southern Antelope Valley*
03.08a Antelope Valley California Poppy State Natural Reserve
03.09 Palm Oasis: *Desert wetland habitat*
03.10 Mojave's Signature Yucca: *Notes on the Joshua tree*
03.11 Great Basin's Perfect Plant: *Notes on sagebrush*
03.12 Fire and Food in the Desert Forest: *Piñon-juniper woodland*
03.13 Biological Wonder of the World: *Notes on creosote*
03.14 Life in Shifting Mountains: *Sand dune habitat*

04. Big Desert Parcels of Federal and State Land:
*Parks, monuments, and military inholdings*  163

04.01 The Preservation of Desert Public Lands:
*National and state parks and monuments*
04.02 Anza-Borrego Desert State Park—overview
04.02a Anza-Borrego Desert State Park—quadrangles
04.02b Anza-Borrego Desert State Park—
NW mountains and water
04.02c Anza-Borrego Desert State Park—
NE mountains and water
04.02d Anza-Borrego Desert State Park—
SW mountains and water
04.02e Anza-Borrego Desert State Park—
SE mountains and water
04.03 Castle Mountains National Monument
04.04 Death Valley National Park—overview
04.04a Death Valley National Park—quadrangles
04.04b Death Valley National Park—NW mountains and water
04.04c Death Valley National Park—NE mountains and water
04.04d Death Valley National Park—SW mountains and water
04.04e Death Valley National Park—SE mountains and water
04.05 Joshua Tree National Park—overview
04.05a Joshua Tree National Park—quadrangles
04.05b Joshua Tree National Park—western mountains and water
04.05c Joshua Tree National Park—eastern mountains and water
04.06 Mojave National Preserve—overview
04.06a Mojave National Preserve—quadrangles

04.06b Mojave National Preserve—western mountains
    and water
04.06c Mojave National Preserve—eastern mountains
    and water
04.07 Mojave Trails National Monument—overview
    04.07a Mojave Trails National Monument—
        western mountains and water
    04.07b Mojave Trails National Monument—
        eastern mountains and water
04.08 Red Rock Canyon State Park
04.09 Sand to Snow National Monument
04.10 Santa Rosa and San Jacinto National Monument
04.11 Military Inholdings of the California Deserts—overview
    04.11a China Lake Naval Air Weapons Station (Navy)
    04.11b Fort Irwin National Training Center (Army)
    04.11c Edwards Air Force Base (Air Force)
    04.11d 29 Palms Air Ground Combat Center (Marines)
    04.11e Chocolate Mountains Gunnery Range (Marines)
    04.11f El Centro Naval Auxiliary Air Station (Navy)

## 05. Of Sagebrush and Solitude: *The Great Basin Desert in California*  239

05.01 Endorheic Basin and Range Lands: *Exploring America's largest desert*
05.02 Dry Forests, Sage Fields, and New Mountains:
    *Regional overview of the southeastern Great Basin Desert in California*
05.03 Dry Lakes, Black Rock, and Big Sagebrush:
    *Regional overview of the Great Basin Desert in northeastern California
    and northwestern Nevada*
05.04 Ecological Sensitivities: *Wilderness study areas of the southeastern
    Great Basin Desert in California*
05.05 Panamint Valley's West Side: *Argus Range Wilderness*
05.06 Gateway to Panamint Springs: *Darwin Falls Wilderness*
05.07 In the Rain Shadow of the Panamint Range:
    *Funeral Mountains Wilderness*
05.08 In View of Mono Lake: *Granite Mountain Wilderness*
05.09 Riparian Jewel over Searles Lake: *Great Falls Basin Wilderness*
05.10 High Mountains between the Owens and Saline Valleys:
    *Inyo Mountains Wilderness*
05.11 Volcanic Terminus of the Inyo Mountains: *Malpais Mesa Wilderness*
05.12 Southernmost Peak of the Panamint Range: *Manly Peak Wilderness*
05.13 Between the White and Inyo Mountains: *Piper Mountain
    Wilderness*

05.14  At the Western Foot of Telescope Peak: *Surprise Canyon Wilderness*

05.15  Remote Ridgeline at the State Border: *Sylvania Mountains Wilderness*

05.16  The Tallest of All Desert Ranges: *White Mountains Wilderness*

06. Of Resilience and Fragility: *The Mojave Desert in California*    285

06.01  A Desert Cut in Half: *The Mojave across four states*

06.02  Wilderness, Parks, Preserves, and Military Land:
*Land designations within the ecological Mojave in California*

06.03  Desert Peripheries: *Wilderness areas of the western Mojave*

06.04  At the Bend of the Amargosa River: *Avawatz Mountains Wilderness*

06.05  Cactus Lands South of the Mojave National Preserve:
*Bigelow Cholla Garden Wilderness*

06.06  Woodlands of the Southern Antelope Valley:
*Bighorn Mountain Wilderness*

06.07  Northeastern Antelope Valley: *Black Mountain Wilderness*

06.08  Western Continuance of the Mojave National Preserve:
*Bristol Mountains Wilderness*

06.09  Wild Gardens near the Colorado River:
*Chemehuevi Mountains Wilderness*

06.10  Dry Lakes North of Joshua Tree: *Cleghorn Lakes Wilderness*

06.11  Lonely Mountains South of the Mojave National Preserve:
*Clipper Mountain Wilderness*

06.12  Volcanic Plateau South of Owens Lake: *Coso Range Wilderness*

06.13  Between the Mojave National Preserve and the Colorado River:
*Dead Mountains Wilderness*

06.14  Mountain Range on the Garlock Fault: *El Paso Mountains Wilderness*

06.15  Wildlife Corridor South of Searles Valley: *Golden Valley Wilderness*

06.16  Desert Prairie North of Barstow: *Grass Valley Wilderness*

06.17  Between the Mojave National Preserve and Fort Irwin:
*Hollow Hills Wilderness*

06.18  North of the Bend in the Armargosa River: *Ibex Wilderness*

06.19  Bristol Mountains West of the Mojave National Preserve:
*Kelso Dunes Wilderness*

06.20  Mountainous Habitat Southeast of Death Valley:
*Kingston Range Wilderness*

06.21  Low Mountains East of the Kingston Range: *Mesquite Wilderness*

06.22  Craggy Mountains South of the Mojave River:
*Newberry Mountains Wilderness*

06.23  Dry Mountains East of Shoshone: *Nopah Range Wilderness*

06.24 Low Hills North of Clark Mountain:
  *North Mesquite Mountains Wilderness*
06.25 Between the Mojave and the Sonoran:
  *Old Woman Mountains Wilderness*
06.26 Bajadas North of Kingston Range: *Pahrump Valley Wilderness*
06.27 Sharing the Northern Border of Joshua Tree:
  *Pinto Mountains Wilderness*
06.28 Across the Fenner Valley, South of Mojave National Preserve:
  *Piute Mountains Wilderness*
06.29 Eastern Flank of the Amargosa Watershed:
  *Resting Spring Range Wilderness*
06.30 Lava Lands South of the Mojave River:
  *Rodman Mountains Wilderness*
06.31 Tiny Wilderness near the South of Death Valley:
  *Saddle Peak Hills Wilderness*
06.32 Two Mountain Ranges North of Joshua Tree:
  *Sheephole Valley Wilderness*
06.33 Critical Habitat North of Mojave National Preserve:
  *Soda Mountain Wilderness*
06.34 Small Peaks East of Tecopa: *South Nopah Range Wilderness*
06.35 Cave-Filled Hills North of Clark Mountain: *Stateline Wilderness*
06.36 Northern Chemehuevi Valley: *Stepladder Mountains Wilderness*
06.37 Lone Range North of Cadiz Valley: *Trilobite Wilderness*
06.38 Transitional Desert East of Joshua Tree:
  *Turtle Mountains Wilderness*

07. Of the Remote and the Rugged: *The Colorado-Sonoran Desert in California*   375

  07.01 The Northern Edge of a Larger System:
    *The Sonoran Desert in California*
  07.02 California's Unique Piece of the Sonoran Desert:
    *The Colorado Ecozone*
  07.03 Peaks West of the Colorado River: *Big Maria Mountains Wilderness*
  07.04 Low Hills North of the Chocolate Mountains:
    *Buzzards Peak Wilderness*
  07.05 Sandy Habitat at the Center of Cadiz Valley:
    *Cadiz Dunes Wilderness*
  07.06 Highlands Southeast of Anza-Borrego Desert State Park:
    *Carrizo Gorge Wilderness*
  07.07 Between Joshua Tree National Park and the Chocolate Mountains:
    *Chuckwalla Mountains Wilderness*
  07.08 Fossil Range on the West Side of the Imperial Valley:
    *Coyote Mountains Wilderness*
  07.09 Mountains on the East Side of Anza-Borrego Desert State Park:
    *Fish Creek Mountains Wilderness*

07.10 Riverside Wilderness in Two States: *Imperial Refuge Wilderness*
07.11 Southern Chocolate Mountains on the Colorado River:
       *Indian Pass Wilderness*
07.12 Ridges and Valleys North of the Mexican Border: *Jacumba Wilderness*
07.13 Dry Mountains North of the Chocolate Mountains:
       *Little Chuckwalla Mountains Wilderness*
07.14 Southernmost Wilderness on the Colorado River:
       *Little Picacho Wilderness*
07.15 Labyrinthine Mountains over Eastern Coachella Valley:
       *Mecca Hills Wilderness*
07.16 Sonoran Woodland South of the Palo Verde Mountains:
       *Milpitas Wash Wilderness*
07.17 Sand Mountains along the Eastern Imperial Valley:
       *North Algodones Dunes Wilderness*
07.18 Between the Salton Sea and Joshua Tree National Park:
       *Orocopia Mountains Wilderness*
07.19 Many Ranges East of Joshua Tree National Park:
       *Palen/McCoy Wilderness*
07.20 Mountains West of Cibola Refuge: *Palo Verde Mountains Wilderness*
07.21 Rich Habitat near the Colorado River: *Picacho Peak Wilderness*
07.22 Dunes North of Big Maria Mountains: *Rice Valley Wilderness*
07.23 West Bank of the Colorado River: *Riverside Mountains Wilderness*
07.24 Steep Mountains West of Anza-Borrego Desert State Park:
       *Sawtooth Mountains Wilderness*
07.25 Easternmost Mountains of California: *Whipple Mountains Wilderness*

08. Philosophies of What Comes Next: *California's Tomorrow Desert*  443

08.01 Mapping Unintended Consequences: *A causal web of ecological stress*
08.02 Magic, Plunder, and Portend: *California's valley desert*
08.03 Hotter Summers: *Mapping increasing temperature averages*
08.04 Habitat Dysconnectivity: *Desert fragmentation by infrastructure*
08.05 Sun, Wind, and Steam: *The value and cost of energy*
08.06 What Remains Intact: *Finding the desert's core habitat areas*
08.07 Understanding the Game of Inches: *A biological conservation framework*
08.08 Tracking the Pollinators: *Predicting rare plant biogeography*
08.09 An Essential Character: *Habitat for the desert tortoise*
08.10 Inside an Emerging Designation: *Areas of critical environmental concern*
08.11 A Circuit Complete: *The reunited desert*

Acknowledgments  487
Glossary  491
Notes  495
Selected Bibliography  515
About the Author  523

Doll's sphinx moth
Sphinx dollii

the moth's beaten wings
never exhaust of their energy
to rake mountains of ash

looking west from Imperial valley

# INTRODUCTION

*A Promise of Life and Death: Journey into the desert heart*

This is an adventure story.

These maps could have been painted in my own sweat and blood. For decades, it was a happy albeit singular obsession of mine to make pilgrimages of ever-deeper expeditions into California's arid backcountry. Across thousands of miles, I hiked through the heart of the desert, searching for the poetry that only the daily reality of disaster's looming threat could deliver. Life meant more when death surrounded me as a promise, clearly written everywhere across this, one the world's most arid landscapes. Salvation was found every day in every drop of precious water, in every sliver of afternoon shade, and in every desert wildflower, whose delicate truths spoke to me in dreams. Compelled by the whispered stories from trusted flowers, narratives that also seemed to emanate from deep in the warmed earth and that echoed across the empty sky, my desert years were spent as a walking piece of the desert land. It wasn't that I was looking for death—the desert will give you death if you ask for it. I was looking for the edge of resil-iency in my own body and my own mind. As I moved through the desert, I invited it to move through me. We had secrets to share. After returning to my modern life after each adventure, back in what seemed to be the anesthetized, urban landscape of my home, I was inoculated against the spirit-numbing virulence of modernity with the simple yet profound truths revealed to me, out there in the ancient dust.

Greater roadrunner.
*Geococcyx californianus*

Mojave tarantula
aphonopelma mojave

When compared to the rest of California's cool and damp country, the deserts may seem like an alien planet, desolate to the eye that is accustomed to read green as the visual signifier of a thriving landscape, when in actual fact, the desert teems with life forms that view the greener places of the world as similarly intolerable. Gathered in the east, outside California's mountainous wall that holds the cooling force of the Pacific to the west, the deserts of California exist inside an arid reality of their own ecological character. Where all manner of being acquiesces to the dictates of the constant sun, the land adopts an endemic palette of chalk, tan, and shadow accented by green-grays, ruddy siennas, and burnt ochers. Indulgent, saturated colors seem only ever to make brief albeit impressive, defiant appearances in the vernal bloom, in the iridescence of Mono Lake, or in other, anomalous places, when the dream of abundance belies the constancy of desiccation. Perhaps the most apparent expression of color in the desert is reserved for the celestial domain, in those twilight moments when perfectly infinite swaths of gradient genius spread across heaven's dome. In those moments of grace, when I am enjoying good, bitter morning coffee at dawn, or at dusk when I am removing my dust-caked boots after hiking just a bit too far in the heat, when I find myself distracted from the constant attention needed to address the pervading lethality of my environment, lost in a moment of aesthetic arrest, the desert reveals something core and original about itself: a mystery wrapped up in just how beautiful life can be. Although I am tempted to linger, if I am distracted by the reveries for too long, the desert may claim me forever.

The adventure this story holds is not necessarily in the geography it describes but in the tension among the concepts it explores. The contrasting qualities that define the deserts of California reveal the ways I have chosen to tell this story as much as they reflect realities written across the terrain. In the contemplative dance of beauty and danger, drama and stillness, commonality and preciousness, life and death, resistance and fragility, I ask whether I am exploring external phenomena or an internalized projection of myself—how much of the experience of the deserts exists only in my mind? In that context, this book walks a metaphorical line between what is known and what is imagined.

The expedition that I am inviting you to join me on is as philosophical as it is a geophysical journey across California's arid eastern landscapes. This particular trail through the desert heart is blazed across a realm where science and art interact to reveal something greater than either might yield alone. It begins largely as an artistic survey of biogeography and land policy, but it becomes an exercise in sewing together potentially disparate conceptions of knowledge across vocational disciplines. From a poetic frame of reference, across a journalistic mindset, and into the domain of a scientific temper, *The Deserts of California* presents a metaphor for an even greater adventure: the quest for a holistic understanding of the world and our place in it.

Because you have decided to accompany me on this journey through what can be called the heart of the desert, I'll bet that you have some conception of, if not a downright affection, toward these lands, and perhaps you even have some intimacy with many of the specifics that I describe in this book. Maybe you live in the desert and already identify intimately with the desert heart. It is my hope that in the way I describe the deserts, you recognize the knowledge you hold as a lover of the desert. I certainly don't want to present to you a vision that bypasses your experience, but instead one that augments and builds on it in a way that you might not have suspected.

All that being said, I do want to look at the desert with new eyes and in a new context that can be described as anticipatory. From the anticipatory perspective, which is a position that looks to the future, I not only imagine what the deserts might become in the face of climate breakdown but also consider deep time and the truths that a circular vision of history reveals about the ecological character of these arid spaces. What might the deserts' future mean to us? What might their history reveal about the resiliency of our own human ecology in the context of climate breakdown by way of anthropogenic (human-caused) global warming? Will human ecology be able to adapt and adjust its attitude to perhaps become minimally extractive and approach something truly sustainable for the long term?

*flower of*
*Mojave mound cactus*
*Echinocereus triglochidiatus*

I seek a new approach to how we talk about "natural" spaces. Certain elements of our vocabulary have been entrenched in a colonizing attitude toward California, an attitude that deserves to be reckoned with and transformed by the sociological and environmental pressures now being brought to bear. This updating of vocabulary may apply to words like *wilderness* and *management*—words steeped in the policy of today that tend to sequester the concept of nature as something that exists outside of human ecology. The endgame of this exercise is to recontextualize even basic notions of nature and wilderness with regard to our rights and our responsibilities in the emerging Anthropocene. How do we transform the concept of nature, whether we are talking about resources or ecosystems, from being something that can be consumed and destroyed to something we cherish and incorporate into our lives? The question, which is more like a gamble of assumptions than a theory backed by evidence, is twofold: Can the needs of the desert to thrive as a biodiverse ecosystem endure the injury of unlimited urban incursion? And are the limits of urban growth and energy infrastructure in the desert solely determined by technical innovation, or are they bounded by the environmental demands and ecological services that the place imposes and provides?

What emerges is a vision of the deserts—a small piece of the political entity that is California—that begins to offer a unique window of inquiry into humanity's place in the cosmos. My attitude can be described as shamelessly subjective. I'm not here to present a textbook on desert ecology. I attempt to fulfill the original

Mojave rattlesnake
*Crotalus scutulatus*

Red-tailed hawk
Buteo jamaicensis

promise of the long-distance desert trek: the realignment of myself with respect to a greater landscape. To understand the greater landscape, I need to track every footfall across every long and tired mile; and within the terrain, I need to engage every inch of knowledge with an open and energetic mind. This attitude promises a greater understanding not only of the external world—its threats, its qualities of resistance, its structure of internal beauty written across revolutionary time—but also of the way those structures are formed inside me. By the secret trail that I came to navigate, I've become the eye of the desert that perceives the heart of the desert, and the two are made one.

This style of storytelling demands a vigilant guard against imprecision while remaining accessible, multifaceted, and adaptive. Through my wildlife renderings, my expressionistic mapmaking, my researched and cited data, I unpack the potentially myopic role of the specialist. I am happy to revel in the imperfect character that I am—namely, a voracious student of the humanities and of the physical sciences, sensitive to the capacities and the limitations of both.

This is a field atlas, a genre of my own invention. It attempts to be not a cultural history of the landscape but a geographic guide to conservation and to the deep ecology of natural features through time, with specific deference to where and when we are in the twenty-first century.

This is not the first book I've written with this approach. I have produced, over the past seven years, five books (including this one). Each represents a different aspect of

coyote expressions

California's more-than-human world, and they can be experienced in any order. The first was *The California Field Atlas* (Heyday, 2017), which contains hundreds of hand-painted maps and describes the regular regimes of California's natural world over deep spans of time. I followed with a thin book titled *The State of Water* (Heyday, 2019), in which I examined water storage, conveyance, and usage in contemporary society and the ecological effects of the fundamentally altered waterscape.

Next I went back to the woods to begin what I call the California Lands Trilogy, the third volume of which is the book you're holding now. The first to appear was *The Forests of California* (Heyday, 2020), an in-depth survey of arboreal habitats across the state that support the tallest and most massive trees within any forest on the planet. Then, in *The Coasts of California* (Heyday, 2022), I described the ecological processes and the biogeography of California's impressively long shoreline.

*The Deserts of California* is, next to the other books, unique in form and substance but consistent in style and ethical disposition. Throughout my work, I maintain the search for the same quality of character within the landscape regardless of the forms that the landscape takes on, namely its biotic and abiotic features and properties. I am interested in those aspects of California that, for all intents and purposes, have always been, continue to be, and will always exist despite the monumental anthropogenic disturbance imposed over the past five hundred years since contact.

mindful

Since the coming of humans to California, nearly the entirety of its landscape has been altered to such a complete degree that to find landscape not altered by the human hand, you would have to go so far back that you were in a different geologic era. The tension between those aspects of California's evolving character that are relatively recent and those that have a much deeper history is a preoccupation of this work. Much like the coasts, or the forests for that matter, the deserts of California at the beginning of the Holocene were much different than the deserts are today. Now, as we look forward to the evolving shape of the Anthropocene, we wonder what the deserts will become and how the ecologies of California (and the rest of the planet) will weather the industrial storm that rages across the land, water, and sky. The effect of global warming is climate breakdown, a process that

Joyful

affects the biosphere by way of potentially disastrous effects on the hydrosphere. Water is the agent that governs all life on earth, including the resistant yet fragile living systems of the desert.

What this book is not is the manifesto of an apocalyptic environmentalist—some alarmist proclamation of the pending end of life on all but perhaps the most extreme terrestrial environments. This work takes a steadied and unpanicked look at the many stressors that affect habitat structure across the desert biome, including the aforementioned storm that is climate breakdown by way of anthropogenic global warming. This book cautiously presumes that there is a vector by which we get it right—that our best efforts, our best predictions, and our best clever solutions engage extant systems toward their own progenerative capacity. It presumes that we can get to a post-carbon emitting society and that stewardship and mutualism become dominant human paradigms wherein we enter into a mutualized, reciprocal relationship with this precious landscape. Together then, we proceed toward a twenty-second century with a natural world in much better shape than even how we left it at the end of the twentieth century.

This book is not preoccupied with prescribing cures for environmental damage. Instead, it finds its power in the democratization of ecological literacy across many different aspects of space and time within California's complex desert landscape. In some respects, my book *The Forests of California* was about the past—how these unique living systems came to existence, organizing themselves over the past several million years. Similarly, *The Coasts of California*—with its opening line, "This is a time capsule"—represents a snapshot of the right now, of dynamic coastal systems being destroyed and built up constantly, ones that are very different than they were even in recent historical times and are very different from what they will be in the future, given a rapidly changing climate. It follows that *The Deserts of California* is an examination of a more arid future that is different from the California we know now.

## Welcome to the Desert

### *Notes on enjoying* The Deserts of California

1. Think of this as a reference book. What is left unexplained here is explained better by others elsewhere. The table of contents is designed as a map in itself. This book examines patterns across many overlapping maps that examine many different ecological qualities of the landscape. You can dip into this book without reading it from front to back. The story being told has no beginning or end. Just like the land of its subject, the book contains some new bits of insight that can be found with every expedition into it.

2. I wish to breathe life into watercolor paintings. This is not a field guide, and the renderings are not scientific illustrations. My primary vocation is not to document species for identification but to paint.

3. This book is more about understanding places and their natural systems than about navigating the modern human infrastructure on top of them. Towns and roads are largely ignored because I wish to examine what is beneath the impervious pavement.

4. I wrote this book, ultimately, to figure this stuff out for myself. That being said, this is not a book of war stories or a memoir of my time in the desert. I am sharing it with you because I want it to be for you. It assumes a bit of proficiency with biological concepts, and the offered glossary is far from complete.

5. This book doesn't tell you what to look at or what to look for; in fact, it seems to me that it is more about how to think about the desert, or rather, how to develop a deeper, more intimate relationship with the desert than it is a standard travel guide. This book can be for locals and for people who have already fallen in love with the deserts of California.

6. This book was born from the mind of an artist, not a research scientist. Throughout the book there are dozens of poetic and philosophical interludes, asides, and segues. Think of these as a metanarrative, an augmentation of the cited research and where the true heart of this book may lie.

7. The eight chapters of this book are divided by themes that range from temporality to geography to ecology. The book opens with an introduction that explores many historical forces that shaped today's deserts of California. Following the next chapter's discussion of water in the deserts—how it works and where it is—the main body of the book, chapters 03 through 07, are explorations of land designations, from parks to wilderness areas, in all four of California's deserts. Chapter 07 presents the Colorado Desert and the Sonoran Desert in California as the Colorado-Sonoran Desert. Chapter 08 closes the book with a primer on many theories that revolve around potential futures inside which the deserts may yet exist.

This book is shot through with hope. It has to be. On the trail, hope is the best tool there is. Hope is not empty. Hope is actionable. Hope drives the heart forward, assists in finding solutions, and guides the unfocused mind when panic sets in. Hope is an agent that finds meaning in the struggle—the struggle to face injustice, tackle adversity, express compassion, and seek truth. Shouldered by love, love for the deserts and love for the human and the more-than-human community, hope becomes a flower of knowledge that untethers the paralysis of despair. Like sun and shadow, life and death in the desert heart are elemental forces that give as they take, and the razor that cuts the line between one and the other is the prepared mind, knowledgeable of the trail behind and hopeful and not ignorant about what lies ahead.

Obi Kaufmann
California
2022

San Jacinto Peak

where the ground glows the rainbow

...ry environmental law of the twentieth century
...d that the more-than-human world is not a
...ntally integrated network and that its des-
...be mediated by the conceptualized compart-
...of that world into constructs such as
the environment and the word wilderness

Artists Palette
Death Valley National Park
Looking west to
the Panamint
Range

## 00.01 AN ACKNOWLEDGED TRUTH
*Land of the people*

For perhaps tens of thousands of years, the deserts of California were the land of the people, and they still very much are. Map 00.01 is a generalization of primary tribal peoples in historical cultural ranges from before contact with Euro-American settlers through to the present day. The map does not define rigid boundaries between tribal sovereignties or the location of modern reservations and native land, but rather its reference is to the omnipresence of historically diverse cultures everywhere in California's desert regions. Having persisted through the genocidal invasions of the past few centuries, the Indigenous peoples of California's deserts may be experiencing an emergent era of resurgence—one that should be supported by a corresponding cultural reckoning, an acknowledgment of and reparations for the trauma, injustice, and land theft.

Autonym (Ethnonym), Region

01. Moatokni maklaks (Modoc), Modoc Plateau
02. Achomawi (Achomawi), Pit River
03. Cui Ui Ticutta (Northern Piute), Pyramid Lake
04. Kucadikadi (Mono), Mono Lake
05. Nuumu (Owens Valley Paiute), Owens Valley
06. Newe (Owens Valley Shoshone), Owens Valley
07. Nümü Tümpisattsi (Timbisha), Death Valley National Park
08. Nüwüwü or Tantawats (Chemehuevi), northern Sonoran
09. 'Aha Makhav or 'Aha Havasuu (Mojave), Colorado River
10. Taaqtam, Yuhaaviatam, or Maarrénga'yam (Serrano), Joshua Tree National Park
11. Xalychidom Piipaa or Xalychidom Piipaash (Halchidhoma), southern Colorado River
12. Kwatsáan (Quechan or Yuma), southern Colorado River
13. Kumeyaay or Tipai-Ipai (Dieg-ueño), Anza-Borrego Desert State Park
14. Kuupangaxwichem (Cupeño), Anza-Borrego Desert State Park
15. Ivilyuqaletem (Cahuilla), Anza-Borrego Desert State Park
16. Nüwü (Kawaiisu), Tehachapi
17. Kitanemuk (Kitanemuk), Tehachapi

*Cactus wren
Campylorhynchus
brunneicapillus*

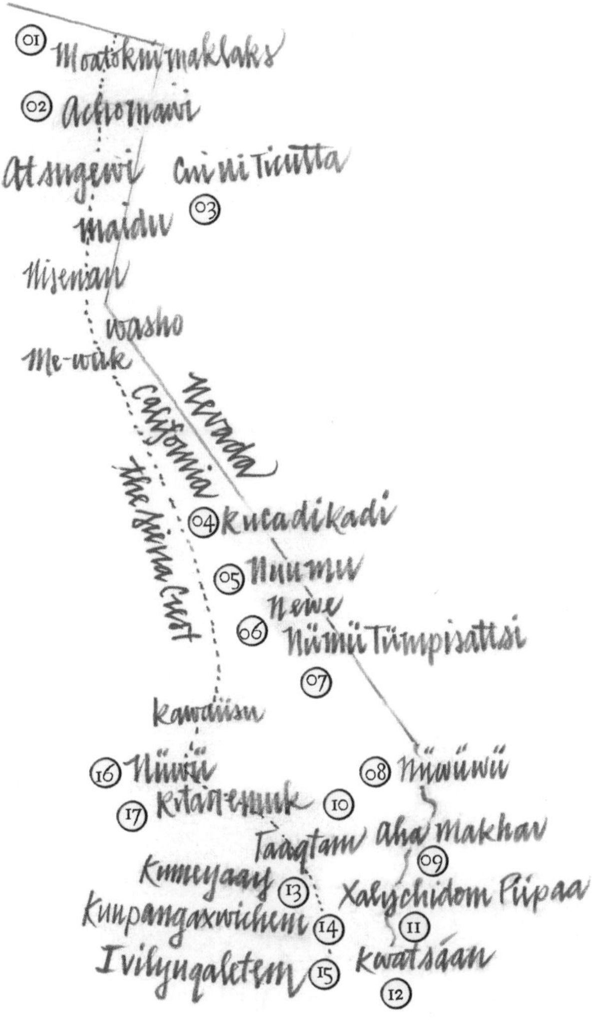
01 Moatokni maklaks
02 Achomawi
Atsugewi
Cui ui Ticutta
03
Maidu
Nisenan
Washo
Me-wuk
Nevada
California
The Sierra Crest
04 Kucadikadi
05 Nuumu
Newe
06
Nümü Tümpisattsi
07
Kawaiisu
16 Nüwü
08 Nüwüwü
17 Kitanemuk
10
Taaqtam
Aha Makhav
09
Kumeyaay
13
Xalychidom Piipaa
Kuupangaxwichem
14
11
Ivilyuqaletem
15
Kwatsáan
12

Map 00.01

| EON | ERA | PERIOD | | EPOCH | TIME SPAN |
|-----|-----|--------|--|-------|-----------|
| Phanerozoic | Cenozoic | Quaternary | | Holocene | 11 KYA–today |
| | | | | Pleistocene | 1.8 MYA–11 KYA |
| | | Tertiary | Neogene | Pliocene | 5.3–1.8 MYA |
| | | | | Miocene | 23.7–5.3 MYA |
| | | | Paleogene | Oligocene | 36.6–23.7 MYA |
| | | | | Eocene | 57.8–36.6 MYA |
| | | | | Paleocene | 66.4–57.8 MYA |
| | Mesozoic | Cretaceous | | | 144–66.4 MYA |
| | | Jurassic | | | 208–144 MYA |
| | | Triassic | | | 245–208 MYA |
| | Paleozoic | Permian | | | 286–245 MYA |
| | | Carboniferous | Pennsylvanian | | 320–286 MYA |
| | | | Mississippian | | 360–320 MYA |
| | | Devonian | | | 408–360 MYA |
| | | Silurian | | | 438–408 MYA |
| | | Ordovician | | | 505–438 MYA |
| | | Cambrian | | | 570–505 MYA |
| Proterozoic | Grouped as the Precambrian | | | | 2500–570 MYA |
| Archean | | | | | 3800–2500 MYA |
| Hadean | | | | | 4500–3800 MYA |

## 00.02 AGES OF THE EARTH

*A geologic history of California's deserts*

MYA—million years ago
KYA—thousand years ago

## Cenozoic

Deserts support cool mesic and woodland vegetation (18-12 KYA)

Last Glacial Maximum (18 KYA)

Mono-Inyo Craters chain develops (50 KYA)

Glass Mountain Volcanic events begin (2.6 MYA)

Sagebrush habitat develops in Great Basin (3 MYA)

Mediterranean climate of California develops (6 MYA)

California Current develops (15 MYA)

San Andreas Fault established (25 MYA)

*Pinus* sp. speciation occurs (40 MYA)

Mohavia Floristic Provence established (50 MYA)

## Mesozoic

Cretaceous-Paleogene mass extinction (66 MYA)

Nevadan orogeny, Inyo-White Mountains (140 MYA)

Dunes in eastern Mojave begin to form (190 MYA)

Triassic-Jurassic mass extinction (200 MYA)

Sonoma orogeny (200 MYA)

## Paleozoic

Subduction of Pacific and Farallon Plates begins (250 MYA)

Permian-Triassic mass extinction (252 MYA)

"Antler" orogeny; Mitchell Caverns, Funeral Mountains (300 MYA)

First conifer trees (320 MYA)

Devonian mass extinction (370 MYA)

Ordovician mass extinction (445 MYA)

Bioherm (proto-reef) of White Mountain Peak (540 MYA)

## Precambrian

Frenchman Mountain, oldest exposed rocks in North America (1,700 MYA)

Formation of granitic and metamorphic basement rocks

Marine deposition along an incipient continental margin

Ecological feature —
anomalous site, point of particular interest

 Human settlement —
town, city, reservation

 Land designation —
wilderness area

 Trail —
unpaved road

 Single peak —
named mountain, outcrop,
distinct peak, or pass

 Mountain range —
ridgeline

 River —
watershed, creek, spring

 Infrastructure —
energy project, dam

 Hills —
discrete land rise

 Park —
national park, state park,
regional park

 Flats —
mesa or meadows

 Ecological refuge —
wildlife preserve

 Canyon —
water-carved land feature

## 00.03 READING THE MAPS
*A key to the map icons*

"Emuu" (mountain sheep) guiding the path of the Milky Way) "Maay hetat kuu" the European star belt constellation orion

Marks the winter solstice from the Maay Uuyow Kumeyaay cosmology) represented in illustration with permission from the author Michael Connolly Miskwish

## 00.04 NATIONAL, STATE, AND REGIONAL LAND MANAGEMENT
*California Desert Conservation Area*

The main characters of this story are the four ecological desert regions of California, including the southeast Great Basin, the Mojave, the Sonoran, and the Colorado.[1] These characters all exist as ecological subregions within the nearly twenty-six-million-acre federally designated California Desert Conservation Area.[2] The Desert Resource Energy Conservation Plan (DRECP, 2016[3]) includes twenty-two million acres of this area (all deserts south of the Mojave–Great Basin border) and is most probably the keystone policy that will determine the ecological fate of the California deserts in the immediate future.

The popularizing, contextualizing, and analysis of the debate between conservation and extraction, between restoration and development, are at the heart of this book. Although this book is about boundaries, ranges, lines in the sand, fences, walls, spaces between designations, corridors, liminal transition zones, and overlapping ecotones, it uses those devices of analysis to present the desert of California as a holistic, ecological singularity.

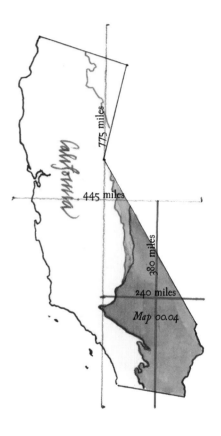

*Map* 00.04

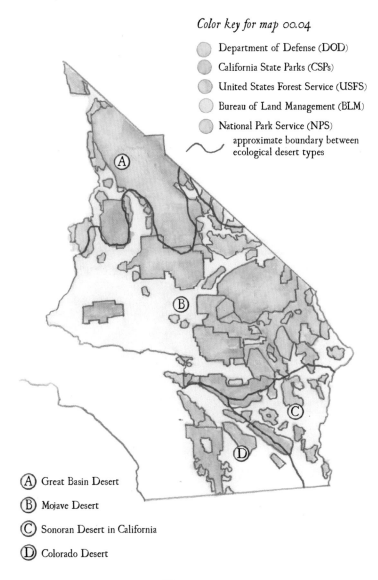

*Color key for map 00.04*

Department of Defense (DOD)

California State Parks (CSPs)

United States Forest Service (USFS)

Bureau of Land Management (BLM)

National Park Service (NPS)

approximate boundary between
ecological desert types

(A) Great Basin Desert

(B) Mojave Desert

(C) Sonoran Desert in California

(D) Colorado Desert

Map 00.04

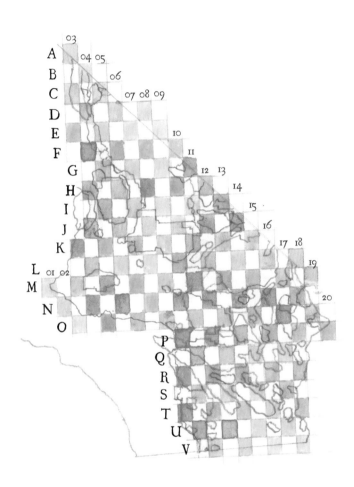

Map 00.05

## 00.05 QUADRANGLE DESIGNATIONS
*USGS California land measurement systems*

Each quadrangle, named by the US Geological Survey, contains 15 minutes of latitude from east to west and approximately 20 minutes of longitude from north to south. Each rectangular area covers approximately 225 square miles.

A.03 Benton
B.03 White Mountain Peak
B.04 Red Mountain
B.05 Piper Peak
C.03 Bishop
C.04 Crystal Peak
C.05 Soldier Pass
C.06 Magruder Mountain
D.03 Big Pine
D.04 Waucoba Mountain
D.05 Waucoba Spring
D.06 Last Chance Range
D.07 Gold Mountain
D.08 Bonnie Claire
D.09 Springdale
E.03 Mount Pinchot
E.04 Independence
E.05 Waucoba Wash
E.06 Dry Mountain
E.07 Tin Mountain
E.08 Grapevine Peak
E.09 Bullfrog Hills
F.03 Mount Whitney
F.04 Alabama Hills
F.05 New York Butte
F.06 Ubehebe Peak
F.07 Marble Canyon
F.08 Stovepipe Wells
F.09 Chloride Cliff
F.10 Big Dune
G.04 Golden Trout

G.05 Keeler
G.06 Darwin
G.07 Panamint Butte
G.08 Emigrant Canyon
G.09 Furnace Creek
G.10 Ryan
G.11 Crystal Reservoir
H.04 Fish Creek
H.05 Haiwee Reservoir
H.06 Coso Peak
H.07 Maturango Peak
H.08 Telescope Peak
H.09 Badwater Basin
H.10 Funeral Peak
H.11 Eagle Mountain
H.12 Stewart Valley
H.13 Pahrump
I.04 Chimney Peak
I.05 Little Lake
I.06 Mountain Springs Canyon
I.07 Trona
I.08 Manly Peak
I.09 Wingate Wash
I.10 Confidence Hills
I.11 Ibex Wilderness
I.12 Tecopa
I.13 Horse Thief Springs
I.14 Shenandoah Peak
J.04 Kiavah Wilderness
J.05 Inyokern
J.06 Ridgecrest
J.07 Searles Lake
J.08 Wingate Pass
J.09 Quail Mountains
J.10 Leach Lake
J.11 Saddle Peak Hills
J.12 Silurian Hills
J.13 Kingston Peak
J.14 Clark Mountain

J.15 Roach Lake
K.03 Emerald Mountain
K.04 Cottonwood Creek
K.05 Saltdale
K.06 Randsburg
K.07 Cuddleback Lake
K.08 Pilot Knob
K.09 Goldstone Lake
K.10 Tiefort Mountains
K.11 Red Pass Lake
K.12 Baker
K.13 Halloran Spring
K.14 Mescal Range
K.15 Crescent Peak
K.16 Searchlight
L.03 Tehachapi
L.04 Horned Toad Hills
L.05 Castle Butte
L.06 Boron
L.07 Fremont Peak
L.08 Opal Mountain
L.09 Lin Mountain
L.10 Alvord Mountain
L.11 Cronise Lake
L.12 Soda Lake
L.13 Old Dad Mountains
L.14 Kelso
L.15 Mid Hills
L.16 Lanfair Valley
L.17 Homer Mountain
L.18 Davis Dam
M.01 Tejon Pass
M.02 Neenach
M.03 Willow Springs
M.04 Rosamond
M.05 Rogers Lake
M.06 Krame
M.07 Hawes
M.08 Barstow
M.09 Daggett
M.10 Newberry

M.11 Cady Mountains
M.12 Broadwell Lake
M.13 Kerens
M.14 Flynn
M.15 Colton Well
M.16 Fenner
M.17 Bannock
M.18 Needles
M.19 Warm Springs
N.02 Liebre Mountain

Bark scorpion
Centruroides
sculpturatus

N.03 Boquet Reservoir
N.04 Palmdale
N.05 Alpine Butte
N.06 Shadow Mountains
N.07 Victorville
N.08 Apple Valley
N.09 Ord Mountains
N.10 Rodman Mountains
N.11 Lava Bed Mountains
N.12 Ludlow
N.13 Bagdad
N.14 Cadiz
N.15 Danby
N.16 Essex
N.17 Stepladder Mountains
N.18 Chemehuevi Mountains

N.19 Topock
O.03 San Fernando
O.04 Mill Creek
O.05 Valyermo
O.06 San Antonio
O.07 Lake Arrowhead
O.08 Lucerne Valley
O.09 Old Woman Springs
O.10 Homestead Valley
O.11 Deadman Lake
O.12 Lead Mountain
O.13 Bristol Lake
O.14 Cadiz Lake
O.15 Milligan
O.16 Turtle Mountains
O.17 Savahia Peak
O.18 Whipple Mountains
O.19 Parker Dam
O.20 Castaneda Hills
P.10 Bartlett Mountains
P.11 Twentynine Palms
P.12 Valley Mountain
P.13 Dale Lake
P.14 Cadiz Valley
P.15 Iron Mountains
P.16 Rice
P.17 Vidal
P.18 Parker
P.19 Black Peak
P.20 Sawnsea
Q.10 Palm Springs
Q.11 Indio Hills
Q.12 Lost Horse Mountain
Q.13 Hexie Mountains
Q.14 Pinto Basin
Q.15 Coxcomb Mountains
Q.16 Palen Mountains
Q.17 Midland
Q.18 Big Maria Mountains
Q.19 Moon Mountain
R.10 Indian Wells

R.11 Coachella
R.12 Cottonwood Spring
R.13 Hayfield
R.14 Chuckwalla Mountains
R.15 Sidewinder Well
R.16 McCoy Spring
R.17 Blythe
R.18 Dome Rock Mountains
S.10 Coyote Creek
S.11 Agua Dulce
S.12 Durmid
S.13 Frink
S.14 Iris Pass
S.15 Chuckwalla Spring
S.16 Palo Verde Mountains
S.17 Cibola
S.18 Trigo Peaks
T.10 Santa Ysabel
T.11 Borrego Springs
T.12 Borrego Mountain
T.13 Kane Spring
T.14 Calipatria
T.15 Iris
T.16 Acolita
T.17 Quartz Peak
T.18 Trigo Mountains
U.11 Sawtooth Mountains
U.12 Carrizo Mountains
U.13 Plaster City
U.14 Brawley
U.15 Holtville
U.16 Ogilby
U.17 Fort Yuma
U.18 Laguna
V.11 Campo
V.12 Jacumba
V.13 Coyote Wells
V.14 Heber
V.15 Calexico
V.16 Midway Well
V.17 Grays Well
V.18 Somerton

## oo.o6 SPECIAL CONCERN FOR THE THREATENED AND ENDANGERED
### Desert animal species conservation

This list was created by cross-referencing the State and Federally Listed Endangered and Threatened Animals of California list[4] with the California state list of species of special concern.[5] Species listed here have distribution ranges that include habitat inside one or more of California's four desert regions discussed in this book.

SSC—Species of special concern, CDFW
FP—Fully protected, CDFW
FT—Federally threatened
FE—Federally endangered
SE—State endangered
CE—Candidate state endangered
ST—State threatened

speckled dace

Amargosa Canyon speckled dace
*Rhinichthys osculus* ssp. 1—SSC

Amargosa pupfish
*Cyprinodon nevadensis amargosae*—SSC

Amargosa vole
*Microtus californicus scirpensis*—SE, FE

American badger
*Taxidea taxus*—SSC

American peregrine falcon
*Falco peregrinus anatum*—FP

Peregrine falcon

American white pelican
*Pelecanus erythrorhynchos*—SSC

Arizona Bell's vireo
*Vireo bellii arizonae*—SE

Arizona myotis
*Myotis occultus*—SSC

arroyo chub

Arroyo chub
*Gila orcuttii*—SSC

Arroyo toad
*Anaxyrus californicus*—FT, SSC

Bald eagle
*Haliaeetus leucocephalus*—SE, SSC

Bank swallow
*Riparia riparia*—ST

Barefoot gecko
*Coleonyx switaki*—ST

Barrow's goldeneye
*Bucephala islandica*—SSC

Bendire's thrasher
*Toxostoma bendirei*—SSC

Big free-tailed bat
*Nyctinomops macrotis*—SSC

Bighorn sheep
*Ovis canadensis*—FP

Black skimmer
*Rynchops niger*—SSC

Black tern
*Childonias niger*—SSC

Blunt-nosed leopard lizard
*Gambelia sila*—SE, FE

Burrowing owl
*Athene cunicularia*—SSC

California black rail
*Laterallus jamaicensis coturniculus*—SSC

California leaf-nosed bat
*Choeronycteris mexicana*—SSC

Barrow's goldeneye

Bendire's thrasher

California black rail

California red-legged frog
*Rana draytonii*—FT, SSC

Cave myotis
*Myotis velifer*—SSC

Coachella Valley fringe-toed lizard
*Uma inornata*—SE, FT

Coastal whiptail
*Aspidoscelis tigris stejnegeri*—SSC

Coast horned lizard
*Phrynosoma blainvillii*—FT, SSC

Colorado Desert fringe-toed lizard
*Uma notata*—SSC

Colorado River cotton rat
*Sigmodon arizonae plenus*—SSC

Cottonball Marsh pupfish
*Cyprinodon salinus milleri*—ST

Couch's spadefoot
*Scaphiopus couchii*—SSC

Desert pupfish
*Cyprinodon macularius*—SE, FE

Desert tortoise
*Gopherus agassizii*—FT, ST

Elf owl
*Micrathene whitneyi*—SE

Flat-tailed horned lizard
*Phrynosoma mcallii*—SSC

Fulvous whistling-duck
*Dendrocygna bicolor*—SSC

Cave myotis

coastal whiptail

elf owl

Gila woodpecker
*Melanerpes uropygialis*—SE

Golden eagle
*Aquila chrysaetos*—FP

Gray vireo
*Vireo vicinior*—SSC

Greater sage-grouse
*Centrocercus urophasianus*—SSC

Greater sandhill crane
*Grus canadensis tabida*—ST

Gull-billed tern
*Gelochelidon nilotica*—SSC

Inyo California towhee
*Melozone crissalis eremophilus*—SE, FT

Inyo Mountains slender salamander
*Batrachoseps campi*—SSC

Jacumba pocket mouse
*Perognathus longimembris internationalis*—SSC

Least Bell's vireo
*Vireo bellii pusillus*—FE, SE

Least bittern
*Ixobrychus exilis*—SSC

Le Conte's thrasher
*Toxostoma lecontei*—SSC

Lesser long-nosed bat
*Leptonycteris yerbabuenae*—FE

Lesser sandhill crane
*Grus canadensis canadensis*—SSC

gray vireo

Inyo California towhee

Jacumba pocket mouse

Loggerhead shrike
*Lanius ludovicianus*—SSC

Long-eared owl
*Asio otus*—SSC

Mexican long-tongued bat
*Choeronycteris mexicana*—SSC

Mohave ground squirrel
*Xerospermophilus mohavensis*—ST

Mohave tui chub
*Siphateles bicolor mohavensis*—SE, FE

Mojave fringe-toed lizard
*Uma scoparia*—SSC

Mojave River vole
*Microtus californicus mohavensis*—SSC

Olive-sided flycatcher
*Contopus cooperi*—SSC

Owens pupfish
*Cyprinodon radiosus*—SE, FE

Owens speckled dace
*Rhinichthys osculus* ssp. 2—SSC

Owens sucker
*Catostomus fumeiventris*—SSC

Owens tui chub
*Siphateles bicolor snyderi*—SE, FE, FP

Owens Valley vole
*Microtus californicus vallicola*—SSC

Panamint alligator lizard
*Elgaria panamintina*—SSC

Mohave ground squirrel

Mohave tui chub

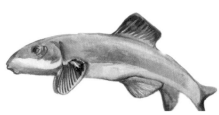

owens sucker

Pallid bat
*Antrozous pallidus*—SSC

Pallid San Diego pocket mouse
*Chaetodipus fallax pallidus*—SSC

Palm Springs pocket mouse
*Perognathus longimembris bangsi*—SSC

pallid bat

Palm Springs round-tailed ground squirrel
*Xerospermophilus tereticaudus chlorus*—SSC

Peninsular bighorn sheep
*Ovis canadensis nelsoni*—ST, FE

Pygmy rabbit
*Brachylagus idahoensis*—SSC

Pocketed free-tailed bat
*Nyctinomops femorosaccus*—SSC

Redhead
*Aythya americana*—SSC

Regal ringneck snake
*Diadophis punctatus regalis*—SSC

San Bernardino flying squirrel
*Glaucomys oregonensis californicus*—SSC

pygmy rabbit

San Bernardino kangaroo rat
*Dipodomys merriami parvus*—SSC

Sandstone night lizard
*Xantusia gracilis*—SSC

Saratoga Springs pupfish
*Cyprinodon nevadensis nevadensis*—SSC

Shoshone pupfish
*Cyprinodon nevadensis Shoshone*—SSC

redhead

Sonoran desert toad
*Icilius alvarius*—SSC

Sonoran mud turtle
*Kinosternon sonoriense*—SSC

Sonoran yellow warbler
*Setophaga petechia sonorana*—SSC

Southern California legless lizard
*Anniella stebbinsi*—SSC

Southern mountain yellow-legged frog
*Rana muscosa*—FE, SE

Southern rubber boa
*Charine umbratica*—ST

Spotted bat
*Euderma masculatum*—SSC

Summer tanager
*Piranga rubra*—SSC

Swainson's hawk
*Buteo swainsoni*—ST

Tehachapi slender salamander
*Batrachoseps stebbinsi*—ST

Townsend's big-eared bat
*Corynorhinus townsendii*—SSC

Tricolored blackbird
*Agelaius tricolor*—CE, SSC

Two-striped garter snake
*Thamnophis hammondii*—SSC

Vermilion flycatcher
*Pyrocephalus rubinus*—SSC

Sonoran mud turtle

Tehachapi slender salamander

Vermilion flycatcher

*white-tailed jackrabbit*

Western spadefoot
*Spea hammondii*—SSC

Willow flycatcher
*Empidonax traillii*—FE, SE

Willow flycatcher ssp. Southwestern flycatcher
*Empidonax traillii extimus*—SE

Western pond turtle
*Emys marmorata*—SSC

Western white-tailed jackrabbit
*Lepus townsendii townsendii*—SSC

Western yellow bat
*Lasiurus xanthinus*—SSC

Western yellow-billed cuckoo
*Coccyzus americanus occidentalis*—FT, SE

Wood stork
*Mycteria amicana*—SSC

Yellow-breasted chat
*Icteria virens*—SSC

*yellow-billed cuckoo*

Yellow-headed blackbird
*Xanthocephalus xanthocephalus*—SSC

Yellow rail
*Coturnicops noveboracensis*—SSC

Yuma clapper rail
*Rallus obsoletus yumanensis*—SE, FE

Yuma hispid cotton rat
*Sigmodon hispidus eremicus*—SSC

Yuma mountain lion
*Puma concolor browni*—SSC

*Yuma hispid cotton rat*

Scolopendra polymorpha

digs burrows under rocks and in logs

common desert centipede

long-lived: 4 years or more

4"–7" in length

Prey: insects, lizards, frogs and rodents

Food for kids of pray and carnivorous mammals

3000 world species of centipede
all centipedes bite
generally, the larger the centipede the more powerful the venom. Painful, not deadly.

By holding this book you have already self-identified, whether you've realized it or not, as a kind of ecological philosopher. You probably already have some relationship with what can be called the more-than-human world. The more-than-human world is the world of Nature—capital $N$—and you exist in and are enveloped by that world. You have already begun questioning your role, your agency, and your place in the world of Nature. Perhaps you are even curious about how you might enter into a reciprocal relationship with an evolving biosphere: How do you shrink your footprint? You are ethically driven to recognize that by attending to corresponding responsibilities, we are honoring the rights we enjoy in a free society. It is a calling to understand Nature.

You are willing to stand up for an abundant and beautiful world, and you are ready to listen to a story about what you already suspect: that this world is able to heal. Historical precedent is that Nature always tends toward regeneration, and in this emerging age, that precedent is called into question. Perhaps you were wondering what the relationship is between understanding and healing and how might that form connective sinew between what is broken and what can be healed inside you and inside Nature.

In your adventure through the material in this book, consider how you explore the trailless landscape of your own metaphorical wilderness. The deserts of California invite you to a deeper understanding of what it is to have a relationship to a place. It could be any place, but the discrete and unique quality of these lands, and their lack of resemblance to any other landscape type in California or across the world, offer a special focus that may seem plain but is really quite mysterious. In an environment like the desert there can be an almost spiritual aspect to the study of ecology and geography. Paradoxes rule the way the desert appears: the desert is as resilient as it is can be fragile, the desert is as dangerous as it can be healing, and the desert is as violent as it can be peaceful. What is in a word? Desert. Abandoned. Desolate. Without. Left. Bereft. So much implied lack. A word from a language that is still adapting to a place where it did not originate. Imagine if we were to embrace that supposed emptiness—a false construct that does not or cannot acknowledge endemic abundance—or if we were to entertain a stripped-down vision of Nature uncluttered by biomass and humidity, and walk into the apparent void. If we did, we may find upon our return a different, stripped-down, forever-altered vision of ourselves.

owens lake (dry) looking west

Great Basin

Mojave

Sonoran

Colorado

Map 01.01

## 01.01 FROM THE ARID TO THE ALPINE
*California's desert regions*

There is nowhere like the deserts of California. Each of the four—the Mojave, the Great Basin, the Sonoran, and the Colorado—exhibit their own characteristics, their own ecological identities across an enormous body of land. But the slippery truth is that they are only partially represented within the geographic boundaries that form the state of California. The Great Basin extends across the interior of the American West. The Mojave is bisected by the California-Nevada border. The Sonoran is only represented here by a small fraction of its whole. And the Colorado is an aspect of the larger Sonoran. While there certainly are a number of physiographic and climatic parallels among the deserts of California (they are all mountainous to a certain degree, they are all arid environments, and they all harbor endemic life forms), there is also so much diversity that any given walkable distance in a day might hold a seemingly opposite environment to encounter. This is exemplified in the names of some regional trails and monuments: palms to pines, cactus to clouds, and sand to snow.

Across space and time, the deserts of California are transforming. Their contemporary ecologies are relatively novel and are currently evolving into something else at great speed. It may be that this adventure story is after all populated with semifictional characters that are only true in the context of the story being told. Each geographic region becomes a character that can be seen as an allegory for some kind of creature, a composite being made of unique ecosystems that presents something alive in its own totality, and something that, having been born at some point in the recent past to its current ecological configuration, may be subject to the forces of death that will end the system as we know it today. California deserts are dynamic entities that exist inside of a life span—a waveform that has come and that will go. Just because there is an element of fiction to these characters, whether we are talking about the deserts as ecological, geographical, or political entities, that doesn't make them any less real. This story is unique to this time and place, and the deserts are the primary protagonists. How humans think about a given subject is based on any number of fictions. The deserts are powerful actors in a grand epic, and to whatever degree contrivances are employed to explain the reality of the situation at hand, so be it.

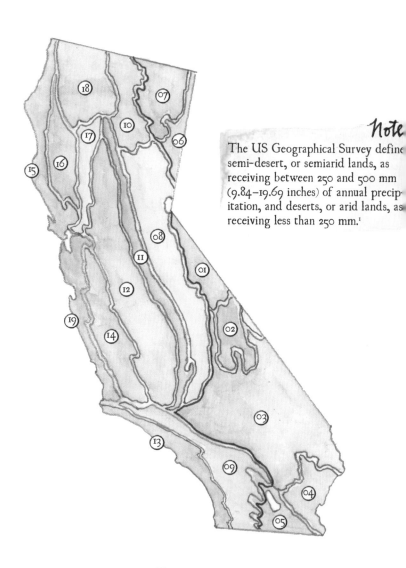

**Note**

The US Geographical Survey define
semi-desert, or semiarid lands, as
receiving between 250 and 500 mm
(9.84–19.69 inches) of annual precipitation, and deserts, or arid lands, as
receiving less than 250 mm.[1]

Map 01.01a

## 01.01a A Plurality of Adaptation
*The ecological sections of California's deserts*

Would the deserts be the deserts if all we knew were the deserts? Despite its generally dry, Mediterranean climate, California is a land of great ecological diversity and contrast. One way to examine California's ecological character is to divide it in two along its most apparent and influential divide: the Sierra Nevada. The Sierra Nevada is North America's longest contiguous mountain range and the highest outside Alaska. All the land to the west of the crest of the Sierra Nevada is of a temperate character; all the land east of the crest is protected from the influence of the Pacific Ocean and kept arid for that reason.

California's ecological sections, as classified by the US Forest Service, constitute a "regionalization, classification, and mapping system" of not necessarily ecological conditions as they are but of their potential.[2] Ecological lines are drawn to describe those areas that share biotic and environmental characteristics such as climate, hydrology, terrain, and vegetative communities.

01. Mono section (intermountain semi-desert and desert)
02. Southeastern Great Basin (intermountain semi-desert and desert)
03. Mojave Desert (American semi-desert and desert)
04. Sonoran Desert (American semi-desert and desert)
05. Colorado Desert (American semi-desert and desert)
06. Northwest Basin and Range (intermountain semi-desert)
07. Modoc Plateau (Sierran forest – alpine meadows)
08. Sierra Nevada (Sierran forest – alpine meadows)
09. Southern California Mountains and Valleys (California coastal range shrub – forest – meadows)
10. Southern Cascades (Sierran forest – alpine meadows)
11. Sierra Nevada foothills (Sierran forest – alpine meadows)
12. Great Valley (California dry steppe)
13. Southern California Coast (California coastal chaparral forest and scrub)
14. Central California Coast Ranges (California coastal range shrub – forest – meadows)
15. Northern California Coast (California coastal steppe – mixed forest – redwood forest)
16. Northern California Coast Ranges (Sierran forest – alpine meadows)
17. Northern California Interior Coast Ranges (Sierran forest – alpine meadows)
18. Klamath Mountains (Sierran forest – alpine meadows)
19. Central California Coast (California coastal range shrub – forest – meadows)

Kingston Peak
7,326'
San Bernardino County)

the desert exudes pressure from
all angles
grinding apprehension
into a clear lens
reflecting a vision
of our own
my own
death

## 01.01b A Landscape of Compromise
*Major land designations of California's deserts*

Five primary public and military (governmental) agencies manage most of California's deserts, an area of over twenty-five million acres, or nearly forty thousand square miles. The citizenry entrusts public and military organizations with the stewarding and management of these lands, which always entails compromise. For example, mining and grazing on public lands have historically been contentious issues, and lawsuits and legislative action are constant in the never-ending fight between economic gain from the extraction, depletion, and degradation of desert resources, and the conservation, restoration, and replenishment of those resources.

Not including the wilderness areas inside parks and monuments, the BLM operates seventy-two wilderness areas that are covered in this book and not delineated on map 01.01b. Land designated as a federal wilderness area is a roadless area of no less than five thousand acres that is managed by USFS, BLM, or NPS (if the wilderness area exists inside a national park). The primary author of the Wilderness Act of 1964, Howard Clinton Zahniser, offered an eloquent definition of wilderness that appears in the text of the law: "A wilderness, in contrast with those areas where man and his own works

dominate the landscape, is hereby recognized as an area where the earth and its community of life are untrammeled by man, where man himself is a visitor who does not remain." Chapters 05 through 07 of this book offer a complete set of maps of California's desert wilderness areas.

The criteria for a local stewardship organization associated with a particular designation are loose, more about locality than function. Other large national or local groups that support and protect desert land include the Wildlands Conservancy, the National Parks Conservation Association, the Sierra Club, the Native American Land Conservancy, Eastern Sierra Land Trust, the Wilderness Society, CalWild, and the Audubon Society.

01. Mono Basin National Forest Scenic Area (USFS); local stewardship organization: Mono Lake Committee
02. Inyo National Forest (USFS); local stewardship organization: Friends of the Inyo
03. Death Valley National Park (NPS); local stewardship organization: Amargosa Conservancy
04. Naval Air Weapons Station China Lake (DOD)
05. Fort Irwin National Training Center (DOD)

o6. Edwards Air Force Base (DOD)

o7. Mojave National Preserve (NPS); local stewardship organization: Mojave National Preserve Conservancy

o8. Mojave Trails National Monument (BLM); local stewardship organization: Mojave Desert Land Trust

o9. Marine Corps Air Ground Combat Center (DOD)

10. Joshua Tree National Park (NPS); local stewardship organization: Joshua Tree National Park Association

11. Chocolate Mountain Aerial Gunnery Range (DOD)

12. Sand to Snow National Monument (BLM/USFS); local stewardship organization: San Gorgonio Wilderness Association

13. Santa Rosa and San Jacinto Mountains National Monument (BLM/USFS); local stewardship organization: Friends of the Desert Mountains

14. Anza-Borrego Desert State Park (CSP); local stewardship organization: Anza-Borrego Foundation

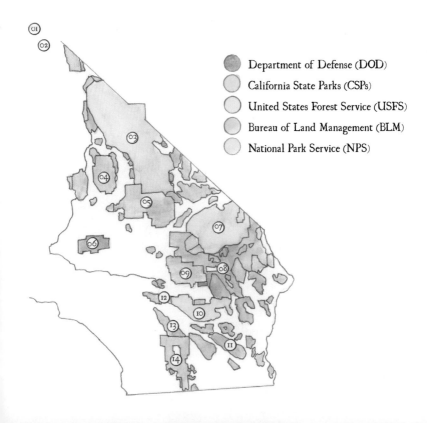

Department of Defense (DOD)

California State Parks (CSPs)

United States Forest Service (USFS)

Bureau of Land Management (BLM)

National Park Service (NPS)

Seven species (and two subspecies) of rattlesnake
live in California's deserts:

A. Northern Mohave rattlesnake, *Crotalus scutulatus scutulatus*
B. Mohave Desert sidewinder, *Crotalus cerastes cerastes*
C. Colorado Desert sidewinder, *Crotalus cerastes laterorepens*
D. Red diamond rattlesnake, *Crotalus ruber*
E. Southwestern speckled rattlesnake, *Crotalus mitchelli pyrrhus*
F. Southern Pacific rattlesnake, *Crotalus oreganus helleri*
G. Great Basin rattlesnake, *Crotalus oreganus lutosus*
H. Panamint rattlesnake, *Crotalus stephensi*
I. Western diamondback rattlesnake, *Crotalus atrox*

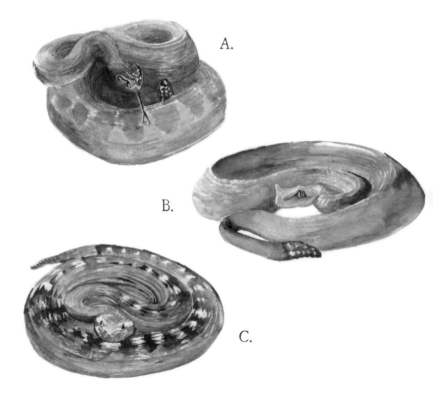

A.

B.

C.

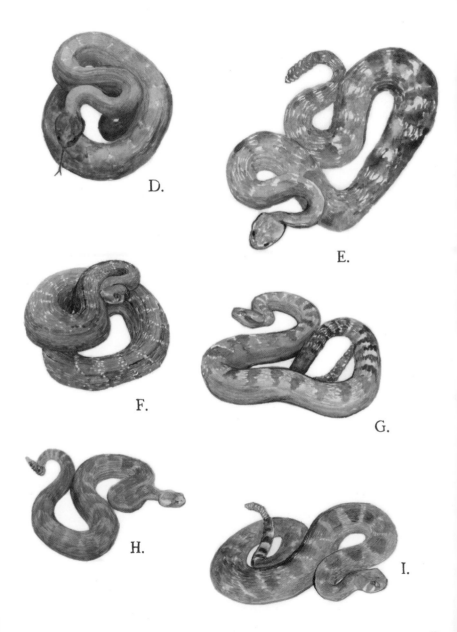

D.

E.

F.

G.

H.

I.

## 01.01c A Trend of Transformation
*The climate regions of California's deserts*

California's climate is as varied as its topography. California is the only region in North America where five climate types (desert, continental, alpine, steppe, and Mediterranean) exist adjacently to one another. Often these climates exist remarkably close to one another, and nowhere is that more apparent than in the desert, where mountain profiles can exceed eleven thousand feet in elevation within less than two dozen linear miles (from the highest point to the lowest in Death Valley National Park), with a corresponding daytime temperature variance of more than 80°F.[3]

A simplification of California's historical seasonal climate patterns[4]

- ○ 01. Cool continental/dry summer
- ○ 02. Cold winter/dry summer and highland/timberline
- ○ 03. Semi-arid steppe (hot)
- ○ 04. Semi-arid steppe
- ● 05. Arid mid-latitude desert
- ○ 06. Arid low-latitude desert (hot)
- ○ 07. California Mediterranean (mixed)

Raven, *Corvus corax*, and crow, *Corvus brachyrhynchos*

Ravens travel and live in pairs; crows travel and live in groups.
Ravens prefer wild habitat; crows prefer proximity to urban communities.
Ravens have a thirty-year life span; crows have an eight-year life span.
Ravens gronk; crows caw.
Ravens have a wedge-shaped tail; crows have a fan-shaped tail.
Ravens have a big, curved beak; crows have a small, flat beak.
Both are extremely intelligent.

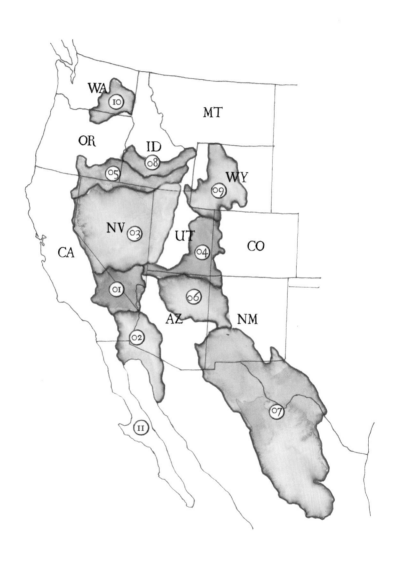

Map 01.02

## 01.02 OF SURVIVAL AND SUN
*Arid lands of the West*

Most geographers describe North America as having four great desert regions: the Mojave, the Great Basin, the Sonoran, and the Chihuahuan. As map 01.02 illustrates, the topographic, climatic, and ecological variation within those deserts deserves further demarcation. Deserts are often divided, climatically, into cold deserts and warm deserts. While all deserts receive relatively low amounts of annual precipitation, cold deserts receive the precipitation in the form of snow, whereas warm deserts receive it as rain.

01. Mojave Desert
02. Sonoran Desert
03. Central Basin and Range
04. Colorado Plateau
05. Northern Basin and Range
06. Arizona/New Mexico Plateau
07. Chihuahuan Desert
08. Snake River Plain
09. Wyoming Basin
10. Columbia Plate
11. Baja California

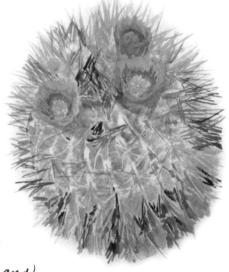

Barrel cactus
Echinocactus sp. and
Ferocactus sp.

*Diameter of inscribed circle, 580 miles*
Map 01.02a

## 01.02a An Ocean of Sagebrush
### *The Great Basin Desert of the West*

At over 157,900 square miles (6,900 in California), the Great Basin Desert sprawls across seven states—the largest desert entirely within the United States. Having no river that makes its way to the ocean, the Great Basin Desert is defined as an endorheic region. Surface water in the Great Basin is fated either to be lost to evaporation or to sink into the earth. In California, it is the smallest of the deserts within the state's borders. The Great Basin crosses into California from the east in two locations: in California's extreme northeast corner, including the Modoc Plateau, and south near Mono Lake and into Death Valley National Park.[5] The primary vegetation type of this desert is sagebrush, *Artemisia tridentata*; piñon, *Pinus* spp.; and juniper, *Juniperus* spp.

Great Basin sagebrush
Artemisia tridentata

*Diameter of inscribed circle, 360 miles*
Map 01.02b

## 01.02b An Expanse of Yucca
### *The Mojave Desert of the West*

At over 54,000 square miles (27,400 in California), the high desert of the Mojave is what most people think of when they imagine the California desert. The ecological Mojave extends into Nevada, Utah, and Arizona and is defined by being, on average, higher in elevation than the surrounding deserts, and because of this, has distinct patterns of botanical life. The eastern Mojave in California, including the Kingston Range, tends to have the Mojave's highest locations. The northern Mojave has the greatest richness of plant species in the California deserts. The southern Mojave is the only location in the world where the Joshua tree, *Yucca brevifolia*, and the giant saguaro, *Carnegiea gigantea*, share habitat. The western Mojave of Antelope Valley is the watershed of the Mojave River. The primary drivers of Mojave's ecological diversity are climate differentials, extreme elevation amplitudes, and volcanic activity.[6]

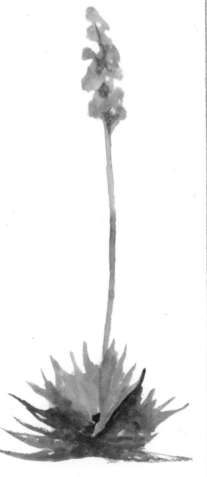

Desert agave
*Agave deserti*

*Diameter of inscribed circle, 700 miles*
Map 01.02c

## 01.02c An Empire of Cactus
### *The Sonoran Desert of the West*

At 106,000 square miles (11,300 in California), the low desert of the Sonoran Desert, of which the Colorado is a subset, is more associated with cactus and other succulent plants than any other of the West's deserts. The number of cactus species is highest in California's Sonoran and Colorado Deserts, contributing the most to the deserts' total population of cactus species, now over eighteen hundred.[7] The Salton Sea, the largest body of water in the California deserts, was preceded by Lake Cahuilla, the largest of the Pleistocene lakes that defined the variegated landscape when this land was much less arid.

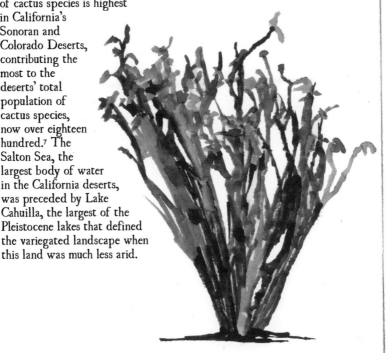

Ocotillo
*Fouquieria splendens*

Common in the Sonoran desert outside of California, the tree like Saguaro, Carnegiea gigantea, only exists along the Colorado River inside the State boundary.

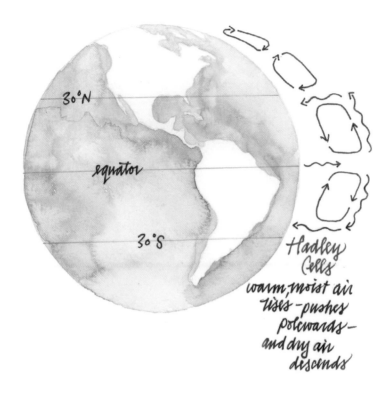

30°N

equator

30°S

Hadley
Cells
warm, moist air
rises—pushes
polewards—
and dry air
descends

## 01.03 GLOBAL BELTS OF WIND AND WEATHER
### *Atmospheric circulation*

As we begin to examine why deserts exist where they do and when they do, we
start with how atmospheric circulation drives global patterns of aridity and how
this circulation is itself directed by the asymmetrical distribution of solar energy.
This energy warms the air most around the equator, where it causes clouds to
form and drop heavy precipitation. This substratospheric air gets pushed poleward
by the ceaseless production of this kind of warmed air. A conveyance occurs as
the air is then unable to escape the troposphere, because as it is pushed north, it
cools and begins to sink. As it sinks it begins to warm again, at about 30 degrees
latitude, but now the air is dry, having already spent its moisture, and arid zones
occur. We know these arid zones as the deserts of the world. A version of this
cyclical, tropospheric conveyance is also responsible for hurricanes, trade winds,
and jet streams across the planet.[8]

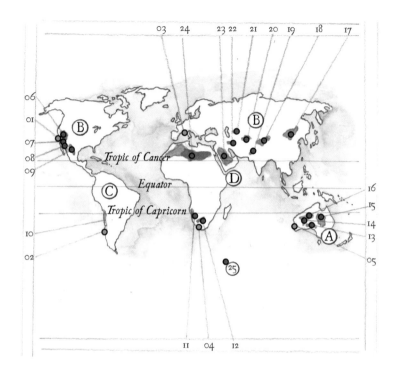

## 01.04 WORLD MAP
*Deserts and botanic realms of the world*

Consistent with map 01.03, arid regions around the world are found in consistent patterns of latitude, often directly adjacent to and east of the world's five Mediterranean climates. Floristic kingdoms are vegetation classifications based on the broadest geographic commonalities, including hemispheric proximity and global tectonic arrangement.

*Tropic of Cancer 23.44°N  Tropic of Capricorn 23.44°S*
*the northern and southern boundaries of the tropics*

## Key 01.04

*Floristic Regions (also called Floristic Realms or Floristic Kingdoms) of the world*

*Source:* Adapted from A. Takhtajan, *Floristic Regions of the World*, trans. T. J. Crovello and A. Cronquist (Berkeley: University of California Press, 1986).

(A) Australian—the most isolated of the world's floristic kingdoms; it includes the titular island continent and New Zealand

(B) Holarctic—the Northern Hemisphere, corresponding to the floristic boreal kingdom

(C) Neotropical—South America, Central America, the Caribbean islands, and southern North America

(D) Paleotropic—Africa, Asia, and Oceania

### Deserts of the world and their aridity causes/temperature type

R—mountain proximity
    cause: rain shadow
E—endorheic
    cause: continental
H—stormless region
    cause: high pressure
O—marine proximity
    cause: ocean temperature
C—cold desert
W—warm desert

### Mediterranean climates of the world

01. California
02. Central Chile
03. Mediterranean Basin
04. Western cape of South Africa
05. Western and south Australia

06. Great Basin (R,E/C)
07. Mojave (R/W)
08. Sonoran (R,H,O/W)
09. Chihuahuan (R/C)
10. Atacama (R,O/C)
11. Namib (O,H/C)
12. Kalahari (R,E/W)
13. Great Victoria (R,H/W)
14. Gibson (R,E,O/W)
15. Simpson (R,O/W)
16. Great Sandy (R,H/W)
17. Gobi (R,E/C)
18. Takla Makan (R,E/C)
19. Thar (R,E,H/C)
20. Kara-Kum (R,E/C)
21. Kyzyl-Kum (R,H/C)
22. Iranian (R,H/C)
23. Arabian (H,O/W)
24. Sahara (H,R,E/W)
25. Antarctic Polar (O/C)

snow geese over the Salton Sea

the greenings of
the Desert
Cahuilla lake bed
Colorado river water
Imperial Valley

## 01.05 LIFE IN THE RAIN SHADOW
*Of physiography and climate*

All of California's deserts exist in what is called a rain shadow. As marine wind moves inland, it picks up moisture from evaporation and transpiration from the sea. When that wind hits the mountains, it cools, which instigates the dumping of all the collected moisture in the form of either rain or snow. Sinking air over the ridgeline becomes relatively drier as it warms, creating a stable desert climate for what is usually thousands of years. With the dramatic difference in elevation from the Mojave to the Sierra Nevada, the conditions are perfect for an unyielding rain shadow effect, and as California is predicted to receive less total precipitation toward the end of the century, so too will the deserts.[9]

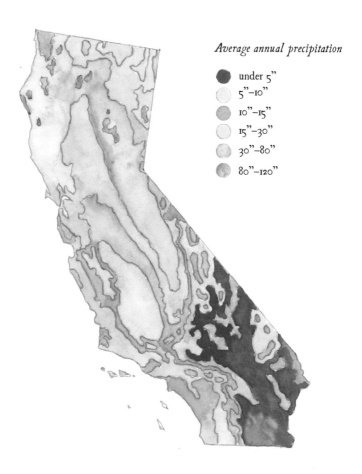

*Average annual precipitation*

● under 5"
○ 5"–10"
◐ 10"–15"
○ 15"–30"
◑ 30"–80"
◕ 80"–120"

The rule of thumb is that you need twenty inches of rainfall per year to maintain agriculture without irrigation. The Imperial Valley in the Salton Slough produces $2 billion a year in agriculture with only three inches of yearly precipitation. The Colorado River is the source of the valley's fecundity.

Map 01.05a

## 01.05a A Disappearing Baseline
*Precipitation patterns in California*

*Climate breakdown* is an appropriate phrase to use when discussing the chaotic long-term patterns of weather that manifest due to anthropogenic global warming. As we move into the second half of the twenty-first century, all patterns teeter on a knife's edge. It may very well be that we will see increased precipitation and simultaneously record increased aridity as patterns defy averages and deluges bring flooding. Because of increasing statewide mean temperature, drought conditions may persist because of the inability of the ground to absorb enough water in time before it evaporates. As conditions exist now, the late-summer monsoon season delivers nearly 25 percent of the yearly precipitation in the Sonoran Desert, and in the Great Basin Desert, 60 percent of its yearly precipitation comes in the form of winter snow.[10]

Harris's Hawk, *Parabuteo unicinctus*, nesting in a saguaro cactus.

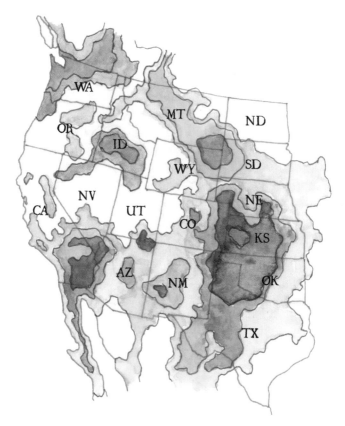

Drought categories (6-month Evaporative Demand Drought Index—spring 2022)

○ ED4 (driest) 98%–100%

○ ED3 95%–98%

○ ED0–ED2 70%–95%

○ unrated 30%–70%

○ EW0–EW2 (wetness categories) 5%–30%

● EW3–EW4 (wettest) 5%–0%

Map 01.05b

## 01.05b Considering Drought in the Desert
### *The West's drying climate*

The Evaporative Demand Drought Index (EDDI), mapped on 01.05b, is a forecasting system for determining ecological and atmospheric dynamics and how they might affect drought conditions.[11] California in the Holocene (the last eleven thousand years) is no stranger to long droughts, and we might be in another one now, although this one is spurred by anthropogenic industry. There have been two such periods of prolonged megadroughts that each lasted for two hundred years. The first was AD 900 to AD 1100, and the other was AD 1200 to AD 1400. Then, as now, the human community seemed to have been more affected than the more-than-human world of Nature, as this was the time of the Ancestral Pueblo collapse, and drought may have been the leading cause. Meanwhile, the deserts and the California Floristic Province retained nearly their entire compliment of biodiversity during such trying times.[12]

Many arthropods have access to physiological survival strategies unavailable to other types of desert fauna. The desert cockroach, *Arenivaga investigata*, survives in the most extreme environments by absorbing water into its body directly from the air in its burrow.[13] Many species of tiny fly (family Chironomidae) enter a state called anhydrobiosis, in which they desiccate into a kind of torpor and reanimate when finally wetted.[14]

There should be a chapter in this book dedicated to invertebrates. The ants, termites, bees, moths, butterflies, spiders, grasshoppers, scorpions, and other insects of the desert—with collectively more total biomass than any faunal type—hold a corresponding share of responsibility for keeping the ecosystem functioning properly. From pollination to decomposition, the ecological role of invertebrate diversity cannot be overstated.

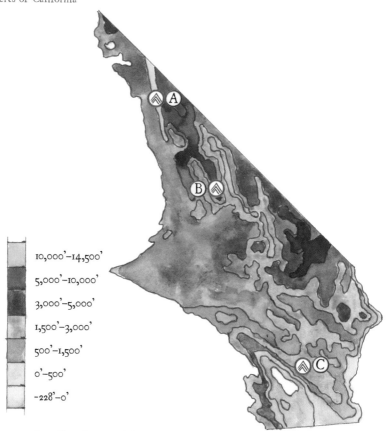

10,000'–14,500'

5,000'–10,000'

3,000'–5,000'

1,500'–3,000'

500'–1,500'

0'–500'

–228'–0'

*Great Basin Desert in California*
(A) Elevation range of basins: 3,800' to 6,000'
Mountains: to 14,246' White Mountain Peak, White Mountains

*Mojave Desert in California*
(B) Elevation range of basins: –280' to 4,500'
Mountains: to 11,049' Telescope Peak, Panamint Range

*Sonoran Desert in California*
(C) Elevation range of basins: –228' to 1,000'
Mountains: to 4,150' Pilot Mountain, Chuckwalla Mountains

Map 01.06

## 01.06 EARTH PROFILE
*Peaks and topography of the desert*

Deep in the earth, under an ancient sea, granitic and metamorphic rocks that
would become the basement rocks for the future Mojave Desert formed almost
two billion years ago and are visible now in the Funeral Mountains near the
Nevada border.[15] The coastal sediment of that ancient sea would eventually form
the five-hundred-million-year-old limestone of the Mitchell Caverns in the Mojave
Preserve.[16] A few periods of volcanism occurred in the last one hundred million
years, forming the Mojave's Cima Dome, among other mountains. Many of the
desert's largest and tallest ranges are known as fault-block ranges, or up-faulted
block ranges. These mountains resulted from a pushing and pulling (rifting and
extensional tectonics) of the ancient parent rock.[17] This process partially describes
the orogeny of the White Mountains, the Panamint Mountains, and the Sierra
Nevada.[18]

Panamint Peak
Death Valley National Park

Map 01.06a

## 01.06a Kingdom of the Bighorn
*Desert-mountain sheep populations*

Today, there are approximately five thousand desert bighorn sheep, *Ovis canadensis nelsoni*, in California's desert mountains. Two other subspecies exist: the endangered California bighorn sheep, *Ovis canadensis californiana*, who survive in just a few herds in the Sierra Nevada, and the threatened peninsular bighorn sheep, *Ovis canadensis cremnobates*, who number under a thousand individuals near Anza-Borrego Desert State Park and whose migration route is threatened by the ill-conceived border wall. These icons of the desert, wondrous ruminant mammals who can weigh more than three hundred pounds and whose horns can weigh over thirty, are masters of the desert and have been grazing these mountains for tens of thousands of years. The mountain cells of map 01.06a are partial or whole mountain ranges wherein known ewe groups, which can number up to a couple of dozen individuals, continue to claim their ancient habitat.[19] Because the sheep's movement is migratory, corridors are critically important for these charismatic wanderers of the desert. The presence of distinct herds of bighorn dictates many conservation policies, and for this reason the map illustrates important biogeographic measures.

01. North White Mountains
02. South White Mountains
03. Deep Springs
04. Inyo Mountains
05. Last Chance/Dry Mountains
06. Grapevine Mountains
07. Funeral Mountains
08. Tin Mountain/Panamint Buttes/ Hunter Mountain
09. Coso Range
10. Argus/Slate Mountains
11. Panamint Range
12. Black Mountains/Greenwater Range
13. Owlshead Mountains
14. Quail/Granite Mountains
15. Eagle Crags
16. Nopah Range
17. Kingston Range/Mesquite Mountains
18. Clark Mountain/Spring Range
19. Avawatz Mountains
20. Soda Mountains
21. Cady Mountains
22. Kelso Peaks/Old Dad Mountains
23. Castle Peaks
24. Piute Range
25. New York Mountains
26. Mid Hills
27. Providence Mountains
28. North Bristol Mountains
29. Granite Mountains
30. South Bristol Mountains
31. Newberry/Rodman Mountains
32. San Gabriel Mountains
33. San Gorgonio Mountains
34. Bullion Mountains
35. Sheep Hole Mountains
36. Marble Mountains
37. Clipper Mountains
38. Old Woman Mountains
39. Dead Mountains
40. Sacramento Mountains
41. Chemehuevi Mountains
42. Whipple Mountains
43. Turtle Mountains
44. Riverside Mountains
45. Iron Mountains

46. Pinto Mountains
47. Little San Bernardino Mountains
48. Coxcomb Mountains
49. Palen Mountains
50. Little Maria Mountains
51. Big Maria Mountains
52. Eagle Mountains
53. Chuckwalla Mountains
54. McCoy Mountains
55. Palo Verde Mountains
56. Peninsular Range
57. Orocopia Mountains
58. Mecca Hills
59. Chocolate Mountains
60. Colorado River
61. Cargo Muchacho

the deserts are always
emerging.
Just as the body
recycles its atomic material
several times over the course of its life,
the deserts are mutable
beings.

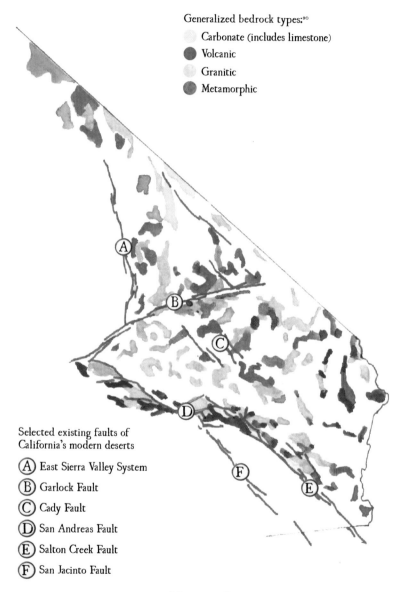

Generalized bedrock types:[20]

- Carbonate (includes limestone)
- Volcanic
- Granitic
- Metamorphic

Selected existing faults of
California's modern deserts

- (A) East Sierra Valley System
- (B) Garlock Fault
- (C) Cady Fault
- (D) San Andreas Fault
- (E) Salton Creek Fault
- (F) San Jacinto Fault

Map 01.06b

## 01.06b Earth Puzzle
*Desert bedrock, faults, and soil*

The San Andreas Fault, between the northward Pacific and the southward North American tectonic plates, formed as a transform fault, or the horizontally moving boundary where the two plates continue to slide past one another, about twenty million years ago. Since then the Pacific Plate has been steadily moving north and slightly away from the continent at a rate of up to two inches per year.[21] The other major fault of the Mojave Desert, the similarly aged Garlock Fault running east–west, has displaced the land forty miles westward relative to the land to its south.[22] The two faults intersect near Tejon Pass. The modern surface geology and soil composition of the Mojave Desert formed through processes of particle erosion, transportation, and deposition.[23]

Soils of the California deserts can be tens of thousands of years old, and for that reason have developed specific chemical features and physical qualities that don't exist in more temperate climates and have a profound influence on local ecology and botany.[24]

Desert varnish: When iron and manganese accumulate on rock surfaces through leaching, disposition, or fungal processes, they form a dark-colored veneer particular to hot desert climates.

Vesicular horizons: Hard, thin layers of wind-deposited silt develop, which hold small pockets of air (vesicles) and prevent rainwater from penetrating the soil.

Desert pavement: The erosion of surface soil and the pushing up of small stones from beneath lead to an accretion and configuration of subsurface rocks that form a rigid shell over desert soil, creating a road-like appearance to many desert landscapes.

Subsurface clay, and carbonate horizons: These are two physical and chemical deterrents to plant growth that affect desert ecology. Subsurface clay prevents roots from reaching deep water, and carbonate layers require specific plant adaptations to tolerate their soil chemistry.

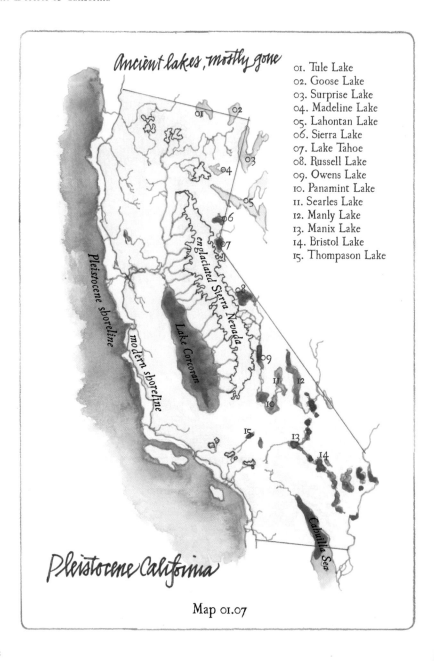

Ancient lakes, mostly gone

01. Tule Lake
02. Goose Lake
03. Surprise Lake
04. Madeline Lake
05. Lahontan Lake
06. Sierra Lake
07. Lake Tahoe
08. Russell Lake
09. Owens Lake
10. Panamint Lake
11. Searles Lake
12. Manly Lake
13. Manix Lake
14. Bristol Lake
15. Thompason Lake

Pleistocene shoreline

modern shoreline

englaciated Sierra Nevada

Lake Corcoran

Cahuilla Sea

Pleistocene California

Map 01.07

## 01.07 THE AGE OF GIANTS AND ICE
*Mapping California's Last Glacial Maximum*

The Last Glacial Maximum ended with the Holocene, which also marked the end of the previous epoch of geologic time, the Pleistocene. During the Pleistocene, so much water was locked in glacial ice that the coastal profile of California was radically different than it is today, and the climate was so different that California's deserts had yet to attain their present characteristics. In the cool, mesic woodlands that was the late-Pleistocene Mojave (around eighteen thousand years ago), Columbian mammoth, *Mammuthus columbi*, whose weight exceeded twice that of an African elephant, roamed alongside the largest camel to have ever lived, *Gigantocamelus*. These two existed, along with at least twenty other herbivorous mammals that weighed more than a ton, for millions and millions of years before the Holocene extinction events that would see the end of their reign with the change in the climate into the world's current interglacial period and with the coming of humanity. Along with the extinction of the megafauna, the great network of lakes that are still detectable as dry beds across California's deserts began to disappear.

The Columbian mammoth, largest of all mammoth species, at home in the Mojave before it was the desert of today

Arizona hairy scorpion
size: up to 7" — toxicity: low
Common

There are at least twenty-five species of scorpions (order Scorpiones) in California's deserts; there are over twenty-five hundred species in the world. Arizona hairy scorpion, *Hadrurus arizonensis*, and stripe-tailed scorpion, *Vaejovis spinigerus*, are common in California's deserts; bark scorpion, *Centruroides exilicauda*, is the most dangerous to humans.

*Paruroctonus conclusus*
size: up to 2" - toxicity: unknown
recently discovered species
extremely rare

Stripe-tailed scorpion
size: up to 2" - toxicity: low
Common

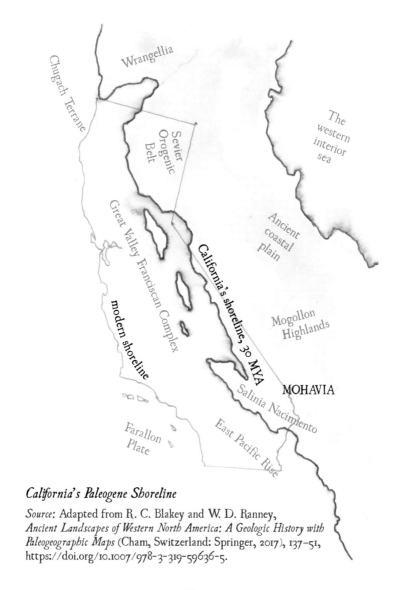

Chugach Terrane

Wrangellia

The western interior sea

Sevier Orogenic Belt

Great Valley Franciscan Complex

Ancient coastal plain

California's shoreline, 30 MYA

modern shoreline

Mogollon Highlands

MOHAVIA

Salinia Nacimiento

Farallon Plate

East Pacific Rise

*California's Paleogene Shoreline*

*Source:* Adapted from R. C. Blakey and W. D. Ranney,
*Ancient Landscapes of Western North America: A Geologic History with
Paleogeographic Maps* (Cham, Switzerland: Springer, 2017), 137–51,
https://doi.org/10.1007/978-3-319-59636-5.

Map 01.07a

## 01.07a Ancient Mohavia
*Paleogene California*

The dawn of the Cenozoic was a tec-
tonically active time in western North
America. Following the extinction of
the dinosaurs, the rise of the mammals
across the paleogeography of what
would eventually become California
took place in a landscape that would
be unrecognizable to us now. By fifty
million years ago, the ancient super-
continent Gondwana had completely
broken up, and it was at about this
time that the Rocky Mountains experienced massive uplift. This period also
saw the establishment of an ancient
floristic province called Mohavia,
marked by the distribution of ancient
palm species. Mohavia existed across
an Oligocene terrane, land that was
displaced by the San Andreas Fault
and eventually carried four hundred
miles northwest in the interim between
then and now.[25]

California fan palm
Washingtonia filifera

ancient California camel skull

## Pleistocene and Current Distribution of Joshua Trees

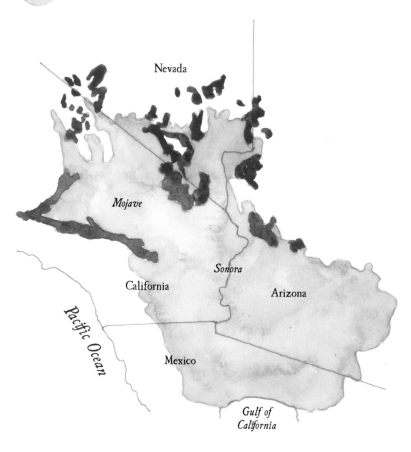

Map 01.07b

## 01.07b Regarding Megafaunal Fruit
*Pleistocene distribution of Joshua trees*

Across what would become the California desert, for millions of years, the black bear–sized Shasta ground sloth, *Nothrotheriops shastensis*, snacked on the fruit of the proto-avocado tree, *Persea coalingensis*.[26] The woodland that the sloth grazed in was thick with Joshua trees, low-elevation bristlecone pines, piñon, and juniper over grasslands of beargrass and sage. In a demonstration of coevolution, the massive seed inside the avocado tree's fruit would pass through the sloth as she wandered her lakeside woodland habitat in the pre-Mojave landscape, ensuring the trees' distribution. It seems that the Shasta sloth and megafaunal herbivores like her were responsible for the distribution of the seeds of many local species, which not only had enormous seeds like that of the avocado but perhaps grew in trees that only they could reach, such as the Joshua tree, *Yucca brevifolia*.[27] Without the megafaunal creatures that they evolved with, how lonely must these ancient trees be in their diminished ranges?

the joshua tree
*Yucca brevifolia*

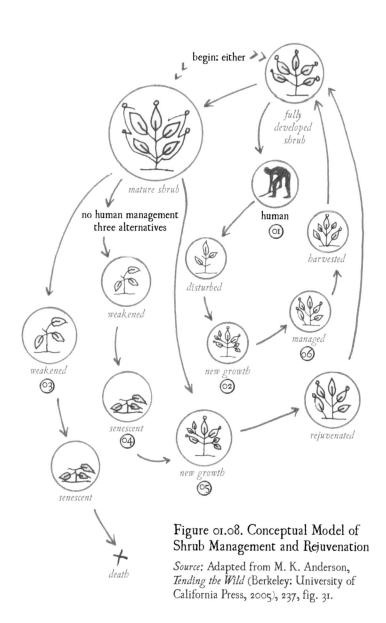

begin: either

*fully developed shrub*

*mature shrub*

no human management
three alternatives

human
⊙1

*disturbed*

*weakened*

*weakened*
⊙3

*harvested*

*managed*
⊙6

*new growth*
⊙2

*senescent*
⊙4

*new growth*
⊙5

*rejuvenated*

*senescent*

death

**Figure 01.08. Conceptual Model of Shrub Management and Rejuvenation**

*Source:* Adapted from M. K. Anderson, *Tending the Wild* (Berkeley: University of California Press, 2005), 237, fig. 31.

## 01.08 INDIGENOUS REGIMES OF RECIPROCITY
*Human–shrub management theory*

For the Kumeyaay, Nature is not a thing full of resources that can be taken but a system that involves people and requires them to give back what they use.[28] Encouraging plant regeneration through the process of harvesting these plants for hundreds of cultural uses, mimicking ecological disturbance regimes, is not only a primary strategy Indigenous peoples of the desert have employed for thousands of years of resiliency and relative prosperity but also a means by which they have shaped ecosystems, fostering fecundity.

01. Human disturbance methods include fire, coppicing, and pruning.
02. New vegetative growth arises from epicormic buds.
03. With no disturbance, shrubs may fade to senescence and death.
04. Senescent shrubs may experience new growth after an extended time period between disturbances.
05. Some nonanthropogenic disturbance such as herbivory, fire, or flood may spur new epicormic growth.
06. A successfully managed shrub is ready for harvest in its adaptive cycle toward becoming again a fully developed shrub.

A Pleistocene bird that still calls the Mojave home
Yellow-headed blackbird, *Xanthocephalus xanthocephalus*

## 02. EVERY SACRED DROP
### *California desert water*

*Sympetrum corruptum*

length 41 mm to 49 mm
(about 1-½")

62 species worldwide

Variegated meadowhawk dragonfly

preys on
aquatic insects
fly larvae, sometimes
fish and tadpoles

live approximately one year

Called darters in the UK

there are 10 quintillion insects alive in the world, that is 200 million insects for every human.

Water means everything in the desert, and its unavailability defines an essential aspect of a desert's ecological character. Where water is, so is life. Where water isn't, neither is life. In the age of climate breakdown, it is likely that exacerbated desiccation of the landscape will continue and probably accelerate. Conceptually understanding the basic historical, spatial, material, and atmospheric dynamics of how water works in the lands to the east of the Sierra Nevada and the mountains of California is instrumental in any talk of future deserts. In addition to water discussed in chapter 01 (01.05), this chapter examines a few important and rudimentary survey aspects of California desert hydrogeography.

Climate breakdown by way of anthropogenic global warming is quickly and radically altering the hydrosphere, and its full effect may be realized soon. The hydrosphere—the dynamic totality of earth's water system in the ocean, ground, and atmosphere, and across the land—has operated within normative, recognizable parameters since the beginning of the interglacial period called the Holocene. In California, after the Last Glacial Maximum approximately eighteen thousand years ago, temperatures had been generally (and slowly) increasing until they plateaued into modern climate patterns about five or six thousand years ago. At a zoomed-out macro scale, California's shoreline has not changed dramatically at all since then. In this period of generally predictable climate patterns, California's forests and deserts began to resemble their contemporary selves. There were occasional megadroughts, and devastating megafires occasionally tore through vast areas of arboreal habitat, but for the most part, California was California. It was about this time that, generally speaking, the peoples of California coalesced into their still-extant tribal identities, proficient in applying landscape-wide resource management techniques that exerted incredible influence on the shape and quality of California's ecosystems. In this time, the deserts of California grew drier and hotter, and took on the shape and character that they still hold. In the Anthropocene, climate change is leading to climate breakdown, and the period of normative predictability is now coming to an end.

Pacific tree frog
of Death Valley
Hyla regilla

At the dawn of what is generally regarded as a new geologic age, the carbon legacy of humanity is so impactful that it may dictate the fate of the biosphere for thousands of years to come. The uncertain fate of the deserts of California is entangled in this inauspicious legacy. Whatever the Anthropocene turns out to be, it is presently replete with paradoxes, and nowhere is that more

Death Valley National Park
Darwin Falls
5.5 meters Tall
Spring fed

apparent than in the deserts of California. A paradox is defined here as an absurd proposition that leads to some piece of truth. Paradoxes are often counterintuitive and also commonly come off as a bit ironic. The primary paradoxes now defining the desert are presented here as questions to stoke contemplation: (1) If the energy development of the desert is wounding the desert, but we need energy development in the form of solar and wind energy to save the world, what world are we saving? (2) If residential development of the desert is occurring because people love the desert, and that development wounds the desert, is love for the desert wounding the desert? (3) If the development of conservation land areas, in the form of sequestering (what is thought of as) nature, isolates what is being protected from any connective habitat, might rethinking policies of development improve conservation goals?

The biggest paradox is wrapped up in the philosophic rhetoric of what the world is and whether or not it may have already ended. Not the world of Nature (capital $N$—your experience of the world right now) but the world that was. When was the moment that the human hand irrevocably deformed the trajectory of the biosphere? Was there a moment when the historical world ended and the Anthropocene began? Are we living after the end of the world? Perhaps the world ended in 1945, deep in the Arizona desert. On July 16, with the testing of the first atomic weapon, humanity became a nuclear-realized, geophysical force. For the next sixty-five years, thousands of nuclear bombs were detonated in Nevada's Mojave Desert at the Nevada Test Site (NTS). Through our depositing of anthropogenic radioactive particles into the biosphere, evidence of the advent of the Anthropocene became detectable and will be so for millions of years to come. By this argument, perhaps it is that in 1945, the world actually ended a second time. The first might have been in 1769, when James Watt patented his steam engine and the first industrial output of carbon forever changed the world's atmospheric chemistry. Considering the end of the world as an metaphorical event that may have already occurred liberates the historical vision about what the world is and what new world might emerge.

This book is not only an exercise in art and the natural history of the desert but an account of the desert of the Anthropocene. After so many centuries of slow buildup of the carbon and then the nuclear particle veneer across the biosphere, humanity is no longer watching but participating. Our interactions with all manner of planetary biology will now be marked by geology.

It may be that the immediate legacy of humanity is continued aridity. All deserts, like all human societies, exist in homeostasis and will adapt to greater aridity in the coming decades, or they won't. Examining the trends and tracing the trickles of water that feed all life in these dry places reveal another great paradox so apparent in the warming desert: Might we love the desert for its lack of water? In that lack, isn't the water we do get that much sweeter?

The world, if it has not already ended,
is beholden to wholly novel stressors,
born of chaos that demand a nuanced understanding
of the strange bottlenecks
that threaten everywhere,
and whisper collapse
at every turn.

Palm grove on fire

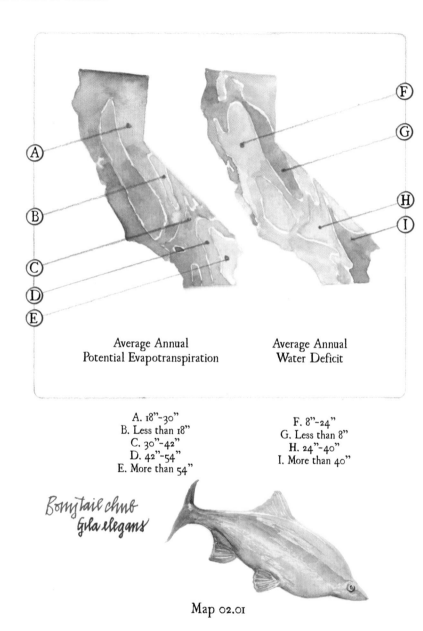

Average Annual
Potential Evapotranspiration

Average Annual
Water Deficit

A. 18"-30"
B. Less than 18"
C. 30"-42"
D. 42"-54"
E. More than 54"

F. 8"-24"
G. Less than 8"
H. 24"-40"
I. More than 40"

Bonytail chub
Gila elegans

Map 02.01

## 02.01 A THIRST ON THE LAND
*Potential evapotranspiration and the water deficit*

Transpiration is best thought of as how a plant breathes. When the plant draws water from the soil, the water serves the plant by facilitating metabolic and physiological functions, including photosynthesis, temperature regulation, and turgor pressure. The water is pulled through the plant and released through specialized pores in the plant's leaves, called stomata. Different plant species transpire different quantities of water, and mitigating rates of transpiration is a key desert plant adaptation (see 03.02). Increased temperature and decreased humidity (both core aspects of desert climate) increase the rate of transpiration.

The rate of evapotranspiration and the accompanying water deficit of the region are important measures of soil aridity and metrics of just how dry the desert actually is, in relation to other land areas of the state. Potential evapotranspiration is the measure of the maximum rate that water is lost both from the soil surface by evaporation and from the regional vegetation via transpiration, measured against the water deficit, which is the amount of water absent that would need to be supplied by irrigation to optimally grow crops. Water deficits of greater than a twenty-four inches begin to define the desert as well as would any measure of precipitation.

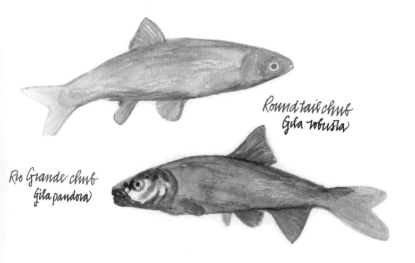

Roundtail chub
Gila robusta)

Rio Grande chub
Gila pandora)

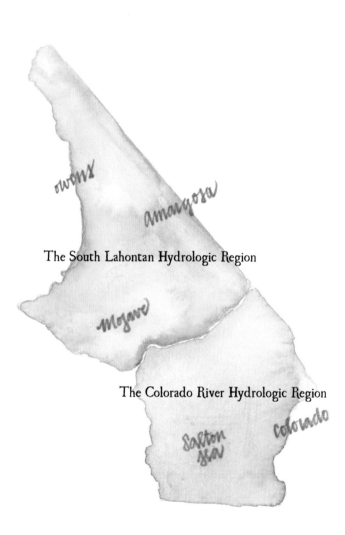

owens

Amargosa

The South Lahontan Hydrologic Region

Mojave

The Colorado River Hydrologic Region

Salton Sea

Colorado

Map 02.02

## 02.02 THE HIGH AND LOW DESERTS
*Hydrologic regions of the Mojave and Sonoran Deserts*

The careful monitoring of water necessary for modern development to occur in California's deserts has resulted in the invention of two management regions: the South Lahontan Hydrologic Region (SLH) and the Colorado River Hydrologic Region (CRH). Both are vast tracts of land and don't necessarily correspond to watershed commonalities but instead represent conglomerates of water-basin provinces divided by demographic, agricultural, and industrial usage. Together, the two hydrologic regions cover more than 26,700 square miles—28 percent of the entire land area of California. The border shared between the two regions is roughly analogous to the ecological zone of the Mojave Desert's southern border, but this correlation is not perfect. The SLH includes the Owens, Mojave, and Amargosa Rivers, as well as the Mono Basin. The CRH includes the watershed of the Colorado River in California, the Salton Trough of the Coachella and Imperial Valleys, and the surrounding basins.

Nearly one million people live in the SLH (most of them in Antelope Valley) in an area that receives only eight inches of annual rainfall. Another million people now live in the CRH (most of them in Coachella Valley) in an area that receives only three inches of annual rainfall. Across the SLH, a bit more than thirteen thousand wells tap 70 percent of an estimated seven hundred thousand acre-feet of water per year that human communities demand for both agricultural and urban uses.[1] Due to a decline in groundwater level, portions of the Antelope Valley Basin have subsided more than six feet in the past one hundred years. That land will never rise again.

In the CRH, water usage is highest in the Coachella Valley and in the Imperial Valley. Despite lack of substantial rainfall, the aquifer under Coachella Valley is large, and in 2021, one hundred thousand acre-feet were pumped to meet urban needs and to make up the difference from the lack of water imported from the Colorado River.[2] Even during the unprecedented, ongoing drought, the Imperial Valley has rights to 3.1 million acre-feet of water from the Colorado River, or 70 percent of California's total allocation.[3] The estimated water budget in the CRH for 2020 was approximately 740,000 acre-feet for urban use and 3.5 million acre-feet for agriculture.[4]

Black skimmer

Black tern

Fulvous whistling-duck

Woodstork

## Birds and waterfowl species of special concern who rely on California's desert wetlands

Redhead, *Aythya americana*
(nesting: Modoc Plateau and Mono
Lake)

Barrow's goldeneye, *Bucephala islandica*
(nesting: Lower Colorado River)

Black skimmer, *Rynchops niger*
(nesting: Salton Sea)

Black tern, *Chlidonias niger*
(nesting: Modoc Plateau)

Fulvous whistling-duck,
*Dendrocygna bicolor*
(nesting: Imperial Valley)

Gull-billed tern, *Gelochelidon nilotica*
(nesting: Salton Sea)

American white pelican,
*Pelecanus erythrorhynchos*
(nesting: Modoc Plateau)

Least bittern, *Ixobrychus exilis*
(nesting: Imperial Valley)

Wood stork, *Mycteria americana*
(nesting: Salton Sea)

Yellow rail, *Coturnicops noveboracensis*
(nesting: Bridgeport Valley)

Lesser sandhill crane,
*Grus canadensis canadensis*
(wintering: Imperial Valley)

Map 02.03

## 02.03 OF AQUIFERS, FLOODPLAINS, AND GEOHYDROLOGY
*Groundwater basin estimates*

There are almost 120 alluvial groundwater basins that lie beneath a bit more than half the entire land area of both the South Lahontan Hydrologic Region and the Colorado River Hydrologic Region. Connected by and reliant on surface-water floodplains for recharge, these groundwater basins are where the desert hides a surprising amount of water. Although there is groundwater everywhere, the groundwater basins under much of rocky and mountainous California are small compared to what the deserts hold. With millions of years of accumulated alluvium and a large number of fractured rock aquifers, the geohydrology of the deserts is such that there are indeed relatively vast and yet precariously dwindling treasure-holds of subterranean water.

A. Light blue: water basin of between 1 and 10 million acre-feet

B. Cadiz Water Basin: potentially between 17 and 34 million acre-feet

C. Light green: undeveloped water basin of unknown size

D. Hydrologic border

Tackstem
*Calycoseris wrightii*

***Estimated Groundwater Capacity per Basin***
*Source:* Adapted from D. Hornbeck and P. S. Kane, *California Patterns: A Geographical and Historical Atlas* (Palo Alto, CA: Mayfield, 1983), 13.

Western spadefoot

### Spadefoots, Scaphiopodidae

True toads are in the family Bufonidae. Spadefoots, often called toads, are in the family Scaphiopodidae. Unlike toads, the burrowing spadefoots have vertical pupils and lack a parotoid gland in their head that toads use to excrete so-called bufotoxins to protect themselves. Species from both of the two genera of Scaphiopodidae live in California's deserts: Couch's spadefoot, *Scaphiopus couchii*, and Western spadefoot, *Spea hammondii*.

Perhaps the world ends
Pretty regularly.
The Mojave has not been the Mojave
for that long,
and in the Anthropocene it will
surely become something
else,
whether this new geologic age
lasts for a long time or is over
quickly.
Perhaps the Mojave
is already unrecognizable
to itself.

Tecopa Hot Springs

Cross section of hillslope: Perched water table and river hydrology

## 02.04 THE MIRACLE OF A SPRING
*Surface saturation dynamics*

A great hydrological truth of groundwater in the desert is the asymmetry between the amount of it in the ground and its inaccessibility. The relatively vast hoard of groundwater in the desert is hidden, accessible only in a relatively few locations. There are thousands of surface seeps (wet areas) and springs (flowing water) across California's desert region. There are over 240 inside Mojave National Preserve alone.[5] Springs, rivers, marshes, creeks, wetlands, seeps, and other habitat environments occur when the water table of the aquifer (composed of alluvium or forming from rock fractures) or the aquiclude (an isolated portion of the aquifer) overlaps with the surface environment. Aquifers recharge only from either rainfall or surface water delivery. When withdrawal outpaces recharge, land subsidence can occur.

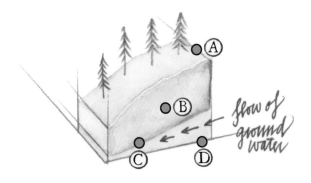

flow of ground water

Cross section of hillslope: Subterranean hydrological zones

A. Surface
B. Unsaturated zone (Vadose zone)
C. Water table (Epiphreatic zone)
D. Saturation zone (Phreatic zone)

*Source:* Adapted from US Geological Survey (USGS), "General Facts and Concepts about Ground Water," https://pubs.usgs.gov/circ/circ1186/html /gen_facts.html

- ◒ Owens pupfish, *Cyprinodon radiosus*
- ● Salt Creek pupfish, *Cyprinodon salinus salinus*
- ◔ Cottonball marsh pupfish, *Cyprinodon salinus milleri*
- ● Amargosa River pupfish, *Cyprinodon nevadensis amargosae*
- ◔ Saratoga Springs pupfish, *Cyprinodon nevadensis nevadensis*
- ◑ Shoshone pupfish, *Cyprinodon nevadensis shoshone*
- ○ Ash Meadows pupfish, *Cyprinodon nevadensis mionectes*
- ◑ Devils Hole pupfish, *Cyprinodon diabolis*
- ○ Warm Springs pupfish, *Cyprinodon nevadensis pectoralis*
- ● Desert pupfish, *Cyprinodon macularius*

*Source:* B. M. Pavlik, *The California Deserts: An Ecological Rediscovery* (Berkeley: University of California Press, 2008), 158.

**Map 02.05**

## 02.05 AN IMPOSSIBLE FISH
### *Pupfish biogeography*

Four species of pupfish, plus one with six subspecies (*Cyprinodon nevadensis*), make for a total of ten taxonomic classifications of this tougher-than-tough little fish in the desert region of southeast California. Over the past twenty thousand years, with the desiccation of Lake Manly and the pluvial network across the region, isolated populations from an original larger population began their march to their present-day speciation.[6]

The pupfish is classified as an extremophilic organism because of its unique adaptations to withstand harsh environmental conditions and huge fluctuations in those conditions. For example, among the arsenal of survival techniques that this two-inch-long fish has uniquely evolved in small bits of watery habitat around the region is the ability to withstand daily water temperature fluctuations of more than 35°F (ten times the temperature fluctuation in a mountain stream or lake), in water temperatures that can reach 111°F.[7] Inside their aqueous habitat, pupfish routinely withstand salinity quotients that are double what they are in the ocean, and they also are able to spend entire winters in anaerobic conditions, buried in sediment, waiting for spring rain.[8]

Devil's Hole pupfish, *Cyprinodon diabolis*—isolated species population for approximately one million years at what is now Ash Meadows National Wildlife Refuge, Nevada

Cottonball marsh pupfish, *Cyprinodon salinus milleri*—isolated species population in the basin of Death Valley

Salt Creek pupfish, *Cyprinodon salinus salinus*—isolated species population endemic to one tributary of the Amargosa River

Amargosa pupfish, *Cyprinodon nevadensis*—six subspecies: 1. Amargosa River pupfish, *C. n. amargosae*, 2. Tecopa pupfish, *C. n. calidae* (extinct), 3. Ash Meadows pupfish, *C. n. mionectes*, 4. Saratoga Springs pupfish, *C. n. nevadensis*, 5. Warm Springs pupfish, *C. n. pectoralis*, 6. Shoshone pupfish, *C. n. shoshone*

## 02.06 THE SWEETNESS OF THE BITTER WATER
### *The Amargosa River*

Near the bend in the Amargosa River, where the river makes its turn from flowing southward to flowing northward toward its denouement in the Badwater Basin, it travels through a geologic region called the middle Proterozoic Crystal Spring formation, which at nearly one billion years old is the oldest sedimentary rock in California.[9] More than 125 miles of this unique river run underground; it begins its 185-mile run to Badwater (which at 282 feet below sea level is the lowest point in North America) from its headwaters at four thousand feet near the Ash Meadows Wildlife Refuge (AMWR) in the Nevadan Mojave, to the west of Death Valley National Park.

The Amargosa River represents some of the most varied and rich desert riverine and riparian habitat in the Mojave. It is speculated that with more than fifty endemic species that exist nowhere else on the planet, AMWR contains more endemic terrestrial species than any other comparatively sized area in the United States.[10] The Amargosa watershed covers a vast 3.52 million acres or fifty-five hundred square miles, with only 60 percent of that area able to contribute to the river's flow.[11] A twenty-eight-mile segment from Shoshone to Dumont Dunes is protected as a Wild and Scenic River—the nation's highest standard of watercourse protection.

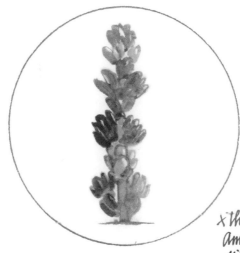

x threatened x
Amargosa niterwort
Nitrophila
Mohavensis

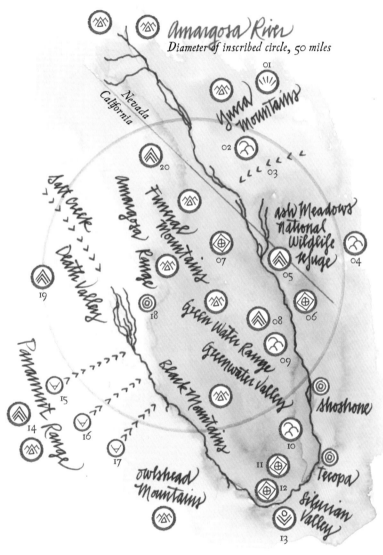

Amargosa River

*Diameter of inscribed circle, 50 miles*

Nevada
California

Yucca Mountains

Ash Meadows National Wildlife Refuge

Salt Creek

Amargosa Range

Funeral Mountains

Death Valley

Green Water Range

Greenwater Valley

Black Mountains

Panamint Range

Shoshone

Tecopa

Owlshead Mountains

Silurian Valley

Map 02.06

01. Jackass Flats
02. Striped Hills
03. Rock Valley Wash
04. Devils Hole Hills
05. Eagle Mountain (3,806')
06. Resting Spring Range Wilderness
07. Funeral Mountains Wilderness
08. Brown Peak (4,497')
09. Dublin Hills
10. Sperry Hills
11. Ibex Wilderness
12. Saddle Peak Hills Wilderness
13. Amargosa Canyon Dumont Dunes
    Natural Area
14. Telescope Peak (11,049')
15. Trail Canyon
16. Hanaupah Canyon
17. Johnson Canyon
18. Furnace Creek
19. Tucki Mountain (6,732')
20. Chloride Cliff (5,279')

x endangered x
amargosa vole
Microtus
californicus
scirpensis

x threatened
Swainson's
hawk
Buteo
swainsoni

California

amargosa
watershed

Map 02.07

## 02.07 RESERVES AND RESERVOIRS
*The Colorado River in California*

Water that falls in the form of snow in the far Rocky Mountains feeds a substantial portion of modern California's need for the stuff. It is delivered and collected in a string of reservoirs along California's border with Arizona by the Southwest's greatest river: the Colorado. The five dams along the border and their reservoir capacity, from north to south, are (07) Parker Dam/Lake Havasu/647,000 acre-feet; (08) Headgate Rock Dam/Lake Moovalya/less than 50,000 acre-feet; (10) Palo Verde Dam/Diversion dam for irrigation only—no storage; (17) Imperial Dam/Imperial Lake/160,000 acre-feet; and Laguna Dam/ Diversion dam for irrigation only.

### National wildlife refuges

a-01. Havasu National Wildlife Refuge—37,516 acres
a-02. Cibola National Wildlife Refuge—18,444 acres
a-03. Imperial National Wildlife Refuge—25,768 acres

An additional eighteen conservation areas that are typically one-to-two thousand acres in size are managed as part of the Lower Colorado River Multi-Species Conservation Program, in turn managed by the Bureau of Reclamation and the Department of the Interior.[12]

### Indigenous water rights of the Colorado

There are thirty federally recognized tribes that depend on the Colorado River for water and together represent seniority rights to 2.9 million acre-feet of river water—almost one-quarter of the river's total annual flow, although lack of infrastructure is often cited as the reason that they are prevented from collecting their allotment.[13] Of these thirty tribes, five are on the Arizona-California border:[14]

A. Fort Mojave Indian Tribe
B. Chemehuevi Indian Tribe
C. Colorado River Indian Tribes
D. Quechuan Tribe
E. Cocopah Tribe of Arizona

01. Mohave Valley
02. Needles
03. Topock Gorge
04. Mohave Canyon
05. Lake Havasu
06. Chemehuevi Reservation
07. Parker Dam
08. Headgate Rock Dam
09. Colorado River Reservation
10. Palo Verde Dam
11. Palo Verde Valley
12. Cibola Valley/Cibola National Wildlife Refuge
13. Indian Pass Wilderness
14. Picacho Peak Wilderness
15. Picacho State Recreation Area
16. Little Picacho Peak Wilderness
17. Imperial Dam/Laguna Dam
18. Morelos Dam
19. Laguna Grande
20. Isla Montague

77

Colorado pikeminnow

Ptychocheilus lucius
federally endangered
endemic to the Colorado
River Basin
family Cyprinidae

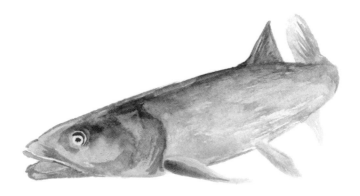

Can live up To 50 years
~ 80 pounds
historically grew to six feet in length
the longest one captured in recent
years was four feet long.

Yuma Clapper Rail
or Yuma Ridgway's rail
Rallus longirostris yumanensis
federally endangered but under
review as to whether
it will continue to be

pre-molt adult bodies (may-august) leave
adults flightless          eats crayfish
Needs wet ground in riparian habitat
for nesting and foraging —
about the size of a chicken
one of seven North american rail species

the Colorado River
across the western
United States

Diameter of inscribed circle, 900 miles

Map 02.07a

## 02.07a Desperately Needed, Desperately Taxed
### *The Colorado River watershed*

In the summer of 2022, as the West continued to experience what is called a megadrought that seems to have lasted for the entire twenty-first century as yet (twenty-two years), the capacity of water storage infrastructure in the Colorado is at a historic low of 34 percent. Despite that, California is set to receive its full allotment of the water it has a right to: more than 4.5 million acre-feet (MAF)—1.1 MAF for agricultural use and 3.4 MAF for urban use.[15] An acre-foot is generally thought of as what a family of four uses in one year; therefore, 3.4 MAF

equates to potentially enough water for 13.5 million people across Southern California. As the drought continues— as it is expected to due to the virulent force that is climate breakdown by way of anthropogenic global warming—California's seniority rights guaranteeing the largest portion of any state to the water of the Colorado may be as tenuous as they are certainly contentious.

01. Green River
02. Big Sandy River
03. Hams Fork
04. Blacks Fork
05. Flaming Gorge Reservoir
06. Little Snake River
07. Yampa River
08. White River
09. Duchesne River
10. Strawberry Reservoir
11. Price River
12. San Rafael River
13. Dirty Devil River
14. Escalante River
15. Blue River
16. Eagle River
17. Gunnison River
18. Dolores River
19. San Juan River
20. Animas River
21. White River Wash

22. Meadow Valley Wash
23. Virgin River
24. Grand Canyon
25. Little Colorado River
26. Polacca Wash
27. Puerco Wash
28. Zuni Wash
29. Colorado River Aqueduct
30. Central Arizona Project
31. Gila River
32. Hassayampa Wash
33. Aqua Fria
34. Verde River
35. Salt River
36. Santa Cruz Wash
37. San Pedro River
38. San Simon Wash
39. Gila River
40. San Francisco River

*Crenichthys baileyi albivallis*
Preston white river springfish
one of three subspecies
of small pool fish endemic
to the white River
white pine County
Nevada
× not listed ×

Endemic California Desert fish families

- ✓ Pupfish  Cyprinodon
- ✓ Poolfish  ~~Empetrichythys~~
- ✓ Dace  Rhinichthys
- ✓ Chubs  Siphateles
- ✓ Suckers  Catostomus and Xyrauchen

Birds of the Imperial wilderness on the
Colorado River

Abert's towhee (breeds)

Bald eagle (winter)

Black rail

Canada goose

Clapper rail (breeds)

Clark's grebe

Common poorwill (breeds)

Crissal thrasher (breeds)

Gila woodpecker (resident)

Ladder-backed woodpecker

Least bittern (breeds)

Lucy's warbler (early spring)

Peregrine falcon

Phainopepla

Prairie falcon (winter)

Sage sparrow

Sandhill crane (rare; migration/winter)

Summer tanager

Tundra swan (rare; winter)

Verdin

Warblers
(winter; migrant)

Western grebe
(breeds)

white-fronted
goose

Willow
flycatcher
(migrant)

## 02.08 THE DESERT'S UNDERGROUND ARTERY
*The Mojave River*

The Mojave River comes to the surface in the San Bernardino Mountains in two forks. The west fork meets Deep Creek; the other fork is near a flood control dam called the Mojave Forks. The Mojave River emerges from the mountains into a floodplain that sits on a massive alluvial fan of Pliocene (5 MYA) deposits that is up to two thousand feet thick.[16] Through the Antelope Valley, the Mojave River travels north until it turns right near Barstow and fades into the desert at the Mojave River Wash, an inland delta east of the Mojave National Preserve. Except for years of deluge, the Mojave River flows mostly underground, only surfacing at a few points near Victorville and in the Afton Canyon.

The river and the riparian habitat it supports are threatened by water usage in the Antelope Valley. Pumping in the last decades of the twentieth century caused the water table of the Mojave River to decline by more than five feet and resulted in the devastating die-off of up to 95 percent of native Fremont cottonwood, *Populus fremontii*, and the habitat this keystone species supports, leaving it vulnerable to the incredibly destructive and difficult to remediate salt cedar tamarisk, *Tamarix chinensis*, an incredibly invasive species that destroys habitat by monopolizing light, water, soil nutrients, and space.[17]

Yellow bullhead.
*Ameiurus natalis*

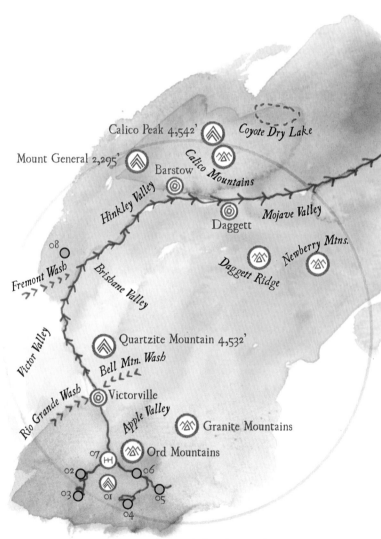

Calico Peak 4,542'

Coyote Dry Lake

Mount General 2,295'

Calico Mountains

Barstow

Hinkley Valley

Mojave Valley

Daggett

Fremont Wash

Brisbane Valley

Daggett Ridge

Newberry Mtns.

Victor Valley

Quartzite Mountain 4,532'

Bell Mtn. Wash

Rio Grande Wash

Victorville

Apple Valley

Granite Mountains

Ord Mountains

o7

o2

o6

o3

o1

o5

o4

o8

*Diameter of inscribed circle, 55 miles*

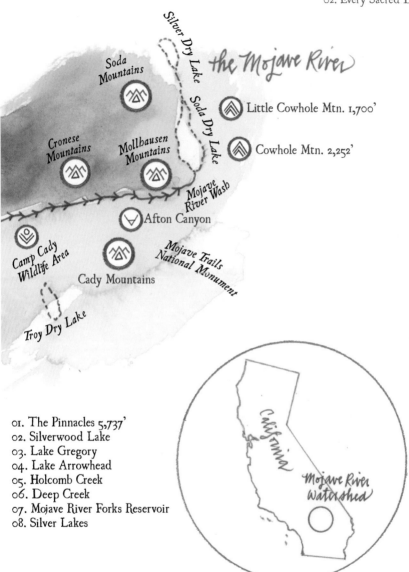

the Mojave River

Silver Dry Lake

Soda Mountains

Little Cowhole Mtn. 1,700'

Soda Dry Lake

Cronese Mountains

Mollhausen Mountains

Cowhole Mtn. 2,252'

Mojave River Wash

Afton Canyon

Camp Cady Wildlife Area

Mojave Trails National Monument

Cady Mountains

Troy Dry Lake

01. The Pinnacles 5,737'
02. Silverwood Lake
03. Lake Gregory
04. Lake Arrowhead
05. Holcomb Creek
06. Deep Creek
07. Mojave River Forks Reservoir
08. Silver Lakes

California

Mojave River watershed

Map 02.08

*Mojave tui chub*
*Gila bicolor ssp. mohavensis*

The only endemic fish in the Mojave River, the Mohave tui chub, *Gila bicolor* ssp. *mohavensis*, is extremely endangered. These large members of the minnow family (Cyprinidae) grow to seven inches and are now found only at a few conservation locations, and only two of those locations are on their ancestral river. Sensitive to pollution, these fish are a piece of the Pleistocene Mojave that thrived when the Mojave River was part of Lake Manix, and are struggling to survive in the Mojave of modern California.

## The Most Common Fish in the Mojave River

Mosquitofish, *Gambusia affinis*
Hitch, *Lavinia exilicauda*
Threespine stickleback, *Gasterosteus aculeatus*
Yellow bullhead, *Ameiurus natalis*

*threespine stickleback*
*1.5"–2" size*

Brine shrimp  Artemia monica

Alkali fly  Ephydra hians

keystone species of Mono Lake ecology

Mono Basin / Scenic area
*Diameter of inscribed circle, 19 miles*

Bodie Hills

Mt. Biedeman 8,981'

08

Conway
Summit
8,138'

Black
Point
6,958'

Mill Creek

Mono Lake 6,402'

Mono
Dome
10,614'

Paoha
Island

02

Williams
Butte
8,431'

04

01

Panum
Crater

Mono Valley

Granite
Mountain
Wilderness

Dry Creek

03

Pumice Valley

Mono
Craters

Sagehen
Summit
8,139'

05

Crater
Mtn.
9,172'

06
07

Aeolian Buttes

Map 02.09

## 02.09 OF BIRDS, BRINE, AND BEAUTY
*Mono Lake*

Millions of birds rely on the biologically rich, saline water of Mono Lake as they migrate between North and South America. Every spring, Mono Lake becomes green with the algae that forms the basis of the lake's ancient food chain. Since its creation by volcanic forces nearly three-quarters of a million years ago, the lake has fostered a unique and fecund biochemistry unlike any other.

The great, modern miracle of the lake is that it actually still exists and was not diverted to oblivion to slake the thirst of Los Angeles in a similar fate that befell Owens Lake to the south. For forty years in the mid-twentieth century, Los Angeles was bent on getting the water from Mono Lake; during that time, the lake level dropped nearly forty-five feet and became three times as salty as the ocean.[18] *Miracle* may be the wrong word; it was (and continues to be) thanks to the fierce determination, organization, and political deployment of a small group of activists who resisted the gluttonous metropolis that we can still witness this singular ecosystem.[19] The debt we collectively owe the community that saved the lake is great, and the lake deserves to be heralded as symbol of hope when evaluated against what might have been lost.

The geology of the Mono Basin is as fascinating as the biological habitat it provides is essential. For a couple of million years, beginning nearly five million years ago, volcanic basalt accumulated across what is now Mono Basin to a depth of almost six hundred feet.[20] The lake formed less than one million years ago and reached its greatest depth of 900 feet in the Pleistocene, as compared to its current greatest depth of 157 feet.[21] The Mono craters remain geologically active; the latest eruption events have occurred in the last 350 years. The predominant Panum Crater, with its massive deposits of obsidian, is evidence of this recent activity and is just a bit older, dating to approximately seven hundred years ago.

01. Mono Lake Tufa State Reserve
02. Lee Vining
03. Rush Creek
04. Walker Creek
05. Grant Lake
06. Silver Lake
07. June Lake
08. Conway Summit Area of Critical Environmental Concern

*Mono Lake Watershed*

red-necked
phalarope
*Phalaropus lobatus*

wilson's
phalarope
*Phalaropus
tricolor*

Common
Birds
of
Mono Lake

Least sandpiper *Calidris minutilla*

California gull
Larus californicus

killdeer
Charadrius vociferus

american avocet
Recurvirostra americana

eared grebe
Podiceps
nigricollis

01 Honey Lake

Pyramid Lake

02

03 04 carson sink
Carson Lake

Lake Tahoe

Walker Lake

Pacific Crest of the Sierra Nevada

Mono Lake

California    Nevada

five rivers
kingdom of the beaver
east of the Sierra

05

owens
Lake

Diameter of inscribed circle, 325 miles

Map 02.10

## 02.10 RIVERS ON THE EDGE
*Five desert rivers in California*

The western edge of the Great Basin Desert is home to five great rivers that form relatively significant flows, draining from the eastern Sierra Nevada. Although these watercourses offer habitat for many endangered and endemic species of fish—perhaps most famously the Lahontan cutthroat trout, *Oncorhynchus clarkii henshawi*—it should be noted that they are all within the ancestral range of the great ecological engineering species of the West: the North American beaver, *Castor canadensis*.

01. Susan River—length, 67 miles; watershed, 1,170 square miles (.75 million acres)
Headwaters: plateau northwest of Honey Lake, Lassen County
Mouth: Honey Lake (intermittent lake)

02. Truckee River—length, 121 miles; watershed, 3,060 square miles (1.90 million acres)
Headwaters: south of Lake Tahoe
Mouth: Pyramid Lake

03. Carson River—length, 131 miles; watershed, 3,930 square miles (2.52 million acres)
Headwaters:
East fork—near Sonora Pass
West fork—near Carson Pass
Mouth: Carson Lake

04. Walker River—length, 62 miles; watershed, 3,134 square miles (2.01 million acres)
Headwaters:
East Walker River—Bridgeport Valley
West Walker River—Tower Lake
Mouth: Walker Lake

05. Owens River—length, 183 miles; watershed, 2,604 square miles (1.67 million acres)
Headwaters: Owens River Wilderness
Mouth: Owens Lake (dry)

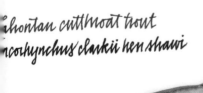

Lahontan cutthroat trout
Oncorhynchus clarkii henshawi

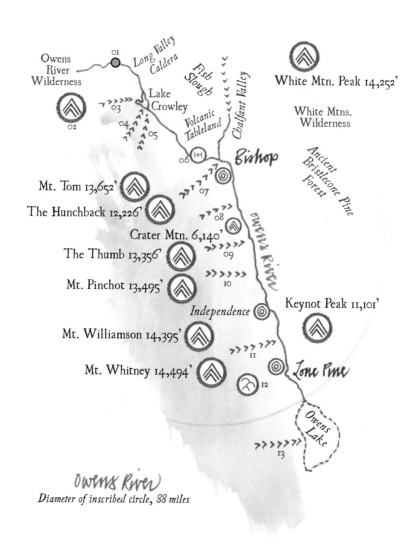

Owens River
Diameter of inscribed circle, 88 miles

Map 02.11

## 02.11 DESICCATION AND DESERTIFICATION
*Owens River, Owens Valley, and Owens Lake*

The Owens River runs along the eastern base of the Sierra Nevada. The river's ridgelines on both sides of its valley rise more than ten thousand feet, to the pinnacles of Mount Whitney to the west and White Mountain Peak to the east. For thousands of years, the Indigenous people of Owens Valley (the Owens Valley Paiute, the Nüümü) have called this valley, their home, the Land of the Flowering Water (Payahuunadü), and that language alludes to the quality of the environment they stewarded and the abundance that this place was able to provide. To say that the practice of irrigation and agriculture that sustained their community in that ocean of time has been dramatically transformed over the past couple of centuries is to downplay an ongoing catastrophe.

The human population of the valley is far greater than it has ever been, and the valley is undergoing a corresponding degradation—a process of desertification based on centuries-old decisions that the colonizing American culture made. Owens Lake, now a desiccated, alkali playa, became that way in 1926, when after thirteen years of diversion to the Los Angeles Aqueduct, it succumbed to lack of inflow. Today, the ancient lake is a major source of pollution as its salt-

rich dust moves north, increasing the aridity of the soil.[22] Added to that, the massive pumping of groundwater is withering riparian habitat of the Owens Valley, and through the process of desertification, native grasslands are vulnerable to conversion by invasives.[23]

01. Deadman Creek
02. Mammoth Mountain (11,053')
03. Hot Creek
04. McGee Creek
05. Hilton Creek
06. Pleasant Valley Reservoir
07. Bishop Creek
08. Big Pine Creek
09. Tinemaha Creek
10. Sawmill Creek
11. Shepherd Creek
12. Alabama Hills
13. Cottonwood Creek

North American beaver
Castor canadensis.

Protecting watersheds
Prioritizing beaver
restoration
wetland engineers

## The North American Beaver

For as long as these rivers have been rivers (at least seven million years) and before the coming of humanity, the North American beaver has been the mammalian steward of the watersheds of the western Great Basin Desert in California. By building its dam, the beaver builds habitat by spreading out the surface area of the water table, and the effect of this is an estimated biodiversity increase of up to fifty times over what the base level of area-wide biodiversity would be without the beaver and its amazing dam.[24] Nearly extirpated in the nineteenth century, beaver have been reintroduced region wide and are tirelessly working at not only augmenting ecological services such as wildland fire remediation and increasing fish-habitat resiliency but also (alas) frustrating human agriculturalists who have their own designs on the land.

*tule elk*

*nannodes*
*Cervus canadensis*

*Tule elk in Owens Valley*

Endemic to California's Central Valley, tule elk, *Cervus canadensis nannodes*, were intentionally introduced to Owens Valley in the mid-twentieth century as part of a larger conservation plan for the species, which had by then diminished nearly to the point of extinction. There are now five managed herds in the valley, with a total population of less than five hundred.

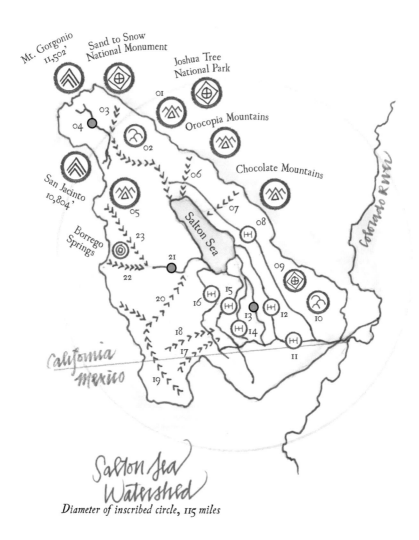

Mt. Gorgonio
11,502'

Sand to Snow
National Monument

Joshua Tree
National Park

01

Orocopia Mountains

02

03

04

Chocolate Mountains

San Jacinto
10,804'

05

06

Salton Sea

07

08

Borrego
Springs

23

21

09

22

20

16

15

13

12

10

18

17

14

11

19

California
Mexico

Colorado River

*Salton Sea Watershed*
*Diameter of inscribed circle, 115 miles*

**Map 02.12**

## 02.12 A HISTORY OF INCESSANT INJURY
*The Salton Sea watershed*

The Salton Trough has a low point that is 278 feet below sea level. The trough was empty of water for at least three hundred years when Lake Cahuilla desiccated and before the accident of 1905 that formed the modern Salton Sea. Today, the Salton Sea holds about 7.5 million acre-feet of water, making it the largest lake in California (besides Lake Tahoe).[25]

The modern Salton Sea was formed when flooding broke the canal system that connected the Colorado River to the Imperial Valley. Where there were only dry washes, the Alamo and New Rivers were carved by the torrent. The lake is fed largely by the two southern rivers and one from the north—the Whitewater River. Originating near

San Gorgonio, the Whitewater makes it way past a hundred golf courses and, like the southern rivers, travels through thousands of farming acres, entering the eutrophic system with a significant and dangerous chemical load. For decades after its accidental creation, this unexpected ecosystem bloomed with productivity and became an essential site for migrating birds. The last half of the twentieth century witnessed its ecological collapse, and today, saying the Salton Sea is a wasteland is not too far from the mark.

*Orangemouth corvina*
*Cynoscion xanthulus*
× extirpated ×

01. Little San Bernardino Mountains
02. Indio Hills
03. Morongo Canyon
04. Palm Springs
05. Santa Rosa Mountains
06. Box Canyon
07. Salt Creek Wash
08. Coachella Canal
09. New Algodones Dunes Wilderness
10. East Mesa
11. All-American Canal
12. East Highline Canal
13. Alamo River
14. Central Canal
15. New River Canal
16. Westside Main Canal
17. Pinto Wash
18. Coyote Wash
19. Carrizo Wash
20. Vallecito Creek
21. San Felipe Creek
22. Borrego Creek
23. Coyote Creek

## Collapsing fish populations in the Salton Sea

Despite the Salton Sea's potential for biological productivity, at the end of the twentieth century only two of the original thirty-four introduced species of fish continued to exist:

Bairdiella, *Bairdiella icistia*, extirpated 2003.[26]

Orangemouth corvina, *Cynoscion xanthulus*, extirpated 2003.[27]

Tilapia, *Oreochromis mossambicus* × *O. urolepis hornorum*, introduced toward the end of the twentieth century and today the dominant species; may be headed toward lake-wide extirpation.[28]

Salton Sea pupfish, *Cyprinodon macularis*; the lake's one endemic fish remains extant in refuge ponds within the Salton Sea Basin.[29]

Tilapia hybrid
oreochromis mossambicus × oreochromis urolepis hornorum

Common poor-will *Phalaenoptilus nuttallii*

The common poorwill, *Phalaenoptilus nuttallii*, the only bird in the world known to hibernate, spends the winter in a state of torpor in the riparian areas of Coachella Valley.[30]

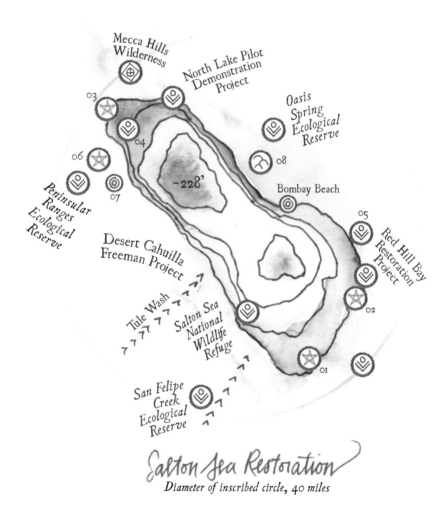

Mecca Hills
Wilderness

North Lake Pilot
Demonstration
Project

Oasis
Spring
Ecological
Reserve

o3

o4

o6

Peninsular
Ranges
Ecological
Reserve

o7

−228'

Bombay Beach

o8

o5

Red Hill Bay
Restoration
Project

Desert Cahuilla
Freeman Project

Tule Wash

Salton Sea
National
Wildlife
Refuge

o2

San Felipe
Creek
Ecological
Reserve

o1

Salton Sea Restoration
*Diameter of inscribed circle, 40 miles*

**Map 02.12a**

## 02.12a Saving the Sea, Saving Ourselves
*Salton Sea restoration*

The eutrophic stew that is the Salton Sea is characterized by a salinity twice that of the ocean, extremely high nutrient concentrations from a century of agricultural pollution, frequent and lethal low oxygen concentrations, and algal blooms that lead to massive fish die-offs. Yet despite all that injury, the Salton Sea is potentially a highly productive ecosystem. There are four hundred marine and terrestrial species that have been recorded living in the lake, including a large number of phytoplankton and invertebrate species.[31]

Because of the negative regional effects that would result, the one million people living in the Coachella and Imperial Valleys cannot let the Salton Sea fade into the desert. Now that irrigation efficiency has largely cut off the primary input of water that keeps the sea from evaporating, the prospect of its destruction is an imminent possibility. The New and Alamo Rivers drain agricultural land from the Imperial and Mexicali Valleys, as well as wastewater from the Mexicali metropolitan area—the Whitewater River does the same, emerging from the Coachella Valley. What little ecological homeostasis remained in the system at the beginning of twenty-first century was sustained by the input from those rivers. Today, with the massive transference of water rights

that redirected much of the Colorado River's water to urban farms and other municipalities, the threat to the Salton Sea is magnified.[32] The Salton Sea is evaporating at an average annual rate of five feet.[33] What is left is a playa of toxic chemical dust exposed to the wind, which will negatively affect the surrounding human communities.[34]

The state's restoration plan to keep the level of the Salton Sea from dropping is off to a shaky start. Although hundreds of millions of dollars are being spent to mitigate the catastrophe over several thousand acres, the promise of restoration is a dream. One economic reality of this terrible predicament is that the restoration plan might very well cost billions of dollars, but that would still be a small amount compared to the potential health care costs for those exposed to the dust left to drape the Coachella Valley by the Salton Sea's continued ecological collapse.[35]

01. New River outlet
02. Alamo River outlet
03. Whitewater River outlet
04. Torres Wetland Project
05. Imperial Valley Wildlife Area Wister Unit
06. Edwards Wash
07. Torres-Martinez Reservation
08. Bat Caves Buttes (100')

Present day
Salton Sea

Colorado River

Pacific Ocean

Gila River

Ancient
Lake Cahuilla
(early 18th century)

Colorado River
Delta

Gulf of
California

Map 02.12b

## 02.12b A Four-Million-Year Pulse
### Lake Cahuilla

Over the past sixty million years, the same tectonic dynamics that have been slowly driving coastal California to the northwest also opened the Gulf of California. Throughout that long period, the Colorado River also moved, cutting different avenues to its delta over a shifting landscape. It went through the Salton Slough. Several times larger than the modern Salton Sea, Lake Cahuilla formed many times in the ancient past and accumulated over a deep sink of alluvium that is often more than three miles thick.[36] Today, the lakebed comprises the fertile fields of the Imperial and

Coachella Valleys, and the blown dust that was the prehistoric lake formed the Algodones Dunes, one of California's largest dune networks.

It is reasonable to suggest that someday, after the ravages of an industrially influenced atmosphere become a memory to the future deserts of California, it may be that Lake Cahuilla will return to its ancient basin. Perhaps it will turn out that the Holocene (and thereby the Anthropocene) are not as cataclysmic in aridifying effect as the consensus of predictions suggests, but rather, the Pleistocene will return and reveal the time of humanity as a small, interglacial moment of warm weather inside surrounding ages of ice.[37]

*Salton Sea Lithium*

Because today's best battery technology requires lithium, lithium is essential for California's plan to become carbon neutral by 2045. Specifically, an estimated 55 gigawatts of electrical storage capacity is required to reliably fulfill California's electrical needs with renewable sources.[38] That is approximately 150 percent of all the electrical storage produced in the last ten years. There may be enough lithium in the briny soil underneath the Salton Sea to supply all of what is needed. By way of what might be the cleanest extraction process yet invented, Salton Sea's lithium is accessible through the eleven geothermal plants in the Salton Sea Basin that are already pumping the lithium-rich soil to the surface to harness the generated steam and thereby produce electricity.[39] Despite not needing the enormous amounts of groundwater that the conventional evaporative process of lithium extraction requires, this new process still generates toxic by-products that include arsenic, barium, and lead, which begs the question of whether we are not merely trading one mortal fate for another.[40]

Latrodectus hesperus — western black widow spider

family Theridiidae
34 species

less than one-half inch long

potent venom containing the neurotoxin latrotoxin; only the bite of the female is dangerous to humans

silk is comparably stronger than steel wire of the same size.

females will often eat their mates

preys on flies, mosquitos, grasshoppers beetles and caterpillars

no death (human) has been reported in america since 1983.

Theoretically, the spatial distribution of life, or biogeography, can be expressed by a complex algorithm that accounts for a great number of biotic, abiotic, physical, evolutionary, and chemical variables. If over time the parameters of the input energy delivered to the land by these variables becomes regular and consistent, ecological predictability becomes traceable from the complex nature of the master algorithm. By grouping some of the variables and making them characters in our story, the wonder of biodiversity that results from species-level, evolutionary adaptation is revealed as potentially infinite. Wherever there is an ecological niche that can be exploited, there seems to be an organism adapted to do exactly that. In the California deserts, from the riverine ecosystems in the middle of the Colorado River to the littoral ecosystems on top of the Algodones Dunes, ancient species exist within a highly specialized framework that is always dependent on the quality of the relationships organisms have with one another and their environment.

The lists, diagrams, and maps of this chapter form a snapshot of the desert world that is contextualized by an evolutionary perspective. The desert world evolved and is evolving within a probability matrix that is dependent on specific conditions in space and time and is therefore irreproducible. Its preciousness and its profound beauty can be revealed, in a sense, through the kind of statistical ecology hinted at here. The patterns of how life forms are linked together, horizontally in terms of botanic alliance and vertically in terms of trophism, or how food webs are structured, suggests a networked world of which humans, as a ubiquitous keystone species, are inescapably a part.

The story of networked life is a story of intrinsic value. A being's intrinsic value refers to what that being (a force, entity, resource, etc.), through its continued existence, adds to the system and that, by way of its absence or its exploitation, would injure the system's ability to function normally. It follows that intrinsic value exists outside and in contrast to the being's value as a resource to be spent, or its utilitarian value. Utilitarian value refers to how much the being (force, entity, resource, etc.) in question is worth in its one-time expendability.

Mojave sand verbena
Abronia pogonatha

Surviving the desert inside patterns
of escape, evasion, and endurance
plant life writhes in pulses of
advance and retreat
based on the Ecosphere's abiotic temperament
And its signature across this demanding
but not unmerciless land
where the evidence of systemic resilience
is a hundred times more tested than
our most brilliant contrivances
to the same end.

Anza Borrego DSP

A popular example of this dynamic, on a global level, might be fossil fuels. The intrinsic value of leaving fossil fuels in the earth may indeed be priceless in avoiding the worst effects of climate breakdown. The utilitarian value of fossil fuel extraction is the sum total of the capital produced during the modern age of industrialization. Painted with broad strokes, intrinsic value will always be greater than utilitarian value. Problems arise in the near impossibility of calculating intrinsic value and pinpointing where it is and how it is embodied.

Perhaps ironically, both of these types of value can be clarified in our generally sloppy use of the word *nature*. Nature can mean two things, and we can differentiate between those two things by capitalizing the $N$. Nature (capital $N$) is what you exist inside of and what you cannot separate yourself from. It is the air you breathe, the water you drink, and the food web that you rely on. Nature is more than just the environment; it is the way the world is put together, and when it is functioning properly, human bodies and human communities thrive. Therefore, Nature can be conceived of as something that is to be cherished, as it is the source of all beauty and invention. The other use of the word nature (lowercase $n$) refers to how everything nonhuman is generally regarded in the modern world. In this sense, nature becomes a thing that exists "out there" and therefore can be disregarded as something that does not include human society. This nature, as opposed to Nature, becomes exploitable, extractable, and degradable with only minimal effect on human society. This falsity is perpetuated to maintain economic growth in a certain form and is ultimately the root of the modern world's unsustainability. To deny the intrinsic value of Nature and to conceive of nature as an inexhaustible well of resources is worse than dangerous—it may just be catastrophic.

What is threatened is the current system of complexity that life in the desert depends on. The catalog of plant alliances (03.06) represents this snapshot in history, which will inevitably change in many key respects. Some of these relationships developed during the ice ages of the Pleistocene. Some have endured despite the fact that a complete inventory of ice age herbivores who grazed the botanical Great Basin Desert, for example, would include twenty-two animal genera that no longer exist. Many of these relationships, these plant alliances, will fail in a relatively brief amount of time due to the staggering rate at which the calamitous matrix of effects that is climate breakdown unfolds, and many will not.

Despite detailed consensus on quantity and quality—how much of what type of system resources must be "saved" to prevent collapse—there are many assumptions that desert policy relies on that will not necessarily turn out to be true. The most important and perhaps disastrous presumption is that there is a bottom limit to how much anthropogenic disturbance desert ecology can take and that desert development and exploitation have not yet hit that bottom. The assumption is that the threshold for collapse has not yet been breached.

There is a direct through line from biodiversity to the well-being of human communities. Increased biodiversity means increased complexity in energy distribution between trophic levels within any given ecosystem. Increased complexity ensures a greater threshold of resiliency in the face of disturbance, and because of that resiliency, the ecosystem is stronger. Strong ecosystems deliver reliable ecosystem services. Ultimately, human communities everywhere, but especially in potentially harsh environments such as the desert, rely on a multitude of ecosystem services to survive at all. From pollination to erosion control, ecosystem service was articulated as a concept in the United Nations' Millennium Ecosystem Assessment, in which four generalized types of services were described: provisioning, regulating, cultural, and supporting. Provisioning services include food, water, fuel, timber, oils, textile material, and medicine.[1] Regulating services include pollination, decomposition, water quality, flood control, carbon storage, and climate normalization. Cultural services include nonmaterial benefits from intellectual and social development. Supporting services are those services that support life in general, including photosynthesis, nutrient cycling (water, nitrogen, carbon, and so on), and soil creation. The grand system of life may react to the absence of any constituent pieces with cascading effects that are impossible to predict. There is no piece of the puzzle that the system can do without. Even the smallest parasites are culling agents that work to make their community stronger. Every piece of biodiversity has a role to play.

Argemone
corymbosa)

Mojave
prickly
Poppy)

## 03.01 MODELING DESERT LIFE
*Conceptual ecology*

The ecological structure of life operates in similar ways across all terrestrial ecosystems, even in environments as unique as the California desert. Abiotic systems—geology, atmospheric chemistry, and climate—interact with a landscape-wide substrate of living soil that transfers and distributes nutrients to a community of what ecologists call autotrophic producers, or plants. This process forms the basis of food webs, in which heterotrophs and decomposers support carbon and nutrient cycles that enable perpetuation of the system.

### Biological soil crust

Plants in the desert are often widely spaced across the landscape. It may seem that the soil between them holds no life, but that couldn't be further from the truth. Nearly everywhere across the floor of the undisturbed desert, a thin layer of biological soil crust has formed from a community of microorganisms that includes cyanobacteria, bacteria, fungi, and green algae, as well as lichens, mosses, and even microarthropods.[2] This phenomenon is central to supporting food webs by providing heat, water, and dust sequestration. The crust also offers sanctuary for seeds and absorbs plant-litter nutrients, distributing the precious resources throughout the botanical community. As important and ubiquitous as these so-called biocrusts are, they are very fragile and only metabolically active when it rains, so recovery from disturbance caused by cars driving on them can be as low at 10 or 20 percent over one hundred years.[3]

### Producers

The majority of this chapter is about what are called macroscopic plant-life patterns. Ecologically, plants are producers, meaning that they produce their own energy in the form of sugar through the process of photosynthesis. Both abiotic and biotic factors influence plant alliances and plant ecology. Abiotic factors greatly affect the biogeography of plants. Soil composition and chemistry, water availability, slope aspect, climate patterns, and atmospheric chemistry are some of the factors that affect botanical communities and species adaptations. Rooting patterns, biocrust affiliation, nurse plant interactions, allelopathic compounds from surrounding plants, and herbivory are all biotic factors that affect the same communities and adaptations.[4]

*Mojave desert bug*
*Cicindelidia haemorrhagica*

## Consumers

Food webs and food chains describe the way that nutrient energy moves up, down, and across the trophic interactions of producers (plants), consumers, omnivores, and predatory consumers. Because up to 90 percent of the energy transferred to higher trophic levels, say from prey to predator, is lost due to physiological inefficiency, there will always be more biomass at the bottom of the food chain than at the top. There will always be more plants than animals. This dynamic is magnified in desert ecosystems.[5] Despite animals' scarcity relative to plants, their adaptations to desert life are robust and varied. Although the spectrum of variation includes adaptations as apparent as body size and as subtle as metabolic regulation, commonalities exist among desert animal survival techniques, both physiological and behavioral—for example, animal body temperature tends to be several degrees warmer than corresponding nondesert animals, most animals are not active during the day, and most burrow to escape the heat.[6]

## Decomposers

Decomposition and detritivory are essential components of any ecosystem, as they are often the primary means of nutrient cycling and distribution and of soil creation.[7] In the desert, fungi are more active than bacteria, and because of their mutualistic relationships with plant root systems and biocrust systems, they tend to congregate around shrubs, creating zones of organic concentration that can be thought of as "islands of fertility."[8] Despite the importance and ubiquity of microorganisms such as bacteria and fungi, as well as macroorganisms, including beetles, invertebrates, and other soil fauna, up to 85 percent of decomposition in California's desert is taken care of by the energy of the sun through photodegradation.[9]

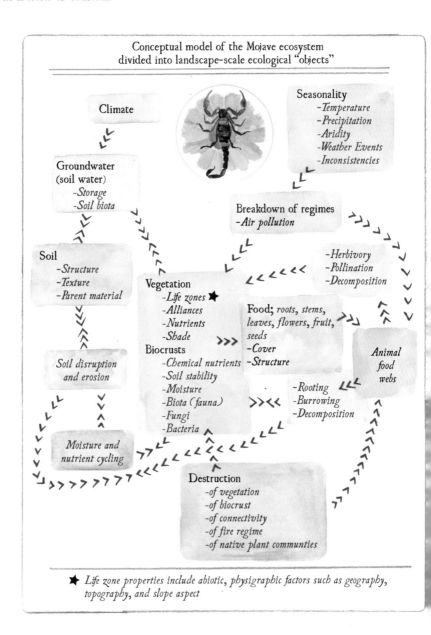

Conceptual model of the Mojave ecosystem
divided into landscape-scale ecological "objects"

Climate

Seasonality
-*Temperature*
-*Precipitation*
-*Aridity*
-*Weather Events*
-*Inconsistencies*

Groundwater
(soil water)
-*Storage*
-*Soil biota*

Breakdown of regimes
-*Air pollution*

-*Herbivory*
-*Pollination*
-*Decomposition*

Soil
-*Structure*
-*Texture*
-*Parent material*

Vegetation
-*Life zones* ★
-*Alliances*
-*Nutrients*
-*Shade*
Biocrusts
-*Chemical nutrients*
-*Soil stability*
-*Moisture*
-*Biota (fauna)*
-*Fungi*
-*Bacteria*

Food; *roots, stems,
leaves, flowers, fruit,
seeds*
-*Cover*
-*Structure*

Soil disruption
and erosion

-*Rooting*
-*Burrowing*
-*Decomposition*

Animal
food
webs

Moisture and
nutrient cycling

Destruction
-*of vegetation*
-*of biocrust*
-*of connectivity*
-*of fire regime*
-*of native plant communties*

★ *Life zone properties include abiotic, physigraphic factors such as geography,
topography, and slope aspect*

Cactus wren
Campylorhynchus brunneicapillus

## 03.02 SURVIVAL TECHNIQUES
*Desert plant adaptations*

When considering how plants survive in the desert, most people think of the common phenotypic traits of mature desert plants, including cactus spines, small and waxy leaves, light coloring, and the rest, but the range of ecological strategies that plant species employ is remarkably wide. One way to classify how plants manage and thrive given the environmental stress generated from the desert's usual arsenal of dry wind, poor soil, low humidity, high temperatures, and arid conditions is to consider three generalized strategic categories: escape, evasion, and endurance.[10] Escapers (forbs and annuals) grow quickly after managing to avoid summer extremes in the form of seeds. Evaders (ocotillo and woody plants with deep tap roots) are able to conserve water by shedding leaves or are able to reach for perennial subterranean water. Endurers (creosote and ambrosia) use combinations of leaf shielding, widespread root systems, and other strategies to defend and conserve their resources. Some plants may use many adaptations, such as palo verde, which is drought-deciduous (evader) and has small leaves to reduce heat loss (endurer).

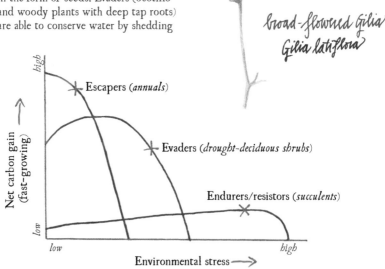

broad-flowered Gilia
Gilia latiflora

*California*

*Botanical Great Basin*

*Mechanical Defense Line*

## 03.02a Spines, Thorns, and Barbs
*The mechanical defense line*

By the end of the Pleistocene (about twelve thousand years ago), the plants of California's modern deserts had evolved and adapted in and to a different world than the one we know today. In the warm deserts, more than one hundred species of plants in twenty-one families evolved to become "tall, armed, and dangerous," whereas in the cold deserts of the north, only six species of plants in six families exist. There is a climatic line that divides the two. It might not have been climate alone that influenced this trend. Herbivory patterns of ice age mammals may have influenced how plant adaptations in the warm deserts included being tall, armed, and dangerous, whereas in the cold deserts, no such armament was needed.[11]

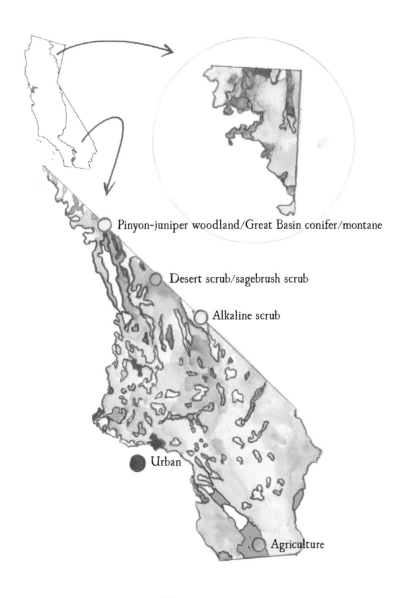

Pinyon-juniper woodland/Great Basin conifer/montane

Desert scrub/sagebrush scrub

Alkaline scrub

Urban

Agriculture

Map 03.03

## 03.03 PLANT PATTERNS ON THE LAND
*Generalized vegetation of California's desert regions*

This map of generalized patterns of vegetation, irrespective of plant alliances, conveys a sense how the scrublands of the desert dominate the geography. This zoomed-out, unfocused view is important because having a sense of the distribution of vegetation is valuable on many levels of interpretation, and we need to note how unsubtle and insensitive vegetation maps are when exploring the ecological character of places as rich as California deserts. Desert scrub, for example, implies little complexity, a homogenized nothing-zone, when in fact it is full of variety, color, and complexity.

Algodones Dunes sunflower
*Helianthus niveus ssp. tephrodes*

*Map 03.03 source:* Adapted from M. Barbour, T. Keeler-Wolf, and A. Schoenherr, eds., *Terrestrial Vegetation of California*, 3rd ed. (Berkeley: University of California Press:, 2007), 1–42.

## 03.04 PLANT PATTERNS AT ELEVATION
*Biozones*

Examining biogeography through the investigation of so-called elevational
biozones, or how botanical patterns appear in stratified layers ascending a
mountain, is to investigate one aspect of the geomorphic units that inform where
all living networks establish themselves.[12] Hillslopes are a regular feature in any
ecosystem; by contrast, geomorphic units that exist only in desert environments
include the following:

### Playas

Ancient lakes from the Pleistocene are now dry, hard clay beds that offer little
habitat to all but the most salt-tolerant plants, such as shadescale, *Atriplex
confertifolia*; four-wing saltbush, *A. canescens*; and the most common salt-tolerant
plant that rings Mojave playas, allscale, *A. polycarpa*. After flooding, which takes
place after vernal storms or late-summer monsoons, amphipods (tiny, shrimp-like
crustaceans) may proliferate and become food for birds, making many of these
playas essential stopovers for migrating birds.[13]

### Eolian features

Sand dune systems exist in localized networks across the Mojave and Sonoran
Deserts, accumulated from the blowing and depositing of the fine silt off the lake
beds. Every dune system has endemic plant species and unique food webs.[14]

### Alluvial fans

Perhaps the most common geomorphic feature in the California desert, and the one
that offers the most potential land area for habitat, is the alluvial fan. The product
of erosion, fans are composed of loose rock and particles that become increasingly
fine the farther they are deposited from their mountain source.

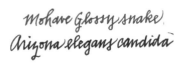

Mohave Glossy snake
*Arizona elegans candida*

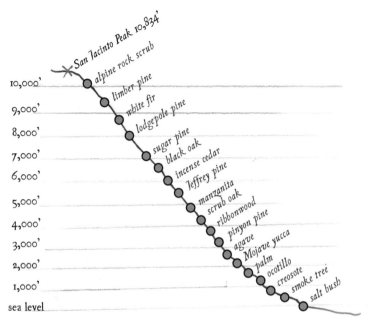

San Jacinto Peak 10,834'

alpine rock scrub
limber pine
white fir
lodgepole pine
sugar pine
black oak
incense cedar
Jeffrey pine
manzanita
scrub oak
ribbonwood
pinyon pine
agave
Mojave yucca
palm
ocotillo
creosote
smoke tree
salt bush

10,000'
9,000'
8,000'
7,000'
6,000'
5,000'
4,000'
3,000'
2,000'
1,000'
sea level

(idealized) botanical biozones of east San Jacinto

## 03.04a One Staircase of the Living Desert
*Botanical biozones of San Jacinto's eastern slope*

The easiest way to see how plant biozones change with increasing elevation from the floor of the Coachella Valley to the alpine San Jacinto Peak (10,834') is to take the tram. The Palm Springs Aerial Tramway provides a quick ride up through these so-called biozones, which are also called biomes, or life zones. The staircase of biomes, a generalized take on how ecological zones exist across large swaths of the West, would include an ascension from the desert biome, up through dry woodlands and chaparral, and finally into the high elevations of the boreal forest.[15] The biozones of San Jacinto begin on the desert floor with the desert grasslands and desert scrub of the Lower Sonoran, and march up through the Upper Sonoran, proceeding through the transition zone of the ponderosa pine forest, then the fir forests of the Canadian life zone, finally up to the subalpine and alpine life zones, called the Hudsonian.[16] The east side of San Jacinto provides an exemplary showcase of how elevation, slope aspect, and other ecological factors coalesce in the living desert.

(idealized) north slope, New York Mountains, Mojave National Preserve

## 03.04b Another Staircase of the Living Desert
*Botanical biozones of the Mojave Desert Preserve*

The same exercise of biozone analysis by elevation that was applied to east San Jacinto can be applied to any mountain slope in the desert. It is best thought of as an idealized thought experiment to make sense of how the puzzle of life across the desert is assembled. From rocky, forest-covered peaks; down the traditional zones of sage, grass, and shrub; and finally into the hot and dry basin of dried lakes, dunes, and volcanic lands, a zonation exists that dictates ecological classifications in a fairly straightforward manner. The New York Mountains of the Mojave National Preserve offer a window into the nature of the Mojave Desert as a transitional desert between the Sonoran Desert to the south and the Great Basin Desert to the north, exhibiting qualities of both and yet also being its own thing.[17] Illustrating this point, Joshua tree alliances of the Mojave exist here often next to sagebrush alliances of the Great Basin.

Let us also praise the common animals — Glory be to those generalists who thrive just as well in some remote canyon as they do by some busy freeway! Glory be to those creatures who can find what they need in the face of so much disturbance! Glory be to the icons, who by their very existence continue to define the place. Praise be to Saint Coyote! To Saint Vulture! To Saint Yellow Jacket! To Saints Skunk, Possum, Raccoon, Crow, Mockingbird, Ground Squirrel, Scorpion, Moth, and Lizard!

New York Peak — Mojave Preserve

## 03.05 WORKING TOGETHER
*Defining ecosections and plant alliances*

Vegetative ecology is essentially the study of plant patterns in the landscape. The term used to describe these patterns is *plant alliance*. While plant biogeography studies where plant life occurs, vegetative ecology is the study of how plant life occurs in observable patterns and communities. A plant alliance is a particular combination of plant species that forms the vegetative basis for a habitat type. The naming conventions of plant alliances are based on a single species that can be either dominant, representative, characteristic, or diagnostic of the local ecology.[18]

This system of alliance classification is useful when conceptualizing the qualities of an ever-shifting landscape. Recognizing patterns of life in the desert and understanding why plants live where they do and what wildlife habitat they can generally offer are more than satisfying thought experiments. They are also an inroad to a deeper relationship with the living desert, developed by recognizing patterns in the landscape based on the ecology in which those patterns have evolved.

The range of many of these plant alliance types extends to other, nondesert ecological sections of California, and some extend into floristic provinces outside the state. The criterion for inclusion on the lists in this section is that the alliance must appear in *A Manual of California Vegetation* (Sawyer, Keeler-Wolf, and Evens; published by the California Native Plant Society) as existing in at least one of the six geographic regions in California: Modoc Plateau, Northwest Great Basin, Southeast Great Basin, or the Mojave, Sonoran, or Colorado Deserts. Provisional and seminatural alliances as detailed in *California Vegetation* have been excluded.

fern bush
*Chamaebatiaria*
*millefolium*

## *Plant alliances in desert forests, woodlands, and bosques*

As I've already noted, all plant alliances have membership criteria. Survey techniques, populations and densities of certain species, and those species' proximate locations and botanical community and growth patterns determine the habitat quality. The following classification summaries are comprehensive reviews of the vocabulary used to describe landscape-scale plant alliance habitat types.[19] The alliances and their habitat descriptions have been divided into three categories: trees (arboreal), shrubs (scrub), and grasslands (herbaceous).

1. Arboreal plant alliance communities
   in desert environments

   Desert big trees
   Forest
   Woodland
   Bosque

2. Shrub plant alliance communities
   in desert environments

   Floristic province
   Scrub
   Chaparral
   Sagebrush
   Thickets
   Patches

3. Herbaceous plant alliance communities
   in desert environments

   Sparsely vegetated alliance
   Grassland
   Fell-fields
   Fields
   Meadows
   Marshes
   Dunes
   Stands
   Beds

yucca

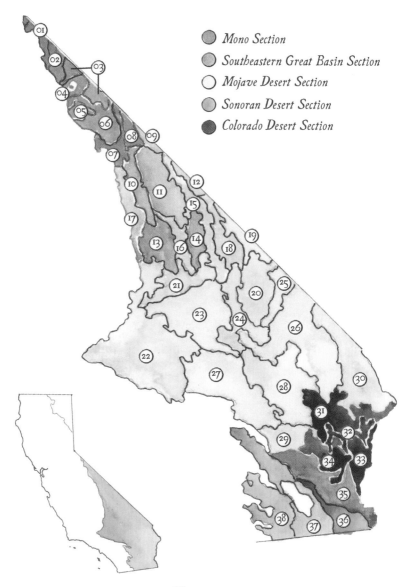

Mono Section

Southeastern Great Basin Section

Mojave Desert Section

Sonoran Desert Section

Colorado Desert Section

**Map 03.05a**

## 03.05a Ecological Subsections of the Deserts of Southeastern California

Ecological subsections, as described by USGS, delineate variation in climate, physiography, lithology, soils, and potential natural vegetation.[20] Map 03.05a is adapted from the USFS rendering of the data and divides the Mono Section from its northeastern continuance described in map 03.05b.[21]

Data of this type enables precise analysis—for example, creosote shrub alliance (*Larrea tridentata*) dominates exactly 67 percent of the central Mojave Desert[22] and 70 percent of the Sonoran Desert in California.[23]

### Mono Section

01. Pine Nut Mountains
02. Sweetwater Mountains; Pine Grove Hills
03. Bodie Hills; Excelsior Mountains
04. Mono Valley
05. Glass Mountain
06. Crowley Flowlands
07. Benton Valley; upper Owens Valley
08. White Mountains

### Southeastern Great Basin Section

09. Silver Peak Mountains; Fish Lake Valley
10. Inyo Mountains
11. Saline Valley; Cottonwood Mountains
12. Northern Amargosa; Grapevine Mountains
13. Cosa-Argus Ranges
14. Panamint Range

### Mojave Desert Section

15. Death Valley
16. Panamint Valley
17. Owens Valley
18. Funeral Mountains; Greenwater Valley
19. Amargosa Desert; Pahrump Valley
20. Kingston Range; Valley Wells
21. Searles Valley; Owlshead Mountains
22. High desert plains and hills
23. Mojave Valley; Granite Mountains
24. Silurian Valley; Devil's Playground
25. Ivanpah Valley
26. Providence Mountains; Lanfair Valley
27. Lucerne; Johnson Valley
28. Bullion Mountains; Bristol Lake
29. Pinto Basin and Mountains
30. Piute Valley; Sacramento Mountains

### Sonoran Desert Section

31. Cadiz; Vidal Valley
32. Palen; Riverside Mountains
33. Palo Verde Valley and Mesa
34. Chuckwalla Valley
35. Chocolate Mountains and Valley

### Colorado Desert Section

36. East Mesa; Sand Hills
37. Imperial Valley
38. Borrego Valley; West Mesa

California leaf-nosed bat
Macrotus californicus

Pocketed free-tailed bat
Nyctinomops femorosaccus

Cave myotis bat
Myotis velifer

### *Bat families*

The following are the most common bat families in California's deserts:

1. Phyllostomidae
(e.g., California leaf-nosed bat, *Macrotus californicus*)

2. Vespertilionidae
(genus *Myotis*, sixteen species—the most common genus)

3. Molossidae
(pocketed free-tailed bat, *Nyctinomops femorosaccus*, and five other species)

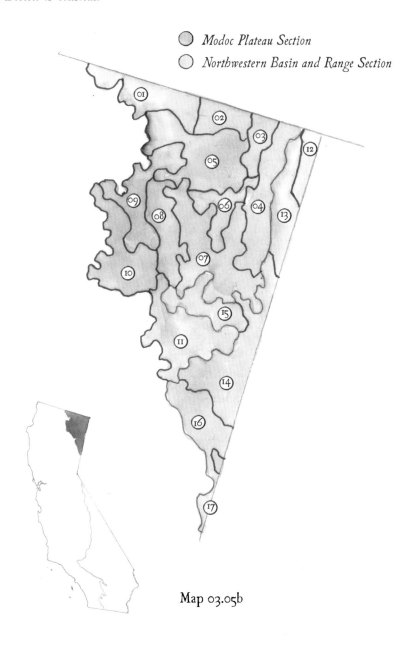

Modoc Plateau Section

Northwestern Basin and Range Section

Map 03.05b

## 03.05b Ecological Subsections of the Deserts of Northeastern California

The Great Basin's westernmost extent in northeast California is a series of fault-block ranges of similar heights across the geologically complex Modoc Plateau. Sagebrush scrub, hardwood woodland alliances, and mountainous chaparral define its vegetation.

### Modoc Plateau Section

01. Klamath Lake basins; Juniper Foot
02. Fremont Pine–Fir Forest
03. Goose Lake Basin
04. Warner Mountains
05. Devil's Garden
06. Pit River Valley
07. Likely Mountain
08. Adin mountains and valleys
09. Big Valley
10. Big Valley Mountains
11. Eagle Lake; Observation Peak

### Northwestern Basin and Range Section

12. High Lava Plains
13. High Desert; Wetlands
14. Cottonwood; Skedaddle Mountains
15. Madeline Plain
16. Honey Lake Basin; Pyramid Lake Basin
17. Fort Sage Mountain; Lemmon Valley

Western Juniper
Juniperus occidentalis

## 03.06 ALL IN THE FAMILY
*Taxonomic families of representative desert plants*

To consider plants as part of botanical families is to take a broad view of plant adaptations and to speculate on their correlation in vegetative ecology. This list details the plant families of each of the 147 representative plant species that are included on the "Dominant Desert Plants of Major Vegetation Alliances" list that follows.

1. Aizoaceae—fig-marigold (1 species)
2. Amaranthaceae—amaranth (10 species)
3. Arecaceae—palm (1 species)
4. Asparagaceae—asparagus (4 species)
5. Asteraceae—sunflower (24 species)
6. Betulaceae—birch (1 species)
7. Bignoniaceae—trumpetvine (1 species)
8. Boraginaceae—borage (2 species)
9. Cactaceae—cactus (1 species)
10. Cornaceae—dogwood (1 species)
11. Cupressaceae—cypress (4 species)
12. Cyperaceae—sedge (10 species)
13. Ericaceae—heath (1 species)
14. Ephedraceae—ephedra (3 species)
15. Fabaceae—legume (7 species)
16. Fagaceae—beech (3 species)
17. Lamiaceae—mint (4 species)
18. Melanthiaceae—bunchflower (1 species)
19. Oleaceae—olive (1 species)
20. Nyctaginaceae—four o'clock (1 species)
21. Papaveraceae—poppy (1 species)
22. Phrymaceae—lopseed (1 species)
23. Pinaceae—pine (7 species)
24. Poaceae—grass (24 species)
25. Polemoniaceae—phlox (1 species)
26. Polygonaceae—buckwheat (2 species)
27. Rhamnaceae—buckthorn (3 species)
28. Rosaceae—rose (8 species)
29. Ruscaceae—butcher's broom (2 species)
30. Salicaceae—willow (11 species)
31. Sarcobataceae—greasewood (1 species)
32. Saururaceae—lizard's tail (1 species)
33. Solanaceae—nightshade (1 species)
34. Typhaceae—cattail (3 species)
35. Zygophyllaceae—caltrop (1 species)

*american bulrush*
*sedge family*

*Black-stem rabbit brush*
*sunflower family*

*blister sedge*
*sedge family*

Although identifying plant alliances is a good way of growing your own relationship with what can be the very mysterious world of desert ecology, the system can be frustrating when you are trying to identify a particular plant species. Because of its broad generalizations, alliance classification is not very good at predicting whether any one species will actually be present or not. It is beyond the scope of this book to delve into a complete inventory of the 2,394 identified plant species that compose the plant alliances detailed in the list that follows.

## Dominant Desert Plants of Major Vegetation Alliances

Agave – Asparagaceae – desert agave, *Agave deserti*
Aspen – Salicaceae – aspen, *Populus tremuloides*
Buckwheat – Polygonaceae – California buckwheat, *Eriogonum fasciculatum*
Buckwheat – Polygonaceae – Wright's buckwheat, *Eriogonum wrightii*
Bunchgrass – Poaceae – alkali sacaton, *Sporobolus airoides*
Bunchgrass – Poaceae – bluebunch wheatgrass, *Pseudoroegneria spicata*
Bunchgrass – Poaceae – deer grass, *Muhlengergia rigens*
Bunchgrass – Poaceae – desert needlegrass, *Achnatherum speciosum*
Bunchgrass – Poaceae – fowl mannagrass, *Glyceria striata*
Bunchgrass – Poaceae – Idaho fescue, *Festuca idahoensis*
Bunchgrass – Poaceae – tall mannagrass, *Glyceria elata*
Cholla cactus – Cactaceae – teddy bear cholla, *Cylindropuntia bigelovii*
Cottonwood – Salicaceae – black cottonwood, *Populus trichocarpa*
Cottonwood – Salicaceae – Fremont cottonwood, *Populus fremontii*
Fir – Pinaceae – white fir, *Abies concolor*
Grass – Poaceae – alkali cordgrass, *Spartina gracilis*
Grass – Poaceae – ashy ryegrass, *Leymus cinereus*
Grass – Poaceae – Baltic rush, *Juncus arcticus* var. *balticus*
Grass – Poaceae – big galleta, *Pleuraphis rigida*
Grass – Poaceae – Cooper's rush, *Juncus cooperi*
Grass – Poaceae – curly blue grass, *Poa secunda*
Grass – Poaceae – desert panic grass, *Panicum urvilleanum*
Grass – Poaceae – ditch-grass, *Ruppia cirrhosa*
Grass – Poaceae – Indian rice grass, *Achnatherum hymenoides*
Grass – Poaceae – James' galleta, *Pleuraphis jamesii*
Grass – Poaceae – meadow barley, *Hordeum brachyantherum*
Grass – Poaceae – Mexican rush, *Juncus arcticus* var. *mexicanus*
Grass – Poaceae – salt grass, *Distichlis spicata*
Grass – Poaceae – tufted hair grass, *Deschampsia caespitosa*
Grass – Poaceae – weak mannagrass, *Torreyochloa pallida*
Grass – Poaceae – widgeon-grass, *Ruppia maritima*
Herb – Asparagaceae – small camas, *Camassia quamash*

Herb – Asteraceae – bugseed, *Dicoria canescens*
Herb – Asteraceae – Pacific alpine gold, *Hulsea algida*
Herb – Boraginaceae – bristly fiddleneck, *Amsinckia tessallata*
Herb – Boraginaceae – Menzies' fiddleneck, *Amsinckia menziesii*
Herb – Nyctaginaceae – desert sand-verbena, *Abronia villosa*
Herb – Phrymaceae – common monkeyflower, *Mimulus guttatus*
Herb – Polemoniaceae – Coville's phlox, *Phlox covillei*
Herb – Saururaceae – yerba mansa, *Anemopsis californica*
Juniper – Cupressaceae – California juniper, *Juniperus californica*
Juniper – Cupressaceae – mountain juniper, *Juniperus grandis*
Juniper – Cupressaceae – Utah juniper, *Juniperus osteosperma*
Juniper – Cupressaceae – western juniper, *Juniperus occidentalis*
Lily – Melanthiaceae – white corn lily, *Veratrum californicum*
Nolina – Ruscaceae – Bigelow's nolina, *Nolina bigelovii*
Nolina – Ruscaceae – giant nolina, *Nolina parryi*
Oak – Fagaceae – canyon live oak, *Quercus chrysolepis*
Oak – Fagaceae – Muller oak, *Quercus cornelius-mulleri*
Oak – Fagaceae – Sonoran live oak, *Quercus turbinella*
Palm – Arecaceae – California fan palm, *Washingtonia filifera*
Pine – Pinaceae – bristlecone pine, *Pinus longaeva*
Pine – Pinaceae – Jeffrey pine, *Pinus jeffreyi*
Pine – Pinaceae – limber pine, *Pinus flexilis*
Pine – Pinaceae – lodgepole pine, *Pinus contorta* ssp. *murrayana*
Pine – Pinaceae – ponderosa pine, *Pinus ponderosa*
Pine – Pinaceae – singleleaf pinyon, *Pinus monophylla*
Reed – Cyperaceae – American bulrush, *Schoenoplectus americanus*
Reed – Cyperaceae – tule reed, California bulrush, *Schoenoplectus californicus*
Reed – Cyperaceae – tule reed, hardstem bulrush, *Schoenoplectus acutus*
Reed – Poaceae – common reed, *Phragmites australis*
Reed – Typhaceae – cattail, *Typha angustifolia*
Reed – Typhaceae – cattail, *Typha dominguensis*
Reed – Typhaceae – cattail, *Typha latifolia*
Sagebrush – Asteraceae – big sagebrush, *Artemisia tridentata*
Sagebrush – Asteraceae – black sagebrush, *Artemisia nova*
Sagebrush – Asteraceae – little sagebrush, *Artemisia arbuscula* ssp. *arbuscula*
Sagebrush – Asteraceae – mountain big sagebrush, *Artemisia tridentata* ssp. *vaseyana*
Sagebrush – Asteraceae – Rothrock's sagebrush, *Artemisia rothrockii*
Sagebrush – Asteraceae – silver sagebrush, *Artemisia cana*
Sedge – Cyperaceae – beaked sedge, *Carex utriculata*
Sedge – Cyperaceae – blister sedge, *Carex vesicaria*
Sedge – Cyperaceae – dark alpine sedge, *Carex subnigricans*
Sedge – Cyperaceae – Nebraska sedge, *Carex nebrascensis*
Sedge – Cyperaceae – needle spike rush, *Eleocharis acicularis*

Bristlecone pine
pine family

common monkeyflower
lopseed family

Coville's phlox
phlox family

desert olive
olive family

desert purple sage
mint family

desert willow
trumpetvine family

Sedge – Cyperaceae – pale spike rush, *Eleocharis macrostachya*
Sedge – Cyperaceae – short-beaked sedge, *Carex simulata*
Shrub – Amaranthaceae – allscale, *Atriplex polycarpa*
Shrub – Aizoaceae – western sea-purslane, *Sesuvium verrucosum*
Shrub – Amaranthaceae – bush seepweed, *Suaeda moquinii*
Shrub – Amaranthaceae – desert holly, *Atriplex hymenelytra*
Shrub – Amaranthaceae – fourwing saltbush, *Atriplex canescens*
Shrub – Amaranthaceae – iodine bush, *Allenrolfea occidentalis*
Shrub – Amaranthaceae – quailbush, *Atriplex lentiformis*
Shrub – Amaranthaceae – shadescale, *Atriplex confertifolia*
Shrub – Amaranthaceae – spinescale, *Atriplex spinifera*
Shrub – Amaranthaceae – spiny hop sage, *Grayia spinosa*
Shrub – Amaranthaceae – winterfat, *Krascheninnikovia lanata*
Shrub – Asteraceae – arrowleaf ragwort, *Senecio triangularis*
Shrub – Asteraceae – arrowweed, *Pluchea sericea*
Shrub – Asteraceae – black-stem rabbitbrush, *Ericameria paniculata*
Shrub – Asteraceae – brittlebush, *Encelia farinosa*
Shrub – Asteraceae – broom baccharis, *Baccharis sergiloides*
Shrub – Asteraceae – California heath-goldenrod, *Ericameria discoidea*
Shrub – Asteraceae – cheesebush, *Ambrosia salsola*
Shrub – Asteraceae – mulefat, *Baccharis salicifolia*
Shrub – Asteraceae – needleleaf rabbitbrush, *Ericameria teretifolia*
Shrub – Asteraceae – net-veined goldeneye, *Viguiera reticulata*
Shrub – Asteraceae – Parish's goldeneye, *Viguiera parishii*
Shrub – Asteraceae – Parry's rabbitbrush, *Ericameria parryi*
Shrub – Asteraceae – rubber rabbitbrush, *Ericameria nauseosa*
Shrub – Asteraceae – scale broom, *Lepidospartum squamatum*
Shrub – Asteraceae – white bursage, *Ambrosia dumosa*
Shrub – Betulaceae – water birch, *Betula occidentalis*
Shrub – Bignoniaceae – desert willow, *Chilopsis linearis*
Shrub – Cornaceae – red osier dogwood, *Cornus sericea*
Shrub – Ephedraceae – California joint fir, *Ephedra californica*
Shrub – Ephedraceae – Mormon tea, *Ephedra virdis*
Shrub – Ephedraceae – Nevada joint fir, *Ephedra nevadensis*
Shrub – Ericaceae – green leaf manzanita, *Arctostaphylos patula*
Shrub – Fabaceae – blue palo verde, *Parkinsonia florida*
Shrub – Fabaceae – catclaw acacia, *Senegalia greggii*
Shrub – Fabaceae – deer weed, *Lotus scoparius*
Shrub – Fabaceae – ironwood, *Olneya tesota*
Shrub – Fabaceae – mesquite, *Prosopis glandulosa*
Shrub – Fabaceae – screwbean mesquite, *Prosopis pubescens*
Shrub – Fabaceae – smoke tree, *Psorothamnus spinosus*
Shrub – Lamiaceae – bladder sage, *Scutellaria mexicana*

Mormon tea
ephedra family

Menzies' fiddleneck
borage family

small camas
asparagus family

spiny hop sage
amaranth family

Stansbury cliffrose
rose family

white corn lily
bunch flower family

Shrub – Lamiaceae – desert lavender, *Hyptis emoryi*
Shrub – Lamiaceae – desert purple sage, *Salvia dorrii*
Shrub – Lamiaceae – white sage, *Salvia apiana*
Shrub – Oleaceae – desert olive, *Forestiera pubescens*
Shrub – Papaveraceae – California poppy, *Eschscholzia californica*
Shrub – Rhamnaceae – deer brush, *Ceanothus integerrimus*
Shrub – Rhamnaceae – mountain white thorn, *Ceanothus cordulatus*
Shrub – Rhamnaceae – tobacco brush, *Ceanothus velutinus*
Shrub – Rosaceae – bitterbrush, *Purshia tridentata*
Shrub – Rosaceae – black brush, *Coleogyne ramosissima*
Shrub – Rosaceae – curl leaf mountain mahogany, *Cercocarpus ledifolius*
Shrub – Rosaceae – desert almond, *Prunus fasciculata*
Shrub – Rosaceae – shrubby cinquefoil, *Dasiphora fruticosa*
Shrub – Rosaceae – small leaf mountain mahogany, *Cercocarpus intricatus*
Shrub – Rosaceae – Stansbury cliff rose, *Purshia stansburiana*
Shrub – Rosaceae – Virgin River brittlebush, *Encelia virginensis*
Shrub – Sarcobataceae – greasewood, *Sarcobatus vermiculatus*
Shrub – Solanaceae – Anderson's boxthorn, *Lycium andersonii*
Shrub – Zygophyllaceae – creosote bush, *Larrea tridentata*
Willow – Salicaceae – arroyo willow, *Salix lasiolepis*
Willow – Salicaceae – Bebb's willow, *Salix bebbiana*
Willow – Salicaceae – Goodding's black willow, *Salix gooddingii*
Willow – Salicaceae – Geyer willow, *Salix geyeriana*
Willow – Salicaceae – Lemmon's willow, *Salix lemmonii*
Willow – Salicaceae – red willow, *Salix laevigata*
Willow – Salicaceae – sandbar willow, *Salix exigua*
Willow – Salicaceae – Sierran willow, *Salix eastwoodiae*
Yucca – Asparagaceae – Joshua tree, *Yucca brevifolia*
Yucca – Asparagaceae – Mojave yucca, *Yucca schidigera*

Ghost flower
*Mohavea confertiflora*

Red Rock Canyon State Park, Calif.

El Paso Mtns.

Lava Mtns

China Lake
(Navy)

Fremont Valley

Cuddle Back Dry Lake

Desert Tortoise Natural area

Harper Dry lake

Barstow

*Northwestern Mojave Desert*
*Diameter of inscribed circle, 52 miles*

Map 03.07

# 03.07 PROTECTED PIECES OF THE WHOLE
*Ecological reserves in the northwestern Mojave Desert*

In the landscape of the northern Antelope Valley, which was for thousands of years the kingdom of the Mohave ground squirrel, the desert tortoise, and the now extirpated pronghorn antelope, humans are today by far the most ubiquitous mammal. From the city of Ridgecrest in the north to the city of Barstow in the south, the region contains only a small checkerboard of eco-reserves and designated natural areas that harbor precious habitat and geologic anomalies.

01. Red Rock Canyon State Park
02. Koehn Dry Lake
03. Fremont Valley Ecological Reserve
04. Rand Mountains
05. Golden Valley Wilderness
06. Black Hills
07. Grass Valley Wilderness
08. West Mojave Desert Ecological Reserve
09. Superior Dry Lake
10. Black Mountain Wilderness
11. Rainbow Bridge National Natural Landmark
12. Barstow Woolly Sunflower (area of critical environmental concern)
13. Harper Lake Wildlife Viewing Area
14. Saddleback Mountain (3,087')
15. Galileo Hill (3,310')
16. Desert Butte (2,849')

Mojave desert tortoise
*Gopherus agassizii*

## 03.08 POPPIES AND PEOPLE
*Southern Antelope Valley*

The urban sprawl of Lancaster and Palmdale lays down a veneer of concrete, stucco, and plastic across the western Mojave's ancient desert woodland. There are only a few land-area designations that offer glimpses into what this landscape was until very recently. The total area of these public lands amounts to far less than 1 percent of the total land area of Antelope Valley.

01. Arthur B. Ripley Desert Woodland State Park
02. Antelope Valley California Poppy State Natural Reserve
03. Fairmont Wash
04. Prime Desert Woodland Preserve
05. Amargosa Creek
06. Little Rock Wash
07. Rock Creek Wash
08. Alpine Butte Wildlife Sanctuary
09. Antelope Valley Indian Museum State Historic Park
10. Saddleback Butte State Park
11. Butte Valley Wildflower Sanctuary
12. Grass Mountain (2,978')
13. Portal Ridge
14. Mt. McDill (5,187')
15. Mt. Emma (5,273')
16. Pleasant View Ridge
17. Pinyon Ridge

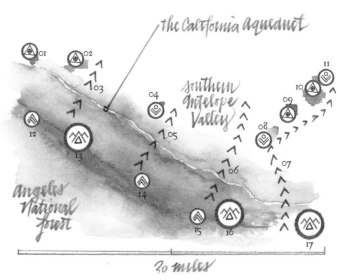

the California aqueduct

southern antelope Valley

angeles National forest

30 miles

Trailmap

Antelope Butte Vntg point

Size of reserve 1,781 acres

diameter: 1 mile

kitanemuk Vista point

Tehachapi Vista point

Lancaster Rd.

## 03.08a Antelope Valley California Poppy State Natural Reserve

The state flower, the California poppy, *Eschscholzia californica*, blooms in the Antelope Valley as it does nowhere else. An unbroken vernal carpet of radiant orange flowers sprawls across thousands of acres. As incredible as the spectacle is, it is indicative of something even more ecologically profound. Just as the name Antelope Valley indicates the now-gone primary grazer of this landscape, the pronghorn antelope, *Antilocapra americana*, so too do these poppy fields suggest an ancient landscape. Across this valley, and indeed the whole California Floristic Province, forbs such as the poppy once dominated what are now grasslands, before the dominance of invasive European plants.[24]

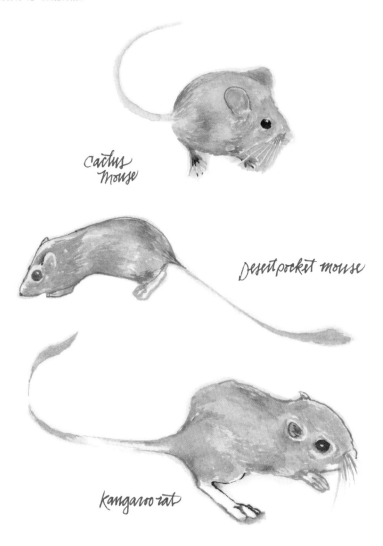

*Eating patterns of desert mice*

Cactus mouse, *Peromyscus eremicus*, is a generalist plant eater.
Desert pocket mouse, *Chaetodipus penicillatus*, only eats seeds.
Kangaroo rat, *Dipodomys microps*, only eats the salty outer
layer of the saltbush, *Atriplex* spp.

*herbaceous alliance of antelope Valley*

California goldfields
*Lasthenia californica*

Purple owl's clover
*Castilleja exserta*

Miniature lupine
*Lupinus bicolor*

*Borrego milkvetch*
*Astragalus lentiginosus*

*Blister beetle larva* m. franciscanus
*on white faced bee* H. pallida

On Borrego milkvetch, *Astragalus lentiginosus*, an endangered desert
forb, large aggregations of the blister beetle, *Meloe franciscanus*, release
pheromones to attract male white-faced bees, *Habropoda pallida*, to their
broods of larvae, who mimic the appearance of female white-faced bees.
The beetle larvae attach themselves to the male bees; when the bees finally
do mate, the larvae are transferred to the female bees. Then the beetle
larvae, unbeknownst to the female bees, are taken to the bees' nest, where
they are fed by the nutrients in the nest.

## 03.09 PALM OASIS
*Desert wetland habitat*

It may be that in the damp, spring-fed shade of California's only native palm—the California fan palm, *Washingtonia filifera*—may be found the richest nodes of biodiversity in the Colorado Desert and the Sonoran Desert in California. In any one of the hundred existing palm oases, several of which contain two thousand or more individual trees, you will find yourself in the company of upwards of eighty species of plants from over thirty different plant families.[25]

*Washingtonia* sp. was already established in the region sixty million years ago in what was then the ancient floristic province called Mohavia—including the Mojave and Sonoran Deserts, just after the dinosaurs died out, when the Imperial and Coachella Valleys were still under the sea.[26] As Lake Cahuilla formed, palm oases developed around the rim of the Pleistocene lake. For many years, academic botanists generally believed that today's palm oases were relict populations left over from the ice age, but now it is understood that they were maintained and cared for with prescriptive burn regimes and germinated by the Kamia and the Cahuilla people.[27] Because of the deep roots of these trees, which retain access to water all year, they are called phreatophytic. They can grow over forty feet tall, and as their trunks don't produce rings, nobody really knows how old they can grow, but certainly they can live for over two hundred years.[28]

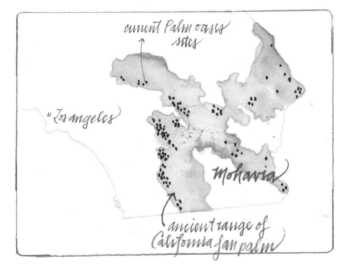

current Palm oases sites

Los angeles

Mohavia

ancient range of California fan palm

# Biodiversity of the California fan palm *(Washingtonia filifera)* oasis woodland alliance

California tree frog
*Pseudacris cadaverina*

White-throated swift
*Aeronautes saxatalis*

Desert spiny lizard
*Sceloporus magister*

Great purple hairstreak
*Atlides halesus*

Ash
*Fraxinus velutina*

California
fan palm
Washingtonia
filifera

White alder
*Alnus rhombifolia*

## 03.10 MOJAVE'S SIGNATURE YUCCA
*Notes on the Joshua tree*

Both varieties of the wild-armed Joshua tree (*Yucca brevifolia*) are endemic to the Mojave Desert, ranging in elevations of 2,000–6,000 feet. The Joshua tree is the only arborescent (tree-like) species of California's four yuccas. The western variety tends to be larger in overall size, although with a shorter primary trunk, than the eastern variety.

Both varietals of Joshua tree are pollinated by moths that are no bigger than a pencil eraser—the western Juniper tree moth, *Tegeticula synthetica*, and the eastern Juniper tree moth, *Tegeticula antithetica*.[29] In exchange for pollination, the larvae of the Joshua tree moths are hosted and nurtured by the growing fruit of the Joshua tree.

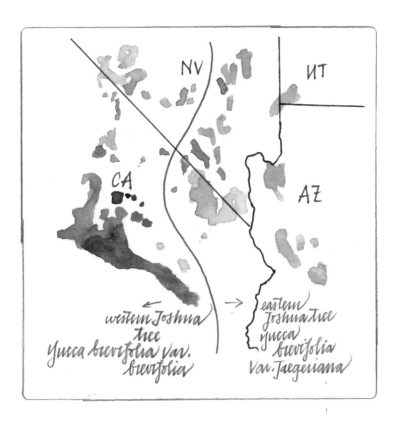

western Joshua tree
Yucca brevifolia var. brevifolia

eastern Joshua tree yucca brevifolia var. Jaegeriana

The current range of Joshua trees is imperiled, not only by rising summer temperatures but by the lack of winter nights when frost forms. Cold snaps are necessary encouragement for the trees to flower.[30] Increased aridity and rising temperatures may cause the Joshua to become extirpated from its current range throughout the Mojave by the end of the twenty-first century. As the environment transforms, the best bet for continuance of the species is likely to be human-assisted migration north, out of the Mojave and into the Great Basin.[31]

Chaparral yucca
*Hesperoyucca whipplei*

Mojave yucca
*Yucca schidigera*

Joshua tree
*Yucca brevifolia*

Joshua trees can grow up to over thirty feet in height, and it has been speculated that they can live for up to one thousand years.

Banana yucca
*Yucca baccata*

## The four yucca species of the California deserts

| White bursage | Desert needle grass | California buckwheat |
| *Ambrosia dumosa* | *Achnatherum speciosum* | *Eriogonum fasciculatum* |

Common shrubs and grasses in the Joshua tree (*Yucca brevifolia*) woodland alliance

# 03.11 GREAT BASIN'S PERFECT PLANT
*Notes on sagebrush*

Oceans of big sagebrush, *Artemisia tridentata*, extend over the Great Basin Desert. Like a wave cresting over the Sierra Nevada and stopped only by marine humidity, sagebrush is as ubiquitous across California's northern deserts and its arid mountain ranges as creosote is in California's southern deserts. These often monotypic shrubs each live for fifty years and are intolerant of regular burn regimes, which is partly why they are most happy in the cold deserts that have historically seen little in the way of massive fire.[32] *Artemisia tridentata* exists with enough genotypic and phenotypic variation in California to be represented by at least five subspecies: ssp. *tridentata*, ssp. *parishii*, ssp. *spiciformis*, ssp. *vaseyana*, and ssp. *wyomingensis*, which explains some of the species' widespread range across many climate types, elevations, and plant alliances.[33] The two-part root structure of sagebrush—shallow roots to grab any surface moisture and a deep tap root to grab deep groundwater—is yet another evolved property of this perfectly adapted, iconic plant.[34]

Big sagebrush
*Artemisia tridentata*

Reaching deep into California from the Great Basin

Even into the Rain Shadow of the Coastal Ranges

Sage sparrow
*Amphispiza belli*

Sage grouse
*Centrocercus urophasianus*

Pronghorn antelope
*Antilocapra americana*

Western scrub-Jay
Aphelocoma californica

Pinyon Jay
Gymnorhinus cyanocephalus

Bushy-tailed woodrat
Neotoma cinerea

*Diameter of inscribed circle, 700 miles*

## Map 03.12

*Juniper*

## 03.12 FIRE AND FOOD IN THE DESERT FOREST
*Piñon-juniper woodland*

Between 3,000 and 9,500 feet across the American West, two genera of long-lived, slow-growing trees who seem to particularly enjoy each other's company form open, short, bushy forests. Three species of piñon (sometimes spelled *pinyon*) and six species of juniper cover a range of more than forty million acres of distinct woodlands. The pine's nuts and the juniper's berries provide food for a cavalcade of animals, including mice, chipmunks, squirrels, birds, coyotes, and foxes who, in reciprocation, distribute the seeds inside that food, increasing the range and distribution of this conifer alliance.

Where there are forests in the West, there is also fire. When fire returns to the piñon-juniper forest in a regular cycle, every ten years or so (as was anthropogenically applied by so many Indigenous nations for thousands of years), it becomes an integrated and necessary component in the healthy maintenance of this ecosystem. When it is suppressed for a century, as it was in the twentieth century, fire returns as a conflagration of catastrophic proportions, and the forest ecosystem is threatened with the inability to regenerate.[35]

01. Parry piñon, *Pinus quadrifolia*
    Singleleaf piñon, *Pinus monophylla*
    California juniper, *Juniperus californica*

02. Singleleaf piñon, *Pinus monophylla*
    Common juniper, *Juniperus communis*
    Western juniper, *Juniperus occidentalis*
    Sierra juniper, *Juniperus grandis*

03. Singleleaf piñon, *Pinus monophylla*
    Rocky Mountain juniper, *Juniperus scopulorum*
    Common juniper, *Juniperus communis*
    Utah juniper, *Juniperus osteosperma*

04. Colorado piñon, *Pinus edulis*
    Utah juniper, *Juniperus osteosperma*
    California juniper, *Juniperus californica* (New York Mountains, eastern Mojave)

*Piñon*

## Generalized Map of Potential Distribution Combinations of Piñon and Juniper Species in the Woodlands of the West

*Source:* Adapted from M. E. Kaufmann, *Conifers of the Pacific Slope* (Kneeland, CA: Backcountry Press, 2013).

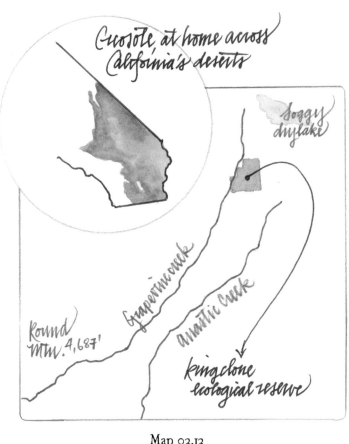

*Creosote at home across California's deserts*

*soggy drylake*

*Grapevine creek*

*Amatic Creek*

*Round mtn. 4,687'*

*kingclone ecological reserve*

Map 03.13

*Creosote Bush grasshopper*
*Bootettix argentatus*

1.5cm

Creosote bush grasshopper, *Bootettix argentatus*, is an example of a monophagous invertebrate, or an organism that only eats one species.

# 03.13 BIOLOGICAL WONDER OF THE WORLD
*Notes on creosote*

In Johnson Valley, at the base of the San Bernardino Mountains, the oldest clonal organism in the world watches geological ages pass. The King Clone creosote bush, growing at one millimeter per year, replaces itself with genetic clones every century or so as it grows in a ring out from a center point. Now roughly seventy feet in diameter and nearly twelve thousand years old, King Clone challenges the distinction between botany and geology in its ability to outlast millennia of erosional processes and persist while the world changes.

A 488-acre ecological reserve, managed by the California Department of Fish and Wildlife, protects this ancient being, one of untold thousands of its brethren across the Mojave, Sonoran, and Colorado Deserts. Covering nearly forty-five million acres, creosote's modern-day range, dominating California's desert regions and in the Mojave, this single species accounts for nearly 30 percent of the entire aboveground biomass.[36] The reasons for this uniquely aromatic, waxy-leafed shrub's success are convoluted, but because cows don't graze on it and it seems to be allelopathic accounts for at least some of it.[37]

creosote flower

eureka

saline

mesquite flats

Panamint

amargosa

Badwater Basin

China Lake

Harper Lake

Kelso Dunes

Antelope Valley

Mojave Valley

Cadiz Sheephole

Landers

Chuckwalla Valley

Sand dune systems
in the Deserts of
California

algodones

east mesa

Map 03.14

## 03.14 LIFE IN SHIFTING MOUNTAINS
*Sand dune habitat*

Most dune systems across California's deserts formed roughly ten thousand years ago, when the climate of the deserts radically transformed the hydrology of the region.[38] Every other plant alliance described in this survey, with the exception of sand dunes, is named after a single plant species. Desert dunes are unique ecosystems—island habitats that each have their own set of plant constituents. The locally adapted plant communities found on dunes tend to be made up of psammophytic (sand-growing) plants and broad-leafed herbs.[39]

Algodones Dunes sunflower
*Helianthus niveus* ssp. *tephrodes*

Dune evening primrose
*Oenothera deltoides*

Desert lily
*Hesperocallis undulata*

Sand verbena
*Abronia villosa*

Spectacle pod
*Dimorphocarpa wislizeni*

Barchan

Transverse seif

Parabolic

whaleback

sandsheet

star

Sand dune types

# 04. BIG DESERT PARCELS OF FEDERAL AND STATE LAND
*Parks, monuments, and military inholdings*

Autographia californica  alfalfa looper moth
wingspan 36-42mm

larvae feed on over 25 taxa of western plants

May cause agricultural defoliation

Several generations per year
active day or/and night

larvae are green with white line

family Noctuidae (owlet-moths)
pollinator of many desert flowers

What qualities of California's true self, independent from the Anthropocene, do we find in the park? The park—any park, monument, or wilderness area—is an invented designation, a fiction based in democratic compromise, a notion of property both public and private that is conceived of as holding some elemental quality of nature. It has very little to do with preserving the world and more to do with fetishizing nature as an external precious object, something that is containable, and something that can be visited and returned from. The park says more about modern culture than it does about nature.

Yet when it is suggested that the national park was America's best idea, heads slowly nod in agreement. Indeed, how can it be argued that the ravenous economic paradigm that ruled the twentieth century—what Wendell Berry calls "industrial fundamentalism"—could not yield such an idea in reaction to it?[1] Set nature aside. Put it away for later. It'll be safe there. By inventing the parks system, we may have inadvertently given the industrial fundamentalists the license they needed to continue the ritual sacrifice of the biosphere to their economic deity.

It is a further irony that the vast tracts of land given to the military, the inholdings of war, are now among the most pristine habitats in the desert, well guarded from the deleterious spoilings of public recreation. It may be that the fight (although it is better thought of as the vision) to designate as much land as off-limits to exploitation, to withhold as much habitat area as possible from the ravages of development and extraction, is the best and highest use of park land.

The account of the parklands in this chapter encourages not casual tourism but instead true identification with these places—understanding the landscapes as reflections of your own heart. This chapter only minimally covers what you might see when visiting your public lands—it is not a tourist guide. Rather, the discussion here concerns a relationship with patterns in the land as a function of some deeper connection, rooted in appreciation and tempered by a love that can only come about by living in this land and letting this land live in you.

## Desert Birds

There are 31 species of birds in the desert that are residents and 220 species that visit as part of their yearly migration.[2] Desert birds are better at retaining water than nondesert birds. The black-throated sparrow, *Amphispiza bilineata*, for example, a common desert bird, concentrates its urine in a specific way to retain water when conditions are especially dry.

a note on the maps going forward

the blue arrow symbols represent
the generalized flow direction of
water in a drainage. These
watercourses rarely hold
flowing water.

the river icon
also represents
spring sites
that may or may
not be active. No information
presented in these maps should be
relied on in survival situations.

black-throated sparrow

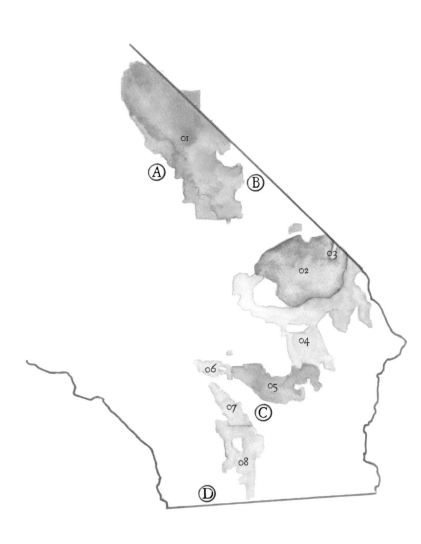

Map 04.01

# 04.01 THE PRESERVATION OF DESERT PUBLIC LANDS
*National and state parks and monuments*

Each of the major parks, monuments, and preserves described in this chapter has up to three map types assigned to its description. The first is a general overview, an at-a-glance map that delineates major land forms. The second is a catalog of the USGS 7.5' quadrangle maps for the land designation in question. The third map in the series illustrating a park will include "mountains and water" in the subtitle and describe basic elements of the park's topography. The watercourses aren't necessarily meant to represent flowing water but instead the general vectors of drainage from the ranges across washes and bajadas.

Edward Abbey says you aren't going to see anything from your car, and he is probably right. Specifically he says that "you've got to get out of the goddamned contraption and walk, better yet crawl, on hands and knees, over the sandstone. . . . When traces of blood begin to mark your trail you'll see something, maybe. Probably not."[3] This sentiment is intended to shock the reader away from the complacency of modern life and to engage the promise, rarely spoken of, that the parks offer. This promise is of adventure that does not guarantee anything but a deeper sense of connection with the ancient and powerful forces of the world beyond the trappings of contemporary society.

01. Death Valley National Park
02. Mojave National Preserve
03. Castle Mountains National Monument
04. Mojave Trails National Monument
05. Joshua Tree National Park
06. Sand to Snow National Monument
07. Santa Rosa and San Jacinto National Monument
08. Anza-Borrego Desert State Park

Potential future national monument designations:

A. Conglomerate Mesa National Monument (Inyo County)
B. Amargosa Basin National Monument (Inyo County)
C. Chuckwalla National Monument (Riverside County)
D. Chaparral Pacific Crest National Monument (San Diego County)

*Bighorn*

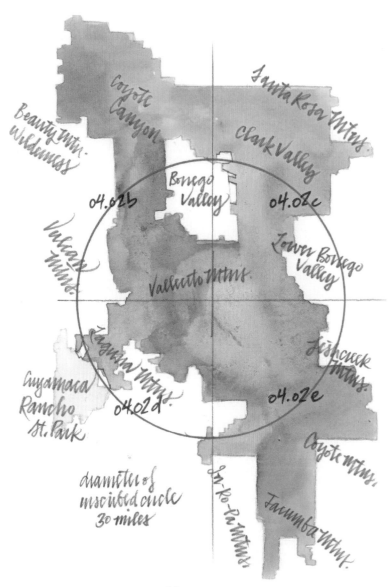

Coyote Canyon

Santa Rosa Mtns

Beauty Mtn. Wilderness

Clark Valley

Borrego Valley

04.02b

04.02c

Lower Borrego Valley

Vulcan Mtns.

Vallecito Mtns.

Laguna Mtns.

Fishcreek Mtns.

Cuyamaca Rancho St. Park

04.02d

04.02e

Coyote Mtns.

diameter of inscribed circle 30 miles

In-ko-pa Mtns.

Jacumba Mtns.

**Map 04.02**

## 04.02 ANZA-BORREGO DESERT STATE PARK—OVERVIEW

Year designated: 1933
585,930 acres/915.51 square miles
Highest peak—Combs Peak, 6,193'

Anza-Borrego Desert State Park, California's biggest state park, extends across the uplands from the Salton Trough to the Peninsular Mountains of San Diego County. Approximately 460,000 acres (719 square miles) of the park is roadless, state-owned wilderness —the largest such state-owned area in California. Surrounding the park are 175,000 acres (274 square miles) of Bureau of Land Management wilderness.

This portion of the California desert is geologically young and seismically active. In the Pleistocene, the peninsular mountain ranges to the park's west had not yet attained their current height, and therefore the rain shadow had not yet developed. For much of the previous geologic age, the Colorado Desert was not a desert at all, but enjoyed a maritime temperate environment and was replete with megafaunal mammals, nearly all of which are long extinct.[4] Fossil evidence of this lost age is evident throughout the park. What is ancient seems to be found everywhere in this young desert. Older than the massive animals of the Pleistocene, fossils of baleen whales are indicative of a time when the desert was under the sea. Today, this arid place still contains anomalous life in the form of the only California habitat for the distinctive elephant tree, *Bursera microphylla*, for example, and blooms of wildflowers that cover thousands of acres with such prismatic splendor that in terms of breathtaking beauty, it rivals any such vernal bloom anywhere in the world.

northern phainopepla
Phainopepla nitens

Author's note: In April of 2018, I gave the keynote address at a board members' conference for the Anza-Borrego Foundation in Borrego Springs. I wrote the brief speech, really a prose poem, over the course of a week before the conference while I was solo backpacking across the park, and am transcribing it here in its original five parts, across this chapter.

Anza-Borrego 01 of 05: I don't move when touching the sun in green and gold, the shadows draw across a somehow perfect angle on this creeping bajada. Today is the landform's one hundred thousandth birthday! Draped in its ancient, ocotillo-spined raiment, where beneath the cloak, all creatures move slow for fear of the dry death and even the eye of the crow holds still her Pleistocene stare. The experience is the opposite of drama as I am now returned to an older, more quiet version of the human that is me. All the trappings and saturations of my digital life desiccate quickly in the desert evening's wind, and cool dreams descend with soft starlight. In the purple of the bat song, I hear what I am sure is an ancestor's voice... (continued)

In praise of vacant
spaces,
I walk an
emptiness
of holy distance
content to be
a disappearing
character
in a timeless
plot

Red-shouldered hawk
Buteo lineatus

Carrizo Gorge

Shakespeare said the purpose of
his art
was to hold a mirror up to nature.
I do no such thing.
I work to bring the perceived forms
of the world
into me
where,
In the eyes of my heart,
these agents become seen and become known
and beloved.

this relationship,
ome part of their reality
in a landscape of eternal
holiness
where nothing is ever lost.

173

## 04.02a Anza-Borrego Desert State Park—quadrangles

01. Bucksnort Mountain
02. Collins Valley
03. Clark Lake NE
04. Rabbit Peak
05. Oasis
06. Hot Springs Mountain
07. Borrego Palm Canyon
08. Clark Lake
09. Fonts Point
10. Seventeen Palms
11. Ranchita
12. Tubb Canyon
13. Borrego Sink
14. Borrego Mountain
15. Shell Reef
16. Julian
17. Earthquake Valley
18. Whale Peak
19. Harper Canyon
20. Borrego Mountain SE

21. Cuyamaca Peak
22. Monument Peak
23. Agua Caliente Spring
24. Arroyo Tapiado
25. Carrizo Mountain SE
26. Sombrero Peak
27. Sweeney Pass
28. Carrizo Mountain
29. Jacumba
30. In-Ko-Pah Gorge

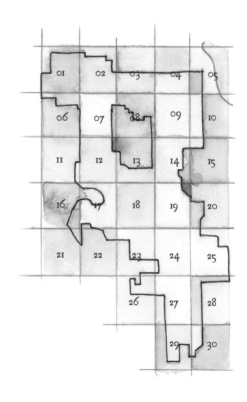

today I fell in love
    with a flower
(its mountain body)
    ~~traced in orange~~
        inside a blue sun

My blue pen — the only traceable stream
disarming my cleverness (without a thought)
I move in
    one hundred degrees

Anza Borrego
Palm Canyon
trail

anza-Borrego 02 of 05: The parade of challenges before this modern culture and this desert exist reflected within the human body as it is across the landscape, and can quickly become an easy course in despair. It is tempting to believe the defensive powers are too fragile and the offending forces are too overwhelming. The tendency is to believe that no amount of added heat can be withstood, that the system is already at its limit ... (continued)

Thousand Palms desert snail
Eremariosta mille palmarum

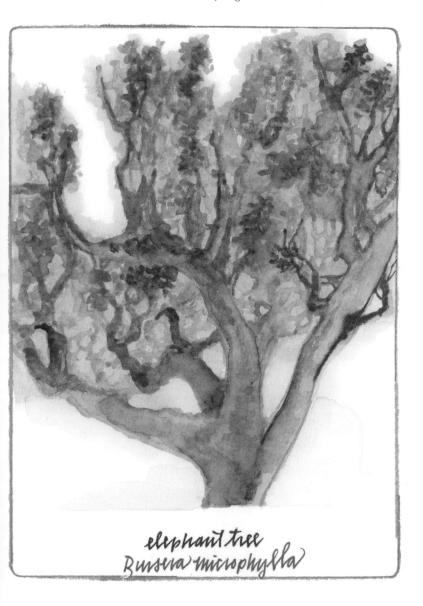

elephant tree
Bursera microphylla

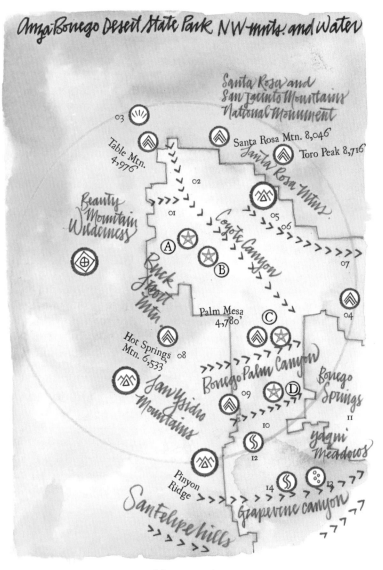

Map 04.02b

## 04.02b Anza-Borrego Desert State Park—NW mountains and water

Two valleys, the Coyote and the Clark, divided by Coyote Mountain (04) and wedged between the San Ysidro Mountains and the Santa Rosa Mountains, make up this quadrant. With piñon- and oak-dotted peaks that top out at 6,000'+, the northwestern quadrant holds the highest elevations in this park. Palm oases exist in this quadrant along tributaries into Coyote Canyon inside of Salvador Canyon (A), Sheep Canyon (B), Borrego Palm Canyon (C), and Hellhole Canyon (D). The seasonal waterfall in Hellhole Canyon is called Maidenhair Falls and is named after the desert-rare fern that grows on its damp walls—maidenhair fern, *Adiantum capillus-veneris*. Galleta grass, *Hilaria rigida*, meadows spread across the mouth of Coyote Creek at Borrego Valley.

01. Tule Canyon
02. Horse Canyon
03. Anza Valley
04. Coyote Mountain (3,192')
05. Buck Ridge
06. Butler Canyon
07. Clark Valley
08. Los Coyotes Indian Reservation
09. San Ysidro Mountain (6,147')
10. Hell Hole Canyon
11. Borrego Sink
12. Pena Spring
13. Yaqui Pass (1,750')
14. Yaqui Well

*Adiantum*
maidenhair fern

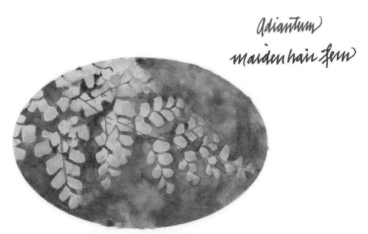

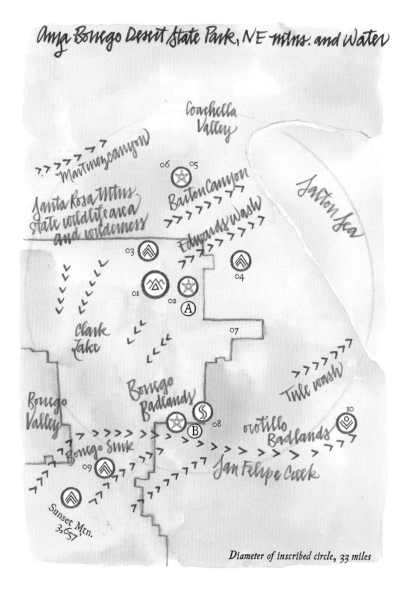

Anza Borrego Desert State Park, NE mtns. and Water

Coachella Valley

Martinez canyon

Santa Rosa Mtns. state wildlife area and wilderness

Barton Canyon

Edwards Wash

Salton Sea

Clark Lake

Bonego Badlands

Tule wash

Borrego Valley

Ocotillo Badlands

Borrego Sink

San Felipe Creek

Sunset Mtn. 3,657'

Diameter of inscribed circle, 33 miles

Map 04.02c

## 04.02c Anza-Borrego Desert State Park—NE mountains and water

The Santa Rosa Mountains cut down to the Carrizo Badlands in the park's northeast interior. East from Borrego Valley, the dry Clark Lake is a large alkali sink that occasionally spawns vernal populations of shrimp and so is habitat for migrating birds. The ancient sedimentary rock holds untold fossil wealth, and many such sites occur in this area. There are palm oases at Travertine Wash (A) and 17 Palms oasis (B). The low-elevation bajadas of the region are shrubland of ocotillo, cholla, yucca, and barrel cactus that come down from piñon-juniper woodlands in the higher lands. Across the sunken areas of Borrego Valley, two threatened plant alliances—mesquite bosque and Sonoran cottonwood willow riparian forest—can be found.

01. Santa Rosa Mountains
02. Anza-Borrego Desert State Wilderness
03. Rabbit Peak (6,640')
04. Travertine Rock (89')
05. Peninsular Ranges Ecological Reserve
06. Torres-Martinez Reservation
07. Desert Cahuilla/Freeman Project
08. 17 Palms Oasis
09. Borrego Mountain (1,207')
10. San Felipe Creek Ecological Reserve

desert thorn
Lycium torreyi

Anza-Borrego 03 of 05: Despite all of this –
the shrinking water tables, cripplingly
expensive conveyance of water, the apparent need
everywhere for some kind of environmental
remediation, and the machinations of
bullying politicians with unwise policies
moving forward despite ecological cost – the
community persists. The community persists
because everywhere there is a treasure of beauty
and desert elegance. The value glints off of
every creosote flower and this wealth,
exalted in the nightly song of the coyote,
and is held in the community's walking
bones and its beating heart. In its
unlimited grace, the Colorado Desert welcomes
respect. The community has the right to
love the desert and also has the responsibility
to protect the desert ... (continued)

Desert iguana
Dipsosaurus
dorsalis

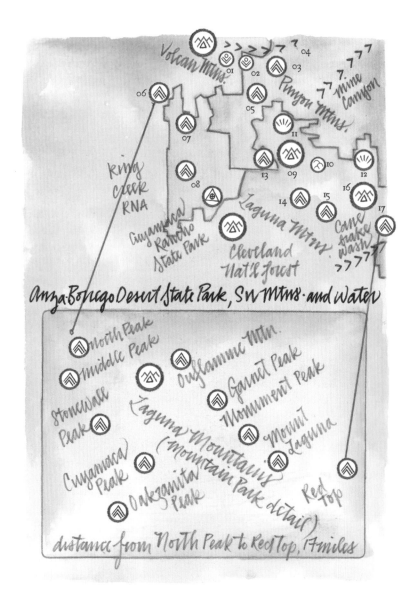

Volcan Mtns.
01 02
03 04
Pinyon Mtns.
05 06
nine canyon
07
King Creek RNA
11
12
13 09 10
08
14 15 16 17
Cuyamaca Rancho State Park
Laguna Mtns.
Cane Brake Wash
Cleveland Nat'l Forest

Anza-Borrego Desert State Park, Sw Mtns. and Water

North Peak
Middle Peak
Oriflamme Mtn.
Gaunt Peak
Monument Peak
Stonewall Peak
Laguna Mountains
(Mountain Park detail)
Mount Laguna
Cuyamaca Peak
Oakzanita Peak
Red Top

distance from North Peak to Red Top, 17 miles

Map 04.02d

## 04.02d Anza-Borrego Desert State Park—SW mountains and water

The Laguna Mountains, the Sawtooth Mountains, and the In-Ko-Pah Mountains define the southwestern border of the park. Rising four thousand feet from the valley floor, the peaks here begin to leave behind their desert identities in exchange for habitat types influenced by coastal environments, such as chaparral and oak woodland. The pine forests and grasslands of the adjacent Cuyamaca Rancho State Park are evidence of this change.

01. Volcan Mountains Wilderness Preserve
02. San Felipe Valley Wildlife Area
03. Granite Mountain (5,633')
04. San Felipe Creek
05. Chariot Mountain (4,644')
06. North Peak (5,993')
07. Stonewall Peak (5,730')
08. Cuyamaca Peak (6,512')
09. Sawtooth Ridge
10. The Portrero
11. Mason Valley
12. Vallecito Valley
13. Garnet Peak (5,909')
14. Monument Peak (6,721')
15. Mount Laguna (5,960')
16. Sawtooth Mountains
17. Red Top (4,425')

Tarantula
Theraphosidae

Anza-Borrego 04 of 05: It was eleven thousand years ago today, that the last mammoth was killed. It may be that by that point, the sixth planet-wide extinction event had already been under way for fifty thousand years or more, sparked by the fiery diaspora of humanity from its origin point. Now, all systems associated with human population growth, both municipal and societal, exhibit bacteria-like mimesis. Something mammalian is slipping from the human mind as its technology attempts to transcend its neolithic emotional core. Yet, in light of the threat, so too a choice emerges like the promise offered by a warm sliver of the orange sun on the horizon after a night chill that is hard to shake... (continued)

wolf's cholla
Cylindropuntia
wolfii

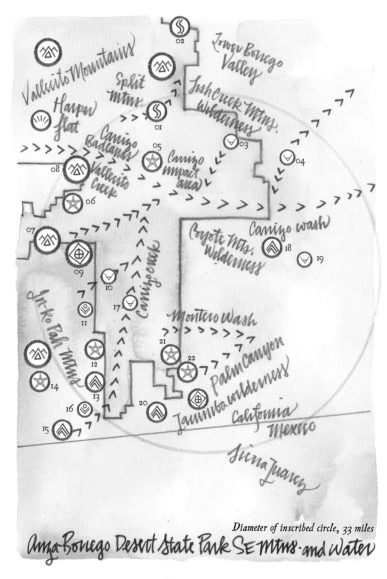

Diameter of inscribed circle, 33 miles

Anza Borrego Desert State Park SE mtns. and Water

Map 04.02e

## 04.02e Anza-Borrego Desert State Park—SE mountains and water

Four physiographic units compose the area shown on map 04.02e: Vallecito Mountains, the Carrizo Badlands (Vallecito Creek), the Coyote Mountains, and the Jacumba Mountains. Flanked by the east–west-running ranges of the Vallecitos to the north and the Coyotes to the south, dozens of bajadas drape both sides of Vallecito Creek. Just north of Palm Spring (05) are the mud caves of Arroyo Tapiado. The ground is composed of gypsiferous claystone, and these fragile, beautiful caves are carved by flooding. One mile from the mud caves is Plunge Pool Cave: a deep cavern formed from volcanic ash 2.5 million years ago.[5] Perhaps the most robust palm oasis in the park is near the confluence of Vallecito and Bow Willow Creeks, near Bow Willow Campground.

01. Fish Creek Wash
02. Elephant Trees Wash
03. Red Rock Canyon
04. Barrett Canyon
05. Palm Spring
06. Mountain Palm Springs
07. Sombrero Mountains
08. Tierra Blanca Mountains
09. Carrizo Gorge Wilderness
10. Rockhouse Canyon
11. McCain Valley National Cooperative Land and Wildlife Management Area
12. Redondo Spring
13. Mt. Tule (4,647')
14. Tecate Divide
15. Boundary Peak (3,921')
16. Walker Canyon Ecological Reserve
17. Carrizo Canyon
18. Carrizo Mountain (2,408')
19. Painted Gorge
20. Table Mountain (4,089')
21. Dos Cabezas Spring
22. Hayden Spring

Say's phoebe
Sayornis saya

Anza-Borrego 5 of 5: Let the community pledge, here, today, and every day, to protect, preserve, and restore as many moments in our legacy landscape as this collective, mortal power by grace will permit. If they still exist, these living moments of habitat represent invaluable resource stores of endemic biodiversity that is not yet lost. The community must never condemn what is not yet lost. With this ethical orientation, empowered with steely resolve for habitat stewardship, restoration, connectivity, and remediation, it may be that the health of the Colorado Desert at the end of the twenty-first century will be stronger and more robust than it was at the end of the twentieth. (end)

Vallerito Creek Anza-Borego desert State Park

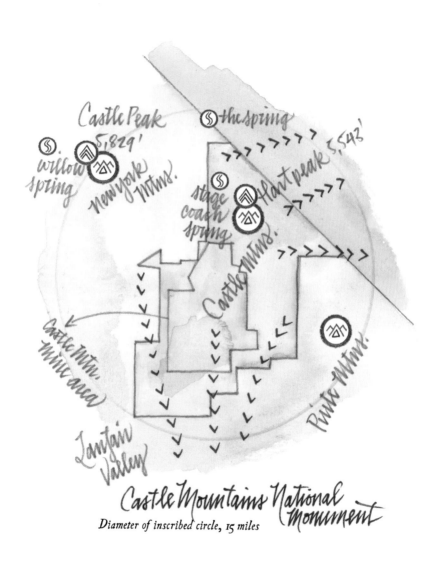

Castle Peak 5,829'

willow spring

New York Mtns.

the spring

Hart peak 5,543'

stage coach spring

Castle Mtns.

Castle Mtns. mine area

Lanfair Valley

Piute Mtns.

Castle Mountains National Monument

Diameter of inscribed circle, 15 miles

Map 04.03

## 04.03 CASTLE MOUNTAINS NATIONAL MONUMENT

Year designated: 2016
20,920 acres/32.69 square miles
Highest peak—Hart Peak, 5,543'

Castle Mountains National Monument has a lot going on for seemingly being in the middle of nowhere. There are no paved roads that access it, and although people are rarely seen there today, its mining scars and numerous ancient art sites are evidence of a long history of human habitation.

The annual grasslands that paint the area with color every spring support wildflower blooms and twenty-eight species of rare plants and desert vegetation, including burro-grass, *Scleropogon brevifolius*, and false buffalo-grass, *Munroa squarrosa*. If it weren't for the historical uses of this land, including gold mining and livestock grazing, it might have been made part of the Mojave National Preserve, which surrounds it on the California side of the state border; instead it was named a national monument decades later.[6]

Nevada
Last Chance Range
Eureka Valley
Saline Range
Saline Valley
04.04b
Last Chance Range
Grapevine Mtns.
04.04c
Death Valley
Amargosa Range
Amargosa Desert
Cottonwood Mtns.
Panamint Range
Inyo Mtns.
Panamint Valley
04.04d
04.04e
Greenwater Valley
Owlshead Mtns.
Amargosa River

Death Valley National Park
diameter of inscribed circle, 80 miles

Map 04.04

## 04.04 DEATH VALLEY NATIONAL PARK—OVERVIEW

Year designated: 1994
3,373,063 acres/5,270.41 square miles
Highest peak—Telescope Peak, 11,043'

*Death Valley*   *Zabriskie Point*

There is nowhere like Death Valley National Park. It is its own principality, governed by climatic and topographic forces that are unwilling to ever compromise or bend toward subtlety or mildness. Every aspect of the world that is Death Valley NP seems wholly alien to more temperate characters elsewhere in the biosphere, as if it has forgotten all memory of milder forms of being and now only knows the boundaries of terrestrial existence. The configuration of features within the local environment —including elevation, climate types, and habitat types supported by the crest-to-trough ecological waveform that is the over eleven-thousand-foot drop across sixteen miles, from the frozen Telescope Peak to the baking Badwater Basin—presents a superlative desert kingdom. Here the conditions exist that rightly place Death Valley on a short list of the world's most extreme environments. The abiotic stress levied from an ancient regime of ceaseless aridity, soaring temperatures, and limited soil nutrients has constructed Death Valley's endemic food webs to be made up of remarkably tough organisms, uniquely adapted to the harshest ecological conditions existing in the world today. As the climate breaks down and Death Valley trends toward greater extremes, however, the obvious question becomes, what is too much? It may be that what we perceive and describe as "tough" characteristics are merely part of a different context of adaptations relative to our own experience. These adaptations are equally as vulnerable to changing conditions as they would be in any other environment, and Death Valley is as vulnerable to changing conditions as any other ecosystem.

## 04.04a Death Valley National Park—quadrangles

These quadrangles are drawn on the USGS 7.5-minute scale—called the "seven and a half minute" map series, or 1:24,000 scale—and each covers about sixty-four square miles (approximately forty-one thousand acres). The scale indicates what a ratio would be for inches when printed to size, meaning that these maps (available from USGS), when printed at 22" × 27", represent an accurate scale where 1" on the map represents 24,000" on the ground. For scale on map 04.04a, from its northern tip to its southern border, Death Valley National Park is approximately 130 miles long.

01. Soldier Pass
02. Horse Thief Canyon
03. Last Chance Mountain
04. Tule Canyon
05. Joshua Flats
06. East of Joshua Flats
07. Hanging Rock Canyon
08. Sand Spring
09. Gold Point SW
10. Gold Point
11. Waucoba Spring
12. East of Waucoba Spring
13. Last Chance Range SW
14. Last Chance Range SE
15. Ubehebe Crater
16. Scotty's Castle
17. Bonnie Claire SW
18. Waucoba Canyon
19. East of Waucoba Canyon
20. Saline Peak
21. Dry Mountain
22. Tin Mountain
23. East of Tin Mountain
24. Grapevine Peak
25. Wahguyhe Peak
26. Bullfrog Mountain
27. Pat Keyes Canyon
28. Lower Warm Springs
29. West of Teakettle Junction
30. Teakettle Junction
31. White Top Mountain
32. Dry Bone Canyon
33. Fall Canyon
34. Thimble Peak
35. Daylight Pass
36. Craig Canyon
37. West of Ubehebe Peak
38. Ubehebe Peak
39. Sand Flat
40. East of Sand Flat
41. Mesquite Flat
42. Stovepipe Well NE
43. Chloride City
44. East of Chloride City
45. Ashton
46. Nelson Range
47. Jackass Canyon
48. Harns Hills
49. Cottonwood Canyon
50. Stovepipe Wells
51. Grotto Canyon
52. Beatty Junction
53. Nevares Peak
54. Lees Camp
55. Leeland
56. Santa Rosa Flat
57. Lee Wash
58. The Dunes

59. Panamint Butte
60. Emigrant Canyon
61. Tucki Wash
62. West of Furnace Creek
63. Furnace Creek
64. Echo Canyon
65. East of Echo Canyon
66. Darwin
67. Panamint Springs
68. Nova Canyon
69. Emigrant Pass
70. Wildrose Peak
71. Devil's Speedway
72. Devil's Golf Course
73. Ryan
74. East of Ryan
75. Maturango Peak NE
76. Jail Canyon
77. Telescope Peak
78. Hanaupah Canyon
79. Badwater
80. Dante's View
81. Greenwater Canyon
82. West of Eagle Mountain
83. Eagle Mountain
84. Ballarat
85. Panamint
86. Galena Canyon
87. Mormon Point
88. Gold Valley
89. Funeral Peak
90. Deadman Pass
91. East of Deadman Pass
92. Manly Fall
93. Manly Peak
94. Anvil Spring Canyon West
95. Anvil Spring Canyon East
96. Shoreline Butte
97. Epaulet Peak
98. Salsberry Peak
99. Shoshone

100. Sourdough Spring
101. Wingate Wash West
102. Wingate Wash East
103. Confidence Hills West
104. Confidence Hills East
105. Ibex Spring
106. Ibex Pass
107. Hidden Spring
108. Quail Spring
109. Owl Lake
110. East of Owl Lake
111. Old Ibex Pass
112. Saddle Peak Hills

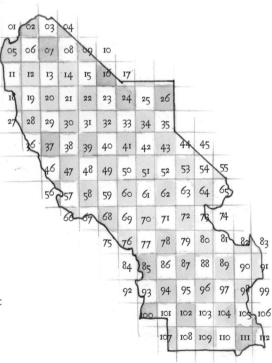

Map 04.04a

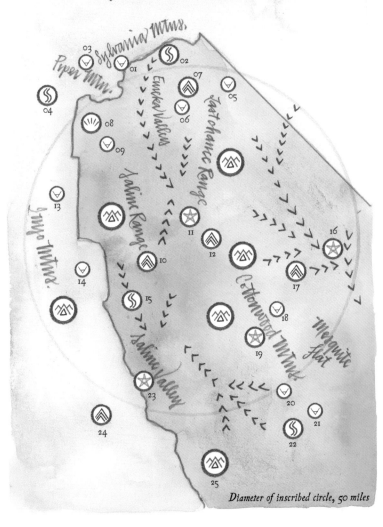

Death Valley National Park, NW mtns. and water

*Diameter of inscribed circle, 50 miles*

Map 04.04b

## 04.04b Death Valley National Park—NW mountains and water

Because of the orientation of the park with the state line of California, a graphic contrivance for map 04.04b must include the entirety of what is actually northern Death Valley National Park. This quadrant contains such notable physiographic features as the Eureka Dunes, some of the biggest and tallest sand dunes in North America, and the Racetrack, a dry lake known for its moving rocks that slide on thin ice, pushed by wind.

01. Horse Thief Canyon
02. Willow Spring; Willow Creek
03. Soldier Pass Canyon
04. Deep Springs Lake; Buckhorn Spring
05. Last Chance Canyon
06. Hanging Rock Canyon
07. Last Chance Mountain (8,456')
08. Cowhorn Valley
09. Marble Canyon
10. Saline Peak (7,063')

11. Eureka Dunes (3,520'); Dedeckera Canyon
12. Dry Mountain (8,674')
13. Waucoba Canyon; Whippoorwill Flat Research Natural Area
14. Piute Canyon from Winnedumah Paiute Monument (8,369')
15. Waucoba Wash
16. Ubehebe Crater; Grapevine Canyon
17. Tin Mountain (8,953')
18. Lost Burro Gap
19. Ubehebe Peak (5,678'); the Racetrack
20. Marble Canyon
21. Cottonwood Canyon
22. Spanish Springs
23. Salt Lake; Saline Valley Dunes (1,203'); Saline Valley Ecological Reserve
24. Cerro Gordo Peak (9,184')
25. Nelson Range

family Solifugae
Solpugids
Sun spiders
up to 4" in length
up to 100 species
in Death Valley

the jaws of Solifugae are called "chelicerae". The largest jaws of any terrestrial invertebrate

Non-venomous

# Death Valley National Park, NE mtns. and Water

the word "over" refers to
elevational proximity
upslope

the word "from" refers to
water flow from an
origin point upslope.

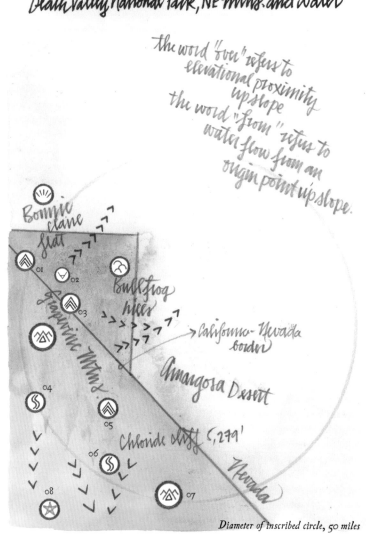

Bonnie claire flat

Bullfrog hills

Grapevine Mtns.

California–Nevada border

Amargosa Desert

Chloride cliff 5,279'

Nevada

*Diameter of inscribed circle, 50 miles*

Map 04.04c

## 04.04c Death Valley National Park—NE mountains and water

Death Valley National Park extends into Nevada along the ridge and eastern bajadas of the Grapevine Mountains. To include the two largest pine-and-juniper-covered peaks in the range, Grapevine Peak and Wahguyhe Peak, both of which are in Nevada, the eastern border of the park jets out in a triangle-like shape that invades the neighboring state for about twelve linear miles on each side of the projecting shape.

01. Grapevine Peak (8,738')
02. Phinney Canyon
03. Wahguyhe Peak (8,628')
04. Death Valley Wash
05. Corkscrew Peak (5,804')
06. Salt Creek
07. Amargosa Range
08. The Dunes at Stove Pipe Wells

coyote family

*Diameter of inscribed circle, 50 miles*

Death Valley National Park, SW mtns. and Water

Map 04.04d

## 04.04d Death Valley National Park—SW mountains and water

Approximately five hundred square miles of the Badwater Basin saltpan is below sea level and the mouth of the Amargosa River. The two mountain ranges that flank the valley are the Amargosa to the east and Panamint to the west. Both are fault-block ranges, and the granite that intruded to become these mountains is dated to 1.4 billion years old.[7]

01. Hunter Mountain (7,365')
02. Panamint Butte (6,585')
03. Darwin Plateau
04. Panamint Dunes (2,672')
05. Panamint Springs (1,940')
06. Tucki Mountain (6,732')
07. Wildrose Wash
08. Furnace Creek
09. Emigrant Canyon
10. Aguereberry Point (6,280')
11. Telescope Peak (11,049')
12. Hanaupah Canyon
13. Six Spring Canyon
14. Rogers Pass (7,160')
15. Anvil Springs Canyon
16. Sugarloaf Peak (4,820')
17. Owlshead Mountains

Telescope Peak from Badwater

Diameter of inscribed circle, 50 miles

Death Valley National Park, SE Mtns. and Water

Map 04.04e

## 04.04e Death Valley National Park—SE mountains and water

The Amargosa River cradles the eastern border of Death Valley National Park. Beginning northeast of the Amargosa Valley, the river make a run south and then turns north again, following the ancient Manly Lake watershed that existed in the Pleistocene.

01. Winters Peak (5,033')
02. Pyramid Peak (6,703')
03. Zabriskie Point
04. Badwater Basin (-282')
05. Dantes View (5,475')
06. Funeral Peak (6,384'); Sheep Canyon

07. Brown Peak (4,947')
08. Amargosa River; Willow Creek
09. Salsberry Pass (4,254')
10. Shoshone (1,569')
11. Ibex Dunes
12. Saddle Peak Hills
13. Round Mountain (472')

Fremont Cottonwood
Populus fremontii

Chuckwalla
genus *Sauromalus*
family *Iguanidae*

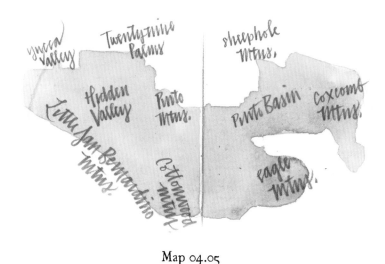

Map 04.05

Joshua Tree National Park
diameter of inscribed circle 60 miles

## 04.05 JOSHUA TREE NATIONAL PARK—OVERVIEW

Year designated: 1994
795,156 acres/1,242.43 square miles
Highest peak—Quail Mountain, 5,816'

In addition to its namesake tree, the first thing to notice about the landscape of Joshua Tree National Park is the array of unusual, massive stones, strangely shaped, ominous, and unique. These enormous structures, called tors, are composed of monzogranite, a type of granitic rock that is the result of a plutonic intrusion (where magma of one type of rock solidifies over time in another type of rock) that occurred nearly one hundred million years ago. In the time since, water has flexed its erosional power by slowly penetrating deep into intrusions, hollowing out the alien rock, effectively cleaving the stone and shaping it into what looks like the piles of rock we find today.[8] Between the trees and the tors, habitat in Joshua Tree National Park across the Little San Bernardino Mountains is unique to the southeastern Mojave Desert. The park is big enough such that it spans two deserts: the Mojave and the Sonoran.

## 04.05a Joshua Tree National Park—quadrangles

Descending from the northwest corner of the park, with its plateau-like prow, the great Pinto Basin opens up into another, fundamentally different kind of desert. Gone are the tors and the Joshua trees; and in the lower elevations, cholla gardens patch the landscape over wide-open vistas with little vegetation until the heights of Eagle Mountains to the south, which harbor riparian ecosystems and other habitat types that in character are more Sonoran than they are of the Mojave.

01. Yucca Valley South
02. Joshua Tree South
03. Indian Cove
04. Queen Mountain
05. Twentynine Palms Mountain
06. Humbug Mountain
07. New Dale
08. Clarks Pass
09. Cadiz Valley SW
10. Cadiz Valley SE
11. Seven Palms Valley
12. East Deception Canyon
13. Keys View
14. Malapai Hill
15. Fried Liver Wash
16. Pinto Mountain
17. San Bernardino Wash
18. Placer Canyon
19. Pinto Wells
20. Coxcomb Mountain
21. West Berdoo Canyon
22. Rockhouse Canyon
23. Washington Wash
24. Porcupine Wash
25. Conejo Well
26. Buzzard Spring
27. Victory Pass
28. East of Victory Pass
29. Thermal Canyon
30. Cottonwood Basin
31. Cottonwood Spring
32. Hayfield
33. Hayfield Spring
34. Desert Center

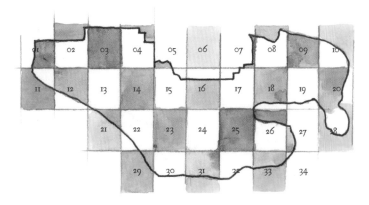

## 04.05b Joshua Tree National Park—western mountains and water

The western Joshua Tree National Park is the most heavily visited portion of the park. Between Yucca Valley to the north and Coachella Valley, the San Bernardino Mountains create a habitat corridor for bighorn that includes Sand to Snow National Monument, extending west to the peak of San Gorgonio.

01. Eureka Peak (5,520')
02. Black Rock
03. Quail Mountain (5,816')

04. Covington Flat; Juniper Flats
05. Queen Mountain (5,677')
06. Quail Springs
07. Ryan Mountain (5,461')
08. Malapai Hill (4,221')
09. Fried Liver Wash
10. Washington Wash
11. Porcupine Wash
12. Smoke Tree Wash
13. Monument Mountain (4,834')
14. Thermal Canyon
15. Fargo Canyon
16. Berdoo Canyon
17. Pushawalla Canyon; Sky Valley Ecological Reserve
18. Fan Hill Canyon
19. East Deception Canyon
20. Long Canyon

*desert quail family*

## 04.05c Joshua Tree National Park—eastern mountains and water

The Pinto Basin, across the eastern half of Joshua Tree National Park, is the park's dominant feature and runs for nearly forty miles. The basin is enclosed on its northern flank by the Pinto Mountains, on the east by the Coxcomb Mountains, and on the south by the Eagle Mountains. The difference exhibited in the vegetation of this landscape in the north and west end of the park compared to its more barren, Sonoran quality in the park's south and east is one of the most readily observable, obvious boundary lines between the two deserts.

01. Humbug Mountain (2,093')
02. Pinto Mountain (2,983')
03. Clark's Pass (1,880')
04. Aqua Peak (4,416')
05. Eagle Mountain (1,280')
06. Pinto Wells
07. Sunrise Well
08. Lost Palms Oasis
09. Hayfield Dry Lake

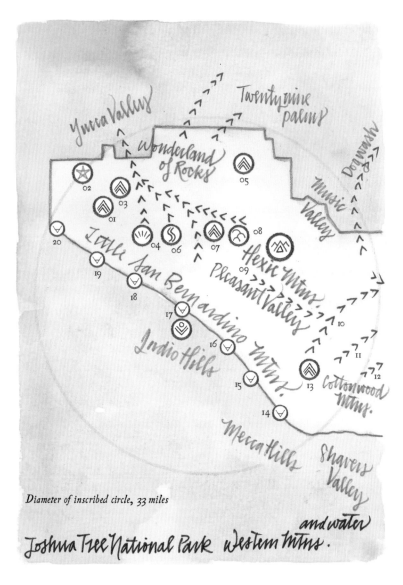

Yucca Valley

Twentynine palms

Wonderland of Rocks

Dogwash?

Music Valley

Little San Bernardino mtns.

Hexie mtns.

Pleasant Valley

Indio Hills

Cottonwood mtns.

Mecca Hills

Shavers Valley

Diameter of inscribed circle, 33 miles

and water

Joshua Tree National Park    Western mtns.

Map 04.05b

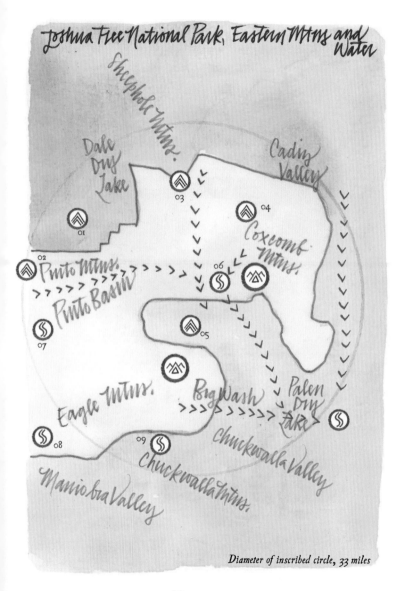

Joshua Tree National Park, Eastern Mtns and Water

Sheephole Mtns.

Dale Dry Lake

Cadiz Valley

03

04

Coxcomb Mtns.

01

02

Pinto Mtns.

06

Pinto Basin

05

07

Eagle Mtns.

Big Wash

Palen Dry Lake

08

09

Chuckwalla Valley

Maniobra Valley

Chuckwalla Mtns.

*Diameter of inscribed circle, 33 miles*

Map 04.05c

213

Shadow Valley
Clark Mtn.
Hollow Hills
Silver Lake
Ivanpah Mtns.
Ivanpah Valley
Cima Dome
New York Mtns.
Castle Mtns. NM
Cinder cone Lava beds
Mid Hills
Lanfair Valley
Soda Lake
Devil's Playground
Kelso Mtns.
Providence Mtns.
Woods Mtns.
Piute Range
Granite Mtns.
Clipper Valley
Fenner Valley
Old Dad Mtns.
Clipper Mtns.

Mojave National Preserve
Diameter of inscribed circle 70 miles

Jackrabbit

Map 04.06

## 04.06 MOJAVE NATIONAL PRESERVE—OVERVIEW

Year designated: 1994
1,542,776 acres/2,410.59 square miles
Highest peak—Clark Mountain, 7,929'

As Death Valley has its austere extremes and Joshua Tree has its incongruous landforms, Mojave National Preserve has an entirely different portfolio of characteristics. As you walk across the Granite Mountains, the Providence Mountains, or even the Cima Dome, there are Joshua tree forests and thick cactus-filled scrublands, songbirds are plenty, and the sensibility can be described as full of life. If there is one area of protected land that can be said to inhabit the ecological quality unique to the Mojave Desert, this is the one.

*in the Providence Mtns. Mojave Preserve*

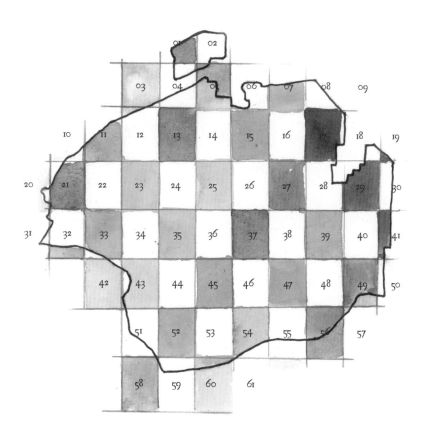

Map 04.06a

anna's hummingbird
(Calypte anna)

## 04.06a Mojave National Preserve—quadrangles

The preserve is bisected by a roughly continuous line of mountain ranges that runs from the Nevada border, heads southwest, and then turns to the northwest across the preserve's western lands. The New York Mountains, Mid Hills, and Providence Mountains form this southwesterly march, and the Granite Mountains form the bottom, slightly turned range to the southwest.

01. Pachalka Spring
02. Clark Mountain
03. Solomons Knob
04. Valley Wells
05. Mescal Range
06. Mineral Hill
07. Nipton
08. Crescent Peak
09. Hopps Well
10. Baker
11. Halloran Springs
12. Granite Spring
13. Cow Cove
14. Cima Dome
15. Joshua
16. Ivanpah
17. Castle Peaks
18. Hart Peak
19. Tenmile Well
20. West of Soda Lake
21. Soda Lake North
22. Seventeenmile Point
23. Indian Spring
24. Marl Mountains
25. Cima
26. Mid Hills
27. Pinto Valley
28. Grotto Hills
29. East of Grotto Hills
30. West of Juniper Mine
31. Crucero Hill
32. Soda Lake South
33. Cowhole Mountain
34. Old Dad Mountain
35. Kelso
36. Hayden
37. Columbia Mountain
38. Woods Mountain
39. Hackberry Mountain
40. Signal Hill
41. Homer Mountain
42. West of Glasgow
43. Glasgow
44. Kelso Dunes
45. Fountain Peak
46. Colton Well
47. Desert Spring
48. Fenner Hills
49. Goffs
50. Homer
51. Budweiser Wash
52. Bighorn Basin
53. Van Winkle Spring
54. West of Blind Hills
55. Blind Hills
56. Fenner
57. Fenner Spring
58. East of Siberia
59. Brown Buttes
60. Van Winkle Wash
61. Castle Dome

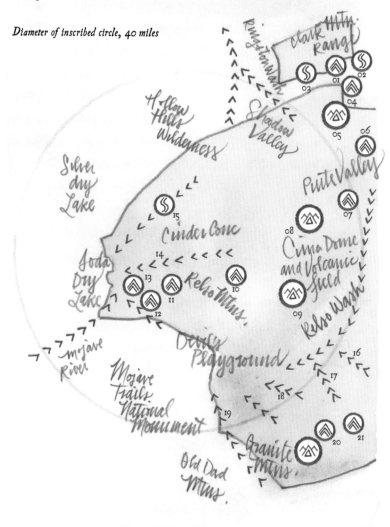

Mojave National Preserve, Western Mtns. and water

*Diameter of inscribed circle, 40 miles*

Map 04.06b

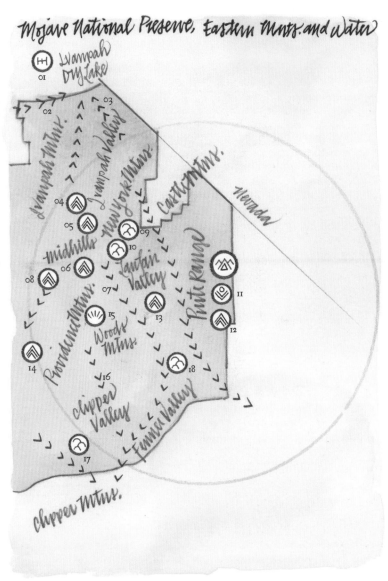

Mojave National Preserve, Eastern Mnts. and Water

Map 04.06c

## 04.06b Mojave National Preserve—western mountains and water

The northwest area of the preserve is dominated by the Cima volcanic field. The field is a sprawling landscape that contains more than forty volcanic cones and covers more than 230 square miles. The area was volcanically active for several million years prior to its last eruption, which was only fifteen thousand years ago.[9] There is no reason to assume that this entire region of the preserve is not volcanically active today.

01. Clark Mountain (7,929')
02. Ivanpah Springs
03. Pachalka Spring
04. Mohawk Hill (5,971')
05. Mescal Range
06. Striped Mountain (5,929')
07. Cima Dome (5,745')
08. Marl Mountains
09. Beale Mountains
10. Kelso Peak (4,764')
11. Old Dad Mountain (4,250')
12. Cowhole Mountain (2,252')
13. Little Cowhole Mountain (1,700')
14. Willow Wash
15. Indian Creek
16. Cedar Wash
17. Winston Wash
18. Cottonwood Wash
19. Budweiser Wash
20. Granite Peak (6,762')
21. Hidden Hill (3,968')

big cougar
always hungry always there

## 04.06c Mojave National Preserve—eastern mountains and water

The eastern half of the Mojave National Preserve is dominated by the tall mountain ranges that run southwest from the Nevada border, and the enormous Fenner and Clipper Valleys that define the southern border. The shrub oak of the Providence Mountains, *Quercus turbinella*, is a tree that makes its habitat in semiarid conditions and is found in the preserve at elevations over four thousand feet. Indicative of the area's regional, biodiverse fecundity, two insects (one 1/10" troglomorphic pseudoscorpion and the 1/8" tawny-hued Niptus beetle) are endemic to Mitchell Canyon in the Providence Mountains.

01. Ivanpah Solar Electric Generating System
02. Wheaton Wash
03. Willow Wash
04. Pinto Mountain (6,144')
05. Table Mountain (6,126')
06. Tortoise Shell Mountain (4,600')
07. Watson Wash
08. Columbia Mountain (5,673')
09. Gotto Hills
10. Lanfair Buttes (4,360')
11. Piute Creek Ecological Reserve
12. Signal Hill (3,600')
13. Hackberry Mountain (5,390')
14. Fountain Peak (6,996')
15. Wildhorse Mesa
16. Black Canyon Wash
17. Blind Hills (2,696')
18. Fenner Hills

Burrowing owl *Athene cunicularia*

## 04.07 MOJAVE TRAILS NATIONAL MONUMENT—OVERVIEW

Year designated: 2016
1,600,000 acres/2,500.00 square miles
Highest peak—Cady Peak, 4,616'

The sprawling and strangely shaped
Mojave Trails National Monument
is a recent addition to our national
catalog of such land designations.
Drawn around existing wilderness
areas, the Mojave Trails NM seems
to take up the negative space, so to
speak, between the Mojave Wildlife
Preserve and Joshua Tree National
Park. The national monument
includes and surrounds seven
wilderness areas and shares a border
with nine others, guaranteeing
the preservation of a broad area
of development-free habitat
connectivity.

Map 04.07

## 04.07a Mojave Trails National Monument—western mountains and water

Between 29 Palms Marine base and the Mojave National Preserve, the neck that is the western half of the Mojave Trails NM extends from Bristol Lake (dry) to the Cady Mountains. In a complex dance of land designations and land management, the central hub of Mojave Trails NM is the privately owned parcel not included in the monument, which is adjacent to both the Marble Mountains Wilderness Area and the lava lands of the Amboy Crater National Natural Landmark.

01. Afton Canyon
02. Broadwell Lake (dry)
03. Sleeping Beauty (3,980')
04. Pisgah Crater and Lava Flow
05. Lavic Lake (dry)
06. Amboy Crater and Lava Flow
07. Bagdad Dry Lake
08. Bristol Lake (dry)
09. Trilobite Wilderness
10. Cadiz Summit (1,319')
11. Sheephole Pass (2,307')

## 04.07b Mojave Trails National Monument—eastern mountains and water

The eastern half of the Mojave Trails NM is of a different ecological character than the desert woodlands of the Providence Mountains of the Mojave National Preserve to the north, across the Clipper Valley. In their sparce, treeless appearance, the small ranges begin to exhibit signs of transition southward into the Sonoran Desert, away from the Joshua tree forests and into the cactus shrublands that extend south into Mexico.

01. Homer Mountain (3,739')
02. Flattop Mountain (3,029')
03. Goffs Butte (3,612')
04. Fenner Spring
05. Barrel Spring
06. Homer Wash
07. Eagle Peak (3,308')
08. Snaggletooth (2,180')
09. Sawtooth Ridge
10. Colton Wash
11. Little Piute Mountains
12. Mercury Mountain (3,720')
13. Hummingbird Spring
14. Chuckwalla Spring
15. Castle Dome
16. Cadiz Dunes Wilderness

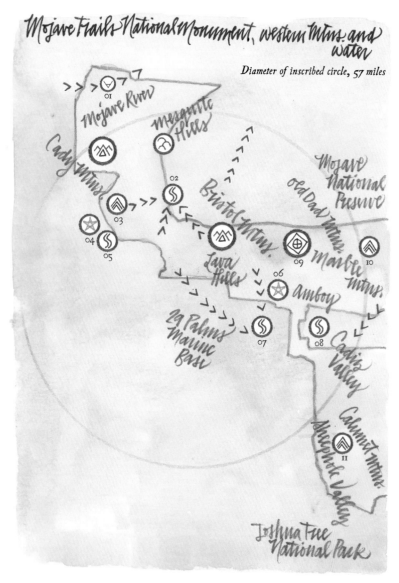

Map 04.07a

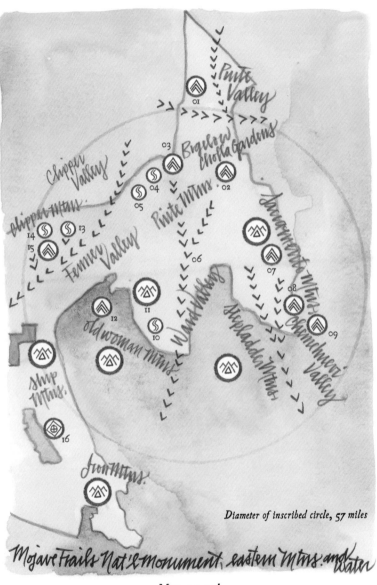

Piute Valley

01

03 Bigelow Cholla Gardens

02

Clipper Valley

04

Clipper Mtns.

05

Piute Mtns.

Sacramento Mtns.

14   13

15

Fenner Valley

06

07

08

Chemehuevi Valley

11

12

10

Ward Valley

09

Old Woman Mtns.

Stepladder Mtns.

Ship Mtns.

16

Iron Mtns.

*Diameter of inscribed circle, 57 miles*

Mojave Trails Nat'l Monument, eastern Mtns. and Water

Map 04.07b

## 04.08 RED ROCK CANYON STATE PARK

Year designated: 1968
27,000 acres/42.19 square miles
Highest peak—Red Rock Canyon State
  Park high point (unnamed), 3,708'

Just south of the El Paso Mountains
wilderness area, tucked into the foothills of the eastern Sierra Nevada, and
adjacent to the Jawbone-Butterbredt

area of critical environmental concern
(ACEC), the relatively small but geologically enthralling Red Rock Canyon
State Park has an ecological identity all
its own. Nearly three million years old,
the canyon itself is full of remarkably
vivid and dynamic sedimentary forms
of white and red sandstone and clay.

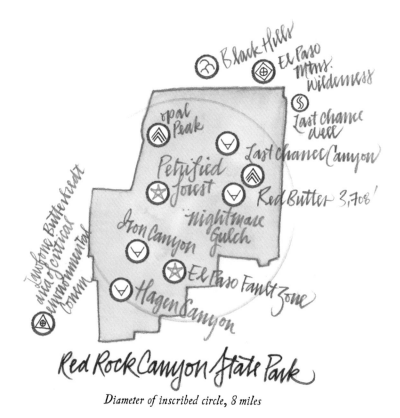

*Diameter of inscribed circle, 8 miles*

# 04.09 SAND TO SNOW NATIONAL MONUMENT

Year designated: 2016
154,000 acres/240.63 square miles
Highest peak—San Gorgonio Peak,
 11,503'

Visible for fifty miles, San Gorgonio, Southern California's tallest peak, is within a number of land designation areas, including Sand to Snow National Monument, the San Bernardino National Forest, and the San Gorgonio Wilderness. For so many different designations to focus on a single geographic feature ensures that multiple management agencies are involved and that appropriate funding goes to its stewardship. The peak represents the end point of a migration corridor from the Little San Bernardino Mountains in Joshua Tree National Park, and it is this corridor that was a key inspiration for the creation of the monument.

01. Onyx Peak (9,120')
02. Little Morongo Creek
03. Little San Bernardino Mountains
04. Little Morongo Canyon
05. Big Morongo Canyon
06. Big Morongo Canyon Preserve
07. Mission Creek
08. Kitching Peak (6,598')
09. Ten Thousand Foot Ridge
10. Fish Creek
11. South Fork Santa Ana River
12. Forsee Creek
13. San Gorgonio Peak (11,503')
14. Anderson Peak (10,840')
15. San Bernardino Peak (10,864')
16. Little San Bernardino Peak (9,133')
17. South Fork Whitewater River
18. North Fork Whitewater River

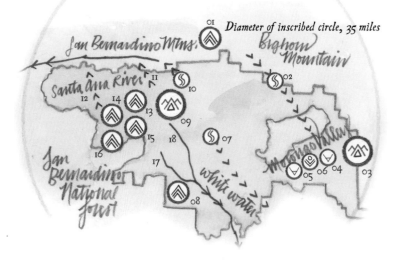

Diameter of inscribed circle, 35 miles

Map 04.10

## 04.10 SANTA ROSA AND SAN JACINTO NATIONAL MONUMENT

Year designated: 2000
280,071 acres/437.61 square miles
Highest peak—Tahquitz Peak, 8,846'

Across two mountain ranges, the national monument extends up from the Cleveland National Forest and Anza-Borrego Desert State Park as the northernmost designation of the landform that is the Peninsula Ranges.

01. Falls Creek
02. Desert Angel (2,356')
03. San Jacinto Peak (10,804')
04. Tahquitz Creek
05. Tahquitz Peak (8,846')
06. Palm Canyon Creek
07. Palm Canyon
08. Murray Hill (2,200')
09. Haystack Mountain (3,808')
10. Bald Mountain (4,454')
11. Palm View Peak (7,160')
12. Deep Canyon
13. Indio Mountain (2,226');
    UC Desert Research Area
14. Lake Cahuilla
15. Sugarloaf Mountain (4,775')
16. Santa Rosa Mountain (8,046')
17. Toro Peak (8,716')
18. Martinez Canyon
19. Rabbit Peak (6,640')
20. Barton Canyon;
    Peninsular Ranges
    Ecological Reserve

*Toro Peak*

## Some endemic species of the Santa Rosa and San Jacinto National Monument

01. Casey's June beetle, *Dinacoma caseyi*
02. Coachella Valley round-tailed ground squirrel,
    *Xerospermophilus tereticaudus*
03. Davidson's stonecrop, *Sedum niveum*
04. Johnston's rockcress, *Arabis johnstonii*
05. Munz's mariposa lily, *Calochortus palmeri*
06. Rock draba, *Draba corrugata*
07. San Jacinto bush snapdragon, *Keckiella rothrockii*
08. Santa Rosa Mountains linanthus, *Leptosiphon floribundum* ssp. *hallii*
09. Shaggy-haired alumroot, *Heuchera hirsutissima*
10. Tahquitz ivesia, *Ivesia callida*

01

02

03

04

05

06

07

08

09

10

## 04.11 MILITARY INHOLDINGS OF THE CALIFORNIA DESERTS—OVERVIEW

Since General Patton drove his tank and marched a million US troops over many fragile dune systems of the Mojave, marring them with scars still visible today, all in preparation for their shipping off to World War II, the US military has come quite a long way with its relationship to the desert.[10] It turns out, in a twist that may seem counterintuitive, the large military inholdings across the Mojave and Sonoran Deserts have become de facto wilderness areas.[11] As mandated by federal law—including the upholding of endangered species statutes and a requirement that they run on their own carbon-free energy as soon as they can—these large land designations remain unassailable to the whims and injuries of recreationalists and resource extraction.

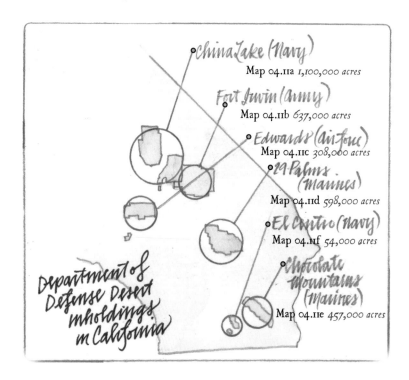

China Lake (Navy)
Map 04.11a *1,100,000 acres*

Fort Irwin (army)
Map 04.11b *637,000 acres*

Edwards (air force)
Map 04.11c *308,000 acres*

29 Palms (marines)
Map 04.11d *598,000 acres*

El Centro (navy)
Map 04.11f *54,000 acres*

Chocolate Mountains (marines)
Map 04.11e *457,000 acres*

Department of Defense Desert inholdings in California

## 04.11a China Lake Naval Air Weapons Station (Navy)

At the center of the northern section of the base (closed to the public) is the Coso Rock Art District (Petroglyph).[12] Across from Searles Lake and the Trona Pinnacles, a second section of China Lake is dominated by Pilot Knob Valley and shares its eastern border with Fort Irwin's western border.

01. Coso Range
02. Coso Peak (8,160')
03. Cactus Peak (5,415')
04. Sugarloaf Mountain (5,126')
05. Volcano Peak (5,352')
06. Airport Lake (dry)
07. White Hills
08. Louisiana Butte (6,826')

09. Wild Horse Mesa (5,260')
10. Coso Rock Art District
11. Wilson Canyon
12. Indian Joe Spring
      Ecological Reserve
13. Argus Range
14. China Lake
15. Searles (dry) Lake
16. Trona Pinnacles
17. Slate Range
18. Wingate Wash
19. Brown Mountain (5,125')
20. Robbers Mountain (4,506')
21. Pilot Knob (5,428')
22. Eagle Crags (5,512')
23. Black Hills

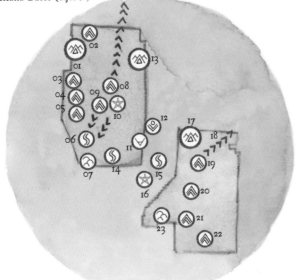

*Diameter of inscribed circle, 45 miles*
China Lake (Navy)

## 04.11b Fort Irwin National Training Center (Army)

At nearly one thousand square miles, Fort Irwin contains parts of the Avawatz Mountains, the Granite Mountains, and Tiefort. The Fort Irwin solar project was the Department of Defense's largest, intended to be capable of producing 500 megawatts (MW) of renewable energy and one billion kilowatt-hours (kWh); for the time being, it is a cancelled project.[13] Were it to be completed, it would be the world's largest solar thermal energy facility.

01. Owlshead Mountain
02. Leach Lake (dry)
03. Drinkwater Lake (dry)
04. Avawatz Mountains
05. Red Pass Lake (dry)
06. Langford Well Lake (dry)
07. Tiefort Mountains
08. Bicycle Lake (dry)
09. Granite Mountains
10. McLean Lake (dry)
11. Nelson Lake (dry)
12. Goldstone Lake (dry)
13. Goldstone Deep Space Communications Complex

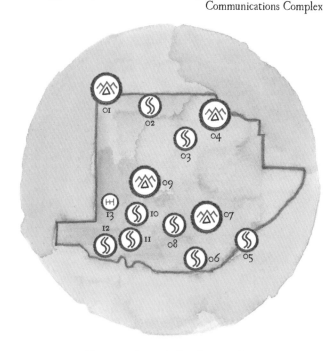

*Diameter of inscribed circle, 50 miles*
Fort Irwin (Army)

## 04.11c Edwards Air Force Base (Air Force)

Near the center of the 470-square-mile air force base is 21-square-mile Rosamond Lake (now dry), which is one of the lowest areas in the Antelope Valley. Because of the Rosamond drainage, the vernal water that does come stirs the lakebed and creates a new flat surface that is an ideal runway for aircraft.[14]

01. Leuhman Ridge
02. Kramer Hills
03. Haystack Butte (3,380')
04. Jackrabbit Hill (2,881')
05. Rogers Lake (dry)
06. Bissell Hills
07. Rosamond Hills
08. Rosamond Lake (dry)
09. Buckhorn Lake (dry)

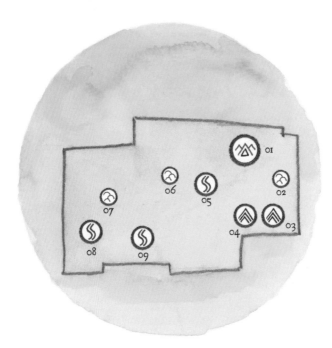

*Diameter of inscribed circle, 33 miles*
Edwards (Air Force)

## 04.11d 29 Palms Air Ground Combat Center (Marines)

As it is officially referred to, Marine Corps Air Ground Combat Center Twentynine Palms is over nine hundred square miles and covers the area north of the town of Twentynine Palms, encompassing the Bullion Mountain Range.

01. Amboy Crater
02. Bagdad Lake (dry)
03. Lead Mountain (2,891'
04. Cleghorn Pass

05. Mesquite Wash
06. Mesquite Lake (dry)
07. Deadman Lake (dry)
08. Bullion Mountains
09. Hidalgo Mountain (4,435')
10. Emerson Lake (dry)
11. Galway Lake (dry)
12. Argos Mountain (4,488')
13. Sunshine Peak (4,421')
14. Lavic Lake (dry)
15. Pisgah Crater
16. Lava Beds Mountains

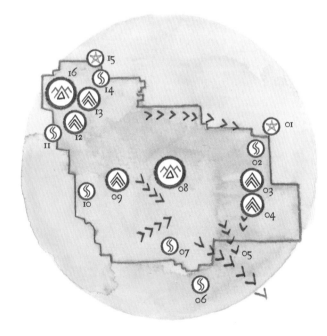

*Diameter of inscribed circle, 38 miles*
29 Palms (Marines)

## 04.11e Chocolate Mountain Aerial Gunnery Range (Marines)

Seven hundred square miles of the Chocolate Mountains east of the Salton Sea are closed to the public and sequestered for live bombing exercises. These mountains have been sacrificed, for all intents and purposes, to be bombed into nonexistence. Perhaps the actual land devastated by ordinance is only a tiny portion of this large area, and what wildland treasure exists there shall persist until new militaristic testing solutions are found.

01. Salt Creek
02. Iris Pass
03. Iris Wash
04. Surveyors Pass
05. Arroyo Seco
06. Little Mule Mountains
07. Mount Barrow (2,475')
08. Mammoth Wash
09. Chocolate Mountains
10. Salton Sea

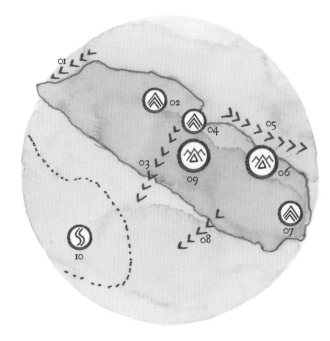

*Diameter of inscribed circle, 45 miles*
Chocolate Mountains (Marines)

## 04.11f El Centro Naval Auxiliary Air Station (Navy)

Between the Imperial Valley and
Anza-Borrego Desert State Park, the
dry plateau of West Mesa is home
to this navy base, also called the El
Centro Naval Reservation.

01. Carrizo Wash
02. San Felipe Creek
03. Superstition Hills
04. Salton Sea
05. West Mesa
06. Superstition Mountain (759')
07. Imperial Valley
08. Yuha Buttes

*Common De
centiped
Scolopendra
Polymorp*

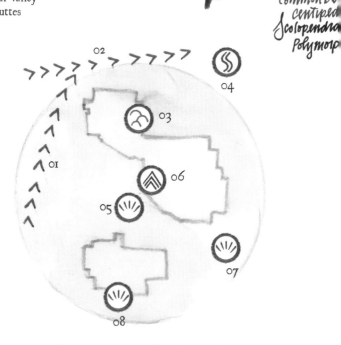

*Diameter of inscribed circle, 30 miles*
El Centro (Navy)

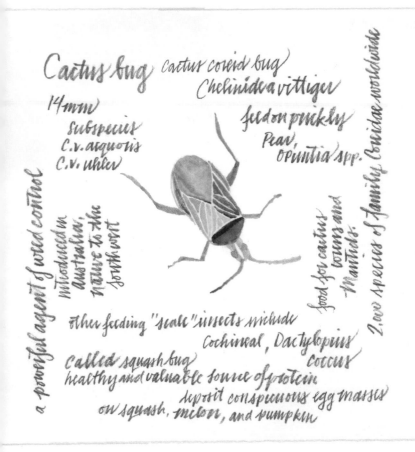

Cactus bug

cactus coreid bug

Chelinidea vittiger

14mm

subspecies
C. v. aequoris
C. v. uhler

feed on prickly
Pear,
Opuntia spp.

a powerful agent of weed control

introduced in
Australia;
native to the
southwest

food for cactus
wrens and
mantids

2,000 species of family Coreidae worldwide

other feeding "scale" insects include
Cochineal, Dactylopius
coccus

called squash bug

healthy and valuable source of protein

deposit conspicuous egg masses
on squash, melon, and pumpkin

There are no signposts between the Great Basin and Mojave Deserts. The walk west across Death Valley from the Ibex Wilderness, across the Badwater Basin, up Telescope Peak, down its western flank into the Surprise Canyon Wilderness, through Darwin Falls Wilderness, and north into Owens Valley across the Malpais Mesa would be on a trail that roughly follows the boundary of these two major desert designations. Perhaps you will note one of the northernmost Joshua tree woodlands of Lee Flat, just east of Malpais Mesa Wilderness—a key plant species in defining the Mojave Desert. Perhaps you will note the sagebrush climbing over the high-altitude knolls of the Inyo Mountains Wilderness—a key plant species in defining the Great Basin Desert, just a few miles from Lee Flat. Whatever the case, the wilderness areas of the next three chapters all exhibit common and yet distinct aspects of their own identity that warrant celebration.

So much of this book relies on drawing boundaries. Lines in the sand. Fences. Walls. Designated spaces and the spaces between those designated spaces. Liminal transitional zones. Overlapping ecotones. This book could have been made with a pair of scissors instead of a paintbrush. All of those boundaries exist only in the collective imaginative mind that is public policy and not because of definitions in the natural world. Although it might encapsulate a mountain range, some piece of connective landscape between other land designations, or a particularly superlative aspect of the terrain, the wilderness area is often a proxy for Nature. The wilderness area is popularly and perhaps even legally thought of as where Nature is and where it can remain untouched by the Anthropocene. Because of this fiction, the land designation of wilderness can also be a cheap receipt—an assumption of a debt having been paid, of a transaction that is over— for the continued devastation wrought by development in the deserts of California.

The story we tell ourselves about Nature (capital $N$—the living systems that support all life) is evolving, and the idea of wilderness should change with it. Based on the Wilderness Act of 1964, the wilderness areas described in the next three chapters are all managed by the Bureau of Land Management and contain at least five thousand acres of roadless terrain.

There is significant overlap in all these maps. The maps extend out into the land that surrounds the designated area in question. This makes two points clear: one, that the natural quality exhibited by the designated space doesn't end at its boundary line; and two, that describing a landscape as a sequestered unit doesn't tell its full story.

The Wilderness Act was the first major piece of national legislation that kicked off a decade of unprecedented lawmaking that has been referred to as a golden era of environmental protection. During this time, Americans witnessed the passage of the Clean Air Act (1970), the Clean Water Act (1972), and the Endangered Species Act (1973), among others, and the creation of the Environmental Protection Agency (1970). The Wilderness Act was evidence of a shift in popular thought about not only what nature (lowercase *n*—everything nonhuman) is and our posture toward it, but also what federal public lands are designed to protect. In this modern context—and the Wilderness Act is the apotheosis of this idea— nature is a construct that needs little but to be left alone in order to thrive, and federal wilderness lands are the setting where this would be allowed to happen. This reasoning—that it is best to leave alone vast and undeveloped spaces that may or may not retain an older piece of California's wild, presettled character—is based in the faulty assumption that ubiquitous Indigenous cultures did not shape the land for thousands of years. To say that this assumption could use an update may be an understatement.

2.5 million year old fossils

Current pop.
~100,000

*Antigone canadensis*
(greater) Sandhill crane

Despite the great gains of the Wilderness Act, there are philosophical inconsistencies, moral problems, historical injustices, and ecological misinterpretations connected with the idea of wilderness that underpins the law. Because the idea of wilderness is an invention that emerged from an American agrarian culture, it remains a culturally biased idea, an idea rooted in colonization. The idea of wilderness requires a land ethic that stands in contrast to the paradigm that dominates so much of Indigenous California's idea of what it is to have a cultural relationship with the land. Doesn't a hands-off relationship to the land result in a lapse of responsibility to the living earth?

From this perspective, wilderness becomes a bad word, emblematic of what happens to the land when it is untended with what is often called traditional ecological knowledge (TEK), or those local systems' kind of reciprocity, a giving back for having accepted the gifts of the land's fecundity.[1] Because of this inconsistency in the cross-cultural concept of wilderness (and the nature/Nature argument), the morality of locking away the land from the ancient mutualism developed over millennia becomes problematic, if not racist. If by proclaiming lands as held in public trust (as wilderness areas are) the lands become off-limits to TEK, then those lands begin to degrade and so do the people, and an injustice becomes apparent. Implicit in the idea of nature is the idea of using nature. The economic system of capitalism and its reliance on the idea of the commodity cause everything to be commodified, including nature. By contrast, Nature (capital $N$) as viewed within the TEK context is part of us and cannot be extracted from, spoiled, or destroyed.

For millennia, all of these wilderness lands were considered part of one connected landscape, sacred and well used—used in a wholly different manner than what the modern mindset would do with it.[2] In the deserts and across California, TEK was a method of maintaining regimes of reciprocity (see 01.08), and in many instances, the species and indeed the whole ecology coevolved to expect the regular disturbance, a kind of pruning that elicited vigorous regrowth in many shrubs, for example.[3] In so many of even what seem to the modernist eye to be desolate landscapes, the ancient human mind, hand, and heart were carefully at work and in relationship with a system of living forces within the desert.

Warner Mountains
from Surprise Valley
Modoc County, Calif.

For each wilderness area, I have chosen two animals and two wildflowers (or fungi/mushrooms) that were locally confirmed, whenever possible, on iNaturalist .org. I've chosen animals that are not necessarily uncommon, or even endemic to the area; rather, I'm letting them stand as iconic, even emblematic of the subject wilderness. Whenever possible, this data is adapted from iNaturalist, a naturalist's app that maps wildlife sightings. Each listing for each wilderness area is unique, so when it wasn't possible to list species from iNaturalist, comparably probable species are noted, based on range data from other published sources.

This criticism is not offered as a condemnation of wilderness or the Wilderness Act—far from it. In the twenty-first century, we have the prescience of such great protective legislation as the Wilderness Act to thank for quite a bit of the remaining habitat spaces in California's backcountry, however isolated, potentially degraded, and exposed to global patterns in the Anthropocene climate they may be. On the mountains, peaks, and other high places of the deserts' wilderness areas, there are already large swaths of habitat classified as climate refugia that will become more and more valuable in the decades to come. In wilderness, there is hope.

In wilderness, a resurgent facet of California's older, biodiverse character remains, and this character aligns with a growing sense of reckoning with what it means to be from a place, any place that allows itself to become postcolonial and embrace its Indigenous design. As we learn more about the connective wiring of habitat, of the aspects of corridor ecology necessary to maintaining biodiversity, it is in wilderness (and other land and water designations, such as those protected in the Wild & Scenic Rivers Act, 1968) that a repository of what is most rare and most precious remains. In wilderness, a seed waits to grow in the postcommodified fertile soil of what Nature is, between what it needs from us and what we need from it. It is because of this hope, as it exists across wilderness, that so much of this book (beginning with map 05.05) is invested in a mapped catalog of the deserts' wilderness areas.

Pronghorn
antilocapra americana

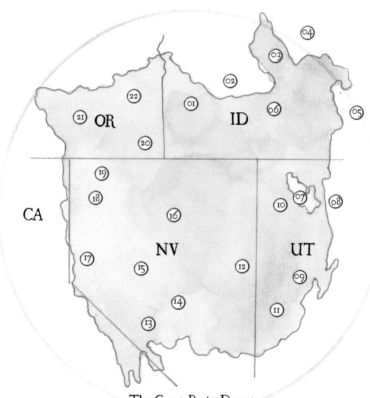

The Great Basin Desert
*Diameter of inscribed circle, 540 miles*

Map 05.01

# 05.01 ENDORHEIC BASIN AND RANGE LANDS
*Exploring America's largest desert*

The Great Basin Desert, also called the Central Basin and Range, centers in northern Nevada and the great vein of the Humboldt River, which at three hundred miles in length can be seen as the desert's primary watercourse. Utah's Bear River, which is the Great Salt Lake's largest tributary, and the Sevier River on the desert's southeast border, are both longer than the Humboldt, but the Humboldt does not mark the desert's border. The Humboldt runs right through the desert's middle and is distinctively emblematic of the fate of every watershed in the Great Basin, in that it runs from the mountains to its denouement in a lonely, sandy sink and does not find its way to the ocean.

01. Columbia Plateau
02. Snake River Plain
03. Lemhi Range; Lost River Range
04. Targhee National Forest
05. Caribou National Forest
06. Bruneau Desert
07. Great Salt Lake;
    Great Salt Lake Desert
08. Wasatch Range
09. Sevier River
10. Booneville Salt Flats
11. Escalante Desert
12. Great Basin National Park
13. Nellis Air Force Base
14. Monitor Range
15. Shoshone Mountains
16. Humboldt River
17. Pyramid Lake
18. Black Rock Desert
19. Sheldon National Wildlife Refuge
20. Owyhee River
21. Harney Basin
22. Malheur River

Greater Roadrunner
*Geococcyx californianus*

Roadrunners prefer to run rather than fly.
Their top speed is about twenty miles per hour.[4]

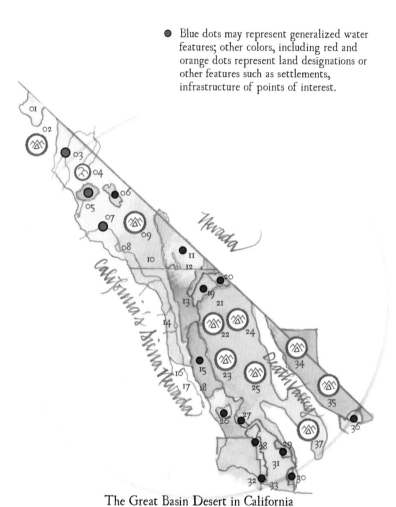

Blue dots may represent generalized water features; other colors, including red and orange dots represent land designations or other features such as settlements, infrastructure of points of interest.

Nevada

California's Sierra Nevada

Death Valley

The Great Basin Desert in California
*Diameter of inscribed circle, 250 miles*

Map 05.02

## 05.02 DRY FORESTS, SAGE FIELDS, AND NEW MOUNTAINS
*Regional overview of the southeastern Great Basin Desert in California*

The ecological story of the Great Basin in California is of ancient lakes and new mountains. Mono Lake, for example, dates back to three-quarters of a million years ago as a basin lake that is fed by many mountain creeks and is a terminal sink for those creeks in a manner typical of lakes in this desert. The mountains to the south of the lake, including Panum Crater, which is very close to the lake, are only seven hundred years old. Although the geologic processes that continue to spur the activity in what are called the Mono-Inyo Craters (from Mono Lake to the Volcanic Tableland north of Bishop) began a few million years ago, regional hydrology and vulcanology contend for venerability.

01. Slinkard Wilderness Study Area;
    Topaz Lake
02. Sweetwater Mountains
03. East Walker River;
    Bridgeport Reservoir
04. Bodie Hills
05. Mono Lake
06. Granite Mountains Wilderness
07. Owens River
08. Crowley Lake
09. Benton Range
10. Volcanic Tableland
11. White Mountains Wilderness
12. Inyo-Mono County line
13. Inyo National Forest
14. Crater Mountains
    Wilderness Study Area
15. Inyo Mountains Wilderness
16. Symmes Wilderness Study Area
17. Independence Creek
    Wilderness Study Area
18. Southern Inyo
    Wilderness Study Area
19. Piper Mountains Wilderness
20. Sylvania Wilderness
21. Eureka Valley
22. Saline Range
23. Cottonwood Range
24. Last Chance Range
25. Panamint Range
26. Malpais Mesa Wilderness
27. Darwin Falls Wilderness
28. Argus Range Wilderness
29. Surprise Canyon Wilderness
30. Manly Peak Wilderness
31. Panamint Valley
32. Great Falls Basin Wilderness
33. Searles Valley
34. Grapevine Mountains
35. Funeral Mountains
36. Funeral Mountains Wilderness
37. Black Mountains

Desert kit fox
*Vulpes macrotis arsipus*

## Fish species of special concern of the Great Basin Desert in California

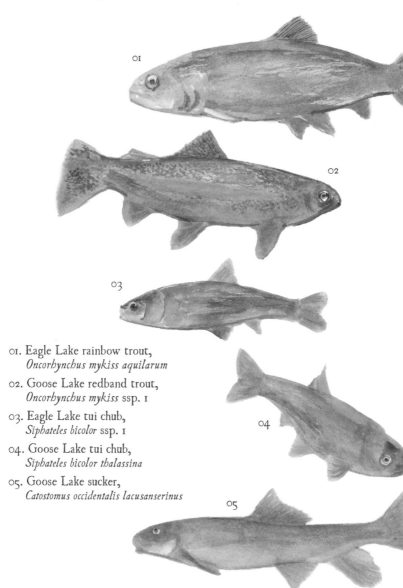

01

02

03

01. Eagle Lake rainbow trout,
    *Oncorhynchus mykiss aquilarum*

02. Goose Lake redband trout,
    *Oncorhynchus mykiss* ssp. 1

03. Eagle Lake tui chub,
    *Siphateles bicolor* ssp. 1

04. Goose Lake tui chub,
    *Siphateles bicolor thalassina*

04

05. Goose Lake sucker,
    *Catostomus occidentalis lacusanserinus*

05

## Plant alliances of the Great Basin Desert in southeastern California, including the Mono section

Alkali cordgrass marsh
Alkali sacaton grassland
Allscale scrub
American bulrush marsh
Anderson's boxthorn scrub
Arrowweed thicket
Arroyo willow thicket
Ashy ryegrass meadows
Aspen groves
Baltic and Mexican rush marshes
Beaked sedge and blister sedge meadows
Big sagebrush
Bitterbrush scrub
Black bush scrub
Black cottonwood forest
Black sagebrush scrub
Black-stem rabbitbrush scrub
Bluebunch wheat grass grassland
Bristlecone pine woodland
Brittlebush scrub
Broom baccharis thicket
Bush seepweed scrub
California buckwheat scrub
California buckwheat–white sage scrub
California bulrush marsh
Cattail marsh
Cheesebush scrub
Coville's phlox fell-fields
Creosote bush–brittlebush scrub
Creosote bush scrub
Curl leaf mountain mahogany scrub
Curly blue grass grassland
Dark alpine sedge turf
Desert almond scrub
Desert dunes
Desert olive patches
Desert panic grass patches
Ditch-grass or widgeon-grass mats

Allscale, *Atriplex polycarpa*

Arrowweed, *Pluchea sericea*

Cheesebush, *Ambrosia salsola*

Fell-fields with California heath-
    goldenrod and Pacific alpine gold
Floating mats of weak manna grass
Fourwing saltbush scrub
Geyer willow thicket
Greasewood scrub
Greenleaf manzanita chaparral
Hardstem bulrush marsh
Herb-rich meadows
Idaho fescue grassland
Indian rice grass grassland
Iodine bush scrub
James' galleta shrub-steppe
Jeffrey pine forest
Limber pine woodland
Little sagebrush scrub
Lodgepole pine forest
Meadow barley patches
Mormon tea scrub
Mountain big sagebrush
Mountain juniper woodland
Mountain white thorn chaparral
Mulefat thicket
Nebraska sedge meadows
Needleleaf rabbitbrush scrub
Nevada joint fir scrub
Pale spike rush marshes
Parry's rabbitbrush scrub
Ponderosa pine forest
Quailbush scrub
Red osier thicket
Rothrock's sagebrush
Rubber rabbitbrush scrub
Salt grass flats
Sandbar willow thicket
Shadescale scrub
Shrubby cinquefoil scrub
Silver sagebrush scrub
Singleleaf pinyon woodland
Small camas meadows

Fourwing saltbush, *Atriplex canescens*

Greasewood, *Sarcobatus vermiculatus*

Lodgepole pine, *Pinus contorta*

Small leaf mountain mahogany scrub
Spiny hop scrub
Stansbury cliff rosa scrub
Tobacco brush chaparral
Tufted hair grass meadows
Utah juniper woodland
Virgin River brittlebush scrub
Water birch thicket
Western juniper woodland
White bursage scrub
White corn lily patches
Winterfat scrubland
Wright's buckwheat patches

Mulefat, *Baccharis salicifolia*

Salt grass, *Distichlis spicata*

Genus *Lasioglossum* sweatbee one of 87 species in California

Water birch, *Betula occidentalis*

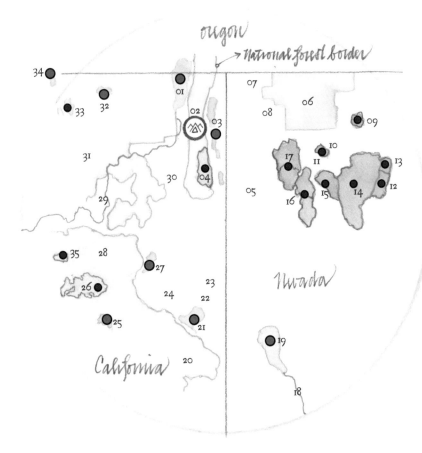

oregon

→ National forest border

Nevada

California

The Great Basin Desert in Northeastern California
and Northwestern Nevada
*Diameter of inscribed circle, 180 miles*

Map 05.03

## 05.03 DRY LAKES, BLACK ROCK, AND BIG SAGEBRUSH
*Regional overview of the Great Basin Desert in northeastern California and northwestern Nevada*

One of the significant geographic questions that haunt this book's maps of the arid and semiarid regions of northeast California is whether or not the Modoc Plateau is included as part of the Great Basin Desert. The argument that the plateau, with its patchwork of forested areas and expansive grasslands, is not part of the desert is so salient that it points to the general deficiency of hard-bordered land designations, and to when debating ecology in the borderland is much more relevant as a process of biological inquiry. With its physiographic connectivity, immediate adjacency, and climatic symmetry to the desert lands to the east, the Modoc Plateau is included in this book as contiguous with the Great Basin, albeit begrudgingly.

01. Goose Lake
02. Warner Mountains
03. Surprise Valley
04. South Warner Wilderness
05. Wall Canyon Wilderness Study Area
06. Sheldon National Wildlife Refuge
07. Sheldon Contiguous Wilderness Study Area
08. Massacre Rim Wilderness Study Area
09. Pine Forest Range Wilderness
10. Lahontan Cutthroat Trout Instant Study Area
11. North Black Rock Range Wilderness
12. South Jackson Mountains Wilderness
13. North Jackson Mountains Wilderness
14. Black Rock Desert Wilderness
15. Pahute Peak Wilderness
16. High Rock Lake Wilderness; Calico Mountains Wilderness
17. Little High Rock Canyon Wilderness; High Rock Canyon Wilderness
18. Truckee River
19. Pyramid River
20. Plumas National Forest
21. Honey Lake
22. Skedaddle Wilderness Study Area
23. Five Springs Wilderness Study Area; Dry Valley Rim Wilderness Study Area
24. Tunnison Mountain Wilderness Study Area
25. Lake Almanor
26. Lassen Volcanic National Park; Caribou Wilderness
27. Eagle Lake
28. Lassen National Forest
29. Pit River; Modoc National Wildlife Refuge
30. Tule Mountain Wilderness Study Area
31. Modoc National Forest
32. Clear Lake Reservoir
33. Lava Beds Wilderness; Lava Beds National Wilderness
34. Tule Lake Sump; Tule Lake National Wildlife Refuge; Lower Klamath National Wildlife Refuge
35. Thousand Lakes Wilderness

# Plant alliances of the Great Basin Desert in northeastern California

## Called the Northwestern Basin and Range ecoregion, including the Modoc Plateau (excluding the Warner Mountains)

American bulrush marsh
Arroyo willow thicket
Aspen groves
Baltic and Mexican rush marshes
Beaked sedge and blister sedge meadows
Bebb's willow thicket
Big sagebrush
Bluebunch wheat grass grassland
California bulrush marsh
Cattail marsh
Common monkeyflower seeps
Curl leaf mountain mahogany scrub
Curly blue grass grassland
Deer brush chaparral
Geyer willow thicket
Greasewood scrub
Hardstem bulrush marsh
Idaho fescue grassland
Iodine bush scrub
Jeffrey pine forest
Lemmon's willow thicket
Little sagebrush scrub
Manna grass meadows
Meadow barley patches
Mountain big sagebrush
Nebraska sedge meadows
Needle spike rush stands
Pale spike rush marshes
Ponderosa pine forest
Rubber rabbitbrush scrub
Salt grass flats
Sandbar willow thicket
Short-beaked sedge meadows
Shrubby cinquefoil scrub

Sierran willow thicket
Silver sagebrush scrub
Tobacco brush chaparral
Tufted hair grass meadows
Water birch thicket
Western juniper woodland
White fir forest

Deer brush, *Ceanothus integerrimus*

Needle spike rush, *Eleocharis acicularis*

Northern leopard frog, *Lithobates pipiens*, once existed near the Owens Valley and on the Modoc Plateau.[5] Across California, this frog finds habitat in only a few areas of the Central Valley and along the south coast, and many of those populations are introduced and are not in their historical range.

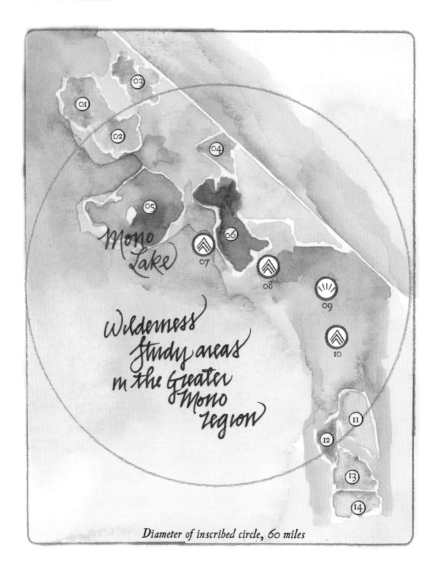

Mono Lake

Wilderness Study areas in the Greater Mono region

Diameter of inscribed circle, 60 miles

Map 05.04

## 05.04 ECOLOGICAL SENSITIVITIES
*Wilderness study areas of the southeastern Great Basin Desert in California*

On its way to becoming a full-fledged wilderness area, a wilderness study area is any area that has been recognized by the Bureau of Land Management as having the characteristics of a wilderness area—roadlessness, size, and naturalness—and that may in time become designated as a federally protected wilderness. Around the Mono Lake area, there are a number of wilderness study areas, a small portion of the BLM's larger catalog of over eleven million wilderness study areas across the western United States.

01. Bodie Mountains Wilderness Study Area
02. Mount Biedeman Wilderness Study Area; Mt. Biedeman (8,981')
03. Bodie Mountains Wilderness Study Area (Bodie Creek)
04. Excelsior Wilderness Study Area; East Mono Valley
05. Mono Lake; Mono Lake Tufa State Natural Reserve
06. Granite Mountain Wilderness Area; Granite Mountain (8,920')
07. Cowtrack Mountain (8,852')
08. Adobe Valley; Black Lake; Trafton Mountain (7,617')
09. Benton Valley (5,387')
10. Blind Spring Hill; Diana Peak, (7,080')
11. Chidago Canyon Wilderness Study Area; Red Canyon Petroglyphs
12. Casa Diablo Wilderness Study Area; Casa Diablo Mountain (7,888')
13. Fish Slough Wilderness Study Area; Fish Slough Petroglyphs
14. Volcanic Tablelands Wilderness Study Area; Chalk Bluff (4,564')

*View of the Sierra Nevada from Cowtrack Mountain*

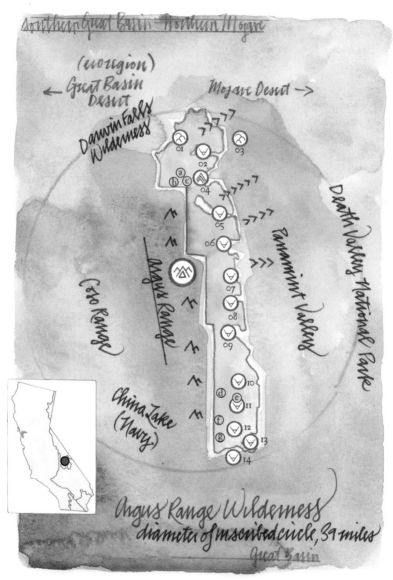

Map 05.05

## 05.05 PANAMINT VALLEY'S WEST SIDE
*Argus Range Wilderness*

The Argus Range Wilderness is configured as a long, narrow strip that extends north from Homewood Canyon nearly forty miles until the border of Death Valley National Park, only one mile from Panamint Springs. The Argus Range forms a divide from the Darwin Wash to the west, inside China Lake navy base, and Panamint Valley to the east, and also a divide between the cold desert of the elevated Great Basin and the warm desert of the lower Mojave. The wilderness area is the east face of nearly the entire Argus Range, and what lands remain unprotected between the southern border of the Argus Range Wilderness and the town of Trona are mostly accounted for by the Great Falls Basin Wilderness.

01. Zinc Hill (5,584')
02. Osborne Canyon
03. Ash Hill (2,595')
04. Lookout Mountain (4,100')
05. Snow Canyon
06. Revenue Canyon
07. Knight Canyon
08. Bendire Canyon
09. Shepherd Canyon
10. Water Canyon
11. Bruce Canyon
12. Orondo Canyon
13. Homewood Canyon
14. Crow Canyon

a. Jack Gunn Spring
b. French Maiden Spring
c. Thompson Spring
d. Smooky Spring
e. Rock Spring
f. Rainy Spring
g. Benko Spring

*... home to creosote, riparian, and desert scrub*
*... essential bighorn corridor of east-facing canyons*
*... dramatic biozone variation by elevation from sandy valley floor to piñon woodland*

Generalized elevation range
2,800–7,500 feet

Land area
47,890 acres
74.83 square miles

Inyo California towhee
*Pipilo crissalis eremophilus*

Wilson's warbler
*Cardellina pusilla*

Rabbit thorn
*Lycium pallidum*
var. *oligospermum*

Thomas's wild buckwheat
*Eriogonum thomasii*

*Inyo California towhee*
*Pipilo crissalis eremophilus*

Great Basin

Santa Rosa
Wash

Death Valley
National Park

Darwin Plateau

Talc
city
hills

★ 5,578'

▽ O2

Eagle
Point
5,160'

★ 6,120'

ⓐ ▽ O1

Darwin
Falls

ⓑ

Ⓐ Ophir Mtn.
6,010'

Ⓗ Darwin

Angus
Range
Wilderness

8,189 acres
12.80 square miles
Darwin Falls
Wilderness

diameter of inscribed circle
14 miles

Map 05.06

## 05.06 GATEWAY TO PANAMINT SPRINGS
*Darwin Falls Wilderness*

The watercourse that includes this wilderness area's namesake waterfall has its headwaters and its drainage inside the wilderness boundary, although the waterfall itself is inside the adjacent Death Valley National Park. The wilderness is dominated by a Joshua tree–covered plateau that measures over fifteen square miles.

01. Darwin Canyon
02. Rainbow Canyon

a. China Garden Spring
b. Millers Spring

*… Darwin Falls is an eighteen-foot-tall Perennial waterfall with habitat for ferns and amphibians*

*… known hotspot for vernal wildflowers*

*… most of the wilderness is volcanic rock; Canyons contain cottonwood and willow*

The white-tailed antelope squirrel, *Ammospermophilus leucurus*, is able to forage in the middle of the desert day and endure inner body temperatures of 111°F before needing to find a burrow.

Generalized elevation range
2,300–5,400 feet

Land area
8,189 acres
12.80 square miles

Alfalfa looper moth
*Autographa californica*

Green bird grasshopper
*Schistocerca shoshone*

Parrot's feather
*Myriophyllum aquaticum*
(nonnative)

Cottontop cactus
*Homalocephala polycephala*
ssp. *polycephala*

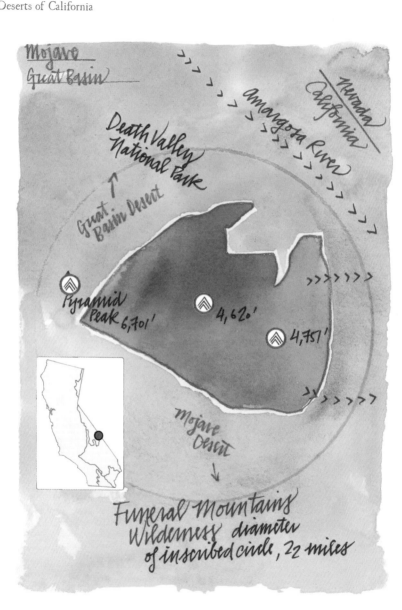

Mojave
Great Basin

Nevada
California

Amargosa River

Death Valley
National Park

Great.
Basin Desert

Pyramid
Peak 6,701'

4,620'

4,757'

Mojave
Desert

Funeral Mountains
Wilderness diameter
of inscribed circle, 22 miles

Map 05.07

## 05.07 IN THE RAIN SHADOW OF THE PANAMINT RANGE
*Funeral Mountains Wilderness*

Although the Funeral Mountain Range is very dry, Travertine Springs, near Furnace Creek, is the largest spring in the park and supplies the community of Furnace Creek with its water. This wilderness is directly west of Ash Meadows National Wildlife Refuge, where the Amargosa Desert of Nevada becomes the Mojave Desert in California, exemplified by the bottleneck between the Funeral Mountains and the Devil's Hole Hills to the east, where the Amargosa River watershed becomes discrete and well defined.

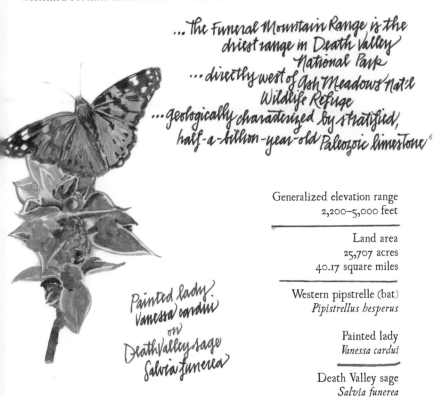

... The Funeral Mountain Range is the driest range in Death Valley National Park
... directly west of Ash Meadows Nat'l Wildlife Refuge
... geologically characterized by stratified, half-a-billion-year-old Paleozoic limestone [6]

Painted lady.
*Vanessa cardui*
on
Death Valley sage
*Salvia funerea*

Generalized elevation range
2,200–5,000 feet

Land area
25,707 acres
40.17 square miles

Western pipstrelle (bat)
*Pipistrellus hesperus*

Painted lady
*Vanessa cardui*

Death Valley sage
*Salvia funerea*

Dainty desert hideseed
*Eucrypta micrantha*

California's Great Basin Desert
east / southeast of Mono Lake

Nevada
California
Mono County

Mono Valley

Mono Basin

Dobie Meadows

8,127'

Cowtrack spring

Inyo Nat'l Forest

Adobe Hills

Adobe Valley

Cowtrack Mtn. 8,852'

Granite Mtn. 8,924'

Inyo Nat'l Forest

Adobe Creek

Granite Mountain Wilderness
diameter of inscribed circle 15 miles

Map 05.08

264

## 05.08 IN VIEW OF MONO LAKE
*Granite Mountain Wilderness*

Granite Mountain Wilderness divides the Mono Valley watershed from Adobe Valley to the east. The Mono-Inyo Craters volcanic chain is a new geologic complex, having formed with eruptions that occurred between 100,000 and 6,000 years ago. In the past two hundred years, cattle grazing has transformed the vegetation from bunch grass that fed herds of antelope and bighorn to bitterbrush and sagebrush that feed the summer migrations of the Mono Lake herd of Rocky Mountain mule deer.[7]

*... exists inside a geologically complex area of Mono-Inyo Craters volcanic chain ... terrain includes uplifted basalt mesas, granite outcrops, and alluvial flats ... an important deer migration corridor*[8]

Two-colored phacelia

Rocky mountain mule deer
*Odocoileus hemionus hemionus*

Generalized elevation range
6,400–9,000 feet

Land area
31,059 acres
48.53 square miles

Rocky mountain mule deer
*Odocoileus hemionus hemionus*

Nuttall's cottontail
*Sylvilagus nuttallii*

Two-colored phacelia
*Phacelia bicolor*

Scale bud
*Anisocoma acaulis*

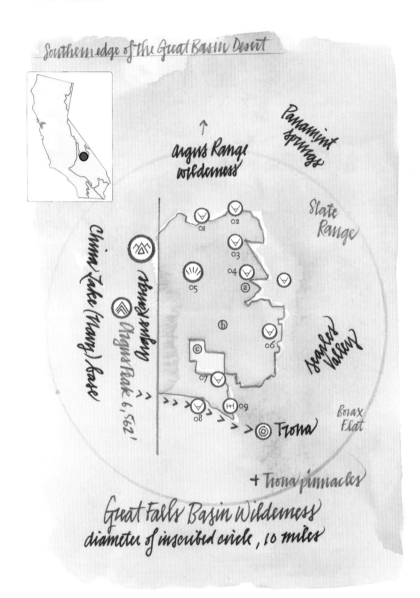

Southern edge of the Great Basin Desert

Panamint springs

Argus Range wilderness

Slate Range

China Lake (Navy.) Base

Argus Peak 6,562'

Searles Valley

Borax Flat

Trona

+ Trona pinnacles

Great Falls Basin Wilderness
diameter of inscribed circle, 10 miles

Map 05.09

## 05.09 RIPARIAN JEWEL OVER SEARLES LAKE
*Great Falls Basin Wilderness*

Between the Argus Range to the west—mountains inside China Lake naval base—Searles Lake (dry) and the town of Trona to the south, and Argus Range Wilderness to the north, Great Falls Basin Wilderness is a relatively small tract of ecologically important land. Indian Joe Spring is regarded as a high-diversity shrub community and includes riparian habitat of Narrowleaf willow, *Salix exigua*, and desert baccharis, *Baccharis sergiloides*.

01. Crow Canyon
02. Homewood Canyon
03. Munford Canyon
04. Rattlesnake Canyon
05. Great Falls Basin
06. Bainter Canyon
07. Indian Joe Canyon
08. Wilson Canyon
09. Panamint Rock Quarry

a. Mumford Springs
b. Bainter Springs
c. Indian Joe Springs

*... habitat for fifty mammal species, including thirteen bat species*
*... habitat for thirty-six amphibian species, including the slender salamander Batrachoseps sp.*
*... home to ninety-nine bird species, including at least eight species of special concern*[9]

Generalized elevation range
2,000–4,500 feet

Land area
7,810 acres
12.20 square miles

Cactus coreid bug
*Chelinidea vittiger*

Northern desert nightsnake
*Hypsiglena chlorophaea*
ssp. *deserticola*

Threadleaf groundsel
*Senecio flaccidus*

Mojave Desert parsley
*Lomatium mohavense*

Narrowleaf willow

desert baccharis

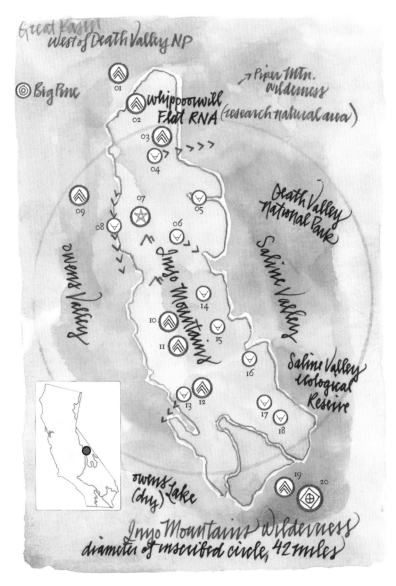

Great Basin
West of Death Valley NP

Big Pine

01

02 Whippoorwill
Flat RNA (research natural area)

Piper Mtn.
Wilderness

03

04

>>>

07

05

09

08

06

Death Valley
National Park

Saline Valley

Owens Valley

Inyo Mountains

14

10

11

15

12

13

16

Saline Valley
Ecological
Reserve

17

18

19    20

Owens Lake
(dry)

Inyo Mountains Wilderness
diameter of inscribed circle, 42 miles

Map 05.10

## 05.10 HIGH MOUNTAINS BETWEEN THE OWENS AND SALINE VALLEYS
*Inyo Mountains Wilderness*

The Inyo Mountains are a fault-block range, meaning that they were created by tensional forces pulling apart pieces of the earth's crust and lifting large pieces of bedrock. The mountains rise in elevation, to dramatic effect, over eleven thousand feet in less than seven miles.

01. Andrews Mountain (9,460')
02. Sawabü Peak (10,358')
03. Waucoba Mountain (11,123')
04. Waucoba Canyon
05. Lead Canyon
06. Paiute Canyon
07. Winnedumah Paiute Monument (8,369')
08. Mazourka Canyon
09. Maxourka Peak (9,410')
10. Mt. Inyo (11,107')
11. Keynot Peak (11,101')
12. New York Butte (10,668')
13. Long John Canyon
14. Pat Keyes Canyon
15. McElvoy Canyon
16. Beverage Canyon
17. Hunter Canyon
18. Craig Canyon
19. Cerro Gordo Peak (9,184')
20. Cerro Gordo Wilderness Study Area

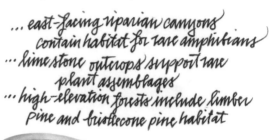

... east-facing riparian canyons contain habitat for rare amphibians

... limestone outcrops support rare plant assemblages

... high-elevation forests include limber pine and bristlecone pine habitat

Inyo Mountains Salamander
*Batrachoseps campi*

Generalized elevation range
1,000–11,200 feet

Land area
205,020 acres
320.34 square miles

Inyo Mountains salamander
*Batrachoseps campi*

Chukar
*Alectoris chukar*

Death Valley beardtongue
*Penstemon fruticiformis*

White stem blazing star
*Mentzelia albicaulis*

Chukar
*Alectoris chukar*

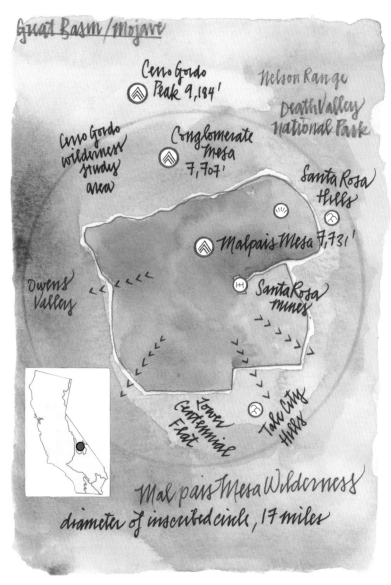

Great Basin / Mojave

Cerro Gordo
Peak 9,184'

Nelson Range

Death Valley
National Park

Cerro Gordo
wilderness
study
area

Conglomerate
Mesa
7,707'

Santa Rosa
Hills

Malpais Mesa 7,731'

Owens
Valley

Santa Rosa
mines

Lower
Centennial
Flat

Talc City
Hills

Mal pais Mesa Wilderness
diameter of inscribed circle, 17 miles

Map 05.11

## 05.11 VOLCANIC TERMINUS OF THE INYO MOUNTAINS
*Malpais Mesa Wilderness*

Rocks in the Inyo-White Mountains are either among the oldest rocks in North America (Precambrian—700 million years) or, as is the case at Malpais Mesa, among the youngest (Holocene eruptions—10,000 years).[10] Bordering the north of the Malpais Mesa Wilderness is a potential wilderness area called Conglomerate Mesa—a significant wildlife corridor whose designation is being stalled by mining interests.[11]

… Primarily an erosion-resistant volcanic mesa resultant from recent eruptions

… dense Joshua tree forest grows on the east end of the mesa

… southernmost point of the seventy-mile-long Inyo-White Mountains

Rock wren
*Salpinctes obsoletus*

Savannah sparrow
*Passerculus sandwichensis*

Generalized elevation range
4,200–7,800 feet

Land area
32,360 acres
50.56 square miles

Savannah sparrow
*Passerculus sandwichensis*

Rock wren
*Salpinctes obsoletus*

Showy gilia
*Gilia cana* ssp. *triceps*

Brownplume wirelettuce
*Stephanomeria pauciflora*

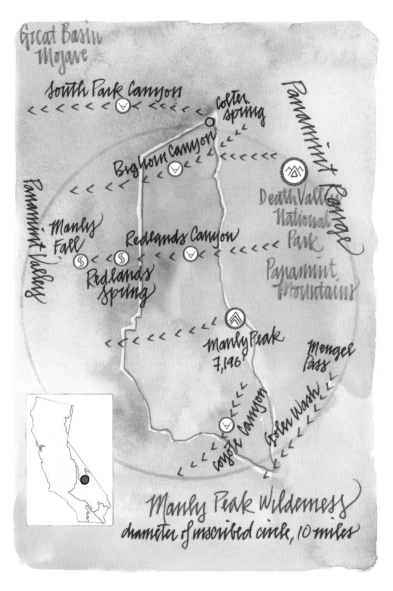

Great Basin
Mojave

South Park Canyon

Colter Spring

Panamint Range

Bighorn Canyon

Death Valley National Park

Panamint Valley

Manly Fall

Redlands Canyon

Redlands Spring

Panamint Mountains

Manly Peak
7,196

Menge Pass

Coyote Canyon

Goler Wash

Manly Peak Wilderness
diameter of inscribed circle, 10 miles

Map 05.12

## 05.12 SOUTHERNMOST PEAK OF THE PANAMINT RANGE
*Manly Peak Wilderness*

With two thousand feet of prominence over the surrounding range, Manly Peak is considered an exemplary California wilderness high point.[12] Although Manly Peak is separated from the main ridgeline of the Panamint Range to the north by Coyote Canyon, it remains part of the range—its southernmost point. The Manly Peak ridgeline separates Panamint Valley to the west and Butte Valley to the east.

... like the Inyo-white Mountains, the
Panamint Range is a fault-block range,
typical in the formation of ranges in
the Great Basin Desert region

... like the view from Telescope Peak, on
Manly Peak both the highest point
(Mt. Whitney) and the lowest point
(Badwater Basin) on the North
American continent are visible
at the same time

... Manly Peak
rises from the Panamint Valley
through creosote shrubland to
piñon woodland

Fringed myotis (bat)
*Myotis thysanodes*

Generalized elevation range
1,100–7,200 feet

Land area
16,105 acres
25.16 square miles

Deer mouse
*Peromyscus maniculatus*

Fringed myotis (bat)
*Myotis thysanodes*

Mojave spurge
*Euphorbia schizoloba*

Whitemargin sandmat
*Chamaesyce albomarginata*

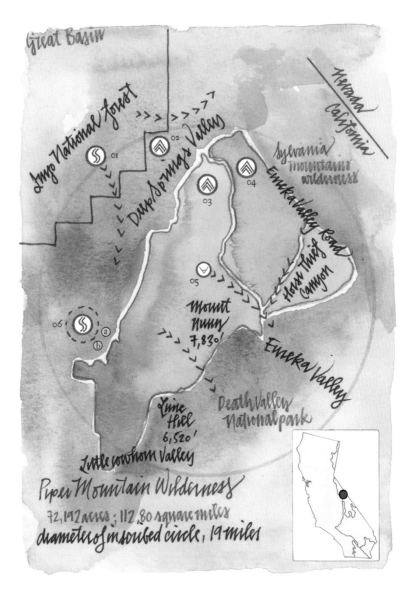

Great Basin

Inyo National Forest

Nevada
California

01

02

Deep Springs Valley

Sylvania
mountains
wilderness

03

04

Eureka Valley Road

Horse Thief Canyon

05

Mount
Nunn
7,830'

Eureka Valley

06

ⓐ
ⓑ

Death Valley
National Park

Lime
Hill
6,520'

Little Cowhorn Valley

Piper Mountain Wilderness

72,192 acres ; 112.80 square miles
diameter of inscribed circle, 19 miles

Map 05.13

## 05.13 BETWEEN THE WHITE AND INYO MOUNTAINS
*Piper Mountain Wilderness*

Between the White Mountains to the north and Last Chance Range to the east, the Piper Mountain Wilderness comprises the northernmost peaks in the Inyo Mountain range. Arranged as an inverted horseshoe, the ridgeline wraps around many square miles of alluvial fans within the northern extent of the Eureka Valley at the northern border of Death Valley National Park. Piper Mountain is sometimes called Chocolate Mountain.

01. Wyman Creek
02. Sentinel Peak (7,000')
03. Piper Mountain (7,703')
04. Sugarloaf Mountain (6,520')
05. Soldier Pass Canyon
06. Deep Springs Lake

a. Carrot Springs
b. Buckhorn Springs

*... a small mountain range east of the Inyo mountains that has no perennial streams*

*... Deep Springs Ecological Reserve, in Deep Springs Valley, is habitat for the endemic black toad, Anaxyrus exsul*

*... habitat for one of the northernmost stands of Joshua tree*

Lilac sunbonnet
Langloisia setosissima

Generalized elevation range
1,000–7,700 feet

Land area
72,575 acres
113.40 square miles

Great Basin
collared lizard
*Crotaphytus bicinctores*

Ladder-backed
woodpecker
*Dryobates scalaris*

Rose heath
*Chaetopappa ericoides*

Lilac sunbonnet
*Langloisia setosissima*

Deep Springs black toad
Anaxyrus exsul

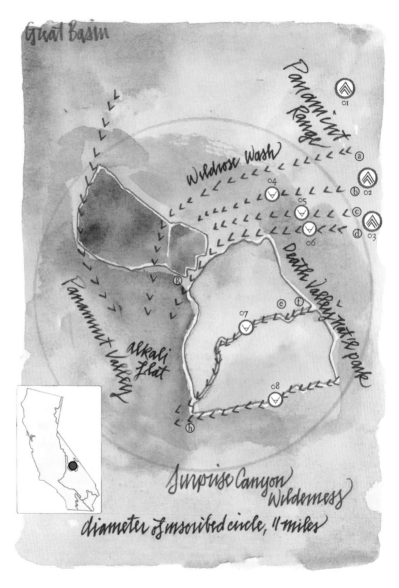

Map 05.14

# 05.14 AT THE WESTERN FOOT OF TELESCOPE PEAK
*Surprise Canyon Wilderness*

A ladder of east–west, knife-edge canyons defines the wilderness area that cuts watersheds down from Telescope Peak, which at 11,049 feet is the tallest mountain in Death Valley National Park. These steep canyons ascend from Panamint Valley, often at a rate of a thousand feet per mile. Because the Panamint Range is so tall, the mountains capture all available moisture and create many perennial streams that fill these canyons.

a. Hummingbird Spring
b. Tuber Spring
c. Jail Spring
d. Eagle Spring
e. Limekiln Spring
f. Brewers Spring
g. Warm Sulphur Springs
h. Post Office Spring

01. Wildrose Peak (9,064')
02. Bennett Peak (9,980')
03. Telescope Peak (11,049')
04 Tuber Canyon
05. Jail Canyon
06. Hall Canyon
07. Surprise Canyon
08. Happy Canyon

*... steep canyons full of perennial streams and riparian habitat*

*... slightly over seven miles of watercourse in the wilderness protected as a Wild and Scenic River* [14]

*... habitat for the rare Panamint alligator lizard, Elgaria panamintina, and Panamint daisy, Enceliopsis covillei*

Generalized elevation range
1,000–7,000 feet

Land area
24,433 acres
38.18 square miles

Lazuli bunting
*Passerina amoena*

Gray buckeye
*Junonia grisea*

Pedicellate phacelia
*Phacelia pedicellata*

Western white clematis
*Clematis ligusticifolia*

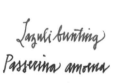

Lazuli bunting
*Passerina amoena*

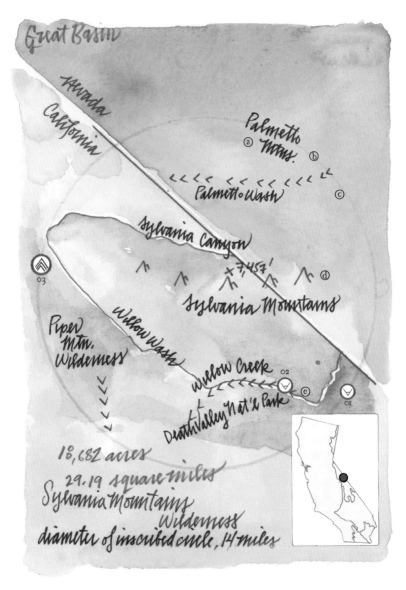

Great Basin

Nevada

California

Palmetto
ⓐ Mtns. ⓑ

ⓒ

Palmetto Wash

Sylvania Canyon

03

+ 7457' ⓓ

Sylvania Mountains

Piper
Mtn.
Wilderness

Willow Wash

Willow Creek  02

ⓔ

01

Death Valley Nat'l Park

18,682 acres
29.19 square miles
Sylvania Mountains
Wilderness
diameter of inscribed circle, 14 miles

Map 05.15

# 05.15 REMOTE RIDGELINE AT THE STATE BORDER
*Sylvania Mountains Wilderness*

Flanked by Sylvania Canyon to the north and Cucamonga Canyon to the south, the Sylvania Mountains Wilderness is a craggy ridgeline that cuts from east to west across the Nevada-California border, north of Death Valley National Park. The west side of the wilderness is an expansive bajada, blanketed in sagebrush.

a. Mud Spring
b. Log Spring
c. Cucamonga Spring
d. Owl Spring
e. Willow Spring

01. Last Chance Canyon
02. Cucamonga Canyon
03. Sugarloaf Mountain (6,520')

*... no permanent trails*
*... no established springs – Willow Spring at the border of Death Valley National Park is the only accessible groundwater*
*... Piñon-juniper woodlands cling to the north face of the ridgeline*

Generalized elevation range
5,000–8,000 feet

Land area
18,682 acres
29.19 square miles

Desert cottontail
*Sylvilagus audubonii*

Desert horned lizard
*Phrynosoma platyrhinos*

Whitedaisy tidytips
*Layia glandulosa*

Yelloweyes
*Lupinus flavoculatus*

*Desert horned lizard*
*Phrynosoma platyrhinos*

*Desert horned lizard –*
*about four inches long*
*lives for five years*
*90% of diet is ants*

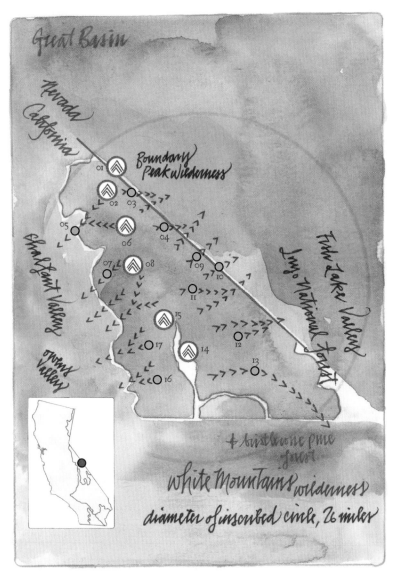

Map 05.16

## 05.16 THE TALLEST OF ALL DESERT RANGES
*White Mountains Wilderness*

This large wilderness area not only is within the tallest range in California's desert regions but contains two other qualities of earth's ancient character: some of its oldest fossils, and habitat for some of its oldest living organisms. Fossils from an ocean reef called a bioherm—a structure that contains organisms, including trilobites, inside of dolomite (a sedimentary rock) deposits—date back nearly six hundred million years.[15] Inside what is called the Ancient Bristlecone Pine Forest, surrounded by the wilderness area, there are at least eight other tree and conifer species that find habitat near the bristlecone—remarkable arboreal diversity for a desert mountain in California. The dramatic topography of the White Mountains Wilderness is exemplified by the elevation drop from White Mountain Peak to Chalfant Valley of 9,700 feet in only seven miles.

... Includes White Mountain Peak (14,246')
the third-highest peak in California

... although the wilderness receives less
than fifteen inches of annual precipitation,
the wilderness has more than one hundred
perennial streams.

... habitat for the world's oldest living
tree, the bristlecone pine,
*Pinus longaeva*

01. Boundary Peak (13,147')
02. The Jumpoff (13,484')
03. Middle Creek
04. Chiatovich Creek
05. Marble Creek
06. Mount Dubois (13,559')
07. Pellisier Creek
08. Mount Hogue (12,751')
09. Davis Creek
10. Indian Creek
11. Leidy Creek; Cabin Creek
12. Perry Atken Creek
13. Cottonwood Creek
14. Mt. Bancroft (13,040')
15. White Mountain Peak (14,246')
16. Millner Creek
17. Lone Treek Creek

Generalized elevation range—4,000–14,300 feet
Land area—230,966 acres/360.88 square miles

Clark's nutcracker
*Nucifraga columbiana*

Yellow-bellied marmot
*Marmota flaviventris*

Great Basin bristlecone pine
*Pinus longaeva*

White Mountains sky pilot
*Polemonium chartaceum*

## The Ecological History of the World's Oldest Tree

Saying that the history of the bristle-cone pine, *Pinus longaeva*, is an old story is an understatement. The reasons the nearly five-thousand-year-old grove of Great Basin bristlecones exists where it does and how it does (for how is the central question of ecology) are part of a story that reaches back more than six hundred million years.

Near the shore of the Proterozoic sea that would become, in the unimaginable future, the White Mountains, sedimentary dolomite was deposited. Today, the old trees at eleven thousand feet above sea level depend on that particular soil, now called reed dolomite.[16]

To further set the scene, three successive mountain-building events (orogenies) occurred in the Paleozoic and Mesozoic eras that pushed and pulled at the land area destined to become the Great Basin Desert. What was left at the dawn of the Cenozoic was the Nevadaplano, an extensive volcanic plateau that was again transformed by shifting tectonic regimes and expansional forces leading to the development of the current inventory of the three hundred fault-block mountain ranges in the Great Basin region. At the beginning of the Quaternary period, two million years ago, California had its modern subalpine roster of trees in place, among them the bristlecone pine.[17]

The final piece of our puzzle in the telling of this story involves a discussion of the history of tree families, or phylogeny. It is generally agreed that at nearly five thousand years old, the bristlecone pine is the oldest living nonclonal organism on the planet. The bristlecone pine is a conifer (cone-bearing plants, e.g., pine, cedar, and redwood), conifers are all gymnosperms (ancients plants without pollinators), and gymnosperms trace their genetic lineage back three hundred million years, to the early Carboniferous period. The first pine (genus *Pinus*) made its evolutionary debut in the late Cretaceous (150 MYA), but trees were still speciating, and further phylogenetic splits needed to occur before we would see the bristlecone. By forty million years ago, the world was on its way to having its full complement of over one hundred species of pine tree, and it was at about this time that the Great Basin bristlecone pine (*P. longaeva*) split off from piñon pines (*Pinus* subsection *Cembroides*), and along with foxtail pine (*P. balfouriana*) formed a distinct lineage (*Pinus* subsection *Balfourianae*) on its way to becoming its own species.[18]

The soil patterns, tectonic activity, and phylogenetic history all coalesce into a recipe for the particular form of California desert life that is the bristlecone pine. Inside the climate and fire regime of modern California, the bristlecone is a product of its specific ecological context. Without any one piece of this ecological epic, the resilient and precious species that is *Pinus longaeva* might not have come into being. Despite these protestations that this story is unique, a similar tale appears to have been told in South America, where in Chile there is a specimen of Patagonian cypress, *Fitzroya cupressoides*, that may be older than California's bristlecone. If this is a pan-American phenomenon, was the development of such long-lived subalpine trees in the Quaternary a fluke of evolution, or was it part of a long chain of events that made their appearance inevitable?

Bristlecone Pine, California, *Pinus longaeva*

Desert Orangetip butterfly
subfamily Pierinae

anthocharis
cethura

Appear early in spring
larvae feed on mustard family

wingspan
2.6 - 4 cm
(1 - 1½ inch)

many subspecies across California
and other species, including
overwintering chrysalis  a. sara
males patrol all day

"Mojave"—endonym Hama Kaave <beside the Water>[1]

Three global forces needed to align for the Mojave Desert to come into existence. The first took place over the past several hundred million years: the rise of the Sierra Nevada. The second was the tectonic configuration of Southern California's Peninsular and Transverse Ranges and the establishment of the San Andreas Fault, which finally decided on its current form between the North American and the Pacific Plates about thirty million years ago. The third force that conjured the modern Mojave into being was the establishment of the California Current in the eastern Pacific Ocean, which helped to regulate California's Mediterranean climate west of the Pacific Crest in the middle Pliocene, about three million years ago. Since then, variances in hydrology and atmospheric conditions set the stage against the geologic backdrop of the landscape for the drama of natural selection to play out. Inside extreme regimes of heat, ice, fire, aridity, and deluge that played out over millennia, biological forms adapted, as did the ecological relationships, to always endure. Despite the potentially countless extinctions this land has faced, and despite how the sometimes fickle climate always, gradually changed, the totality of the Mojave ecosystem may have never faced so wickedly virulent a challenge to its viability as the one presented by the crush of disturbances that is the Anthropocene.

desert tortoise     Gopherus agassizii

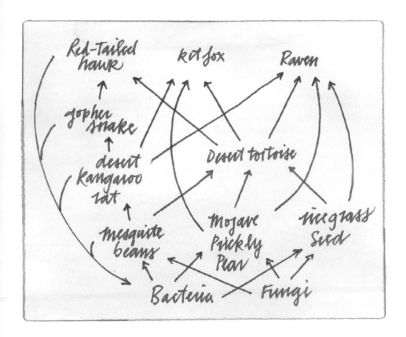

## Simplified food web of the desert tortoise

The tortoise genus *Gopherus* sp. has been moving west across ancient America for the past forty million years. The genus split into the modern desert tortoise, *Gopherus agassizii*, about ten million years ago, and modern lineages that divide this icon of the Mojave and Sonoran Deserts between the two different geographies date to about half that age.[2] The tortoise has walked the mountains of the Mojave long before primates in Africa evolved to become bipedal. What multitude of species—bird, mammal, reptile, plant, and insect—has the tortoise seen come and go?

This simplified diagram represents a common food web that plays out every day across the modern Mojave. The diagram is drawn with the desert tortoise as the hub and does not include the specific role of detritus or of biocrust, both of which may be fundamental to the ecology of the shelled desert steward.

## 06.01 A DESERT CUT IN HALF
*The Mojave across four states*

With more than three thousand plant species, over five hundred of which are found nowhere else, and almost four hundred vertebrate animal species, over sixty of which are endemic, the greater Mojave bioregion exhibits world-class biodiversity. The Mojave is delineated by the plants, their distribution and their mix, across the landscape. Toward the desert's southern border, shrublands of ocotillo, *Fouquieria splendens*; palo verde, *Parkinsonia* ssp.; smoke tree, *Psorothamnus spinosus*; and ironwood,

*Olneya tesota*, become more common as Joshua tree woodlands become less frequent. Toward the eastern edge, the lack of summer rain may stop the common proliferation of saguaro cactus west of the Colorado River, indicating the border with the Sonoran Desert in Arizona. To the north, the vegetation across the blackbrush shifts from Joshua tree dominant to sagebrush dominant; and from the Mojave to the Great Basin, the common precipitation type shifts from rain to snow.

Map 06.01

## Plant alliances of the Mojave Desert in southeastern California

Allscale scrub
American bulrush marsh
Anderson's boxthorn scrub
Arrow weed thicket
Big galleta shrub-steppe
Big sagebrush
Bitterbrush scrub
Black brush scrub
Black-stem rabbitbrush scrub
Black willow thickets
Bladder sage scrub
Brittlebush scrub
Broom baccharis thicket

Broom baccharis, *Baccharis sarothroides*

Bush seepweed scrub
California buckwheat scrub
California buckwheat–white sage scrub
California juniper woodland
California poppy fields
Canyon live oak forest
Catclaw acacia thorn scrub
Cattail marsh
Cheesebush scrub
Common reed marshes
Cooper's rush marsh
Creosote bush–brittlebush scrub
Creosote bush scrub
Creosote bush–white bursage scrub

Catclaw acacia, *Senegalia greggii*

Curly blue grass grassland
Deer grass beds
Desert almond scrub
Desert dunes
Desert holly scrub
Desert lavender scrub
Desert needlegrass grassland
Desert olive patches
Desert panic grass patches
Desert purple sage scrub
Desert willow woodland
Ditch-grass or widgeon-grass mats

Desert lavender, *Hyptis emoryi*

Fiddleneck fields
Fourwing saltbush scrub
Fremont cottonwood forest
Greasewood scrub
Indian rice grass grassland
Iodine bush scrub
James' galleta shrub-steppe
Joshua tree woodland
Mesquite bosque
Mesquite thicket
Mojave yucca scrub
Mormon tea scrub
Mountain big sagebrush
Muller oak chaparral
Needleleaf rabbitbrush scrub
Net-veined goldeneye scrub
Nevada joint fir scrub
Nolina scrub
Parish's goldeneye scrub
Quailbush scrub
Red willow thickets
Rubber rabbitbrush scrub
Sagebrush scrub
Salt grass flats
Sandbar willow thicket
Shadescale scrub
Singleleaf pinyon woodland
Smoke tree woodland
Sonoran live oak scrub
Spinescale scrub
Spiny hop sage scrub
Stansbury cliff rose scrub
Teddy bear cholla patches
Utah juniper woodland
Virgin River brittlebush scrub
Western sea-purslane marshes
White bursage scrub
Winterfat scrubland
Wright's buckwheat patches
Yerba mansa meadows

Iodine bush, *Allenrolfea occidentalis*

Net-veined goldeneye,
*Bahiopsis reticulata*

Western sea-purslane,
*Sesuvium verrucosum*

## Focal Species of the Mojave Connectivity Project

A. Yucca moth, *Tegeticula synthetica*,
   wingspan 17 to 21 mm
B. Desert green hairstreak, *Callophrys
   comstocki*, wingspan 22 to 29 mm
C. Bernardino dotted blue, *Euphilotes
   bernardino*, wingspan 11 to 13 mm
D. Desert ("Sonoran") metalmark,
   *Apodemia mejicanus*,
   wingspan, approx. 28 mm
E. Ford's swallowtail, *Papilio indra
   fordi*, wingspan 62 to 72 mm

C.

A.

D.

B.

E.

*Source:* K. Penrod, P. Beier, E. Garding, and C. Cabañero, *A Linkage Network
for the California Deserts*, produced for the Bureau of Land Management and the
Wildlands Conservancy (Fair Oaks, CA: Science and Collaboration for Connected
Wildlands, and Flagstaff: Northern Arizona University, 2012), http://www
.scwildlands.org/reports/ALinkageNetworkForTheCaliforniaDeserts.pdf.

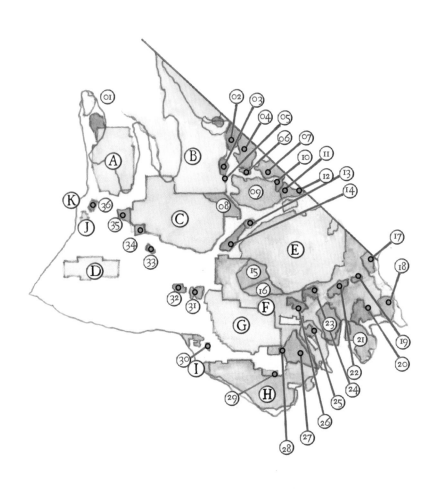

Map 06.02

## 06.02 WILDERNESS, PARKS, PRESERVES, AND MILITARY LAND
*Land designations within the ecological Mojave in California*

The area described by map 06.02 is roughly continuous with the distribution range of the Joshua tree. Often called the high desert, the Mojave has also been called "America's Definitive Desert" because in contrast to the sagebrush of Nevada's Great Basin, the cactus lands of Mexico's Sonoran, or even the scrublands of the Southwest's Chihuahuan, the desert scrub, woodlands, and lava fields of the Mojave are as unique as they are diverse, extending across the majority of southeastern California's ancient, rugged terrain.

01. Coso Range Wilderness
02. Resting Spring Range Wilderness
03. Ibex Wilderness
04. Nopah Range Wilderness
05. Saddle Peak Hills Wilderness
06. South Nopah Range Wilderness
07. Pahrump Valley Wilderness
08. Avawatz Mountains Wilderness
09. Kingston Range Wilderness
10. North Mesquite Mountains Wilderness
11. Mesquite Wilderness
12. Stateline Wilderness
13. Hollow Hills Wilderness
14. Soda Mountain Wilderness
15. Kelso Dunes Wilderness
16. Bristol Mountains Wilderness
17. Dead Mountains Wilderness
18. Chemehuevi Mountains Wilderness

19. Bigelow Cholla Garden Wilderness
20. Stepladder Mountains Wilderness
21. Turtle Mountains Wilderness
22. Piute Mountains Wilderness
23. Old Woman Mountains Wilderness
24. Clipper Mountain Wilderness
25. Cadiz Dunes Wilderness
26. Trilobite Wilderness
27. Sheephole Valley Wilderness
28. Cleghorn Lakes Wilderness
29. Pinto Mountains Wilderness
30. Bighorn Mountain Wilderness
31. Rodman Mountains Wilderness
32. Newberry Mountains Wilderness
33. Black Mountain Wilderness
34. Grass Valley Wilderness
35. Golden Valley Wilderness
36. El Paso Mountains Wilderness

A. China Lake navy base
B. Death Valley National Park
C. China Lake navy base/ Fort Irwin army base
D. Edwards Air Force Base
E. Mojave National Preserve
F. Mojave Trails National Monument
G. 29 Palms marine base
H. Joshua Tree National Park
I. Sand to Snow National Monument
J. Red Rock Canyon State Park
K. Wilderness areas of the desert periphery (see map 06.03)

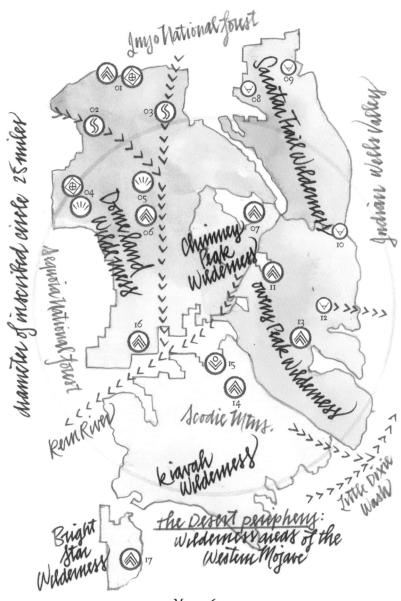

Map 06.03

## 06.03 DESERT PERIPHERIES
*Wilderness areas of the western Mojave*

Although annual precipitation rates in many of the Sierra Nevada's southeastern wilderness areas indicate that you may still be in a desert environment, the proximity of these lands to the snowpack of the Sierra Nevada, coupled with soil types of mountainous and nondesert chemistries, reveal that indeed, this region is a transitional area that is certainly not quite montane, but also not desert.

01. Bald Mountain Botanical Area;
    Bald Mountain (9,382')
02. Trout Creek
03. Fish Creek
04. Church Dome Research
    Natural Area;
    Manter Meadow
05. Rockhouse Meadow
06. White Dome (7,555')
07. Chimney Peak (7,990')
08. Sacatar Canyon
09. Portuguese Canyon
10. Deadfoot Canyon
11. Lamont Peak (7,510')
12. Sand Canyon
13. Owens Peak (8,453')
14. Pinyon Peak (6,805')
15. Canebrake Ecological Reserve
16. Pilot Knob (6,200')
17. Kelso Peak (5,080')

Bright Star Wilderness

Elevation range—3,300–5,500 feet
Land area—9,520 acres/14.88 square
    miles

Chimney Peak Wilderness

Elevation range—6,000–8,035 feet
Land area—13,700 acres/21.41 square
    miles

Domeland Wilderness

Elevation range—3,000–9,730 feet
Land area—130,986 acres/204.67
    square miles

Kiavah Wilderness

Elevation range—3,000–7,096 feet
Land area—88,290 acres/137.95 square
    miles

Owens Peak Wilderness

Elevation range—3,000–8,453 feet
Land area—74,640 acres/116.63 square
    miles

Sacatar Trail Wilderness

Elevation range—3,000–
    7,800 feet
Land area—51,900
    acres/81.09 square
    miles

### Desert fox, Vulpes *sp.*

Two of North America's four true fox species find widespread habitat in California's deserts. One of them, the eleven-pound gray fox, *Urocyon cinereoargenteus,* is the only member of the dog family that can climb trees. Smallest of the North American foxes, the kit fox, *Vulpes macrotis,* is the other. The other two true foxes are the red fox, *Vulpes fulva,* who lives in Chihuahua Desert, and the swift fox, *Vulpes velox,* a nondesert dweller.

*California leaf-nosed bat,* Macrotus californicus

The California leaf-nosed bats of the Avawatz Mountains Wilderness are one hundred miles north of the next-nearest roost.[3]

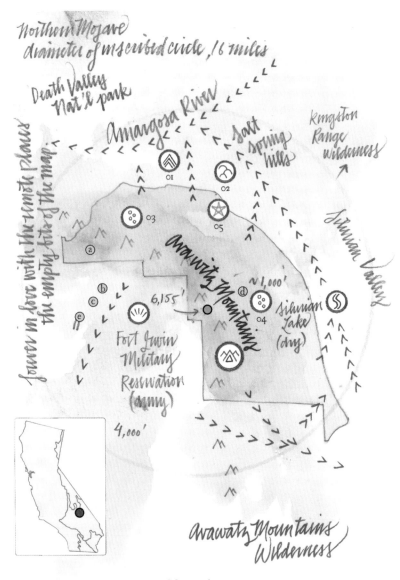

Northern Mojave
diameter of inscribed circle, 16 miles

Death Valley
Nat'l park

Amargosa River

Salt
Spring
hills

Kingston
Range
wilderness

Sirwan Valley

forever in love with the remote places
the empty sites of the map.

Avawatz Mountains

~1,000'

Silurian
Lake
(dry)

6,155'

Fort Irwin
Military
Reservation
(army)

4,000'

Avawatz Mountains
Wilderness

Map 06.04

## 06.04 AT THE BEND OF THE AMARGOSA RIVER
*Avawatz Mountains Wilderness*

The ridgelines that follow the eastern border of Fort Irwin from Death Valley National Park are the Avawatz (Paiute: *iva-watz*—white mountain sheep[4]) Mountains. Reaching from Death Valley to the Soda Mountains and then onto Mojave National Preserve, the Avawatz form an essential wildlife linkage for migratory bighorn.[5] Salt Creek, tributary of the Amargosa River, and the Salt Creek Hills area of critical environmental concern (ACEC), just outside the wilderness area, are the only habitats of the rare and endemic Salt Creek pupfish, *Cyprinodon salinus*.

01. Round Mountain (313')
02. Salt Spring Hills (1,769')
03. Sheep Creek Springs Trail
04. Renoville Trail
05. Salt Creek Hills ACEC

a. Denning Spring
b. Arrastre Spring
c. Cave Springs
d. Old Mormon Spring
e. Avawatz Pass

... *nine springs feed riparian watercourses within the Amargosa watershed*
.. *forms the western border of the Silurian Valley / Salt Creek watershed*
... *the southern border of the Amargosa watershed*

Generalized elevation range
600–6,200 feet

Land area
89,500 acres
139.84 square miles

Western harvest mouse
*Reithrodontomys megalotis*

White-throated swift
*Aeronautes saxatalis*

Golden desert-snapdragon
*Mohavea breviflora*

Schott's pygmy cedar
*Peucephyllum schottii*

*white-throated swift*
*Aeronautes saxatalis*

*white-throated swift*
*Aeronautes saxatalis*

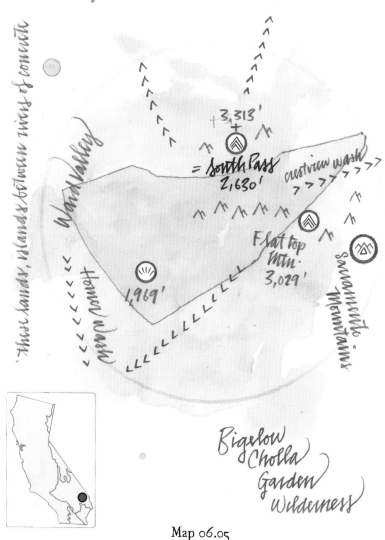

eastern Mojave, south of the Preserve
diameter of inscribed circle, 9 miles

'these sands, islands between rivers of concrete'

Ward Valley

+ 3,313'

South Pass
2,630'

crestview wash

Watson wash

1,969'

Flat top
Mtn.
3,029'

Sacramento Mountains

Bigelow
Cholla
Garden
Wilderness

Map 06.05

## 06.05 CACTUS LANDS SOUTH OF THE MOJAVE NATIONAL PRESERVE
*Bigelow Cholla Garden Wilderness*

Rising to the north of Ward Valley, between the Piute and the Sacramento Mountains, the low hills that make up this wilderness establish the northern end of the south-flowing Homer Wash. Flattop Mountain, to the south of the wilderness, is the northernmost peak of the volcanic Sacramento Mountains. There are no established trails through this creosote-covered wilderness. The wilderness is entirely within the Mojave Trails National Monument.

... the thickest stands of Bigelow cholla,
*Cylindropuntia bigelovii* in California
grow here

... provides critical habitat for the desert
tortoise across scrubland and cactus
gardens

... smoketree, acacia and mesquite
wash/riparian habitat exist
throughout

Branched pencil cholla
*Cylindropuntia ramosissima*

Generalized elevation range
500–2,000 feet

Land area
14,645 acres
22.88 square miles

Coachwhip
*Masticophis flagellum*

Desert orangetip
*Anthocharis cethura*

Desert dandelion
*Malacothrix glabrata*

Branched pencil cholla
*Cylindropuntia ramosissima*

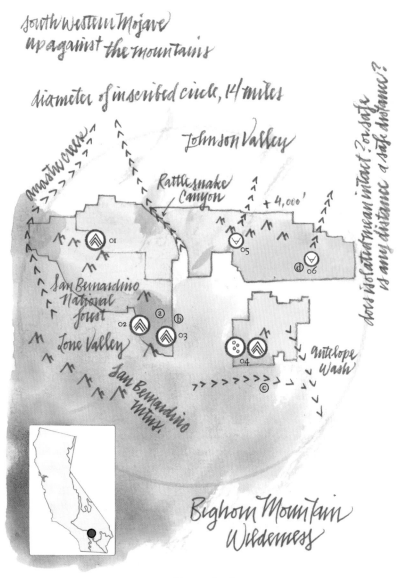

south western Mojave
up against the mountains

diameter of inscribed circle, 14 miles

Johnson Valley

Rattlesnake
Canyon

+ 4,000'

does not attract tourists? or safe
is any distance a safe distance?

San Bernardino
National
forest

Lone Valley

San Bernardino
Mtns.

Antelope
Wash

Bighorn Mountain
Wilderness

Map 06.06

## 06.06 WOODLANDS OF THE SOUTHERN ANTELOPE VALLEY
*Bighorn Mountain Wilderness*

Saddling two distinct woodland types, from Joshua tree habitat to higher-elevation Jeffrey pine forest, the Bighorn Mountain Wilderness presents a broad range of habitat types for a wealth of biodiversity, including hundreds of bird species and large mammals—for example, mountain lion and California black bear. The mountain range namesake of the wilderness area is the northeasternmost edge of the San Bernardino Mountains, part of the Transverse Mountains of Southern California.

01. Granite Peaks (7,527')
02. Tip Top Mountain (7,623')
03. Mineral Mountain (7,238')
04. Black Mountain Trail;
    2.3 miles long,
    5,558'–6,139'
05. Bighorn Canyon
06. Ruby Canyon

a. Viscera Spring
b. Vaughn Spring
c. Burns Spring
d. Ruby Spring

*...the perennial stream through Rattlesnake Canyon attracts migrating birds*

*...part of the larger designation known as the Bighorn Mountain and Whitewater River National Recreation Lands*

*...the bighorn population has been extirpated*

Desert larkspur
*Delphinium parishii*

Generalized elevation range
2,000–7,000 feet

Land area
38,599 acres
60.31 square miles

Gray vireo
*Vireo vicinior*

Thicket hairstreak
*Callophrys spinetorum*

Desert larkspur
*Delphinium parishii*

Desert mariposa lily
*Calochortus kennedyi*

## Rare carbonate endemic plants of the San Bernardino Mountains

Being derived from limestone, carbonate soils are chemically unique. The plants that grow in the habitats these soils provide are specially adapted to do so.

Cushenbury buckwheat, *Eriogonum ovalifolium* var. *vineum*
Cushenbury milkvetch, *Astragalus albens*
Cushenbury oxytheca, *Oxytheca parishii* var. *goodmaniana*
San Bernardino Mountains bladderpod, *Physaria kingii* var. *bernardina*
Parish's daisy, *Erigeron parishii*

Cushenbury buckwheat
Eriogonum ovalifolium var. vin

Cushenbury milkvetch
Astragalus albens

Cushenbury oxytheca
Oxytheca parishii var. goodmaniana

San Bernardino Mountains
bladder-pod
Physaria kingii ssp. bernardina

Parish's daisy
Erigeron parishii

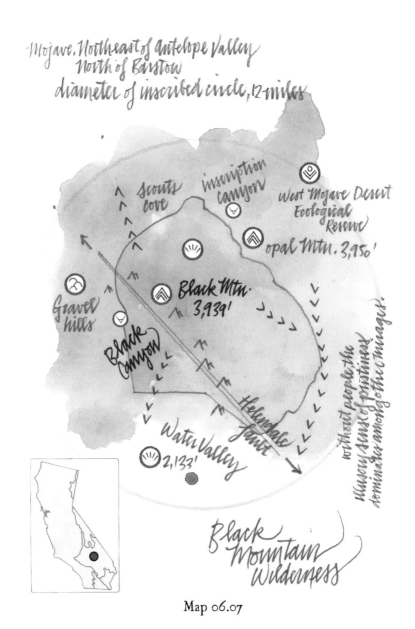

Mojave. Northeast of Antelope Valley
North of Barstow
diameter of inscribed circle, 12 miles

scouts cove

inscription canyon

West Mojave Desert Ecological Reserve

opal Mtn. 3,950'

Gravel hills

Black Mtn. 3,939'

Black Canyon

Helendale fault

Water Valley 2,133'

without people the illusory sense of pristineal nominates among other mirages.

Black Mountain Wilderness

Map 06.07

## 06.07 NORTHEASTERN ANTELOPE VALLEY
*Black Mountain Wilderness*

On the south end of Gravel Hills, Black Mountain is a mesa surrounded by volcanic flows that date from as recently as ten thousand years ago and back to the Early Jurassic, almost two hundred million years ago.[6] Surrounded by private land holdings, the piece of public land has no trails. The Helendale Fault is one of the central Mojave's chief fault lines and runs right through the wilderness area.

*... volcanic soil makes this wilderness a vernal wildflower hotspot*

*... contains a variety of rocky landscapes, including sandy plots*

*... adjacent to primary n corridors in the Fremont-Kramer area of critical environmental concern*[7]

Chick lupine
*Lupinus microcarpus*

Dyebush
*Psorothamnus emoryi*

Desert hairy scorpion
*Hadrurus arizonensis*

Common side-blotched lizard
*Uta stansburiana*

Land area
20,548 acres
32.11 square miles

Generalized elevation range
2,000–4,000 feet

*e-blotched lizard*
*ta stansburiana*

Mojave's Heart, east of the Preserve
(its geographic heart, anyway)

Maximum height 3,874'

diameter of inscribed
circle, 24 miles

Devil's Playground
Wash

Mojave
National
Preserve

Kelso Dunes
Wilderness

2,100'

ⓐ
ⓑ
Old Dad Mountains
ⓒ

Bristol Mountains

Bristol
Mountains
Wilderness

Map 06.08

## o6.o8 WESTERN CONTINUANCE OF MOJAVE NATIONAL PRESERVE
*Bristol Mountains Wilderness*

Two parallel-running mountain ranges define the dry, trailless Bristol Mountains Wilderness. One is the Bristol Mountains range, which runs for approximately thirty miles from the Kelso Dunes Wilderness in the north to the Mojave Trails National Monument in the south. The other is the volcanic Old Dad Mountains, whose basalt boulders were created in an orogeny at least one hundred million years ago.[8]

a. Budweiser Wash
b. Orange Blossom Wash
c. Old Dad Mountains Wash

*... a tilted, volcanic plain of rolling hills in dark red and rust-colored stone*

*... no springs, no trails, and yet abundant wildlife and wildflower blooms*

*... contiguous habitat with the Granite Mountains of the Mojave National Preserve to the east*

Desert lily
*Hesperocallis undulata*

Generalized elevation range
2,200–4,500 feet

Land area
71,389 acres
111.54 square miles

Desert iguana
*Dipsosaurus dorsalis*

Desert night lizard
*Xantusia vigilis*

Wallace's wooly daisy
*Eriophyllum wallacei*

Desert lily
*Hesperocallis undulata*

Glossy snake
western Mojave
Arizona elegans candida

---

### Glossy snakes, Arizona elegans *sp.*

Western Mojave glossy snake, *Arizona elegans candida*, native to the Mojave

Desert glossy snake, *Arizona elegans eburnata*, native to the Sonoran and the Colorado

California glossy snake, *Arizona elegans occidentalis*, native to Southern California, nondesert, species of special concern

The loggerhead shrike, *Lanius ludovicianus*, is a small songbird that resembles a mockingbird, although it prepares its prey, a broad mix of species, in a unique way. The shrike skewers the prey, often much larger than itself, on plant spikes and thorns, and once it is secure, the bird picks off pieces of it with its beak. Its Latin name, *Lanius*, means "butcher."

Loggerhead shrike
Lanius ludovicianus

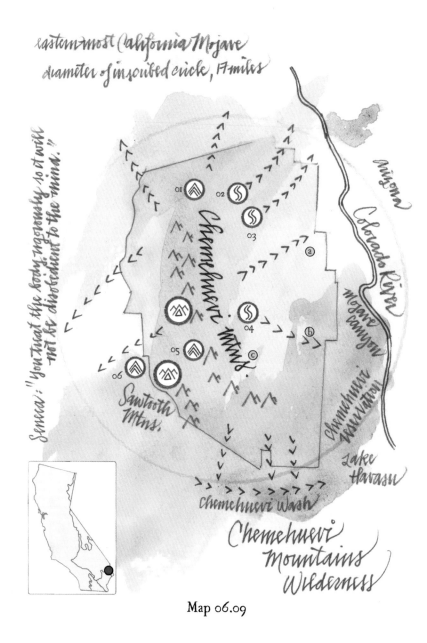

eastern-most California Mojave
diameter of inscribed circle, 17 miles

Seneca: "You treat the body ingorously so it will not be disobedient to the mind."

Chemehuevi Mtns.

Arizona

Colorado River

Mojave Canyon

Chemehuevi Reservation

Lake Havasu

Sawtooth Mtns.

Chemehuevi Wash

Chemehuevi Mountains Wilderness

Map 06.09

## 06.09 WILD GARDENS NEAR THE COLORADO RIVER
*Chemehuevi Mountains Wilderness*

The eastern border of this wilderness is shared with the Havasu National Wildlife Refuge in the north and the Chemehuevi Indian Reservation, on the western shore of Lake Havasu, in the south. Flanked on its west and south by the Chemehuevi Valley Wash, the wilderness is primarily composed by its namesake mountains that form a U-shaped valley facing east, toward the Colorado River.

01. White Mountain (2,774')
02. Bat Cave Wash
03. Mojave Wash
04. Trampas Wash
05. Chemehuevi Peak (3,550')
06. Snaggletooth (2,180')

a. Red Rock Falls
b. Trampas Wash
c. Studio Spring

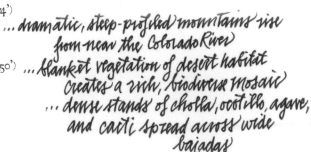

*... dramatic, steep-profiled mountains rise from near the Colorado River*
*... blanket vegetation of desert habitat creates a rich, biodiverse mosaic*
*... dense stands of cholla, ocotillo, agave, and cacti spread across wide bajadas*

*Southwestern willow flycatcher*
*Empidonax traillii extimus*

Generalized elevation range
500–3,800 feet

Land area
85,864 acres
134.16 square miles

Southwestern willow flycatcher
*Empidonax traillii extimus*

Greater roadrunner
*Geococcyx californianus*

Littleleaf ratany
*Krameria erecta*

Largebract spiderling
*Boerhavia wrightii*

Mojave - north of Joshua tree park
and the town of
Twentynine Palms

Southern
end of the
Bullion Mtns.

diameter of inscribed circle, 12 miles

Bristol dry lake

air Ground Combat Center

Marine corps AGCC
Twentynine Palms

what is humanity also, but a product of a natural world?

Bullion Mtns.

Cleghorn Dry Lakes

Mesquite Wash

Valley Mtn
2,311'

Sheephole
Pass
2,307'

Dale Dry
Lake

Cleghorn
Lakes
Wilderness

Map 06.10

# 06.10 DRY LAKES NORTH OF JOSHUA TREE
*Cleghorn Lakes Wilderness*

At the southern end of the Bullion Mountains south of the 29 Palms Marine Corps base and north of the neighborhood called Wonder Valley, Cleghorn Lakes Wilderness is named for dry lakes near its center. A large bajada spreads along the western half of the wilderness and is the site for regular, spectacular wildflower blooms.

*... granitic geology here resembles the boulder landscape of Joshua Tree National Park*

*... one of the northernmost extents of habitat for the smoke tree,*
*Psorothamnus spinosus* [9]

*... includes habitat for a distinct population of crucifixion thorn*
*Castela emoryi* [10]

Crucifixion thorn
*Castela emoryi*

Generalized elevation range
1,400–4,100 feet

Land area
39,167 acres
61.20 square miles

Pallid-winged grasshopper
*Trimerotropis pallidipennis*

Southwestern speckled rattlesnake
*Crotalus mitchellii pyrrhus*

Parish's poppy
*Eschscholzia parishii*

Lilac sunbonnet
*Langloisia setosissima*

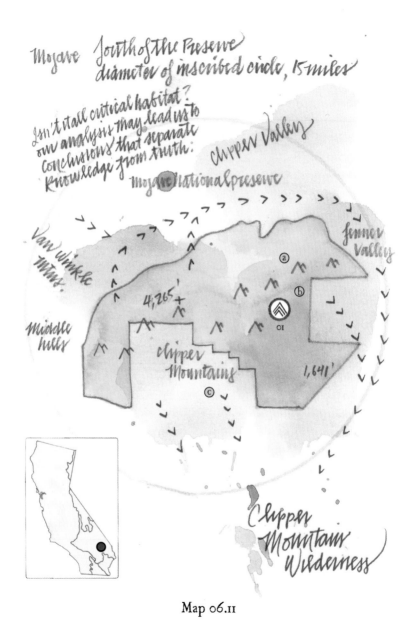

Mojave South of the Preserve
diameter of inscribed circle, 15 miles

Isn't it all critical habitat?
our analysis may lead us to
conclusions that separate
knowledge from truth.

Mojave National Preserve

Clipper Valley

Van Winkle Mtns.

Fenner Valley

(a)

(b)

01

4,265'

Middle Hills

Clipper Mountains

(c)

1,641'

Clipper Mountain Wilderness

Map 06.11

# 06.11 LONELY MOUNTAINS SOUTH OF THE MOJAVE NATIONAL PRESERVE
*Clipper Mountain Wilderness*

Rising between Fenner Valley to the south and Clipper Valley, within the Mojave National Preserve, to the north, the Clipper Mountains form an isolated range that orients from the northeast to the southwest. Located in the Mojave Trails National Monument, these jagged mountains and striped mesa date back to the Jurassic.[11]

01. Castle Dome (3,299')

a. Chuckwalla Spring
b. Hummingbird Spring
c. Bonanza Spring, one of the
   largest freshwater springs
   in the Mojave Desert

... home to a localized population of fifty
bighorn sheep
... essential habitat for desert tortoise,
Gopherus agassizii
... Vernal blooms
of brittle bush, Encelia farinosa,
blanket the mountain washes
in yellow

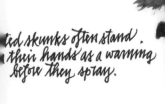

western spotted skunk
Spilogale gracilis

...ted skunks often stand
their hands as a warning
before they spray.

Generalized elevation range
2,000–4,600 feet

Land area
33,843 acres
52.88 square miles

Badger
*Taxidea taxus*

Western spotted skunk
*Spilogale gracilis*

Clearwater cryptantha
*Cryptantha intermedia*

Desert willow
*Chilopsis linearis*

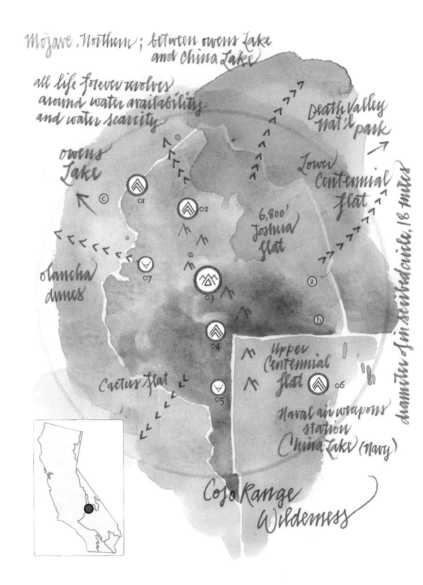

Mojave, Northern; between owens Lake
and china Lake

all life forever revolves
around water availability
and water scarcity

owens
Lake

olancha
dunes

Cactus flat

Death Valley
Nat'l park

Lower
Centennial
flat

6,800'
Joshua
flat

Upper
Centennial
flat

Naval air weapons
station
China Lake (Navy)

diameter of inscribed circle, 18 miles

Cofo Range
Wilderness

Map 06.12

# 06.12 VOLCANIC PLATEAU SOUTH OF OWENS LAKE
*Coso Range Wilderness*

The uplifted volcanic mesa that is the Coso Range lies between Lower Centennial Flat to its east and the great expanse of the now desiccated Owens Lake to its north and west. The approximately four-square-mile Joshua Flat sprawls across the roof of the wilderness area, and from that vantage point, noble views of the tallest peaks of the Sierra Nevada are to be had.

01. Red Ridge (3,806')
02. Sugar Loaf (5,232')
03. Coso Range
04. Silver Mountain (7,492')
05. Thorndyke Canyon
06. Coso Peak (8,160')
07. Vermillion Canyon

a. Lower Centennial Spring
b. Upper Centennial Spring
c. Dirty Socks Hot Spring

*... generally has higher elevations than those of other wilderness areas in the high desert*

*... Volcanic mountains that developed over a long history of volcanic activity, most recently forty thousand years ago* [12]

*... northern edge of the Coso Range; the largest portion of the Coso Range is inside China Lake naval base to the southeast*

California ground squirrel

Generalized elevation range
4,000–7,500 feet

Land area
49,296 acres
77.03 square miles

California ground squirrel
*Spermophilus beecheyi nesioticus*

Sagebrush sparrow
*Artemisiospiza nevadensis*

Saltlover
*Halogeton glomeratus*

California coreopsis
*Leptosyne californica*

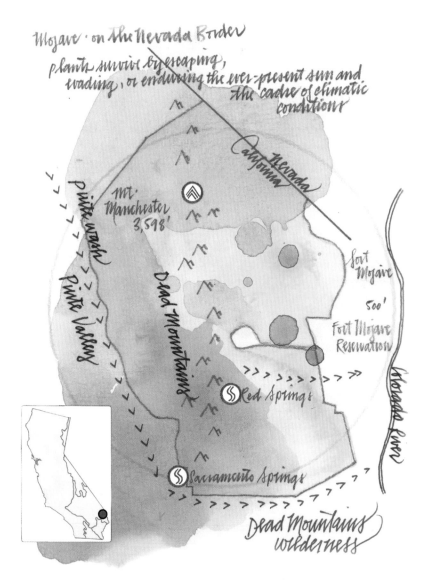

Mojave · on the Nevada Border

plants survive by escaping,
evading, or enduring the ever-present sun and
the cache of climatic
conditions

Mt.
Manchester
3,598'

Dead Mountains

Piute wash

Piute Valley

California

Nevada

Fort
Mojave

500'

Fort Mojave
Reservation

Colorado River

Red Springs

Sacramento Springs

Dead Mountains
wilderness

Map 06.13

## 06.13 BETWEEN THE MOJAVE NATIONAL PRESERVE AND THE COLORADO RIVER
*Dead Mountains Wilderness*

The Dead Mountains are a single ridgeline, about twelve miles in length, that separates the Piute Wash to the west and the Colorado River Basin to the east. Sweeping, dark bajadas fan down to the west of the mountains into Piute Valley. To the east, Fort Mojave Indian Reservation sits between the wilderness and the river.

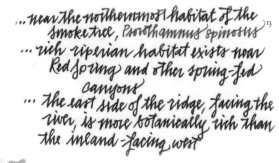

... near the northernmost habitat of the smoke tree, *Psorothamnus spinosus*[13]
... rich riparian habitat exists near Red Spring and other spring-fed canyons
... the east side of the ridge, facing the river, is more botanically rich than the inland-facing, west

Desert tobacco
*Nicotiana obtusifolia*

Generalized elevation range
500–3,600 feet

Land area
47,158 acres
73.69 square miles

Dark-eyed junco
*Junco hyemalis*

Black harvester ant
*Veromessor pergandei*

Desert rock nettle
*Eucnide urens*

Desert tobacco
*Nicotiana obtusifolia*

Dark-eyed junco
*Junco hyemalis*

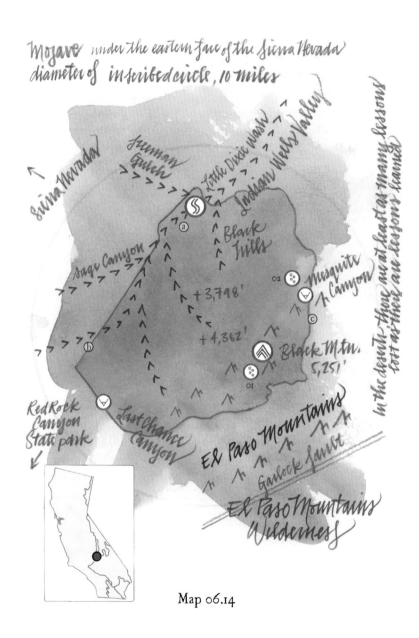

Mojave *under the eastern face of the Sierra Nevada*
diameter of *inscribed circle, 10 miles*

Sierra Nevada

Freeman Gulch

Little Dixie Wash

Indian Wells Valley

Black Hills

Sage Canyon

+ 3,798'

+ 4,362'

Mesquite Canyon

Black Mtn.
5,251'

Red Rock Canyon State Park

Last Chance Canyon

El Paso Mountains

Garlock Fault

El Paso Mountains Wilderness

*In the desert, there are at least as many lessons taught as there are lessons learned*

Map 06.14

## o6.14 MOUNTAIN RANGE ON THE GARLOCK FAULT
*El Paso Mountains Wilderness*

This area is included as part of the El Paso to Golden Valley Wildlife Corridor area of critical environmental concern.[14] The craggy, labyrinthine, seismically active wilderness area offers landscape habitat contiguous with Red Rock Canyon State Park, with which it shares a border.

o1. Black Mountain Trail; more of a route than a trail, the way up Black Mountain from Mesquite Canyon Road is a tough hike up fifteen hundred vertical feet in two and a half miles.

o2. El Paso Mountains Trail; this quiet place full of birds has no trail where maps indicate that one should be.

*... home to some of the highest and densest populations of golden eagles and prairie falcons in the Mojave[15]*

*... inside the Garlock Fault zone, which built the fault-block El Paso Mountains*

*... site of the oldest cenozoic fossils in the Mojave[16]*

a. Freeman Wash Well (spring)
b. Black Hills Well (spring)
c. Sheep Spring

Generalized elevation range
2,800–5,300 feet

Land area
23,679 acres
37.00 square miles

Long-nosed leopard lizard
*Gambelia wislizenii*

Sagebrush sparrow
*Artemisiospiza nevadensis*

White fiesta flower
*Pholistoma membranaceum*

Browneyes
*Chylismia claviformis*

*Prairie falcon*
*Falco mexicanus*

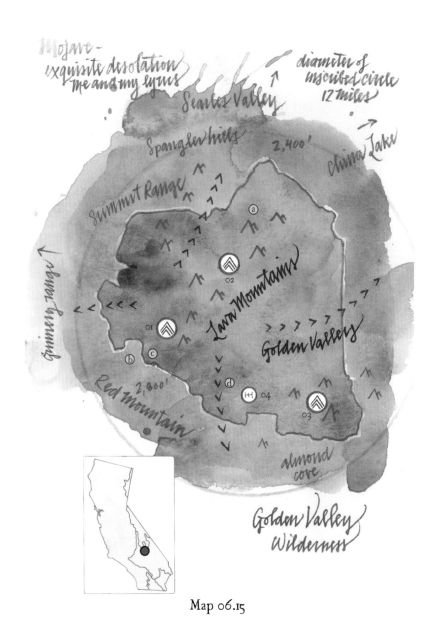

Mojave –
exquisite desolation
me and my lizards

diameter of
inscribed circle
12 miles

Searles Valley

China Lake

Spangler hills

2,400'

Summit Range

Gunnery range

Lava Mountains

Golden Valley

Red Mountain

2,400'

almond cove

Golden Valley
Wilderness

Map 06.15

## 06.15 WILDLIFE CORRIDOR SOUTH OF SEARLES VALLEY
*Golden Valley Wilderness*

Named for the land expanse between Almond Mountain in the south and the
Lava Mountains to the north, both ranges inside the wilderness boundary, Golden
Valley is renowned for its wildflower blooms. The wilderness rises to an elevation
of 4,974 feet above the Searles Valley to the north of Golden Valley, Cuddleback
Lake to the south, and Fremont Valley to the west.

01. Klinker Mountain (4,562')
02. Dome Mountain (4,974')
03. Almond Mountain (4,155')
04. Steam Wells Road

a. Bedrock Spring
b. Sking Well (spring)
c. Mountain Well (spring)
d. Steam Well (spring)

... a core linkage area wilderness connectivity
from China Lake to Edwards Air Force
Base

... core habitat for the Mohave ground
squirrel, *Xerospermophilus
mohavensis*

... a landscape that is best described as
regularly cut by steep, multicolored
canyons built of sedimentary rock

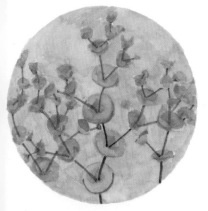

Roundleaf oxytheca
*Oxytheca perfoliata*

Generalized elevation range
3,000–5,000 feet

Land area
37,789 acres
59.04 square miles

Variegated meadowhawk (dragonfly)
*Sympetrum corruptum*

Say's phoebe
*Sayornis saya*

Roundleaf oxytheca
*Oxytheca perfoliata*

White horehound
*Marrubium vulgare* (nonnative)

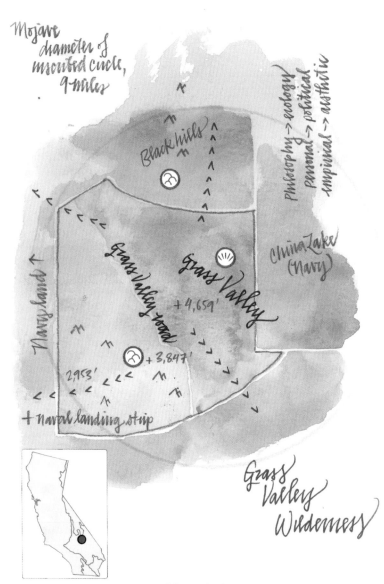

Mojave
diameter of
inscribed circle,
9 miles

Black hills

Philosophy → ecology
personal → political
empirical → aesthetic

China Lake
(Navy)

Grass Valley

+ 4,659'

Grass Valley road

Navy lands

+ 3,847'

2,953'

+ naval landing strip

Grass
Valley
Wilderness

Map 06.16

# o6.16 DESERT PRAIRIE NORTH OF BARSTOW
*Grass Valley Wilderness*

The Barstow–Red Mountain Road runs diagonally down the middle of the wilderness and is the only trail across these low mountains. The wilderness shares its eastern border with China Lake navy base's South Range, and it is easy to see Slocum Mountain (5,124') inside the base, three miles from the wilderness boundary.

*... core habitat for the black-tailed gnatcatcher, Polioptila melanura, a non-migratory bird and a species of special concern*
*... a rolling landscape with no peaks and extensive creosote shrublands and wildflower meadows*
*... unique desert prairie grassland offers habitat to a variety of raptor species*

Black-tailed gnatcatcher

Generalized elevation range
3,000–4,700 feet

Land area
30,186 acres
47.17 square miles

Chisel-toothed kangaroo rat
*Dipodomys microps*

Desert green hairstreak
*Callophrys comstocki*

Thistle sage
*Salvia carduacea*

Sandblossom
*Linanthus parryae*

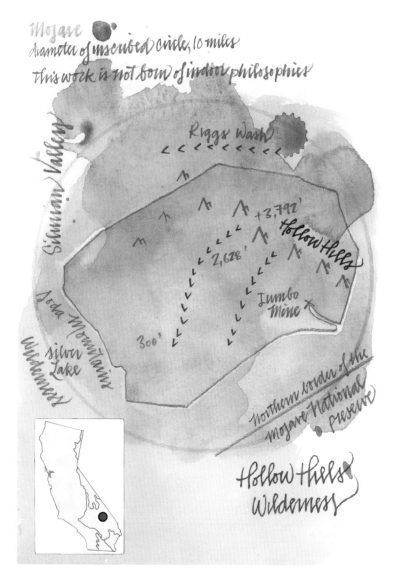

Mojave
diameter of inscribed circle, 10 miles
this work is not born of indoor philosophies

Riggs Wash

Siberian Valley

+3,792'

Hollow Hills

2,628'

Soda Mountains

Jumbo Mine

Silver Lake Wilderness

300'

Northern border of the
Mojave National Preserve

Hollow Hills
Wilderness

Map 06.17

## 06.17 BETWEEN THE MOJAVE NATIONAL PRESERVE AND FORT IRWIN
*Hollow Hills Wilderness*

Just a couple of miles north of the little town of Baker, on the road to Death Valley, the first wilderness area north of the Mojave National Preserve is the Hollow Hills Wilderness. The bajada that fans southwest from the mountains inside the wilderness area descends into the dry lake basin known as Silver Lake. Silver Lake is part of a dry lake network that includes Soda Lake to the south.

... Silver Lake and Soda Lake were once part of
Lake Mojave, a Holocene lake that dried up
approximately nine thousand years ago [17]
... no trails penetrate the mountains except
for the faded route to the abandoned gold
mine called Jumbo Mine
... Precambrian mountains include deposits
of metamorphic rock called gneiss that is
at least two billion years old. [18]

Rosy boa
*Lichanura trivirgata*

Generalized elevation range
1,600–3,900 feet

Land area
22,366 acres
34.97 square miles

Rosy boa
*Lichanura trivirgata*

Bernardino dotted-blue
*Euphilotes bernardino*

Paper bag bush
*Scutellaria mexicana*

Spiny menodora
*Menodora spinescens*

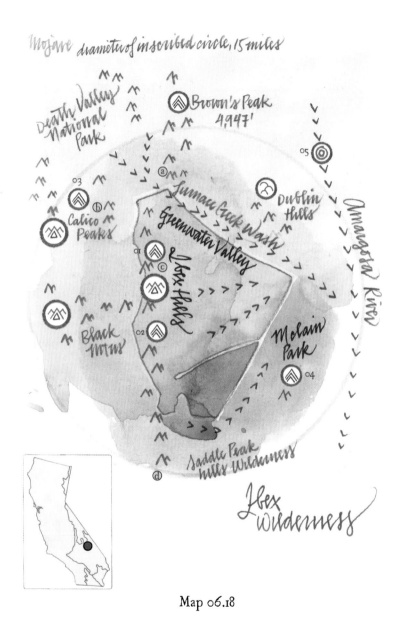

Mojave diameter of inscribed circle, 15 miles

Death Valley National Park

Brown's Peak 4,947'

○5

○3

Calico Peaks

Furnace Creek Wash

Dublin Hills

Greenwater Valley

Ibex Hills

Amargosa River

Black Mtns

○2

Molvin Park

○4

Saddle Peak Hills Wilderness

Ibex Wilderness

Map 06.18

## 06.18 NORTH OF THE BEND IN THE ARMARGOSA RIVER
*Ibex Wilderness*

The northern, taller half of the Ibex Hills lies within the Ibex Wilderness Area, and the rest of it is inside the Death Valley Wilderness Area. The craggy mountains—which they are, not "hills"—are a divide between the Death Valley–Amargosa River watershed to the west and the Furnace Creek Wash to the east (which itself is a tributary of the Amargosa).

01. Sheephead Mountain (4,270')
02. Ibex Peak (4,752')
03. Salsberry Peak (4,254')
04. Tecopa Peak (2,671')
05. Shoshone

a. Miller Spring
b. Montgomery Spring
c. Sheephead Spring
d. Saratova Spring

*... Ibex is a reference to the bighorn, who are most likely extirpated from the region and this range*

*... The Amargosa river forms a U shape around the Ibex hills and switches from flowing north-south from its headwaters to flowing south-north through Death Valley*

*... most of the wilderness is occupied by McLain Park, an east-facing bajada, west of Tecopa and Shoshone, both on the Amargosa river*

Generalized elevation range
3,000–4,800 feet

Land area
28,822 acres
45.03 square miles

Southern grasshopper mouse
*Onychomys torridus*

Great Basin collared lizard
*Crotaphytus bicinctores*

Catclaw acacia
*Senegalia greggii*

Desert plantain
*Plantago ovata*

Southern grasshopper mouse
*Onychomys torridus*

331

Mojave
diameter of inscribed circle, 24 miles

Mojave River Wash

Devil's Playground

Mojave Nat'l Preserve

Kelso Wash

Mesquite Hills

Bristol Mtns.

Broadwish Wash

Broadwell Lake (dry)

2,494'

3,379'

Bristol Mtns.

Old Dad Mtns.

Kelso Dunes Wilderness

Map 06.19

# 06.19 BRISTOL MOUNTAINS WEST OF THE MOJAVE NATIONAL PRESERVE
*Kelso Dunes Wilderness*

The Kelso Dunes system rises from the surrounding desert several miles to the east of the wilderness area and is completely within the Mojave National Preserve. Encompassing the northern end of the Bristol Mountains, Kelso Dunes Wilderness is surrounded by the Mojave Trails National Monument to its west and north, the Mojave National Preserve to its east, and the Bristol Mountains Wilderness to its south.

01. McGorman Peak (3,225')
02. Natural arch
03. Broadwell Mesa (2,893')
04. Crucero Hill (1,568')

a. Hyten Spring

*... there are no sand dunes inside the wilderness area*

*... mountainous areas are granite spires surrounded by sweeping bajadas*

*... centrally located and part of essential connectivity habitat for dozens of species*

*Dune evening primrose*
*Oenothera deltoides*

Generalized elevation range
1,000–3,300 feet

Land area
144,915 acres
226.43 square miles

Western whiptail
*Aspidoscelis tigris*

LeConte's thrasher
*Toxostoma lecontei*

Dune evening primrose
*Oenothera deltoides*

Gilia beardtongue
*Penstemon ambiguus*

*western whiptail*
*Aspidoscelis tigris*

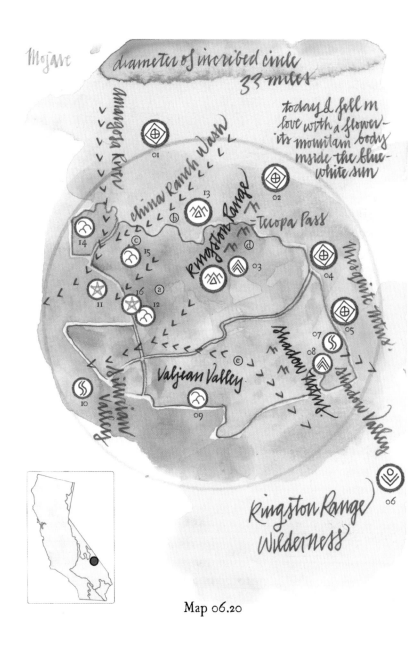

Mojave

diameter of inscribed circle
33 miles

today I fell in
love with a flower —
its mountain body
inside the blue-
white sun

Amargosa River

China Ranch Wash

Kingston Range

= Tecopa Pass

Mesquite Mtns.

Shadow Valley

Shadow Mtns.

Silurian Valley

Valjean Valley

Kingston Range
Wilderness

Map 06.20

## 06.20 MOUNTAINOUS HABITAT SOUTHEAST OF DEATH VALLEY
*Kingston Range Wilderness*

One of the great peaks of the Mojave Desert, Kingston Peak attains an elevation of 7,323 feet, rising between the Silurian Valley to the south and the Pahrump Valley to the north. A refugia habitat for many species for millennia, the wilderness area continues to be so, as it is today one of a small handful of sites in the California desert where you can find such species as white fir, *Abies concolor*, and the Gila monster, *Heloderma suspectum*.

01. South Nopah Range Wilderness
02. Pahrump Valley Wilderness
03. Kingston Peak (7,323')
04. North Mesquite Mountains Wilderness
05. Mesquite Wilderness
06. Mojave National Preserve
07. Kingston Wash
08. Shadow Mountain (4,197')
09. Silurian Hills (3,707')
10. Silurian Lake (dry)
11. Dumont Sand Dunes (1,238')
12. Valjean Hills (2,168')
13. Livingston Range
14. Sperry Hills
15. Dumont Hills
16. Valjean Dunes (1,150')

a. Rabbit Holes Spring
b. Tule Spring
c. Willow Spring
d. Horse Thief Springs
e. Kingston Springs

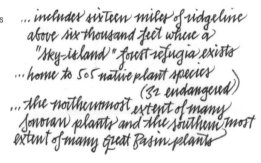

*... includes sixteen miles of ridgeline above six thousand feet where a "sky-island" forest-refugia exists*

*... home to 505 native plant species (32 endangered)*

*... the northernmost extent of many Sonoran plants and the southernmost extent of many Great Basin plants*

Generalized elevation range
1,500–7,400 feet

———

Land area
252,149 acres
393.98 square miles

———

Zebra-tailed lizard
*Callisaurus draconoides*

Inflated beetle
*Cysteodemus armatus*

———

Wallace's woolly daisy
*Eriophyllum wallacei*

Lilac sunbonnet
*Langloisia setosissima*

*Inflated beetle
Cysteodemus armatus*

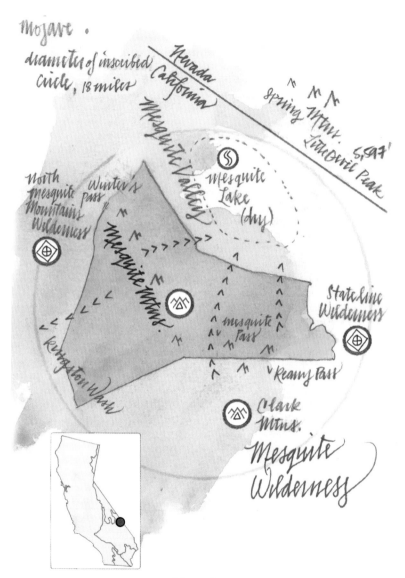

Mojave .

diameter of inscribed
circle, 18 miles

Nevada
California

Spring Mtns. 5,597'
Little Devil Peak

Mesquite Valley

Mesquite
Lake
(dry)

North
mesquite pass
Mountains
Wilderness

Winter's
Pass

Mesquite Mtns.

Mesquite Mtns.

Stateline
Wilderness

mesquite
Pass

Kingston Wash

Kearny Pass

Clark
Mtns.

Mesquite
Wilderness

Map o6.21

## o6.21 LOW MOUNTAINS EAST OF THE KINGSTON RANGE
*Mesquite Wilderness*

Part of a wilderness network that dominates the land area east of Death Valley and north of the Mojave National Preserve, this wilderness is flanked by several wilderness areas that ensure the preservation of this land's ancient character. Species of special concern included in the vernal bloom include Rusby's desert mallow, *Sphaeralcea rusbyi* var. *eremicola*.

... comprising low limestone hills dotted
with dense stands of Joshua tree
... dominated by shrubland that explodes
with color in the vernal wildflower bloom
... many species of bat make habitat in
the many caves of this mountainous
wilderness

phainopepla
*Phainopepla nitens*

Rusby's desert mallow
*Sphaeralcea rusbyi*
var. *eremicola*

Generalized elevation range
3,000–4,600 feet

Land area
44,804 acres
70.00 square miles

Phainopepla
*Phainopepla nitens*

Schinia ligeae moth
*Schinia ligeae*

Desert larkspur
*Delphinium parishii*

Notch-leaf scorpion-weed
*Phacelia crenulata*

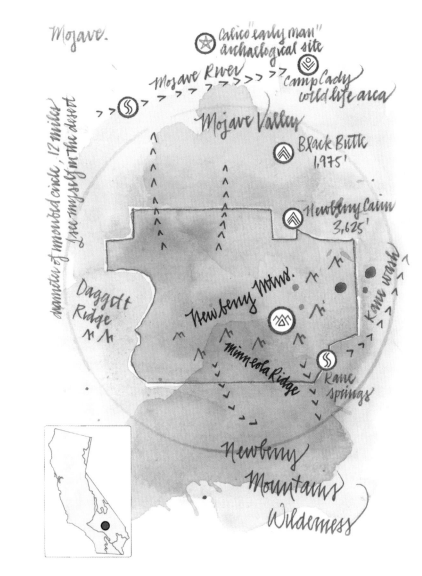

Mojave.

Calico "early man" archaeological site

Mojave River

Camp Cady wild life area

Mojave Valley

Black Butte 1,975'

Newberry Cairn 3,625'

diameter of imaginal circle, 12 miles lose myself in the desert

Daggett Ridge

Newberry Mtns.

Kane wash

Minneola Ridge

Kane springs

Newberry Mountains Wilderness

Map 06.22

## o6.22 CRAGGY MOUNTAINS SOUTH OF THE MOJAVE RIVER
*Newberry Mountains Wilderness*

South of the Mojave River—twenty miles after the elbow in the Mojave Desert's primary watercourse where it begins to flow to the east—the Newberry Mountains Wilderness, a maze of sedimentary and volcanic stones, sits at the eastern border of the Antelope Valley.

*... there are no trails but those of the bighorn, who migrate from here to Rodman Mountains and back*

*... critical habitat for many species integral to desert connectivity, including potential habitat for the Mojave mountain lion, Puma concolor*

*... this range is an uplifted tangle of Miocene volcanic rocks south of the Mojave River valley*

Desert bluebells
*Phacelia campanularia*

Generalized elevation range
2,200–5,100 feet

Land area
26,102 acres
40.78 square miles

Red-tailed hawk
*Buteo jamaicensis*

Desert tarantula
*Aphonopelma iodius*

Desert bluebells
*Phacelia campanularia*

Desert snow
*Linanthus demissus*

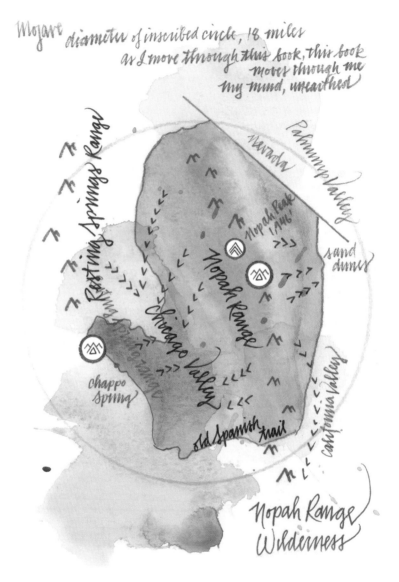

Mojave diameter of inscribed circle, 18 miles
as I move through this book, this book
moves through me
my mind, unearthed

Nevada

Pahrump Valley

Resting Springs Range

Nopah Peak
1,946'

sand dunes

Nopah Range

Chicago Valley

Resting Springs Range

Chappo Spring

Old Spanish Trail

California Valley

Nopah Range
Wilderness

Map 06.23

## 06.23 DRY MOUNTAINS EAST OF SHOSHONE
*Nopah Range Wilderness*

Like its neighboring wilderness area the Kingston Range, the Nopah Range also has a long ridgeline, albeit a few thousand feet lower than the Kingston ridgeline to the south, that offers a bit of habitat refugia over its eighteen-mile length. The ancient limestone Nopah Range rises over four thousand feet above the Pahrump Valley to the east and the Chicago Valley to the west.

*... yucca and cactus landscapes climb bajadas east of the Amargosa River*

*... provides corridor linkage and core habitat for lizard and bat species*

*... old Spanish Trail separates this wilderness from the South Nopah Range*

Generalized elevation range
1,800–6,400 feet

Land area
106,623 acres
166.59 square miles

California mantis
*Stagmomantis californica*

Ground snake
*Sonora semiannulata*

Three hearts
*Tricardia watsonii*

Stansbury's cliffrose
*Purshia stansburyana*

California mantis
*Stagmomantis californica*

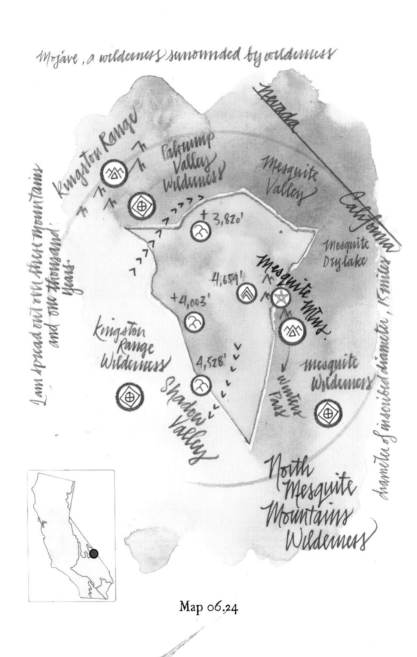

Mojave, a wilderness surrounded by wilderness

North
Mesquite
Mountains
Wilderness

Map 06.24

## 06.24 LOW HILLS NORTH OF CLARK MOUNTAIN
*North Mesquite Mountains Wilderness*

A wedge-shaped land designation between the Kingston Range and the larger body of the Mesquite Mountains, the North Mesquite Mountains Wilderness is separated from the rest of the range at Winters Pass.

*... limestone, dolomite, and gneiss stones
compose these hills
... extensive Joshua tree forest
... mining activity has left roads
scarring the land*

*Ceraunus blue
Hemiargus ceraunus*

*Dorr's sage
Salvia dorrii*

Generalized elevation range
500 to 4,200 feet

Land area
28,955 acres
45.24 square miles

Ceraunus blue
*Hemiargus ceraunus*

Creosote bush bagworm
*Thyridopteryx meadii*

Cooper's dogweed
*Adenophyllum cooperi*

Dorr's sage
*Salvia dorrii*

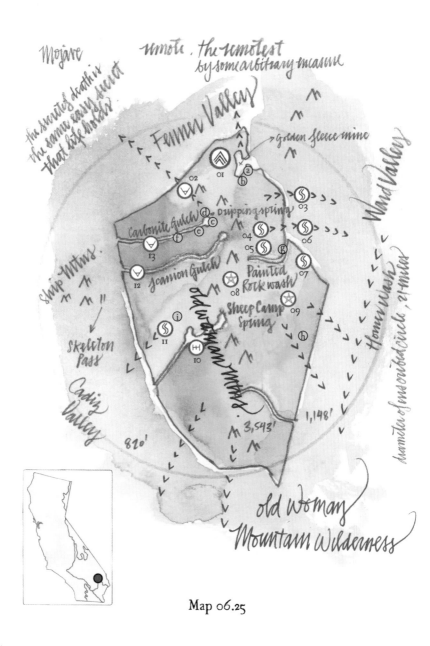

Mojave

remote. the remotest
by some arbitrary measure

the secretest death is
the same easy secret
that life holds

Fermen Valley

green fleece mine

Ward Valley

o2

01

a

b

o3

Dripping spring

Carbonite Gulch

d

c

o4

o6

f

o5

g

13

o7

Ship Mitns.

12

Scanion Gulch

Painted
Rock wash

o8

Sheep Camp
Spring

o9

old woman mtns

Homer Wash

diameter of inscribed circle, 21 miles

i

11

Skeleton
Pass

h

10

Cadiz
Valley

820'

3,543'

1,148'

old Woman

Mountain Wilderness

Map 06.25

344

# 06.25 BETWEEN THE MOJAVE AND THE SONORAN
*Old Woman Mountains Wilderness*

Between two enormous valleys, Fenner Valley to the west and Ward Valley to the east, the Old Woman Mountains exhibit an enormous variety of biodiversity and habitat types. Near the center of this 35-mile-long, 28-mile-wide range is a large granite boulder called Old Woman Statue, the namesake of the wilderness.

01. Mercury Mountain (3,720')
02. Willow Spring Wash;
    Willow Spring Canyon
03. Big Wash
04. Paramount Wash
05. Sunflower Spring
06. Sunflower Wash
07. Painted-Rock Wash
08. Old Woman Statue
09. Painted Rock
10. Black Metal Mine
11. Browns Wash
12. Scanion Gulch
13. Carbonite Gulch

a. Weaver Well
b. Honeymoon Spring
c. Paramount Spring
d. Sweetwater Spring
e. Willow Spring
f. Dripping Spring
g. Sunflower Spring
h. Wilhelm Spring
i. Sheep Camp Spring

*... lone mountain range holds a variety of habitat types in the transition zone between the Mojave and Sonoran Deserts*

*... numerous springs and juniper woodland refugia at higher elevations*

*... extensive historical mining of metals, including tungsten, lead, and mercury*

old woman statue

Generalized elevation range
800–5,300 feet

Land area
165,172 acres
258.08 square miles

Black swallowtail
*Papilio polyxenes*

Cactus wren
*Campylorhynchus brunneicapillus*

Bigfoot hybrid rockcress
*Boechera xylopoda*

California barrel cactus
*Ferocactus cylindraceus*

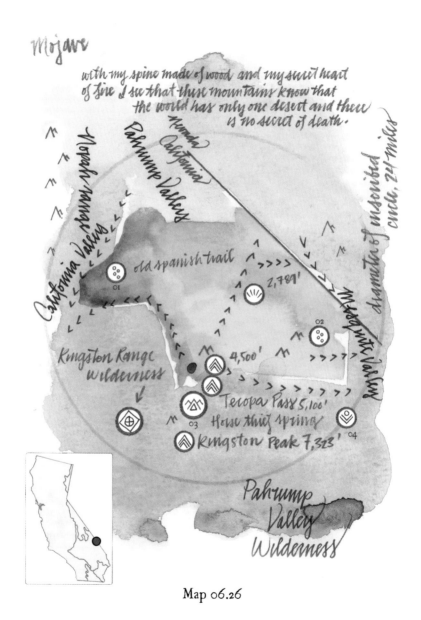

Mojave

with my spine made of wood and my sweet heart
of fire I see that these mountains know that
the world has only one desert and there
is no secret of death.

Nevada
California

Pahrump Valley

Nopah Range

California Valley

old spanish trail

2,789'

01

02

diameter of inscribed
circle, 24 miles

Mesquite Valley

Kingston Range
wilderness

4,500'

Tecopa Pass 5,100'
Horse thief spring
03
Kingston Peak 7,323'

04

Pahrump
Valley
Wilderness

Map 06.26

## 06.26 BAJADAS NORTH OF KINGSTON RANGE
*Pahrump Valley Wilderness*

Three valleys make up the land area of this wilderness: the California, the Mesquite, and the south end of the Pahrump. The wilderness includes the northern washes of the Kingston Range, and its northern border is the Nevada state line.

01. Spanish National Trail
02. Old Traction Road
03. Kingston Range
04. State Burro Sanctuary

*... contains numerous yucca-filled valleys on the northern edge of the kingston range*

*... mostly rolling bajadas and easy to walk across*

*... transected by the Old Spanish-National Historic Trail; the wilderness has no other trails*

*Western big-eared bat*
*Plecotus townsendii*

*burro skeletons are common in the backcountry*

Generalized elevation range
2,720–4,600 feet

Land area
73,726 acres
115.20 square miles

Feral burro
*Equus asinus*

Western big-eared bat
*Plecotus townsendii*

White fiesta flower
*Pholistoma membranaceum*

Mojave aster
*Xylorhiza tortifolia*

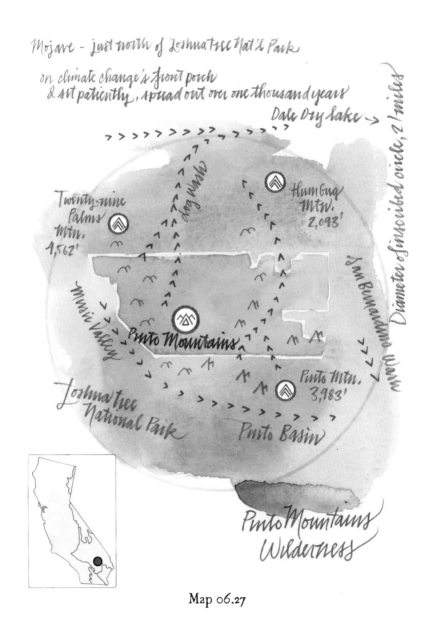

Mojave - just north of Joshua Tree Nat'l Park

on climate change's front porch
& sit patiently, spread out over one thousand years

Dale Dry Lake →

Diameter of inscribed circle, 21 miles

Dog Wash

Twenty-nine
Palms
Mtn.
4,562'

Hum Bug
Mtn.
2,093'

San Bernardino

Music Valley

Pinto Mountains

Joshua Tree
National Park

Pinto Mtn.
3,983'

Pinto Basin

Pinto Mountains
Wilderness

Map 06.27

## 06.27 SHARING THE NORTHERN BORDER OF JOSHUA TREE
*Pinto Mountains Wilderness*

Sharing its southern border with Joshua Tree National Park, Pinto Mountains Wilderness does not hold the lion's share of the Pinto Mountains themselves. Most of the range is inside the park. Rising from the Pinto Basin, a sprawling alluvial wash to their south, the Pinto Mountains are generally a series of sharp spines that reach a height of 4,560 feet at Twentynine Palms Peak, north of the wilderness area.

... provides essential desert tortoise habitat and ecological connectivity with Joshua Tree National Park

... remains largely untouched although much of the range has been degraded by historical mining

... range composed mostly of gneiss, a metamorphic rock

Bendire's thrasher
*Toxostoma bendirei*

Generalized elevation range
2,200–4,000 feet

Land area
24,348 acres
38.04 square miles

Bendire's thrasher
*Toxostoma bendirei*

California leaf-nosed bat
*Macrotus californicus*

Evening snow
*Linathus dichotomus*

Strigose bird's-foot trefoil
*Ottleya strigosa*

349

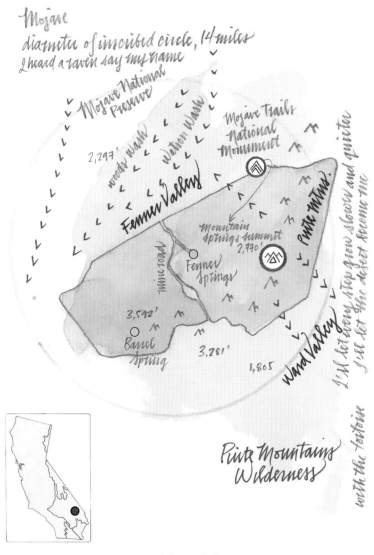

Mojave
diameter of inscribed circle, 14 miles
I heard a raven say my name

Mojave National
Preserve

woody wash

watson wash

2,297'

Fenner Valley

Mojave Trails
National
Monument

Pinto mtns.

mine road

Mountain
springs summit
2,770'

Fenner
Springs

3,592'

Barrel
Spring

3,281'

1,805

Ward Valley

I'll let every step grow slower and quieter
I'll set the desert become time

Pinto Mountains
Wilderness

with the tortoise

Map 06.28

## o6.28 ACROSS THE FENNER VALLEY, SOUTH OF MOJAVE NATIONAL PRESERVE
*Piute Mountains Wilderness*

The southern half of the Piute Mountains is designated wilderness, and the northern half lies just south of the Mojave National Preserve. Between two broad, alluvial washes—Fenner Valley to the north and Ward Valley to the south—the Piute Mountains and the much smaller Little Piute Mountains (south of the wilderness) run parallel to each other northeast of Old Woman Mountains.

... home to a relatively high density of desert
tortoise - up to fifty per square mile [19]
... these mountains are a Paleozoic metamorphosed
range, not a standard fault-block range [20]
... shrubland ecology, rich in diversity,
includes plants of both the Mojave
and Sonoran deserts

Thisbe's tarantula-hawk wasp
*Pepsis thisbe*

chia
*Salvia columbariae*

Generalized elevation range
1,000–3,700 feet

Land area
48,080 acres
62.63 square miles

Gopher snake
*Pituophis catenifer*

Thisbe's tarantula-hawk wasp
*Pepsis thisbe*

Chia
*Salvia columbariae*

Plain mariposa lily
*Calochortus invenustus*

Mojave northern-most Mojave in California
the valleys that exit Mecho.

diameter of the inscribed circle, 17 miles

Nevada
California

+2,500'

Resting Springs
wilderness
Study Area
+3,000'

Shadow
Mountain
5,067'

+2,000'

Eagle
Mountain
3,806'

dry lake

Stewart
Valley
2,400'

5,753'

Death
Valley
National
Park

Amargosa River

old mine road

Resting Springs Range

desert river in my dreams

Nopah
Range
wilderness

Resting Springs
Range
Wilderness

Map 06.29

## 06.29 EASTERN FLANK OF THE AMARGOSA WATERSHED
*Resting Spring Range Wilderness*

South of the Funeral Mountains, east of Death Valley National Park, the promontory peak, Eagle Mountain, stands over the Amargosa River on the western border of the Resting Spring Range Wilderness. The Nevada state line is the northeasterly border, and the Nopah Range Wilderness to the east completes the surrounding land areas of the wilderness.

*... no trails cut through this remote and colorful mountain wilderness*

*... contains significant populations of wild horse, wild burro, and bighorn*

*... shares connective ecology with the Nopah range to the south*

*wild horses of the mojave*

Generalized elevation range
2,000–5,300 feet

Land area
76,312 acres
119.24 square miles

Sawfinger scorpions
*Serradigitus* spp.

Metallic
wood-boring beetle
*Gyascutus planicosta*

Bigelow's
monkeyflower
*Diplacus bigelovii*

Granite prickly phlox
*Linanthus pungens*

353

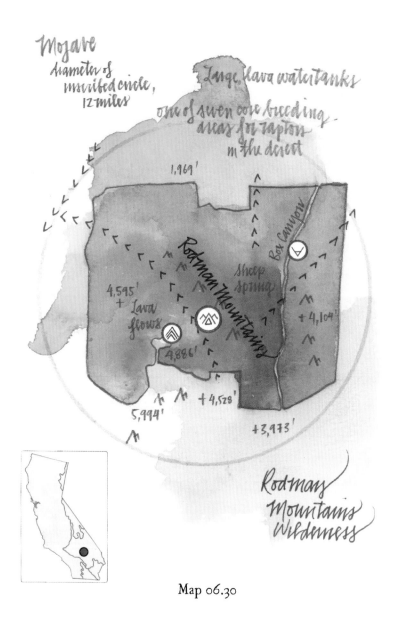

Mojave
diameter of
inscribed circle,
12 miles

Large lava water tanks

one of seven core breeding
areas for raptors
in the desert

1,969'

Box Canyon

Rodman Mountains

Sheep
Spring

4,595'
+ Lava
flows

+ 4,104'

4,886'

+ 4,528'

5,994'

+ 3,973'

Rodman
Mountains
Wilderness

Map 06.30

## 06.30 LAVA LANDS SOUTH OF THE MOJAVE RIVER
*Rodman Mountains Wilderness*

South of the Mojave River valley in the tangle of mountains west of the Bullion Mountains, the Rodman Mountains comprise fault-block ridges and volcanic mesas. A geologic anomaly accounts for the presence of a couple of large water reservoirs inside hollow spaces of cooled lava stone within the wilderness. Both reservoirs hold thousands of gallons of ancient water.

*... provides wildlife linkage with the Bullion Mountains and the Newberry Mountains*

*... the bighorn population has been extirpated, but may be reintroduced from the adjacent population in the Newberry Mountains*

*... core breeding habitat for many species of raptor*

lesser nighthawk
*Chordiles acutipennis*

Generalized elevation range
2,000–5,000 feet

Land area
34,264 acres
53.54 square miles

American pipit
*Anthus rubescens*

White-bowed
smoothwing (fly)
*Scaeva affinis*

Desert globemallow
*Sphaeralcea ambigua*

Desert bluebell
*Phacelia campanularia*

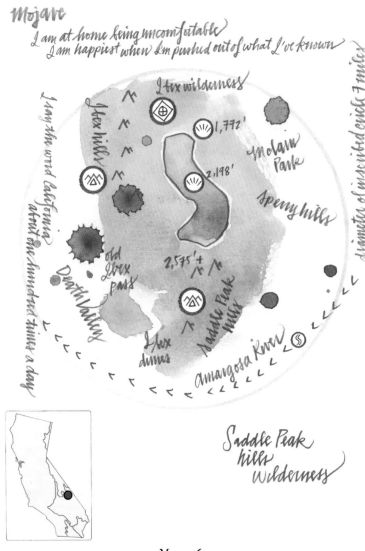

Mojave

I am at home being uncomfortable
I am happiest when I'm pushed out of what I've known

Ibex wilderness

Ibex hills

1,772'

Molasm Park

2,198'

Sperry hills

I say the word California about one hundred times a day

diameter of inscribed circle 7 miles

old Ibex pass

Death Valley

2,575' +

Saddle Peak hills

Ibex dunes

Amargosa River

Saddle Peak hills Wilderness

Map 06.31

## 06.31 TINY WILDERNESS NEAR THE SOUTH OF DEATH VALLEY
*Saddle Peak Hills Wilderness*

At just a few square miles, the Saddle Peak Hills Wilderness is a nexus of several physiographic features: the northwestern end of the Silurian Valley, the northern tip of the Ibex Hills, and the southern end of the Greenwater Valley.

... land designation between the Saddle
Peak hills and the Ibex hills
... also the boundary between Furnace
Creek and Amargosa River watersheds
... the Saddle Peak hills are northwest of
the Kingston Range, and the wilderness
area is the northern corner of this low,
north-south-running range

young mojave bobcat

Generalized elevation range
500–2,500 feet

Land area
1,530 acres
2.39 square miles

Black-tailed jackrabbit
*Lepus californicus*

Bobcat
*Lynx rufus*

Desert shaggy mane
(mushroom)
*Podaxis pistillaris*

Yellow cups
*Chylismia brevipes*

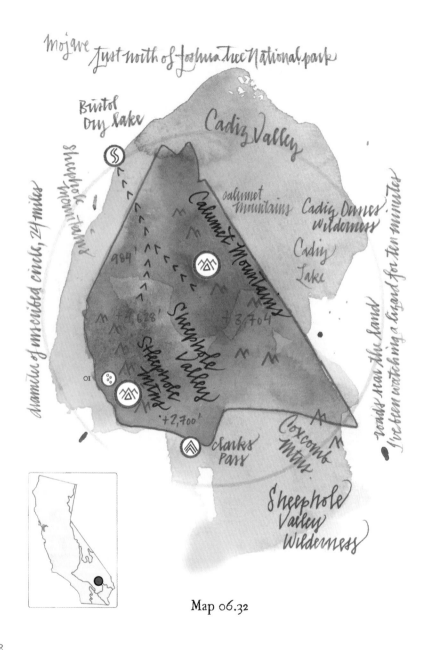

Mojave

Just north of Joshua Tree National park

Bristol Dry Lake

Cadiz Valley

Sheephole Mountains

diameter of inscribed circle, 24 miles

calumet mountains

Calumet Mountains

Cadiz Dunes Wilderness

Cadiz Lake

984

+1,628'

+3,704'

Sheephole Valley

Sheephole Mtns

+2,700'

01

Clarks Pass

Coxcomb Mtns

roads near the sand

I've been watching a lizard for ten minutes

Sheephole Valley Wilderness

Map 06.32

# 06.32 TWO MOUNTAIN RANGES NORTH OF JOSHUA TREE
*Sheephole Valley Wilderness*

Sheephole Valley runs between two mountain ranges, both of which are inside the boundaries of its namesake wilderness. The Calumet Mountains, the eastern range, rise to an elevation of 3,723 feet. The Sheephole Mountains, the western range, rise to an elevation of 4,613 feet.

01. Sheep Hole Mountain Trail, a five-mile scramble route around what has been described as a "pile of rocks"[21] that extends from 2,226' to 4,746'.

*... until 1950, the Sheephole mountains were part of Joshua Tree National Park*

*... there are sand dune ecosystems at several locations, and include the plant Borrego milkvetch, Astragalus lentiginosus var. boreganus*

*... mesozoic granite mountains rise two thousand feet from the valley floor*

Generalized elevation range
2,000–4,700 feet

Land area
188,169 acres
294.01 square miles

Golden eagle
*Aquila chrysaetos*

Merriam's kangaroo rat
*Dipodomys merriami*

Cleveland's beardtongue
*Penstemon clevelandii*
var. *mohavensis*

Alverson's pincushion cactus
*Coryphantha vivipara*
var. *alversonii*

*alverson's pincushion cactus (Coryphantha vivipara var. alversonii*

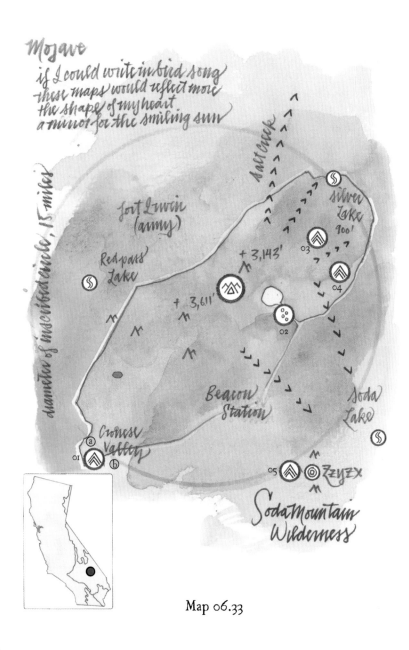

Mojave

if I could write in bird song
these maps would reflect more
the shape of my heart.
a mirror for the smiling sun

Fort Irwin
(army)

Red pass
Lake

Ant creek

silver
Lake
900'

○3

○4

+ 3,143'

+ 3,611'

○2

Beacon
Station

Soda
Lake

diameter of inscribed circle, 15 miles

Crouese
Valley

○ a

or

○ b

○5

Zzyzx

Soda Mountain
Wilderness

Map 06.33

# 06.33 CRITICAL HABITAT NORTH OF MOJAVE NATIONAL PRESERVE
*Soda Mountain Wilderness*

The Soda Mountain range constitutes the main body of the Soda Mountain Wilderness. South of the Soda Mountains, across a small valley, is an even smaller, independent mountain range called the Cronise Mountains. The Soda Mountains rise over Soda Lake, a dry lake inside the Mojave National Preserve and the mouth of the Mojave River.

01. Cronise Mountain (2,209')
02. Zzyzx trail
03. Otto Mountain (1,725')
04. Nickel Mountain (1,395')
05. Noels Knoll (1,572')

a. West Cronise Lake (1,148')
b. East Cronise Lake

*... two intermittent, pluvial lakes allow habitat for migratory birds, including the endangered Yuma clapper rail Rallus obsoletus yumanensis*

*... essential connectivity habitat for bighorn*

*... the area is the site of a long-running debate over a contentious potential Solar energy array*

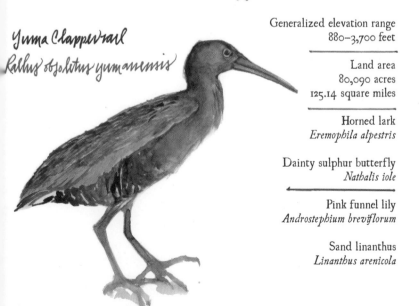

*Yuma Clapper rail*
*Rallus obsoletus yumanensis*

Generalized elevation range
880–3,700 feet

Land area
80,090 acres
125.14 square miles

Horned lark
*Eremophila alpestris*

Dainty sulphur butterfly
*Nathalis iole*

Pink funnel lily
*Androstephium breviflorum*

Sand linanthus
*Linanthus arenicola*

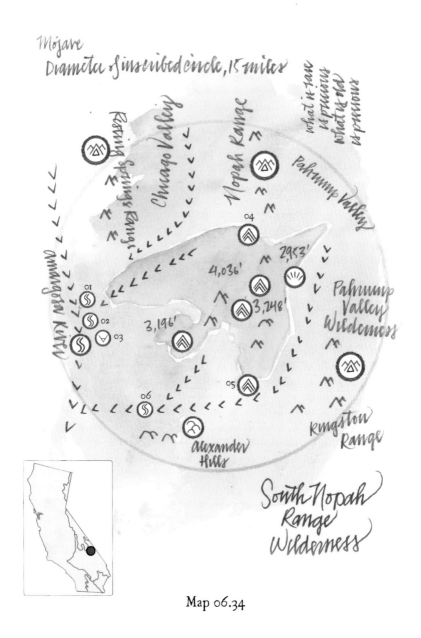

Mojave

Diameter of inscribed circle, 15 miles

what it rare
is precious
what is not
is precious

Resting Springs Range

Chicago Valley

Nopah Range

Pahrump Valley

04

2,953'

4,036'

Pahrump Valley Wilderness

01

3,248'

02

03

3,196'

3,148'

05

06

Alexander Hills

Kingston Range

Amargosa River

South Nopah Range Wilderness

Map 06.34

## 06.34 SMALL PEAKS EAST OF TECOPA
*South Nopah Range Wilderness*

This is a keystone piece of wilderness land surrounded on three of its four sides by other wilderness areas: Nopah Range Wilderness to the north, Pahrump Valley Wilderness to its east, and Kingston Range Wilderness to its south. The wilderness is irregularly shaped, as its boundaries were drawn around historical mining operations.

01. Tecopa Hot Springs
02. Grimshaw Lake
03. Amargosa Canyon
04. Emigrant Pass
05. Tecopa Pass
06. China Ranch Wash

... the southern tip of the Nopah Range,
which divides the Chicago Valley from
the California Valley

... sedimentary rocks and long, low
bajadas define the land's profile

... there are no permanent trails and
no dependable springs

Western banded gecko
*Coleonyx variegatus*

Generalized elevation range
1,500–4,200 feet

Land area
17,059 acres
26.65 square miles

Western banded gecko
*Coleonyx variegatus*

Blue dasher
*Pachydiplax longipennis*

Tuber anemone
*Anemone tuberosa*

Mojave sage
*Salvia mohavensis*

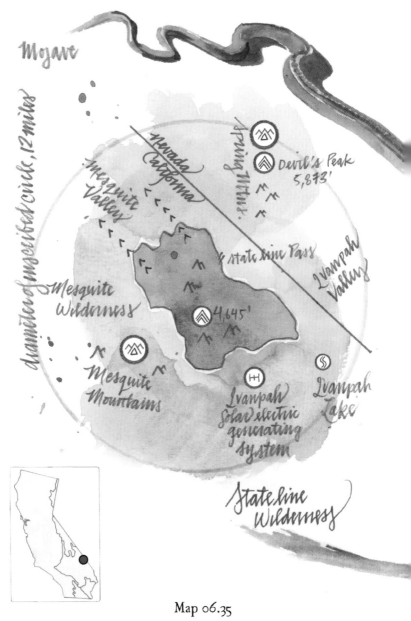

Mojave

diameter of inscribed circle, 12 miles

Nevada / California

Spring Mtns.

Devil's Peak
5,873'

Mesquite Valley

State Line Pass

Ivanpah Valley

Mesquite Wilderness

4,645'

Mesquite Mountains

Ivanpah Solar electric generating system

Ivanpah Lake

State line Wilderness

Map 06.35

# 06.35 CAVE-FILLED HILLS NORTH OF CLARK MOUNTAIN
*Stateline Wilderness*

The Stateline Wilderness comprises a few north–south-running ridgelines that rise 1,500 feet from the valley floor. This small wilderness area separates two Holocene lakes: Mesquite Lake (dry) to the north, and Ivanpah Lake (dry) to the south.

... there are no permanent springs in these dry, ancient mountains
... a creosote-covered landscape in soil composed of Paleozoic limestone and dolomite
... encompasses the easternmost extent of the Clark Range

m) Patch-nosed snake
*Salvadora hexalepis*

Mojave kangaroo rat
*Dipodomys deserti*

Generalized elevation range
2,500–4,700 feet

Land area
6,964 acres
10.88 square miles

White desert moth
*Schinia ligeae*

California myotis bat
*Myotis californicus*

Fishhook cactus
*Ferocactus wislizeni*

Woolly bursage
*Ambrosia eriocentra*

Mojave

our species is unique in the history of life on earth in being able to embody our animal natures outside of our physical selves and transfer that nature to other members of our community in the form of Story.

homer wash

Ward Valley

Chemehuevi Valley

stepladder mountains

2,926'

Chemehuevi Wash

turtle Mountains wilderness

Stepladder Mountains Wilderness

diameter of inscribed circle, 18 miles

Map 06.36

## 06.36 NORTHERN CHEMEHUEVI VALLEY
*Stepladder Mountains Wilderness*

The Stepladder Mountains are only about twelve thousand acres of the total land area this wilderness is named after. The mountains divide two of the largest washes in the Mojave Desert: the Chemehuevi Wash to the east and the Ward Valley/Homer Wash to the west.

*... home to gardens of crucifixion thorn Castela emoryi*

*... critical tortoise habitat and contains high population densities of the threatened species*

*... ravines full of paloverde, smoke tree, and catclaw riparian habitat*

*blue paloverde*
*Parkinsonia florida*

Generalized elevation range
1,300–3,000 feet

Land area
83,195 acres
129.99 square miles

Black-tailed
gnatcatcher
*Polioptila melanura*

White-throated
wood rat
*Neotoma albigula*

Crucifixion thorn
*Castela emoryi*

White rhatany
*Krameria bicolor*

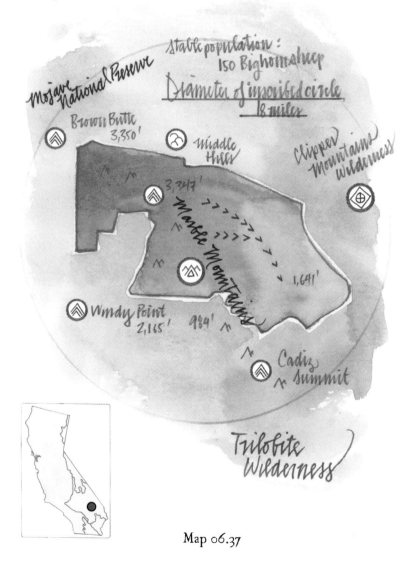

Mojave

Mojave National Preserve

stable population:
150 Bighornsheep

Diameter of inscribed circle
18 miles

Brown Butte
3,350'

Middle Hills

Clipper Mountains Wilderness

3,347'

Marble Mountains

1,641'

Windy Point
2,165'        989'

Cadiz Summit

Trilobite Wilderness

Map 06.37

## 06.37 LONE RANGE NORTH OF CADIZ VALLEY
*Trilobite Wilderness*

The Marble Mountains make up the totality of the land area of the Trilobite Wilderness. These dry mountains have only a few outcrops of actual marble, but appear white and marble-like. The Marble Mountains are a lone mountain range between the Granite Mountains of Mojave National Preserve to the north and the sprawling Cadiz Valley to the south.

*...named for fossils of Paleozoic marine arthropods*
*...the wilderness is inside an eighteen-mile-long volcanic mountain ridge without many springs*
*...the bighorn population of about 150 individuals is the largest local herd*

*desert chicory*
*Rafinesquia neomexicana*

*Monoptilon belioides*
*mojave desert star*

Generalized elevation range
1,000–3,500 feet

Land area
37,308 acres
58.29 square miles

Desert kangaroo rat
*Dipodomys deserti*

Cactus mouse
*Peromyscus eremicus*

Mojave desert star
*Monoptilon bellioides*

Desert chicory
*Rafinesquia neomexicana*

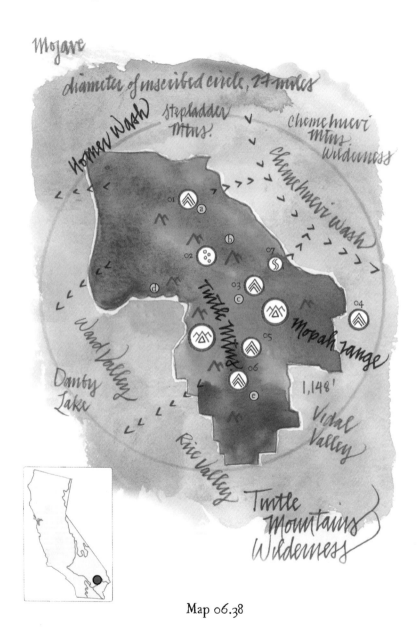

Map 06.38

# 06.38 TRANSITIONAL DESERT EAST OF JOSHUA TREE
*Turtle Mountains Wilderness*

Only a dirt road separates this wilderness from Stepladder Mountains Wilderness to the north. Ward Valley to its west, Chemehuevi Valley to its northeast, Vidal Valley to its southeast, and Rice Valley to its south bound the larger-than-average Turtle Mountains Wilderness.

01. Mexican Hat (2,686')
02. Heritage Trail
03. Mopah Peaks (3,541')
04. Pyramid Butte (1,848')
05. Castle Rock (2,979')
06. Horn Peak (3,737')
07. Gary Wash

a. Mohawk Spring
b. Coffin Springs
c. Mopah Spring
d. Martins Well (spring)
e. Horn Spring

*... Inside the Sonoran Desert Transition zone, the Turtle Mountains are noted for their dramatically composed mountain profiles*

*... Most of the accessible springs in the range are located where modern development established itself prior to the wilderness designation*

*... Northern Sonoran habitat is evident throughout, including palo verde and cactus shrub*

Generalized elevation range
1,000–4,300 feet

Land area
177,309 acres
277.05 square miles

Queen butterfly
*Danaus gilippus*

Desert horned lizard
*Phrynosoma platyrhinos*

Desert penstemon
*Penstemon pseudospectabilis*

Desert milkweed
*Asclepias subulate*

*Queen butterfly*
*Danaus gilippus*

*Desert penstemon*
*Penstemon pseudospectabilis*

Today's environmental rhetoric issues the refrain that the world will end if we don't somehow act now. The Mojave serves as a reminder that the world regularly endures its own end.

the Mojave desert exists as a nested object
inside a larger system of conceptual constructs
like The American West, and the ecosphere.
It is ancient, but it is impermanent.
It is subject to definition.

# 07. OF THE REMOTE AND THE RUGGED
## The Colorado-Sonoran Desert in California

From all directions, you descend into the Colorado Desert, often called the Salton Sink (the basin that was Lake Cahuilla). From the Little San Bernardino Mountains of Joshua Tree National Park, you descend over three thousand feet into the Coachella Valley—the northern Colorado Desert. From the Laguna Mountains, you descend over two thousand feet into the Borrego Valley of Anza-Borrego Desert State Park—the western Colorado Desert. From the Chocolate Mountains, you descend over two thousand feet to the Salton Sea—the eastern Colorado Desert. East of the Chocolate Mountains, a step up from the Colorado and a step down from the Mojave, are the desert mountains and playas of their own identity, the Sonoran Desert in California.

western zebra-tailed lizard
Callisaurus dracoppides

there are nine recognized subspecies across the southwest United States

Font's Point
and the Badlands
Anza-Borrego Desert State Park

What is called the Colorado-Sonoran Desert in this chapter is a compromising naming convention to describe the intersection of desert geographies and ecological subsections. In California, the northern end of the vast Sonoran Desert (see 01.02C) is called the Colorado Desert. Because this unique area encompasses the Lower Colorado River Valley and mainly because the giant saguaro is not found here (except for a few specific places), the desert deserves its own identity as a subsection of the Sonoran.[1] The Colorado Desert has alternate boundaries, depending on which agency is consulted:

The US Environmental Protection Agency (EPA) does not name the Colorado Desert as a bioregion separate from the Sonoran, although it does describe the Chocolate Mountains and the Chuckwalla Mountains as "Central Sonoran/Colorado Desert Mountains and Basins." Notably, all lands west of the Salton Sink in the EPA's analysis of level III and IV ecoregions are called "Western Sonoran."[2]

The California Department of Forestry and Fire Protection (CAL-FIRE) denotes all desert lands in California south of the Mojave Desert in California as the Colorado Desert.[3]

In the *Manual of California Vegetation*, the US Department of Agriculture (USDA) draws a line down the spine of the Chocolate Mountains, separating the Salton Sink and the lands dominated by Anza-Borrego Desert State Park, called the Colorado Desert ecological section, from the lands east of the Chocolate Mountains to the Colorado River, called the Sonoran Desert ecological section.[4]

Does the Colorado Desert exist?

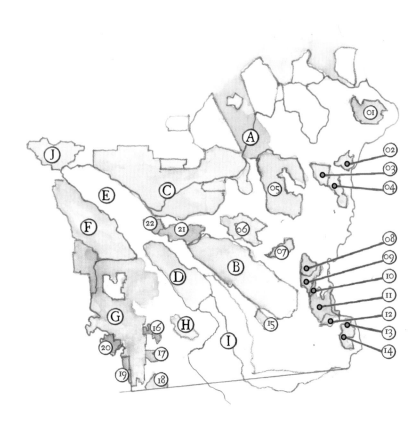

Map 07.01

# 07.01 THE NORTHERN EDGE OF A LARGER SYSTEM
*The Sonoran Desert in California*

The typical botanical landscape of the Sonoran Desert bajada might include creosote, *Larrea tridentata*; burrobush, *Ambrosia dumosa*; ocotillo, *Fouquieria splendens*; beavertail cactus, *Opuntia basilaris*; chollas, *Cylindropuntia* spp.; and barrel cactus, *Echinocactus* sp. and *Ferocactus* sp. In canyons and washes, the plant list might include blue palo verde, *Parkinsonia florida*, and desert ironwood, *Olneya tesota*.

01. Whipple Mountains Wilderness
02. Riverside Mountains Wilderness
03. Rice Valley Wilderness
04. Big Maria Mountains Wilderness
05. Palen/McCoy Wilderness
06. Chuckwalla Mountains Wilderness
07. Little Chuckwalla
    Mountains Wilderness
08. Palo Verde Mountains Wilderness
09. Milpitas Wash Wilderness
10. Buzzards Peak Wilderness
11. Indian Pass Wilderness
12. Picacho Peak Wilderness
13. Imperial Refuge Wilderness
14. Little Picacho Wilderness
15. North Algodones Dunes Wilderness
16. Fish Creek Mountains Wilderness
17. Coyote Mountains Wilderness
18. Jacumba Wilderness
19. Carrizo Gorge Wilderness
20. Sawtooth Mountains Wilderness
21. Orocopia Mountains Wilderness
22. Mecca Hills Wilderness

A. Mojave Trails National Monument
B. Chocolate Mountain
   Aerial Gunnery Range
C. Joshua Tree National Park
D. Salton Sea
E. Coachella Valley
F. Santa Rosa and San Jacinto
   National Monument
G. Anza-Borrego Desert State Park
H. Naval Air Facility El Centro
I. Imperial Valley
J. San Gorgonio Wilderness

*flowers of the barrel cactus*
*Echinocactus sp.*

## Plant alliances of the Sonoran Desert in California

Alkali sacaton grassland
Allscale scrub
American bulrush marsh
Arrow weed thicket
Big galleta shrub-steppe
Bitterbrush scrub
Black-stem rabbitbrush scrub
Black willow thickets
Bladder sage scrub
Brittlebush scrub
Bush seepweed scrub
California bulrush marsh
California fan palm oasis
California joint fir scrub
Catclaw acacia thorn scrub
Cattail marsh
Cheesebush scrub
Creosote bush–brittlebush scrub
Creosote bush scrub
Deer grass flats
Desert almond scrub
Desert dunes
Desert holly scrub
Desert lavender scrub
Desert purple sage scrub
Desert willow woodland
Fourwing saltbush scrub
Fremont cottonwood forest
Iodine bush scrub
Ironwood woodland
James' galleta shrub-steppe
Mesquite bosque
Mesquite thicket
Mojave yucca scrub
Net-veined goldeneye scrub
Nolina scrub
Parish's goldeneye scrub
Salt grass flats

Sandbar willow thickets
Smoke tree woodland
Sonoran live oak
Spinescale scrub
Teddy bear cholla patches
White bursage scrub

Deer grass, *Muhlenbergia rigens*

Sonoran live oak, *Qyercus turbinella*

Although the Colorado doesn't contain the iconic saguaro, the western
Sonoran Desert does have its own mysterious and iconic plants. The endangered elephant tree, *Bursera microphylla*, is a squat, aromatic, semisucculent,
drought-deciduous tree that finds its northernmost range in a few out-of-the-
way canyons of Anza-Borrego Desert State Park.

Sonoran Bumblebee
Bombus sonorus

Coachella Valley

Chocolate Mountains
live bombing

Salton Sea

North Algodones
Dunes Wilderness Area

Cargo Muchacho Mountains

04
05
09
08
06

Anza Borrego
Desert
State Park
01
Imperial Valley
west mesa

east mesa

N

10  11

12

02

03  07

Imperial Sand dunes
Recreation Area

Mexico
Baja California Norte

Pysiographic and geographic localities
Protective land designations
in California's Colorado desert

Map 07.02

## 07.02 CALIFORNIA'S UNIQUE PIECE OF THE SONORAN DESERT
*The Colorado Ecozone*

Because of its extremely low elevation, the physiographic feature that keeps the Gulf of California from invading the Salton Sink is the Colorado River Delta. At 275 feet below sea level, the Salton Basin is only 7 feet higher than Badwater Basin in Death Valley National Park, the lowest point on the North American continent. The Colorado River has changed its path many times, creating proto versions of what is today the Salton Sea.

The accident that caused the Salton Sea to form (see 02.12) was the only time the Colorado River altered its course because of the will of a single species, the human. The Salton Sea, the Imperial Valley, and the rivers that flow through the valley are Anthropocene ecosystems; the unique desert that surrounds them, existing as a much less arid place before the Holocene, is also not ancient. It was only twelve thousand years ago, when humanity had already established itself in these valleys, that the bighorn sheep that today still climb and play on craggy ridgelines gazed down on grasslands that were fecund enough to be grazing fields for mammoth.

01. Fish Creek Mountains; Fish Creek Mountains Wilderness; Lower Borrego Valley; Carrizo Impact Area (closed to public), Anza-Borrego Desert State Park
02. Coyote Mountains; Coyote Mountains Wilderness; Yuha Desert Recreation Area
03. Jacumba Mountains Wilderness; In-Ko-Pah Gorge; Valley of the Moon Trail
04. Ocotillo Wells State Vehicle Recreation Area; Tule Wash; US Navy Salton Sea Test Base
05. San Felipe Creek Ecological Reserve; San Felipe Creek
06. Superstition Hills; US Navy bombing area
07. Yuha Desert; Yuha Buttes; Vista De Anza Historical Monument; Crucifiction Thorn Natural Area
08. New River; Central Main Canal; Westside Canal
09. Alamo River; Imperial State Wildlife Area (Finney-Ramer Unit); West Lake County Park
10. Fort Yuma-Quechan Indian Reservation; Araz Wash; Picacho Wash
11. Colorado River
12. All American Canal

Crotch's bumble bee
*Bombus crotchii*

## Plant alliances of the Colorado Desert of California

Allscale scrub
American bulrush marsh
Arrow weed thicket
Big galleta shrub-steppe
Black-stem rabbitbrush scrub
Black willow thickets
Bladder sage scrub
Brittlebush scrub
Bush seepweed scrub
California bulrush marsh
California fan palm oasis
California joint fir scrub
Catclaw acacia thorn scrub
Cattail marsh
Cheesebush scrub
Creosote bush–brittlebush scrub
Creosote bush scrub
Creosote bush–white bursage scrub
Deer weed scrub
Desert agave scrub
Desert dunes
Desert holly scrub
Desert lavender scrub
Desert panic grass patches
Desert willow woodland
Ditch-grass or widgeon-grass mats
Fourwing saltbush scrub
Fremont cottonwood forest
Mesquite bosque
Mesquite thicket
Mojave yucca scrub
Parish's goldeneye scrub
Quailbush scrub
Salt grass flats
Sandbar willow thickets
Smoke tree woodland
Teddy bear cholla patches
Virgin River brittlebush scrub
White bursage scrub

Bush seepweed, *Suaeda nigra*

Quailbush
*Atriplex lentiformis* ssp. *breweri*

Virgin river brittlebush
*Encelia virginensis*

*Heloderma sp. in the Santa Maria Mtns.*

## Gila monster, *Heloderma suspectum*

At almost two feet long, the Gila monster, the only venomous lizard in the United States (there are four species of closely related venomous bearded lizards in Mexico)[5], is also the largest extant lizard north of the Mexican border.

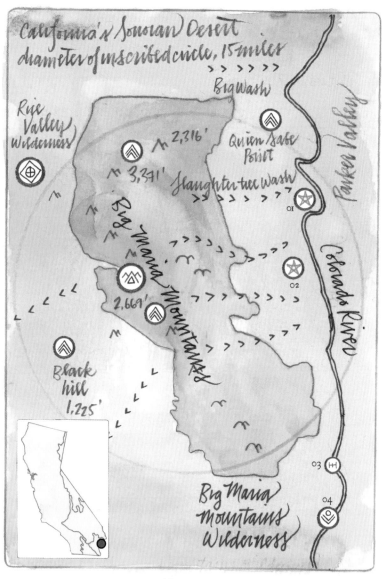

Map 07.03

## 07.03 PEAKS WEST OF THE COLORADO RIVER
*Big Maria Mountains Wilderness*

After one hundred million years of being pushed and pulled inside a geologic region called the Maria Fold and Thrust Belt, the Big Maria Mountains are today a series of craggy peaks and steep canyons.[6] South of the Big Wash Valley and to the west of Slaughter Tree Wash, the Big Maria Mountains are also being eroded to the south across the McCoy Wash.

01. Hall Island
02. Blythe Intaglios
03. Palo Verde Dam
04. Palo Verde Ecological Reserve

*... these mountains are covered with cactus gardens composed of many species, including foxtail cactus Conyphantha alversonii*

*... can be described as disjointed canyon lands that support herds of burro deer*

*... riparian habitat drains to the Colorado River and supports water birds and amphibians*

american kestrel

Generalized elevation range
500–3,400 feet

Land area
45,384 acres
70.91 square miles

American kestrel
*Falco sparverius*

Burro mule deer
*Odocoileus hemionus* var. *eremicus*

Gravel ghost
*Atrichoseris platyphylla*

Bigelow's nolina
*Nolina bigelovii*

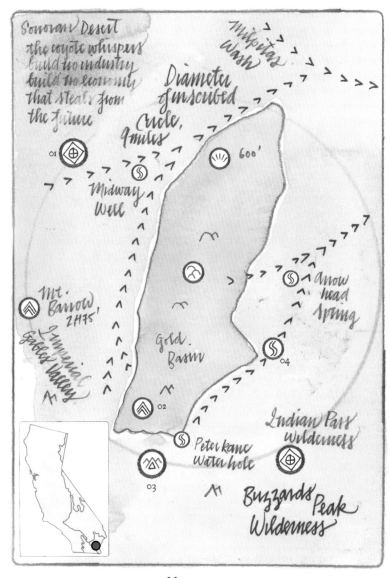

Sonoran Desert
the coyote whispers
build no industry
build no economy
that steals from
the future

Milpitas Wash

Diameter
of inscribed
Circle,
9 miles

600'

01

Midway Well

Mt. Barrow, 2475'

Imperial Gabbes Valley

Gold Basin

Arrow head Spring

04

Indian Pass Wilderness

02

Peter kane Water hole

03

Buzzards Peak Wilderness

Map 07.04

## 07.04 LOW HILLS NORTH OF THE CHOCOLATE MOUNTAINS
*Buzzards Peak Wilderness*

The Quechan people have known these rich and colorful hills well. From Buzzards Peak, in the south of the wilderness area, the low ridgeline inclines down toward the north, perpendicular to the Chocolate Mountains dividing the Milpitas Wash from the Vinagre Wash.

01. Milpitas Wash Wilderness
02. Buzzards Peak (1,400')
03. Chocolate Mountains
04. Vinagre Wash

... ample water exists in this wilderness for amphibians including Colorado River toad, *Incilius alvarius*, and Great Plains toad, *Anaxyrus cognatus*

... mountain lions hunt mule deer inside the remote riparian habitat around Buzzards Peak

... site of the rare perennial herb California ditaxis
*Ditaxis serrata var. californica*

Generalized elevation range
600–1,400 feet

Land area
11,840 acres
18.5 square miles

Red-lined grasshopper
*Poecilotettix sanguineus*

Forsebia moth
*Forsebia cinis*

American threefold
*Trixis californica*

Pebble pincushion
*Chaenactis carphoclinia*

Red-lined grasshopper
*Poecilotettix sanguineus*

389

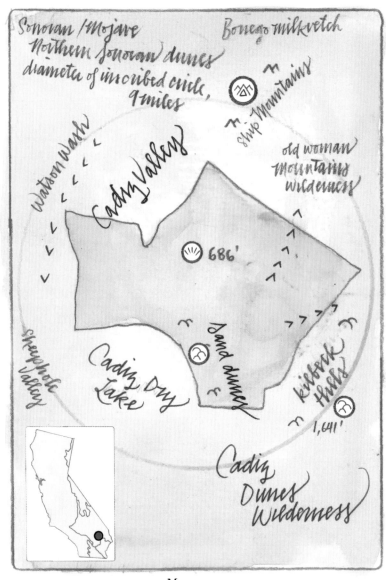

Sonoran / Mojave
Northern Sonoran dunes
diameter of inscribed circle,
9 miles

Borrego milkvetch

Ship Mountains

Watson Wash

Cadiz Valley

old woman
mountains
wilderness

686'

sand dunes

Cadiz Dry
Lake

Sheephole
Valley

kilbeck
hills

1,641'

Cadiz
Dunes
Wilderness

Map 07.05

## 07.05 SANDY HABITAT AT THE CENTER OF CADIZ VALLEY
*Cadiz Dunes Wilderness*

Between the Calumet Mountains of Sheephole Valley Wilderness to the west and
Old Woman Mountains to the east, Cadiz Dunes Wilderness sits in the center of
Cadiz Valley. The ice age pluvial lake that was Cadiz Lake, now desiccated, is
part of the erg-sand sheet—a littoral designation of shifting sands across the south
Mojave and northern Sonoran Deserts in California.

*... a largely flat wilderness with small
dunes that are fed sand from the
ancient dry Cadiz Lake
... coyotes and rattlesnakes chase jackrabbits
and kangaroo rats across dunes and shrubland
... Rare plants grow across the dune network
that also provides habitat for desert tortoise*

Borrego milkvetch
*Astragalus lentiginosus var. borreganus*

Generalized elevation range
1,000–1,500 feet

Land area
19,935 acres
31.15 square miles

Dune scorpion
*Smeringurus mesaensis*

Ophryastes weevil
*Ophryastes argentatus*

Fan-leaved tiquilia
*Tiquilia plicata*

Borrego milkvetch
*Astragalus lentiginosus*
var. *borreganus*

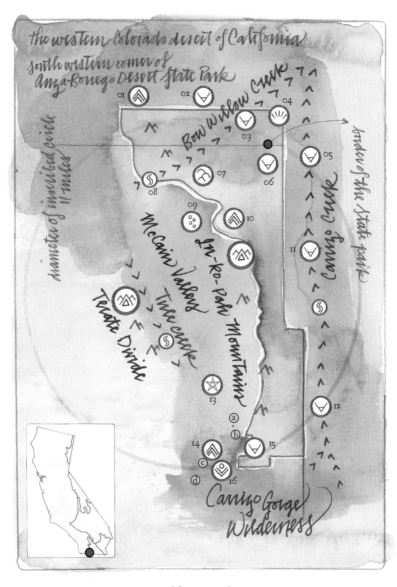

the western colorado desert of California

south western corner of
Anza-Borrego Desert State Park

Bow Willow Creek

border of the State park

diameter of inscribed circle
11 miles

McCain Valley

Tule Creek

In-Ko-Pah Mountains

Tecate Divide

Carrizo Creek

Carrizo Gorge
Wilderness

Map 07.06

## 07.06 HIGHLANDS SOUTHEAST OF ANZA-BORREGO DESERT STATE PARK
*Carrizo Gorge Wilderness*

Within the greater San Andreas Fault zone, the In-Ko-Pah Mountains that make up the Carrizo Gorge Wilderness were part of the same geologic process that spanned the last 150 million years and was also responsible for the slumping of the Salton Trough.[7] Throughout the wilderness, desert palm canyons and catclaw canyons provide habitat for bighorn.

01. Sombrero Peak (4,180')
02. Indian Gorge
03. Bow Willow Canyon
04. Unnamed hills (1,739')
05. Carrizo Canyon
06. Rockhouse Canyon
07. Unnamed flats (1,542')
08. Bow Willow Creek
09. Carrizo Overlook to Peak Trail
10. Carrizo Overlook Peak (4,186')
11. Goat Canyon
12. Carrizo Gorge; Carrizo Creek
13. McCain Valley National Cooperative Land & Wildlife Management Area
14. Mount Tule (4,636')
15. Tule Canyon
16. Walker Canyon Ecological Reserve

a. Redondo Spring
b. Sacotone Spring
c. Tule Lake
d. Bunchhead Spring

*...Carrizo Gorge is west of the wilderness in the Jacumba Mountains*

*...raised uplands provide vistas of the entire Colorado Desert region to the east*

*... Redshank, Adenostoma sparsifolium and chamise chaparral, Adenostoma fasciculatum grow at the western edge of the desert*

Generalized elevation range
1,500–4,600 feet

Land area
14,740 acres
23.03 square miles

Swainson's hawk
*Buteo swainsoni*

Pacific-slope flycatcher
*Empidonax difficilis*

Chuparosa
*Justicia californica*

Rock hibiscus
*Hibiscus denudatus*

*Swainson's hawk*
*Buteo swainsoni*

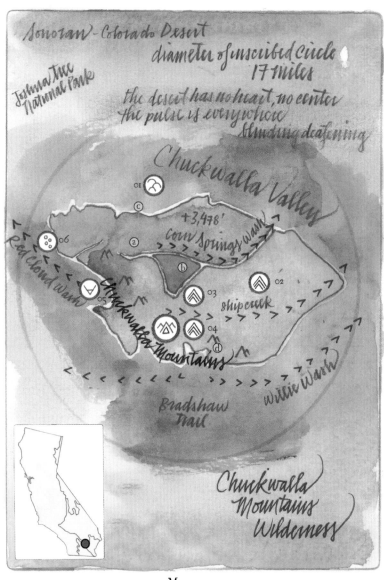

Sonoran - Colorado Desert

diameter of inscribed circle
17 miles

the desert has no heart, no center
the pulse is everywhere
blundering deafening

Joshua Tree
National Park

Chuckwalla Valley

+ 3,478'

Corn Springs Wash

Red Cloud Wash

Chuckwalla Mountains

shipcreck

Bradshaw Trail

Willie Wash

Chuckwalla
Mountains
Wilderness

Map 07.07

## 07.07 BETWEEN JOSHUA TREE NATIONAL PARK AND THE CHOCOLATE MOUNTAINS
*Chuckwalla Mountains Wilderness*

A series of north Sonoran wilderness areas exists in the corridor between Joshua Tree National Park and the Chocolate Mountains (closed to the public), and the Chuckwalla Mountains Wilderness is the largest of them, and perhaps the most varied in both geology and biodiversity. Endemic plants of the Chuckwalla Bench ACEC are Munz's cholla, *Cylindropuntia munzii*; Mecca aster, *Xylorhiza cognata*; and Orocopia sage, *Salvia greatae*.[8]

01. Alligator (1,267')
02. Sharp Peak (2,418')
03. Pilot Mountain (4,216')
04. Black Butte (4,504')
05. Red Cloud Canyon
06. Red Cloud Trail

a. Aztec Well
b. Corn Spring
c. Granite Well
d. Willie Wash Spring

*... this wilderness is part of the Chuckwalla Bench, an area of critical environmental concern (ACEC)*

*... the ridgeline that runs along the entirety of this wilderness is a craggy and colorful landscape with exceptional reptile density per square mile*

*... the final location of the Sonoran pronghorn in the California desert before extirpation*[9]

Generalized elevationn range
800–4,600 feet

Land area
99,548 acres
155.54 square miles

Common chuckwalla
*Sauromalus ater*

Desert pocket mouse
*Chaetodipus penicillatus*

Emory's rockdaisy
*Perityle emoryi*

Star gilia
*Gilia stellata*

Common chuckwalla
*Sauromalus ater*

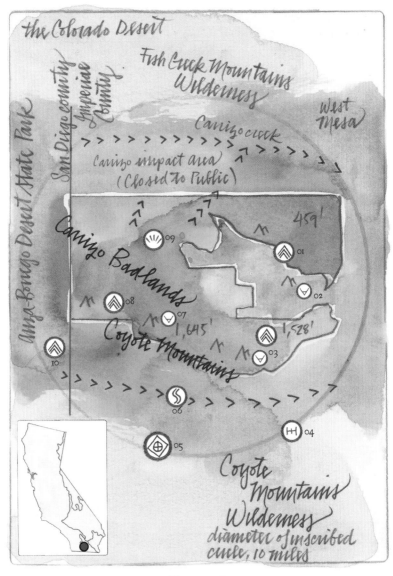

the Colorado Desert

Fish Creek Mountains
Wilderness

West
Mesa

San Diego County
Imperial County

Carrizo creek

Carrizo impact area
(Closed to Public)

Anza-Borrego Desert State Park

Carrizo Badlands

459'

01

02

09

08

1,645'

07

Coyote Mountains

1,528'

03

10

06

05

04

Coyote
Mountains
Wilderness
diameter of inscribed
circle, 10 miles

Map 07.08

## 07.08 FOSSIL RANGE ON THE WEST SIDE
## OF THE IMPERIAL VALLEY
*Coyote Mountains Wilderness*

The Carrizo Badlands, which rise from the Carrizo Valley, come to their eastern
border in the elbow of the Coyote Mountains, which account for almost half of
the wilderness land area. Diverse topography within the Coyote Mountains Wilderness developed over six million years ago when the area was under the ocean.
The submarine sedimentary environment was suitable for the formation of fossils,
which now decorate the landscape.[10]

01. Carrizo Mountain (2,408')
02. Painted Gorge
03. Fossil Canyon
04. Ocotillo Wind Energy
    Facility Project
05. Yuha Desert
    Recreation Area
06. Palm Canyon Wash
07. Andrade Canyon
08. Unnamed mountain (1,773')
09. Unnamed mesa (768')
10. Red Hill (1,720')

*... lower elevations of the Coyote Mountains
are creosote scrub; higher elevations are
agave gardens*

*... deeply varied topography and geology
cover the "badlands" and low mountains*

*... habitat for the rare peninsula
banded gecko Coleonyx switaki switaki*[11]

Generalized elevation range
100–2,000 feet

Land area
18,631 acres
29.11 square miles

Western black widow
*Latrodectus hesperus*

Cahuilla ebony tarantula
*Aphonopelma xwalxwal*

Flatbud prickly poppy
*Argemone munita*

Yuma silverbush
*Ditaxis serrata*

*Yuma silverbush
Ditaxis serrata*

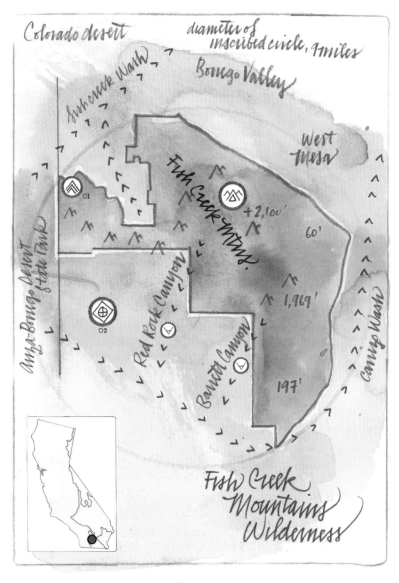

Colorado desert

diameter of inscribed circle, 9 miles

Fishcreek Wash

Borrego Valley

West Mesa

Fish Creek Mtns.

+2,100'

60'

1,969'

Anza-Borrego Desert State Park

O1

O2

Red Rock Canyon

Barrett Canyon

Carrizo Wash

197'

Fish Creek Mountains Wilderness

Map 07.09

## 07.09 MOUNTAINS ON THE EAST SIDE OF ANZA-BORREGO DESERT STATE PARK
*Fish Creek Mountains Wilderness*

Surrounded by expansive lowlands to the east, the ten-mile-long Fish Creek Range reaches from Anza-Borrego Desert State Park across Imperial Valley's West Mesa and offers a unique long view of California's Colorado Desert. Lake Cahuilla's ancient shoreline is evident at certain places in the range.

01. Split Mountain 1,700'
02. Carrizo Impact Area
(closed to public)

*... primarily a limestone plateau.*
*with steep canyons that collect precious water*
*... from the top of the range, vistas stretch south to Mexico and east to the Chocolate Mountains*
*... these low mountains rise outside of essential habitat connectivity corridors for bighorn*

anza horned lizard
Phrynosoma anzaense

Generalized elevation range
sea level–2,400 feet

Land area
21,390 acres
33.42 square miles

Round-tailed ground squirrel
*Spermophilus tereticaudus*

Anza horned lizard
*Phrynosoma anzaense*

Bristle sage
*Salvia vaseyi*

Heartleaf suncup
*Chylismia cardiophylla*

Map 07.10

## 07.10 RIVERSIDE WILDERNESS IN TWO STATES
*Imperial Refuge Wilderness*

Along a thirty-mile, unchanneled section of the Colorado River, the Imperial Refuge Wilderness lies on both the California and Arizona sides of the river. The wilderness area is contiguous with the Little Picacho Wilderness to the south and the Indian Pass Wilderness to the west.

01. Velian Wash
02. Indian Pass Wilderness
03. Julian Wash
04. Para Wash
05. Picacho Peak Wilderness
06. Picacho State Recreation Area
07. Bear Canyon
08. Little Picacho Wash
09. Trigo Mountain Wilderness
10. Rojo Grande (710')
11. Little Picacho Peak (1,193')
12. Little Picacho Wilderness

a. Three Finger Lake
b. Cibola Lake
c. Draper Lake
d. Adobe Lake
e. Taylor Lake
f. Island Lake
g. Nortons Lake
h. Ferguson Lake
i. Martinez Lake
j. Senator Wash Reservoir
k. Imperial Reservoir

*...the refuge contains extensive riparian, marsh, and terrestrial Sonoran habitat ...provides habitat along the Colorado River for at least 275 bird species, not including dozens of waterfowl* [12] *...largemouth bass and channel catfish are among the common fish in this area*

| Generalized elevation range | Arizona |
|---|---|
| 500–600 feet | 9,220 acres |
| | 14.41 square miles |
| Total land area | |
| 15,056 acres | California |
| 23.53 square miles | 5,836 acres |
| | 9.12 square miles |

Abert's towhee
*Melozone aberti*

Peregrine falcon
*Falco peregrinus*

Little gold poppy
*Eschscholzia minutiflora*

Desert starvine
*Brandegea bigelovii*

Abert's towhee
*Melozone aberti*

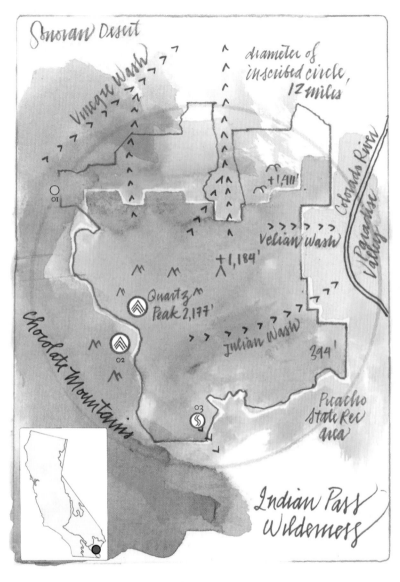

Sonoran Desert

Vinegar Wash

diameter of
inscribed circle,
12 miles

Colorado River

O1

+1,411'

Velian Wash

Paradise Valley

+1,184'

Quartz
Peak 2,177'

O2

Chocolate Mountains

Julian Wash

> > >

394'

O3

Picacho
State Rec
area

Indian Pass
Wilderness

Map 07.11

## 07.11 SOUTHERN CHOCOLATE MOUNTAINS ON THE COLORADO RIVER
*Indian Pass Wilderness*

Part of the Chocolate Mountains range, the Indian Pass Wilderness covers a land area dominated by the Julian Wash, which drains west through the Imperial Wilderness into the Colorado River. The wilderness shares a southern border with both the Picacho Peak Wilderness and the Picacho State Recreation Area.

01. Peter Kane Water Hole
02. Black Mountain (2,164')
03. Gavilan Wash

... habitat for California ditaxis
*Ditaxis serrata var. californica*
a rare perennial plant

... habitat for rare amphibians, including Colorado River toad, *Incilius alvarius*, and Great Plains toad, *Anaxyrus cognatus*

... Quartz Peak (2,177') is corridor habitat for bighorn

Generalized elevation range
300–2,200 feet

Land area
43,279 acres
67.62 square miles

Kit fox
*Vulpes macrotis*

Gambel's quail
*Callipepla gambelii*

Arizona lupine
*Lupinus arizonicus*

Anderson thornbush
*Lycium andersonii*

Gambel's quail
*Callipepla gambelii*

403

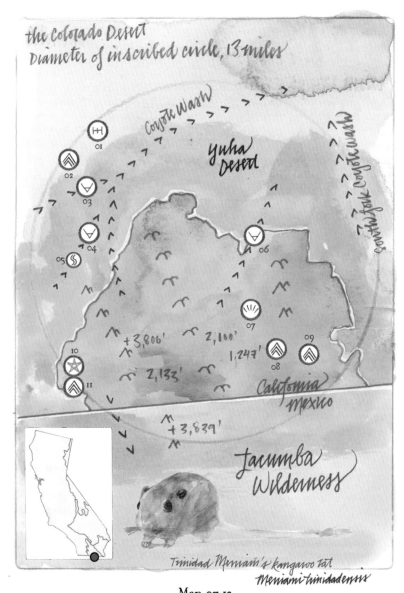

the Colorado Desert
Diameter of inscribed circle, 13 miles

Coyote Wash

South fork Coyote wash

yuha Desert

+ 3,806'   2,100'

1,247'

2,133'

California
Mexico

+ 3,839'

Jacumba
Wilderness

Trinidad Merriam's kangaroo rat
Merriami trinidadensis

Map 07.12

## 07.12 RIDGES AND VALLEYS NORTH OF THE MEXICAN BORDER
*Jacumba Wilderness*

With a southern border that runs for eight miles along the Mexican border, the Jacumba Wilderness contains many ridges in a transition zone between the uplands of Anza-Borrego Desert State Park and the lowlands of California's Colorado Desert.

01. Ocotillo wind energy facility project
02. Sugarloaf Mountain (1,022')
03. Devil's Canyon
04. In-Ko-Pah Gorge
05. Boulder Creek
06. Davies Canyon
07. Davies Valley
08. Kirk (1,424')
09. Bennie (1,516')
10. Smugglers Cave
11. Blue Angels Peak (4,548')

*... portions of the wilderness contain granite outcrops that resemble Joshua Tree National Park*

*... northernmost habitat of Trinidad Merriam's kangaroo rat, merriami trinidadensis*

*... many rare plant species, including Jacumba milkvetch, Astragalus douglasii var. perstrictus grow in this area*

red-spotted toad
Anaxyrus punctatus

Generalized elevation range
500–4,000 feet

Land area
31,358 acres
49.00 square miles

Red-spotted toad
*Anaxyrus punctatus*

Peninsular leaf-toed gecko
*Phyllodactylus nocticolus*

Desert apricot
*Prunus fremontii*

Spanish needle
*Palafoxia arida*

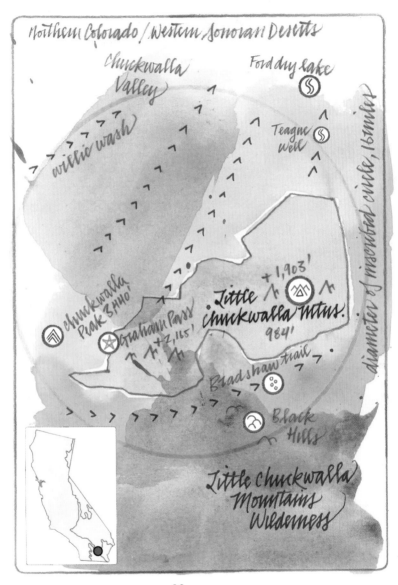

Northern Colorado / Western Sonoran Deserts

Chuckwalla Valley

Ford dry Lake

Teague Well

willie wash

Chuckwalla Peak 3,440'

Graham Pass
+2,165'

Little Chuckwalla Mtns.
+1,903'
984'

Bradshaw trail

Black Hills

Little Chuckwalla Mountains Wilderness

diameter of inscribed circle, 16.5 miles

Map 07.13

## 07.13 DRY MOUNTAINS NORTH OF THE CHOCOLATE MOUNTAINS
*Little Chuckwalla Mountains Wilderness*

Rising from the enormous expanse of the Chuckwalla Valley to its north and the Palo Verde Mesa to its east, and across the Arroyo Seco from the Chocolate Mountains to its west and south, this wilderness spreads across the smallish range that is the Little Chuckwalla Mountains.

... includes shrubland habitat for many potentially rare plant species including California snakeweed, *Gutierrezia californica* and foxtail cactus, *Coryphantha alversonii*

... mineral-rich mountains, potentially in gold and silver, are a favorite site for rock collectors

... no trails, no reliable springs occur in this wilderness

California snakeweed
*Gutierrezia californica*

Generalized elevation range
600–2,200 feet

Land area
28,052 acres
43.83 square miles

Desert spiny lizard
*Sceloporus magister*

California harvester ant
*Pogonomyrmex californicus*

Thickleaf groundcherry
*Physalis crassifolia*

Desert purple mat
*Nama demissa* var. *demissa*

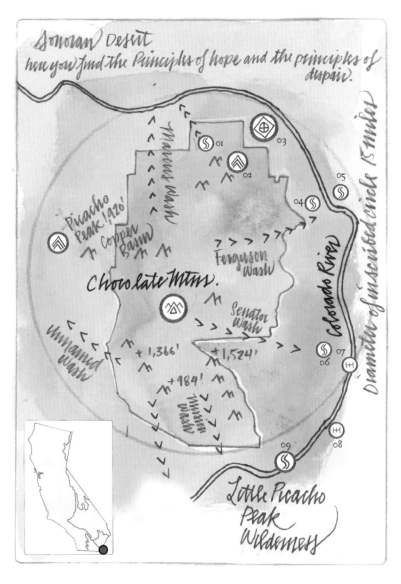

Sonoran Desert
here you find the Principles of hope and the principles of despair.

Picacho Peak 1920'
↗ Copper Basin

Manul Dunndl Wash

Ferguson Wash

Chocolate Mtns.

Senator Wash

Unnamed Wash

+1,366'

+1,524'

+984'

Wwwwl Wash

Colorado River

Diameter of inscribed circle (15 miles)

Little Picacho Peak Wilderness

Map 07.14

## 07.14 SOUTHERNMOST WILDERNESS ON THE COLORADO RIVER
*Little Picacho Wilderness*

West of the Imperial Reservoir, the seventy-mile-long Chocolate Mountains range comes to its southern terminus at the Little Picacho Wilderness. This wilderness is noted for its colorful, geologically diverse peaks that rise above rich desert-riparian habitat.

01. Sortan Wash
02. Little Picacho Peak (1,193')
03. Imperial National Wildlife Refuge
04. Ferguson Lake
05. Martinez Lake
06. Senator Wash Reservoir
07. Imperial Dam; Xanyō Xamshre
08. Laguna Dam; Mittry Lake
09. All American Canal

*... home for a herd of approximately twenty-five to fifty bighorn* [14]
*... other big mammals of this wilderness include an isolated herd of a few dozen wild horses* [15]
*... habitat for rare reptiles and amphibians including the yuma king snake* Lampropeltis getula
*Couch's spadefoot toad* Scaphiopus couchii
*Rocky mountain toad* Anaxyrus woodhousii woodhousii

yuma kingsnake
Lampropeltis getula

Generalized elevation range
200–1,400 feet

Land area
38,216 acres
59.71 square miles

Spotted bat
*Euderma maculatum*

Picacho wild horse
*Equus ferus*

Sweetbush
*Bebbia juncea*

California fagonbush
*Fagonia laevis*

Ocotillo *Fouquieria splendens*
Costa's hummingbird
*Calypte costae*

With increasing temperatures across the Sonoran Desert, the
ocotillo, *Fouquieria splendens*, a primary food source for migrating
hummingbirds, is blooming up to a month earlier than in the past.
This threatens populations of both species and could be indicative
of cascading effects to come.[16]

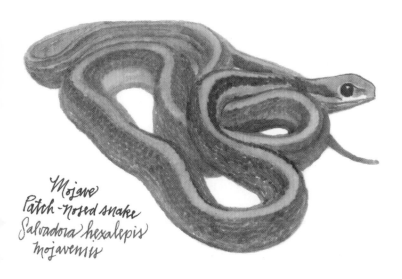

Mojave
Patch-nosed snake
Salvadora hexalepis
mojavensis

---

### Patch-nosed snakes, *Salvadora hexalepis*

Mohave patch-nosed snake, *Salvadora hexalepis mojavensis*,
native to the Mojave

Desert patch-nosed snake, *Salvadora hexalepis hexalepis*,
native to the Sonoran

Coast patch-nosed snake, *Salvadora hexalepis virgultea*,
native to Southern California; nondesert; species of special concern

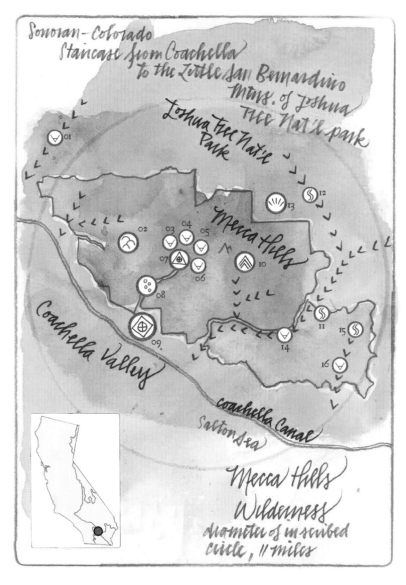

Map 07.15

## 07.15 LABYRINTHINE MOUNTAINS OVER EASTERN COACHELLA VALLEY
*Mecca Hills Wilderness*

Within the San Andreas Rift Zone, along the eastern side of the Coachella Valley, the Mecca Hills rise over the Salton Trough and across Shavers Valley from Joshua Tree National Park. The unique geology of the place has lent itself to the nickname Mud Hills because of their impassability to hiking when it rains.

... these hills contain regionally unique geology, including exposed layers of earth over six hundred million years old [17]
... one of two habitat sites for the endemic wildflower Mecca aster, *Xylorhiza cognata*
... this wilderness is considered a site that may become a vernal wildflower hotspot, including the pink-flowered desert sand verbena, *Abronia villosa*

01. Thermal Canyon
02. Mecca Hills (1,641')
03. Big Painted Canyon
04. Little Painted Canyon
05. Rope Canyon
06. Ladders Canyon
07. Mecca Hills County Park
08. Painted Canyon Road
09. Torres-Martinez Reservation
10. Blake Hill (1,772')
11. Shavers Well
12. Pinkham Wash
13. Shavers Valley
14. Box Canyon
15. Hidden Spring
16. Hidden Spring Canyon

Generalized elevation range
200–1,800 feet

Land area
26,356 acres
41.18 square miles

Loggerhead shrike
*Lanius ludovicianus*

White-tailed antelope squirrel
*Ammospermophilus leucurus*

Smallseed sandmat
*Euphorbia polycarpa*

Trailing windmills
*Allionia incarnata*

*Cryptantha*
*Cryptantha* spp.

## *Cryptantha* spp.

What may be the most common wildflower in the Coachella Valley is the tiny white flower known as *Cryptantha* spp. Thirty-six species in the genus *Cryptantha* live in the deserts of California.[18]

the purple coyotes of Coachella

coyote pup
at dawn

I bring the perceived forms of the world into me
where, in the eyes of my heart, these agents
become seen and become beloved

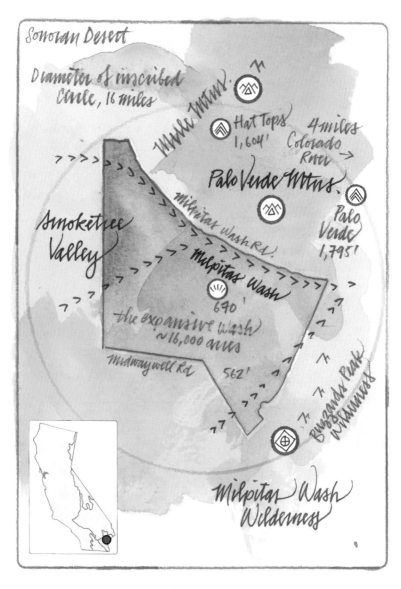

Sonoran Desert

Diameter of inscribed
Circle, 16 miles

Middle Mtns.

Hat Tops
1,604'

4 miles
Colorado
River →

Palo Verde Mtns.

Palo
Verde
1,795'

Smoketree
Valley

Milpitas Wash Rd.

Milpitas Wash
690'

the expansive wash
~16,000 acres

Midway well Rd

562'

Buzzards Peak Wilderness

Milpitas Wash
Wilderness

Map 07.16

## 07.16 SONORAN WOODLAND SOUTH OF THE PALO VERDE MOUNTAINS
*Milpitas Wash Wilderness*

In the Milpitas Wash Wilderness, several species of normally short trees of the Sonoran Desert grow to the unusually tall average height of fifteen feet. Protected and fed with mineral nutrients from the Palo Verde Mountains to the north and the Chocolate Mountains from the south, the rich desert soil biota of the Milpitas Wash supports a wide array of life.

... desert foothills covered with unusually dense Sonoran woodland

... woodland includes ironwood, *olneya tesota*; acacia, *Acacia ssp.*; mesquite, *Prosopis ssp.*; Palo verde, *Parkinsonia ssp.*; and willow, *Chilopsis linearis*

... habitat for the Gila woodpecker *Melanerpes uropygialis* an endangered species in California but whose numbers remain strong in Arizona

Generalized elevation range
500–700 feet

Land area
17,250 acres
26.95 square miles

Funereal duskywing
*Erynnis funeralis*

Gila woodpecker
*Melanerpes uropygialis*

Chinchweed
*Pectis papposa*

Distant phacelia
*Phacelia distans*

funereal duskywing
*Erynnis funeralis*

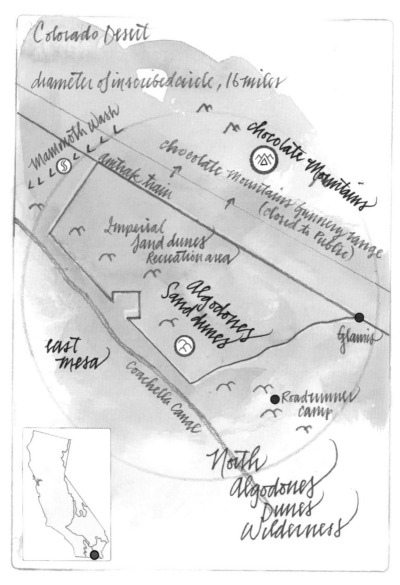

Map 07.17

## 07.17 SAND MOUNTAINS ALONG
## THE EASTERN IMPERIAL VALLEY
*North Algodones Dunes Wilderness*

The ancient lakebed of Lake Cahuilla now exists as California's most extensive dune system, the Algodones Dunes. The North Algodones Dunes Wilderness is only one fragment of the dune system, which spreads over one thousand square miles from the Salton Slough into Mexico.

... east side of the extensive sand dune habitat supports spots of wetland and desert-riparian habitat

... provides habitat for the rare and endemic Andrew's dune scarab beetle
*Pseudocotalpa andrewsi*

... habitat for rare plants including

Peirson's locoweed *Astragalus Magdalenae var. Peirsonii*

silver-leaved dune sunflower *Helianthus niveus*

Giant Spanish needle *Palafoxia arida var. gigantea*

and sand food, *Pholisma sonorae*

Generalized elevation range
300–500 feet

Land area
25,85 acres
40.46 square miles

Sidewinder
*Crotalus cerastes*

Algodones sand
treader cricket
*Macrobaenetes algodonensis*

Many-flowered mentzelia
*Mentzelia longiloba*

Desert sand verbena
*Abronia villosa*

Andrew's dune scarab beetle
*Pseudocotalpa andrewsi*

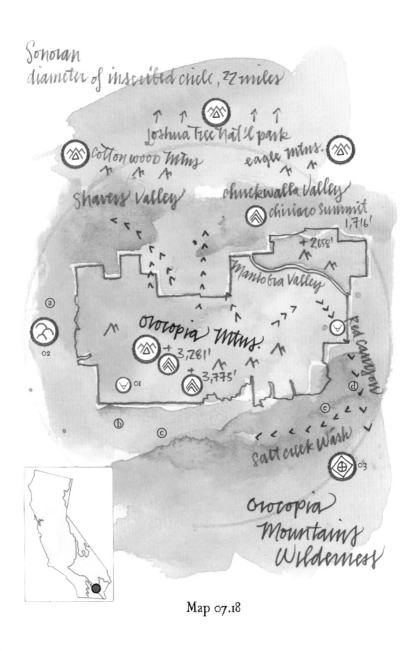

Sonoran
diameter of inscribed circle, 22 miles

Joshua Tree Nat'l Park

Cotton wood Mtns

eagle mtns.

Shavers Valley

chuckwalla Valley

chiriaco Summit
1,716'

+ 2,658'

Maniobra Valley

Orocopia Mtns.

Red Canyon

+ 3,281'

+ 3,775'

(a)

O2

O1

(b)

(c)

(e)

(d)

Salt creek Wash

O3

Orocopia
Mountains
Wilderness

Map 07.18

## 07.18 BETWEEN THE SALTON SEA AND JOSHUA TREE NATIONAL PARK
*Orocopia Mountains Wilderness*

Forming a wildlife corridor that connects habitat with that of the Mecca Hills to its west, the Orocopia Mountains Wilderness is full of colorful canyons teeming with rare plant habitat. To the east, the Bradshaw Trail Wash separates the Orocopia Mountains from the Chuckwalla Mountains to the east and the Chocolate Mountains to the south.

01. Orocopia Canyon
02. Mecca Hill
03. Chocolate Mountains
    Gunnery Range

a. Hidden Spring
b. Dos Palmas Spring
c. Hunters Spring
d. Canyon Springs
e. Clemens Well

... habitat for rare plants including
Orocopia sage, Salvia greatae
foxtail cactus, Coryphantha alversonii
and Orcutt's woodyaster Xylorhiza
orcuttii

... extensive complex of mammal fossils from
the late oligocene to Early Miocene are
located inside what is called the Diligencia
Formation [19]

... dozens of plant alliances are hidden in
deep canyons, including habitat for the
endemic flower Orocopia Mountain spurge,
Euphorbia jaegeri

velvet ant
(ant-like)
flightless
wasp.
Painful
sting

Magnificent velvet ant
Dasymutilla magnifica

| | |
|---|---|
| Generalized elevation range sea level–3,600 feet | Magnificent velvet ant *Dasymutilla magnifica* |
| Land area 51,289 acres 80.14 square miles | California patch butterfly *Chlosyne californica* |
| | Sand blazingstar *Mentzelia involucrata* |
| | Flatbud prickly poppy *Argemone munita* |

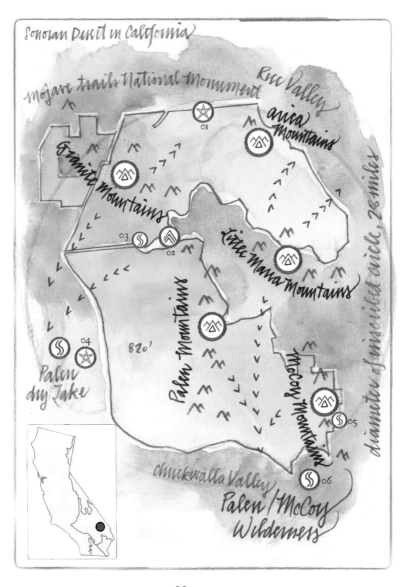

Map 07.19

## 07.19 MANY RANGES EAST OF JOSHUA TREE NATIONAL PARK
*Palen/McCoy Wilderness*

Five mountain ranges—the Arica, Little Maria, Granite, Palen, and McCoy Mountains—extend into and through the Palen/McCoy Wilderness. Extensive washes include the Palen Valley, the Ford Wash, and the McCoy Wash. Bounded by Joshua Tree National Park to the west, Mojave Trails National Monument to the north, Rice Valley to the east, and Chuckwalla Valley to the south, the Palen/McCoy Wilderness contains a substantial land area of essential ecological connectivity.

01. Sand dunes
02. Palen Pass (1,472')
03. Packard Well
04. Sand dunes
05. McCoy Springs
06. Ford Dry Lake

*... extensive riparian habitat exists throughout, along with desert wash systems of robust diversity*

*... includes the midland ironwood forest, among the highest-density ironwood, Olneya tesota, habitats in California*

*... a desert lily, Hesperocallis undulata, preserve is located at Palen Lake, west of the wilderness*

Generalized elevation range
600–3,600 feet

Land area
236,488 acres
369.51 square miles

Long-nosed leopard lizard
*Gambelia wislizenii*

Curve-billed thrasher
*Toxostoma curvirostre*

Wishbone bush
*Mirabilis laevis*

*Heartleaf suncup*
*Chylismia cardiophylla ssp. cardiophylla*

Heartleaf suncup
*Chylismia cardiophylla*
ssp. *cardiophylla*

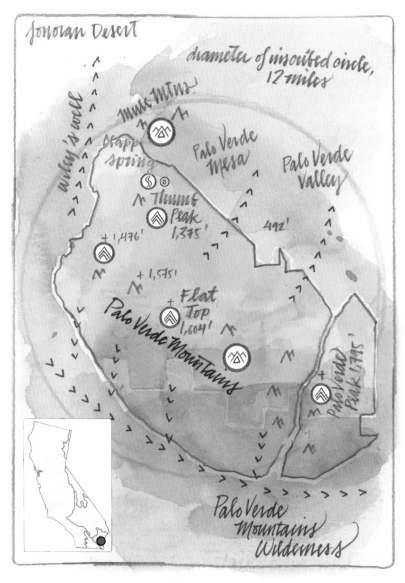

Map 07.20

## 07.20 MOUNTAINS WEST OF CIBOLA REFUGE
*Palo Verde Mountains Wilderness*

At the southern end of Palo Verde Mesa and Palo Verde Valley, the rugged Palo Verde Mountains rise north of Milpitas Wash. In the southeast corner of the wilderness, two miles west of Cibola National Wildlife Refuge on the Colorado River, Palo Verde Peak rises to 1,795 feet.

... Desert palm, Washingtonia filifera,
   habitat exists at Clapp Spring
... these mountains contain rare California
   habitat for the iconic saguaro cactus,
   Carnegiea gigantea, along the southern
   portion of the wilderness
... the wilderness is sparsely vegetated
   throughout except for a few locations
   of desert wash / riparian habitats that
   contain the wilderness's namesake tree,
   Palo verde, Parkinsonia sp.

ornate
checkered
beetle  Trichodes ornatus on
Narrowleaf silverbush
Ditaxis lanceolata

Generalized elevation range
500–1,800 feet

Land area
39,955 acres
62.43 square miles

Black-throated sparrow
*Amphispiza bilineata*

Ornate checkered beetle
*Trichodes ornatus*

Wand holdback
*Hoffmannseggia microphylla*

Narrowleaf silverbush
*Ditaxis lanceolata*

*Palo verde in the Whipple Mtns*

*The Palo Verde beetle, Derobrachus hovorei grows to three and one-half inches*

### Genus *Parkinsonia*

The Sonoran Desert is home to three species of palo verde, *Parkinsonia* sp. Two exist in California: blue palo verde, *Parkinsonia florida*, and little-leaf palo verde, *Parkinsonia microphylla*. A third species, Mexican palo verde, *Parkinsonia aculeata*, is not native to California.[20] All palo verde species are stem photosynthetic.

### Palo verde beetle

The palo verde root borer, *Derobrachus hovorei*, grows up to five inches long and can be found in palo verde, *Parkinsonia* sp., habitat throughout the Sonoran Desert.

I am bats. I am frogs. I am agave.
The desert is a mirror.

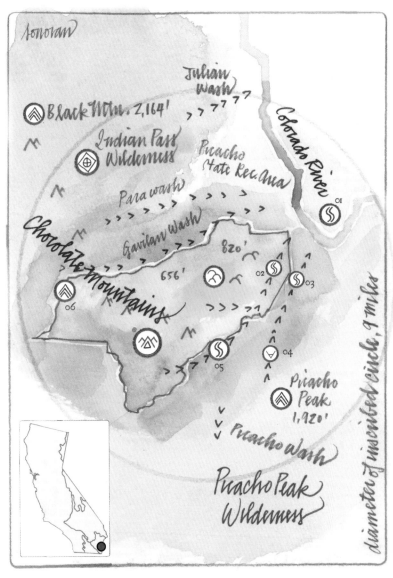

Map 07.21

## 07.21 RICH HABITAT NEAR THE COLORADO RIVER
*Picacho Peak Wilderness*

Picacho Peak (1,922') lies outside its namesake wilderness. Picacho Peak Wilderness is dominated by the Gavilan Wash and is part of a necklace of connected wilderness areas in the proximity of the Colorado River, including Imperial Wilderness, Indian Pass Wilderness, and Little Picacho Peak Wilderness.

01. Adobe Lake
02. Carrizo Falls
03. Bear Canyon Falls
04. Bear Canyon
05. Carrizo Wash
06. Indian Pass

... highest peak is Mica Peak (1,499')
a basaltic mountain)

... habitat for many sensitive species of
flora and fauna is provided by waterfalls
in the Carrizo Wash)

... habitat for a relatively abundant
populations of bighorn and
tortoise

Texas stork's bill
*Erodium Texanum)*

Generalized elevation range
300–1,500 feet

Land area
8,860 acres
13.84 square miles

Curve-billed thrasher
*Toxostoma curvirostre*

Colorado River toad
*Incilius alvarius*

Texas stork's bill
*Erodium texanum*

Little gold poppy
*Eschscholzia minutiflora*

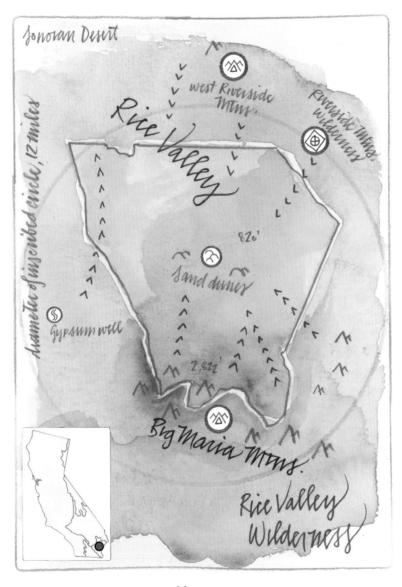

Sonoran Desert

West Riverside Mtns.

Riverside Mtns. Wilderness

Rice Valley

diameter of inscribed circle, 12 miles

826'

Sand dunes

Gypsum well

2,822'

Big Maria Mtns.

Rice Valley Wilderness

Map 07.22

## 07.22 DUNES NORTH OF BIG MARIA MOUNTAINS
*Rice Valley Wilderness*

Most of the Rice Valley Wilderness, north of the Big Maria Mountains, is a broad bajada that runs to a series of sand dunes. These sand dunes are part of what is called the erg-sand sheet (see also 07.05), one of the largest dune networks in California's deserts; it includes the Cadiz Valley and the Ward Valley—both are northwest of Rice Valley.

... noted creosote-shrub biodiversity exists across a secluded alluvial fan that makes up most of the land area

... harbors the world's largest stand of Emory's crucifixion thorn, *Castela emoryi*[21]

... core habitat of the Kit fox, *Vulpes macrotis*[22]

Devil's spineflower
*Chorizanthe rigida*

Generalized elevation range
500–2,900 feet

Land area
41,777 acres
65.28 square miles

Mojave fringe-toed lizard
*Uma scoparia*

Cheeseweed owlfly
*Oliarces clara*

Devil's spineflower
*Chorizanthe rigida*

Sonoran sandmat
*Euphorbia micromera*

## Fringe-toed lizards in California

These dune-adapted lizards have elongated scales on their hind toes that form a "fringe" that enables them to move quickly over loose and sandy soil.

Coachella Valley fringe-toed lizard, *Uma inornata*
Colorado Desert fringe-toed lizard, *Uma notata*
Mojave fringe-toed lizard, *Uma scoparia*
Yuman Desert fringe-toed lizard, *Uma cowlesi*

Mojave
fringe-toed
lizard
Uma scoparia

The great miracle of understanding is the more energy you spend, the more your investment grows, returning the now-transformed energy to you, exceeding what was there before. The danger is in the discrepancy between truth and understanding. I am learning more about my own desire for interconnection, for an antidote to nihilism. I sense it, like something beautiful in the wind, a place of wholeness behind the next turn in the trail.

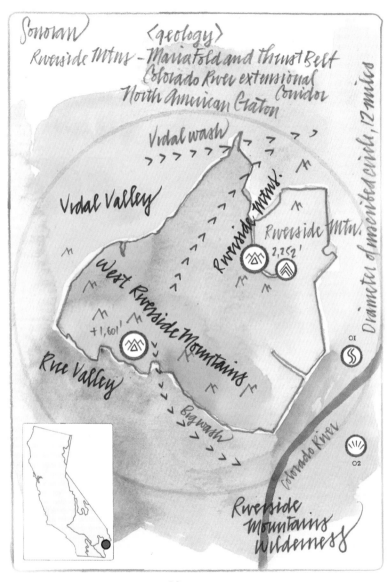

Sonoran

⟨geology⟩

Riverside Mtns - Maria Fold and Thrust Belt
Colorado River extensional
Corridor
North American Craton

Vidal wash

Vidal Valley

Riverside Mtns.

Riverside Mtn.
2,252'

West Riverside Mountains

+1,601'

Rice Valley

Big wash

Diameter of inscribed circle, 12 miles

01

02

Colorado River

Riverside
Mountains
Wilderness

Map 07.23

## 07.23 WEST BANK OF THE COLORADO RIVER
*Riverside Mountains Wilderness*

The Riverside Mountains are so close to the Colorado River and the Arizona border that ducks can be heard from the east side of the mountain slopes and you can see a wide view of Parker Valley on the river's far side. To the south is the taller Big Maria Mountains range, and to the north is the wide Vidal Valley.

01. Lost Lake
02. Parker Valley (400')

*... mountainous habitat for sensitive cactus species*

*... Ironwood and palo verde woodlands throughout*

*... ample habitat for a hearty herd of burro deer, Sonoran mule deer Odocoileus hemionus*

*white-crowned sparrow*
*Zonotrichia leucophrys*

Generalized elevation range
400–2,300 feet

Land area
22,380 acres
34.97 square miles

White-crowned sparrow
*Zonotrichia leucophrys*

Black harvester ant
*Veromessor pergandei*

Parry's false prairie-clover
*Marina parryi*

Desert gold
*Geraea canescens*

Map 07.24

## 07.24 STEEP MOUNTAINS WEST OF ANZA-BORREGO DESERT STATE PARK
*Sawtooth Mountains Wilderness*

On the eastern flank of the Laguna Mountains, a few mountain ranges rise that are at least partially inside the Sawtooth Mountains Wilderness, including the namesake Sawtooth Mountains and the Tierra Blanca Mountains. Due to its proximity to Anza-Borrego Desert State Park and the Cleveland National Forest, this wilderness is part of a larger roadless network of extensive wildland habitat.

01. Sawtooth Mountains
    Wilderness Study Area
02. Troutman Mountain (2,000')
03. Mat Kwa'rar Nemaaw
04. Moonlight Canyon
05. North Wash
06. Canebrake Wash
07. Carrizo Valley
08. Carrizo Gorge Wilderness
09. Cuyapaipe Indian Reservation
10. Monument Peak (6,271')

Generalized elevation range
1,400–5,600 feet

Land area
33,772 acres
52.77 square miles

White-winged dove
*Zenaida asiatica*

Western toad
*Anaxyrus boreas*

Acton brittlebush
*Encelia actoni*

California chicory
*Rafinesquia californica*

... incredible plant diversity, including two hundred different species of flowering plants [23]

... a transition zone between coastal vegetation of the Southern California mountains and the desert vegetation of the Colorado Desert

... habitat for dozens of endangered and threatened animal and plant species, including the San Diego horned lizard *Phrynosoma coronatum* and Jacumba milkvetch *Astragalus douglasii var. perstrictus*

western toad
*Anaxyrus boreas*

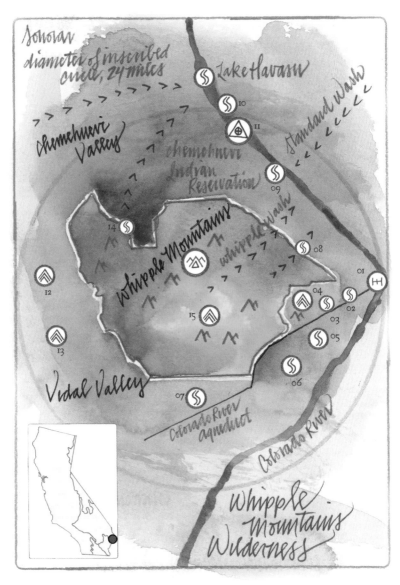

Map 07.25

## 07.25 EASTERNMOST MOUNTAINS OF CALIFORNIA
*Whipple Mountains Wilderness*

A fourteen-mile-long, east–west-oriented mountain range juts out to form the Whipple Mountains, the easternmost peaks in California. The large Whipple Wash bisects the wilderness and drains into the nearby Colorado River. Desert pavement covers large areas of the western half of the desert.

01. Parker Dam
02. Gene Wash Reservoir
03. Copper Basin Reservoir
04. Monument Peak (2,453')
05. Bowmans Wash
06. Bennett Wash
07. Arch Creek
08. Black Metal Wash
09. Whipple Bay
10. Thompson Bay
11. Lake Havasu State Park
12. Pyramid Butte (1,848')
13. Savahia Peak (2,695')
14. Whipple Well
15. Unnamed peak (4,118')

... fossil evidence of middens, as constructed by millennia after millennia of desert pack rat, *Neotoma* spp. (family Cricetidae), offers clues to the ancient climate and vegetation history of Sonora)[24]

... biodiverse washes include rare California habitat for Saguaro cactus, *Carnegiea gigantea*

... high concentrations of desert tortoise, *Gopherus agassizii*, upwards of one hundred per square mile[25]

Generalized elevation range
500–4,200 feet

Land area
76,123 acres
118.94 square miles

Ash-throated flycatcher
*Myiarchus cinerascens*

Yellow-backed spiny lizard
*Sceloporus uniformis*

Parish's goldeneye
*Bahiopsis parishii*

Yellowhead
*Trichoptilium incisum*

Parish's goldeneye
*Bahiopsis parishii*

*Opuntia sp. (beavertail)
in the Whipple Mountains*

the loeal pit, between the nostril
and the eye of family Crotalinae
the pit vipers. extumely sensitive
infared-detecting organs.

# 08. PHILOSOPHIES OF WHAT COMES NEXT
## *California's tomorrow desert*

*Ammopelmatus kelsoensis*
Kelsodunes jerusalem cricket
burrow-dwelling

family Stenopelmatidae

spines (vestigial) on legs, distinguishing from other "related bugs" species

7 genera 50 species in this family
strong jaws - can bite
regularly 2" long
detritivore

When imagining the future of any ecological system in the Anthropocene, it is useful to go beyond polarized judgments about things getting worse or things getting better. Might it be possible for things to be getting worse and getting better at the same time? Depending on the scale of investigation, it certainly is.

However much the desert ecology has transformed over the past two hundred years, it is likely to transform again over the next few centuries, and to a similar degree. We have the opportunity to decide what the character of future deserts will be. Our ability to solve problems, build infrastructure, and facilitate restoration projects is matched by our capacity to demonstrate compassion and empathy, plan for the future, and understand the minute and nuanced implications of our collective action.

The bottleneck that is the twenty-first century is also a bridge between economic paradigms. The State of California is planning to become carbon neutral by 2045. What might a postcarbon economy mean for California Nature?[1] What story is being told, or what story should be told about our rights, our responsibilities, and our relationship to the more-than-human world? A review of the predominant ideas that shaped twentieth-century conservation policy might offer clues about what is happening in the twenty-first century and what may be where the story is headed in the twenty-second century.

In the first half of the twentieth century, the federal government and, to some degree, the state government initiated the first phase of what can be called a land protection paradigm in the form of the National Park System (founded 1916), the National Forest Service (founded 1905), and California State Parks (founded 1927). In this paradigm, nature was imagined as an aspect of the world to be put away, to be stored, to be visited, and to be used. The fetishizing of nature expressed its apotheosis with the Wilderness Act of 1964. In the Wilderness Act, a piece of land designated as wilderness is a discrete object, a piece of public property permanently inhabited only by the thing called nature, and the assumption is that nature's preservation will be guaranteed by its physical sequestration. Roadless lands were attributed the characteristics "intact" and "wild," and therefore deserved to be free from development, exploitation, and disposal. These lands were successfully presented in federal court to be valuable for intrinsic reasons that transcended the utilitarian mindset that until then dominated American attitudes toward nature. Regardless of this kind of particular commentary about how wilderness law prevents engagement of many regenerative cultural practices within local ecological communities, the Wilderness Act represented a seismic shift in land policy.

Great basin bumble bee
Bombus centralis

Upper Centennial Springs
Coso Range Wilderness

every tuneful drop of rain feels like a prayer, a power, and a spirit.

Arguably, the Wilderness Act and the many nature-protecting laws that followed were popularly ushered into the American psyche through the work of two writers: Rachel Carson and Wallace Stegner.

During the second half of the twentieth century, following the Wilderness Act, a series of extremely effective and extremely popular, albeit reactive, laws were passed that proved the United States could correct course when it came to such serious issues as water and air cleanliness and the protection of endangered species.[2] These monumental laws—among them the Clean Air Act (1963), the Clean Water Act (1972), and the Endangered Species Act (1973)—expanded the idea of nature to codify the idea of the environment as an entity of sorts that interfaces with and affects the well-being of human society. The environment was an invented concept that, when coupled with the wilderness idea, presented a modern construct of nature as a quantifiable something that was measurably in decline.

Turkey Vulture
Cathartes aura

In 1994, the US Congress passed a sweeping law that set a benchmark for desert land preservation. The California Desert Protection Act established the boundary designations for the majority of the maps and land descriptions in this book. Included in the bill were the establishment of Death Valley National Park, Joshua Tree National Park, and Mojave National Preserve as well as sixty-nine desert wilderness areas. This law redesignated Death Valley as a national park, after its founding designation as a national monument in 1933. Joshua Tree National Park was also redesignated after its founding in 1936 as a national monument. The East Mojave National Scenic Area, designated as such in 1981, became the Mojave National Preserve.

The California Protection Act of 2010 continued to expand land protection policy by designating 344,000 acres as federal wilderness (much of it in the national parks) and also designating seventy-six miles of watercourse to be protected under the Wild & Scenic Rivers Act, the nation's most stringent protection for

Turkey Vulture
*Cathartes aura*

rivers. These watercourses include Surprise Canyon Creek, west of Death Valley National Park; parts of the Amargosa River; and parts of the Deep Creek/ Whitewater River network that flow east from San Gorgonio in the San Bernardino National Forest. The California Protection Act of 2010 laid the legislative groundwork for the designation of the Mojave Trails National Monument (2016), the Sand to Snow National Monument (2016), and the Castle Mountains National Monument (2016).

In addition to these landmark acts of Congress, the end of the twentieth and the beginning of the twenty-first centuries saw the advent of a grassroots network of land trusts and NGOs (nongovernmental organizations). Land trusts use various legal means, including management of conservation easements (a partnership of public and private interests to preserve land) and fee-simple acquisition (the purchase of inholdings) to protect land, often with the intent of restoring degraded habitat, Indigenous rights, or wildlife connectivity.

With the implementation of the Desert Renewable Energy Conservation Plan (DRECP) in 2016 (see 08.05), the Bureau of Land Management and the State of California are betting that through the massive implementation of solar, wind, and steam-energy production technology on desert lands, significant progress in reducing America's carbon emissions can occur and that wildlife can also be protected. Recognizing that industrial carbon emissions are spurring rapid climate breakdown by way of anthropogenic global warming, California launched an ambitious plan in 2018, through an executive order issued by the governor, to attain carbon neutrality by 2045. This would not be at all possible without the DRECP. Furthermore, in 2020, and again by executive order, the 30×30 initiative, with its stated mission to protect from development, degradation, and extraction 30 percent of California's land and water by 2030, is setting an ambitious agenda for the next decade. In that time, California will ascertain whether the assumption that investing so much land area to renewable energy can be done concurrently with meeting the needs of an ecologically healthy desert, or whether indeed, the outcomes of policy decisions mean that nature is sacrificed to save the environment.

How can we insure a carbon-free future while also preserving the quality of extant biodiversity in the deserts? What if technical, educated, unionized trade labor were put to the task? Might, for example, the establishment of a fully funded Climate Conservation Corps be able to tackle a large range of landscape-scale ecological issues, from removing invasive species, to assisting the migration of at-risk species to habitat refugia, to preventing and abating wildfire? In 2022, the Inflation Reduction Act was signed into national law. Despite its lackluster name, the law promises a huge impact on not only the California deserts but the global atmosphere. Original drafts of the law had included the idea of establishing a Climate Corps, but instead, a funding windfall dedicated to the production of renewable energy infrastructure has been negotiated, risking the delicate balance between development and ensuring that wildlife and wild habitat conditions are maintained and respected.

Establishing something like a publicly financed Climate Corps is one possible approach to integrating the justice-serving application of scientific innovation with sensitivity to and awareness of what is commonly called, in academic, cultural, and political circles, traditional ecological knowledge (TEK). An array of techniques and traditions—the multimillennia-old Indigenous techniques of reciprocity and abundance, including managed disturbance regimes and nonextractive agricultural and harvesting practices—may prove to be essential. Policies that simultaneously draw from both science and TEK may be the key to shifting the balance away from California's dangerous prescription for increasing ecological degradation and toward augmenting endemic systems of resilience. By prioritizing the protection of biodiversity as key to preventing ecological collapse, legal policy in the postcarbon society might expand the Endangered Species Act to protect not only species but endangered phenomena. Natural cycles and aspects of the more-than-human world, such as the season of winter itself, might gain standing in court to continue to exist as an essential component of a functioning desert.

To continue the list of policy moves that may be implemented, it may also be that legal personhood for watersheds will established, acknowledging water's right to exist unmarred. This concept is already being tested in other countries and in some tribal courts in California; might the Amargosa River have its day in court to represent itself against those who would destroy it? It might also be that habitat and migration corridors will become incorporated into every housing development plan as the human and more-than-human worlds integrate to become a single whole. Even given all the progress over the past century toward a holistic vision of the deserts, creative, codifiable insurance against the continued destruction of the deserts' ecosystems has only begun to be imagined, implemented, and fought for. With that in mind, this final chapter inventories some of the challenges and opportunities that the communities of the future deserts are beginning to act on today.

*snow on the joshua tree*

## Climate breakdown

All signs point to increasingly dry conditions over the next one hundred years in the California deserts, especially through winter.[3] Modeling also suggests that there will be increased temperatures region-wide, especially of the important baseline that is the nightly minimum temperature.[4] It may seem counterintuitive that so many desert plants need cool, even cold nights, but it is very much the case. The Joshua tree, *Yucca brevifolia*, for example, needs the disturbance of cold snaps during the winter to produce flowers in the spring.[5] Although some native plants—those able to tap deep water, such as creosote—may do well, perhaps even spread in their range, increased heat and aridity could make for dry soil conditions and threaten native perennials that might be disastrously outcompeted by fast-growing, invasive annuals. The woodlands may not fare better; as increased drought stress continues, piñon becomes susceptible to beetle infestation (piñon beetle, *Ips confusus*) and increasingly vulnerable to fire. Perhaps just as likely is an increase in distribution range for some desert plants as desert-like conditions manifest to the north and west.

Cheatgrass, *Bromus tectorum*

Compact brome, *Bromus madritensis*

Fountain grass, *Pennisetum setaceum*

Kelch grass, *Schismus barbatus*

African mustard, *Brassica tournefortii*

Red brome, *Bromus rubens*

Above are common invasive plant species that radiate out from populated areas, displacing natives, altering the fire regime, and possibly surging in a future Mojave marked by increased numbers of precipitation events, increased aridity, and increased atmospheric carbon and nitrogen.

*Immolation of the Joshua tree*

## Now and Future Fire in the Deserts of California

The fire regime across the pre-Euro-American Mojave and Sonoran Deserts existed in three modalities.[6] The first type was extremely infrequent (up to six hundred years between fire events) in the middle-elevation shrub communities across alluvial bajadas—indicator species: creosote. The second was slightly more frequent (up to 150 years between fire events) in the high-elevation shrublands and woodlands—indicator species: piñon and juniper.[7] The third was the moderately frequent (fifteen to thirty years between fire events) in the spring/oasis sites, where the fire rarely extended out from its source more than a dozen meters—indicator species: desert palm.[8] With increased grass invasivity, fire return intervals shrank, and the landscape became threatened with conversion from shrubland to grassland. In 2005, more than one million acres burned across the Mojave Desert, and in 2020, nearly one-and-a-half million individual Joshua trees were killed in a single conflagration within Mojave National Preserve.[9]

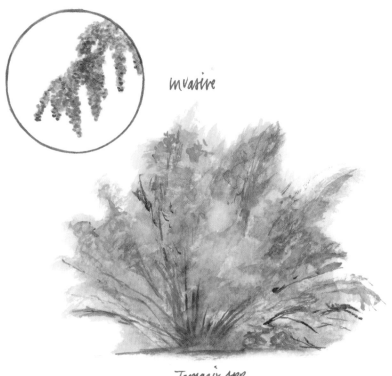

*Invasive*

*Tamarix spp.*
*Tamarix*

## March of the Tamarix

The invasive *Tamarix* spp., called salt cedar, is very good at outcompeting native riparian plants for habitat resources. Tamarix likes to regularly burn. Able to burn with a higher intensity than the high-moisture fuels of the native riparian plant community, tamarix bounces back vigorously postfire and will destroy the recovery attempts of the native flora, creating for itself a monotypic grove.[10]

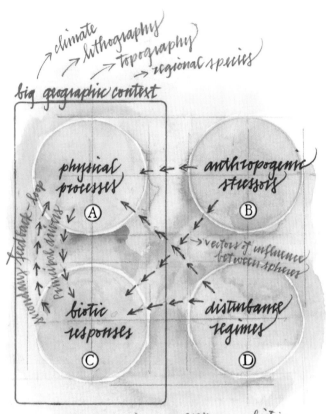

climate
lithography
topography
regional species

big geographic context

physical processes
(A)

anthropogenic stressors
(B)

biotic responses
(C)

disturbance regimes
(D)

anomaly feedback loop
amplified drivers

vectors of influence between spheres

note: resiliency and vulnerability are biotic responses with functional implications rooted in ecological complexity and simplicity in local biodiversity

Stressors and Drivers

Diagram 08.01

## o8.oi MAPPING UNINTENDED CONSEQUENCES
*A causal web of ecological stress*

Fundamental to the study of ecology is the relationship between the living and nonliving forces within an environment, and how they affect each other. Diagram o8.oi imagines a large number of forces, or variables, within four spheres of influence that work together in a network to describe some of the primary factors that determine the deserts' ecological quality. An imbalance in any one of these factors may spark a cascading effect that either moves the whole living network forward in regular succession, like a fire inside a normalized regime moving through a habitat and encouraging renewal; or the effect may result in an unraveling cascade that converts the ecosystem to something else, like an invasive reed destroying a pond through eutrophication that encourages desiccation. The dynamic forces that influence the biogeographic context of life in the modern deserts operate in a matrix of causality directed by regimes. A regime is the return of a disturbance at some regular or nonregular interval. The word *stress*, in an ecological context, refers to the influence of a disturbance on the ecosystem. Understanding how and which anthropogenic stresses and disturbance regimes influence the landscape and then detailing the biotic response to those dynamic networks offer valuable insight into how the living desert maintains itself.[11]

### A. Physical Processes

Hydrology
Sediment
Soil biodiversity
Biogeochemical cycling
Habitat configuration
  and chemistry

### B. Anthropogenic Stressors

Land designation—policy
Habitat degredation/
  restoration/mediation
Water withdrawl
Fire

### C. Biotic Responses

Biomass density
Age structure
Alliance (community) dynamics
Resliency/vulnerability
Physiological adaptations
Genetic diversity
Food web dynamics

### D. Disturbance Regimes

Floods
Fire
Drought
Storms
Disease
Herbivory
Climate
Invasivity

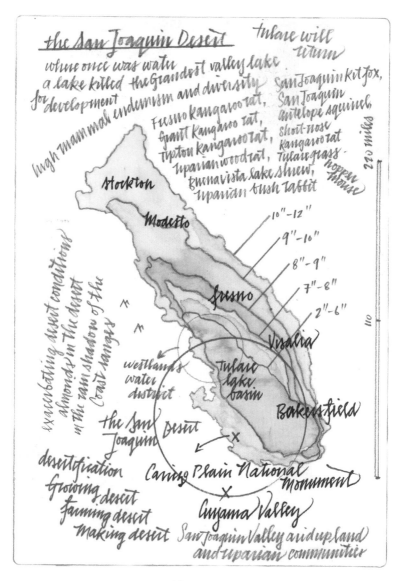

the San Joaquin Desert    Tulare will
                           return
where once was water
a lake killed the Grandest valley lake
for development  high mammal endemism and diversity   San Joaquin kit fox,
                                          San Joaquin
                    Fresno kangaroo rat,   antelope squirrel
                    Giant kangaroo rat,    short-nose
                    Tipton kangaroo rat,   kangaroo rat
                    riparian woodrat,  Tulare grass
                    Buena vista lake shrew,   hopper
                    riparian bush rabbit      mouse

Stockton

Modesto                              10"-12"

                                     9"-10"

                                     8"-9"

                                     7"-8"
                    Fresno
                                     2"-6"

                              Visalia
            westlands
            water       Tulare
exacerbating desert conditions  district   lake
almonds in the desert                basin
in the rain shadow of the
Coast Ranges                              Bakersfield
            the San
            Joaquin  Desert
                           X
desertification
growing desert   Carrizo Plain National
farming desert                   Monument
making desert   X
            Cuyama Valley
            San Joaquin Valley arid upland
            and riparian communities

Map 08.02

## o8.o2 MAGIC, PLUNDER, AND PORTEND
*California's valley desert*

In the rain shadow east of the California's Central Coast ranges sits the misunderstood San Joaquin Desert. At over twice the size of Death Valley National Park, this arid region that includes half the San Joaquin Valley, Cuyama Valley, and Carrizo Plain has long been miscategorized as an annual grassland, when it would be more appropriate for development, research, and popular understanding to call it what it is—a desert.[12] More than half of the San Joaquin Desert is now converted to grassland dominated by invasive species or has been appropriated for agricultural use.[13] With soil composed of rich, Holocene alluvium, the valley has resisted being labeled as a desert. It is the curse and the blessing of the valley that it contains some of the world's best soil, but with less than ten inches of rain per year cannot support irrigated agriculture without imported water.[14] Until the first part of the twentieth century, Tulare Lake, in the middle of the valley, was the largest lake by land area in the state. Fed by the unimpounded Kings, Kaweah, Tule, and Kern Rivers for millennia, the Tulare lakebed was converted in the mid-twentieth century by private interests, backed by the Bureau of Reclamation, to cotton production after the dammed rivers starved the once vast wetlands. The economy based on industrial agriculture in this part of the valley has historically been dominated by a few, whether businesspeople or corporations, and through the apparatus of water district agencies, these few still manage to get the water needed to maintain growth, even in the claypan soils of Westlands, despite the ever-increasingly arid climate.[15]

As profoundly as irrigation has transformed this valley, as fundamentally as modern industry has altered the ecology of this valley, so too will the valley transform again over the next hundred years as the industry and the culture that depends on it wrestle with the local and now global ramifications of anthropogenic desertification—whether that be dam construction for flood control or the ongoing practice of unrecoverable groundwater depletion. The question becomes, is the industry stealing from the future to support an economy whose sustainability is based on an illusion?

*Map o8.o2 Source*: Adapted from "Average Annual Precipitation (Inches) in the San Joaquin Valley," Oregon State University, PRISM Climate Group, http://prism.oregonstate.edu.

kit fox
*Vulpes macrotis*

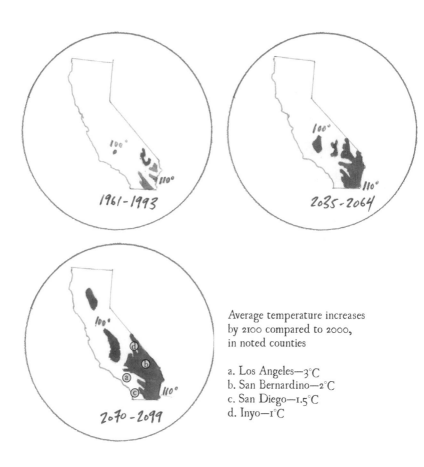

Average temperature increases
by 2100 compared to 2000,
in noted counties

a. Los Angeles—3°C
b. San Bernardino—2°C
c. San Diego—1.5°C
d. Inyo—1°C

## Map 08.03

July Temperature Extremes across California, Historical and Predicted 1961–2099.
*Map 08.03 Source*: Adapted from D. Cayan, M. Tyree, M. Dettinger, H. Hidalgo,
T. Das, E. Maurer, P. Bromirski, N. Graham, and R. Flick, "Climate Change
Scenarios and Sea Level Rise Estimates for the California 2009 Climate Change
Scenarios Assessment," https://www.sciencebase.gov/catalog/item
/51701361e4b05024ef3cd662.

## 08.03 HOTTER SUMMERS
*Mapping increasing temperature averages*

As global warming increases local temperatures across California, the ecology of the deserts will be tremendously affected. More frequent, deeper, and longer droughts, an altered monsoon season, and increased soil aridity will displace historical regimes for a great many organisms thought to be already at their thermal limits.[16] As entire ecologies look for refuge from a warming and desiccating atmosphere, upslope and northward is the place to find it, however temporarily. In the forests of the Santa Rosa Mountains, vegetational biozones have entirely shifted upward in elevation from historical levels by over two hundred feet in the thirty years between 1977 and 2007.[17]

Carrizo

the wall                                                        08.04

California

o1
o2        o3
          o4
          o5      o6
                  o7                          ag

pedestrian fence

vehicle fence

Mexico

Map one
the existing wall in California
diameter of inscribed circle, 160 miles

Ca
        ag      NM
                        Texas

Mexico

Map two
the existing wall across four states
diameter of inscribed circle, 1,000 miles

the ecological improvement of their manifestation of ideology, is tragic and deep

Map 08.04

## 08.04 HABITAT DYSCONNECTIVITY
*Desert fragmentation by infrastructure*

The virulent and deleterious effects of modern infrastructure and development on the desert landscape cannot be overstated. The combined effect of urban and transportation infrastructure has deformed ecological conditions desert-wide. Some of the effects include the accretion of impervious surfaces (asphalt and concrete) across hundreds of thousands of acres of land, thousands of acre-feet of pumped groundwater and the contamination of groundwater reservoirs, habitat degradation through isolation, habitat destruction by off-road vehicle use, nondegradable garbage and plastic pollution, flood expulsion through control basins, invasive landscape plants, predator subsidization, increased carbon and environmental nitrogen promoting the growth of invasive grasses, roadkill, rodenticide pollution, heat-island effects, light pollution, sound pollution, feral pets, and sewage contamination. The cumulative effect may prove to be a wholesale transformation of the desert itself away from the processes and entities that this book depicts as the character of the deserts. With the emergence of the altered, Anthropocene desert, new complex systems will inevitably yield new niche opportunities for novel ecosystems to populate.

In an ultimate act of fragmentation rooted in a divisive paradigm of nationalism, a wall along the southern border of the United States and Mexico remains in various stages of completion. From the Gulf of Mexico to Tijuana, the border runs for 1,933 miles, only 140 of which are inside California. Of the total, 1,279 miles remain unwalled and of that, 654 miles of the so-called wall are only a fence (pedestrian barrier).[18] Because there are twenty-five million acres of protected land within one hundred miles of the border, from Texas to California, the area is full of rich habitat for many threatened and endangered species.[19] In California, dozens of species of migrating animals are negatively impacted by the wall's impassability. Among them are the mountain lion, bighorn sheep, burrowing owl, and Quino checkerspot butterfly, *Euphydryas editha quino*. The Jacumba bighorn subpopulation, which numbered 232 in 2010, migrate seasonally across the border in an unwalled area south of the Jacumba Wilderness.[20]

01. San Diego
02. Tijuana
03. Otay Mountain Wilderness
04. Anza-Borrego Desert State Park
05. Jacumba Wilderness
06. Calexico
07. Mexicali

*Map 08.04 Source*: Adapted from M. Mark, S. Gould, and A. Kiersz, "As the Government Shutdown over Trump's Border Wall Rages, a Journey along the Entire 1,933-Mile US-Mexico Border Shows the Monumental Task of Securing It," *Business Insider*, January 12, 2019, https://www.businessinsider.com/us-mexico-border-wall-photos-maps-2018-5.

Major infrastructure arteries—
a web of dysconnectivity across
counties

## Death from a Thousand Wounds

At least five categories of what can be called municipal infrastructure policy and planning decisions are presently being played out to the detriment of California's desert ecology at different scales of influence. The five categories are as follows (described in more detail following the list):

1. Further transportation fragmentation
   (e.g., a commuter train through the Mojave)
2. Excessive water extraction (e.g., the Cadiz Water Project)
3. "Gentrivacation" (e.g., the economic transformation of Joshua Tree)
4. "Zeroscaping" (e.g., new development styles based on
   nonecological aesthetic decisions)
5. The pointless death of wildlife (i.e., roadkill)

1. A plan to build a railway line from Victorville to Las Vegas would effectively erect a six-foot-high wall down the spine of the Mojave along Highway 15, which could potentially destroy migration routes for bighorn and dozens of other species. This is an example of "green" policy conflicting with ecological reality. The need for fewer cars on the road, which train proponents argue is part of their green agenda, should not come at the cost of desert ecosystems. Adding a few wildlife crossings to the plan to build such a train may solve the dilemma and must be part of the train's design infrastructure.[21]

2. The Cadiz Water Project plans to mine the aquifer under the Mojave Trails National Monument of sixteen billion gallons of water each year for fifty years and sell the water to Los Angeles. The Cadiz project is perhaps the greatest threat the desert ecology of this protected land, which relies on the precious water the aquifer provides, has faced in recent history. Negotiating the dynamics between a growing human community and the quality of the natural environment that that future community inhabits is perhaps the greatest challenge of the twenty-first century.[22]

Quino checkerspot
*Euphydryas editha quino*

Raven

3. *Gentrivacation* is a play on the word *gentrification*, which is an economic term that describes invasive or outside patterns imposed on a particular municipality that often displace communities, their traditions, and their demographic makeup. In Joshua Tree, the popularity of the built community of the area and access to Joshua Tree National Park have inorganically engorged real estate prices and deformed the makeup of neighborhoods, as short-term "vacation" rental properties are now beginning to outnumber permanent residences.[23]

4. *Zeroscaping* is another recently invented word that refers to a design choice of clearing and grading the local landscape around a new residential site of all shrubbery, often based on a minimalist aesthetic.[24] There seems to be a fundamental disconnect at work between what the desert is and the imposed vision of what it could be, visually designed and empty of life. An ethically bereft aesthetic choice, zeroscaping fails to consider the desert as a system worthy of freedom from imposition. Zeroscaping—as opposed to xeriscaping, which is a design style that is sympathetic to the ecological realities of the xeric environments of the desert— perpetuates a colonial view of the desert as empty of life and thereby represents a terribly nihilistic worldview.

5. The statistics on roadkill in California are tough to take. Across the state between 2016 and 2020, approximately 302 mountain lions, 557 black bears, and 27,134 deer were killed by cars.[25] In the deserts, where life is hard enough for wild animals, the idea of a violent death for the sake of transportation seems worse than wasteful. It borders on the nefariously callous. The new awareness of the efficacy of wildlife crossings—the most notable example being the Wallis Annenberg Wildlife Crossing in the Santa Monica Mountains—seems to be spurring a popular cry for this type of remedying connectivity to be built.[26]

Raven

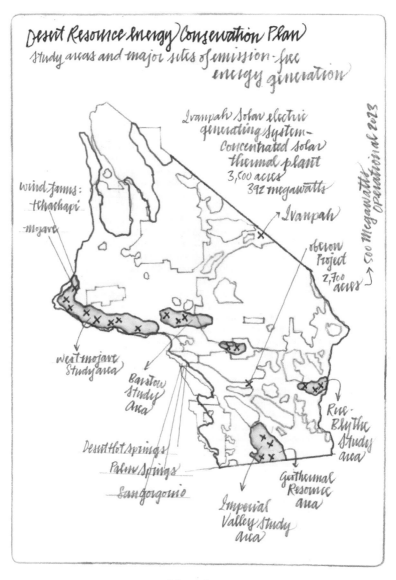

Desert Resource Energy Conservation Plan
study areas and major sites of emission-free energy generation

Ivanpah Solar electric generating system - Concentrated solar thermal plant 3,500 acres 392 megawatts

→ Ivanpah

Oberon Project 2,700 acres

← 500 megawatts Operational 2023

wind farms: Tehachapi Mojave

West mojave study area

Barstow study area

Desert Hot Springs Palm Springs San gorgonio

Imperial Valley study area

Rice-Blythe Study area

Geothermal Resource area

Map 08.05

## 08.05 SUN, WIND, AND STEAM
*The value and cost of energy*

The carbon-based energy economy is rapidly transitioning to emission-free sources of energy, and the primary technologies employed to generate that energy, in the form of electricity, are solar, wind, and geothermal. There is a piece of important legislation that is precariously holding the line between two needs, proposing a compromise. On one side is the desperate need for society to wean itself from carbon-based energy in order to prevent climate catastrophe, and on the other side is the equally desperate need to preserve fragile ecosystems and their rare, endemic desert biodiversity. The legislation, as regulated by the Bureau of Land Management (BLM), is the Desert Resource Energy Conservation Plan (DRECP). The DRECP galvanizes many state and federal agencies to manage the preservation of the deserts and their dismantlement through energy-infrastructure construction. The construction of energy projects impacts the desert ecosystem in many ways, including but not limited to habitat fragmentation and reduction, dust generation, the compaction of desert soil, reduction of plant cover, increased soil erosion, changes in plant production and composition, bird death by thermal solar technology and windmills, and an unknown photovoltaic panel recycling life span and regime.[27]

On September 6, 2022, during a record-breaking heat wave, California broke another record: it demanded fifty-two thousand megawatts (MW) of electricity.[28] The national mandate is now that the country will be generating 100 percent of its electricity through carbon-free technology by 2035.[29] As part of that mandate, the Bureau of Land Management, the agency that manages 10 million acres of the 22 million-acre DRECP, has approved sixty-four new wind, solar, and geothermal projects that will generate an estimated capacity of 41,000 MW. It is reviewing another 140 applications for such projects.[30] Because the BLM is a federal organization, these projects are across the West, not just in California. The DRECP has a goal of producing a capacity of 20,000 MW by 2030 in a network of 250,000 acres of wind, solar, and geothermal infrastructure that will ultimately sprawl across two million acres of land[31]; given the current capacity of about 7,000 MW, the next decade will surely see a massive wave of infrastructure construction in the desert.

*Current renewable energy infrastructure in the desert*

> Five wind farms inside the DRECP generate a capacity of 3,828 MW.

> The thirteen biggest solar plants in the Mojave Desert have a combined capacity of 2,125 MW.[32]

> Ten geothermal power plants in the Imperial Valley Geothermal Resource Area produce a combined capacity of 327 MW.[33]

Map 08.06

## 08.06 WHAT REMAINS INTACT
*Finding the desert's core habitat areas*

In the probably impossible, desperately hopeful, and paradoxically imperative act of trying to preserve the desert while developing it, there are many actors who are negotiating what gets saved and what gets spent in the deserts of California. One of the strategies to this end is the identification of core habitat areas. Deemed by the Nature Conservancy as critical to the preservation of as much species richness as possible, *ecological core areas* seem to be off-limits and must-saves if indeed the actors are sincere in their commitment to preserving biodiversity. *Ecologically intact areas* are one rung down from core areas on a rather arbitrary ladder of designation, but vital nonetheless, providing connective land area between cores such that habitat islands don't wither from within due to lack of energy flow from outside their boundaries. The last two types of landscape designation employ the rather anesthetized labels of *moderately degraded* and *highly converted* and are most probably sacrifice zones if they are not protected already, given the ravenous energy-infrastructure boom occurring now in California's deserts.[34]

Mojave

Prairie Falcon
Falco mexicanus

## The California Desert Conservation Area:
*The ten areas of the DRECP's biological conservation framework*

01. Cadiz Valley and Chocolate
    Mountains
02. Imperial–Borrego Valley
03. Kingston and Funeral Mountains
04. Mojave; Silurian Valley
05. Owens Valley
06. Panamint Death Valley
07. Pinto Lucerne Valley
08. Piute Valley and Sacramento
    Mountains
09. Providence and
    Bullion Mountains
10. West Mojave; eastern slopes

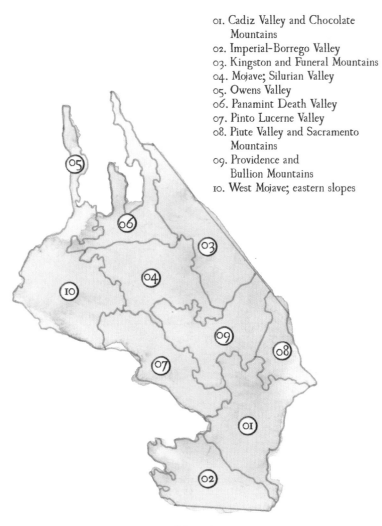

Map 08.07

## 08.07 UNDERSTANDING THE GAME OF INCHES
*A biological conservation framework*

In the twenty-two million acres covered by the DRECP, a game of inches is being played between the actors in power (governmental agencies, corporate interests, activists for the land, Indigenous sovereignties, environmental NGOs, municipalities, land trusts, and public interest at-large) about how much land space the imaginary construct of nature actually needs and how much of that land space can simply be destroyed to feed the equally imaginary construct called modern society.

Further dividing the desert into ten conservation areas, the DRECP employs a geographic system called the California Desert Biological Conservation Framework. This framework is the official scoreboard in this game of inches. It accounts for what are called "general community groupings: natural communities," which are generalized habitat types based on vegetation patterns, and counts how many acres are within each section. What is summarized on the next page are those groupings totaled across all ten of the framework areas. The total biological conservation framework (BCF) acres and percentage protected represent the highest amount possible of recognized habitat that could be saved, a best-case scenario after the DRECP achieves its goals—but only if everything goes as planned.

*Ivanpah*

| Grouping | Total acres | Total acres protected today | Total BCF acres | Percentage with potential protection |
|---|---|---|---|---|
| California forest and woodland | 150,000 | 33,000 | 128,000 | 86 |
| Chaparral and coastal scrub | 109,000 | 16,000 | 71,000 | 65 |
| Desert conifer woodlands | 287,000 | 170,000 | 250,000 | 87 |
| Desert outcrop and bandlands | 1,590,000 | 996,000 | 1,430,000 | 90 |
| Desert scrub | 13,055,000 | 6,985,000 | 11,258,000 | 86 |
| Dunes | 286,000 | 166,000 | 251,000 | 88 |
| Grassland | 237,000 | 26,000 | 115,000 | 48 |
| Riparian | 691,000 | 327,000 | 789,000 | 82 |
| Wetland | 851,000 | 225,000 | 655,000 | 77 |
| Other (agriculture and development) | 1,219,000 | 13,000 | 110,000 | 9 |

*Source*: Adapted from "California Desert Biological Conservation Framework Analysis," in *Desert Renewable Energy Conservation Plan, Land Use Amendment*, 2016, 49–66, https://eplanning.blm.gov/public_projects/lup/66459/133474/163144/DRECP_BLM_LUPA.pdf.

Greater roadrunner
*Geococcyx californian*

## The 30×30 Plan in California's Deserts

California's bold move to sequester from development, extraction, and other forms of degradation (including use of off-highway vehicles, or OHVs) 30 percent of the state's total land area and waterways by 2030 is called the 30×30 plan. The determination of what is and what is not protected is largely based on how disturbances in the ecology, such as fire, are managed at the urban–wildland interface. The land management categories established to gauge the quality of management enacted within a specific designation are referred to as gap status codes (named for the Gap Analysis Project).[35] Gap level 1 is any designated land area managed for diversity wherein disturbance events proceed or are mimicked. Level 2 is any designated land area managed for diversity wherein disturbance events are suppressed. Level 3 is any land area managed for multiple uses—subject to extraction (e.g., mining or logging) or OHVs. Wilderness areas are level 1, whereas many national monuments are level 3. Gap levels 1 and 2 are consistent with the goals of the 30×30 program.[36] Gap levels are a good metric of the legislative quality of preservation on the land. They indicate what legal license human industry retains to disturb the land for profit. As innovative as 30×30 is, the danger is that it gives license to further ransack the other 70 percent of California.

Because enough of it is already protected under the DRECP, the protected land within the California Desert Conservation Area is doing a lot of the heavy lifting for the 30×30 plan across the state. When the goals of the DRECP are met, 17,256,000 acres of the ten habitats described on map 08.07 will enjoy an average of 78 percent protection, working out to approximately 13,459,680 acres, or nearly 13.5 percent toward the state's 30×30 goal.

white-lined sphinx moth
*Hyles lineata*

Rare plant diversity in the California deserts

more rare ← → more common

Map 08.08

## 08.08 TRACKING THE POLLINATORS
*Predicting rare plant biogeography*

All desert plants are rare, but a full 25 percent (152 species) of all rare desert plants (491 species, as designated by the California Native Plant Society) are also endemic.[37] Of these, only 13 are protected by the Endangered Species Act.

As we consider plants species, if they are angiosperms (flowering plants), so too must we consider what is probably a close to corresponding number of pollinators. Pollinators can be any kind of animal, from ant to moth to bat, but perhaps the most ubiquitous and perhaps the most popular is the bee. Taxonomically, bees are in the superfamily Apoidea in the order Hymenoptera, which along with the sphecid wasps (family Sphecidae) form the group known as apiformes.[38] The deserts of the West are home to world-class bee biodiversity. The Mojave Desert counts at least 689 resident species of bee, and in the Sonoran Desert the number of species tops over 1,000.

Threatened by development, invasive competitors (such as the honey bee, *Apis mellifera*), and a growing disruption of the synchrony between seasonal flower blooms and bee activity due to global warming, the bee is a key actor in habitat sustainability going forward because it is the bee that we have to thank for the flowers. Protect the bee and you protect our wild gardens.

*Calochortus flexuosus*
Mojave mariposa lily

*Map 08.08 Source*: Adapted from P. McIntyre, "Applying Species Distribution Modeling to Identify Rare Species Hot Spots," *Fremontia* 42, no. 1 (2014): 15–16

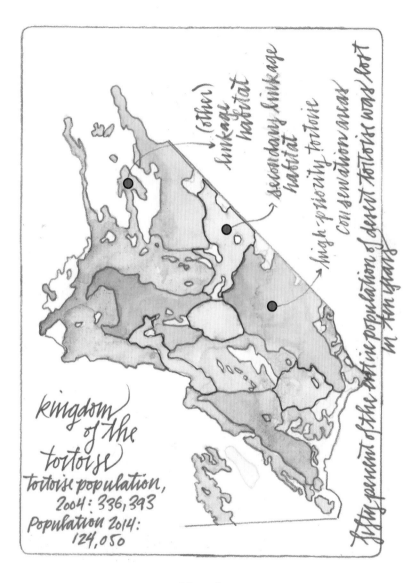

(other) linkage habitat

secondary linkage habitat

high-priority tortoise conservation areas

fifty percent of the entire population of desert tortoise was lost in ten years

kingdom of the tortoise

tortoise population, 2004: 336,393

Population 2014: 124,050

Map 08.09

## 08.09 AN ESSENTIAL CHARACTER
*Habitat for the desert tortoise*

If there is one indicator species that should be regarded as the measure of success in creating a nonfragmented landscape, it is our friend the slow-moving desert tortoise, *Gopherus agassizii*. Universally loved and perhaps universally disrespected, this queen of the desert is as the land: tough but vulnerable, resilient but sensitive. The many vectors of desert fragmentation are together conspiring to threaten the future existence of this icon. Roads, for example, erode tortoise populations not only because of the terrible toll that traffic takes but because of tortoises' reticence to cross them, causing isolation. With the coming wave of solar projects that will devour hundreds of thousands of acres of desert habitat, it is the charismatic tortoise who may feel the impact most. Two predominant threats exacerbated by development include (1) increased predation by ravens, whose populations are growing in developed communities encroaching on tortoise lands; and (2) increased risk of inbreeding, due to habitat fragmentation and thus population isolation.[39] Dozens of desert species—including the burrowing owl and the kit fox, who both den in abandoned tortoise holes—depend on the ecological engineering of the tortoise and her ability to dig relatively deep burrows. What tragic cascade of collapse and disappearance will flow through the heart of the desert if the tortoise is lost?

desert tortoise
*Gopherus agassizii*

*Map 08.09 Source*: Adapted from "20130517_Desert Tortoise_ TCA_Linkage_Master_Layer," US Fish and Wildlife Service and University of Redlands.

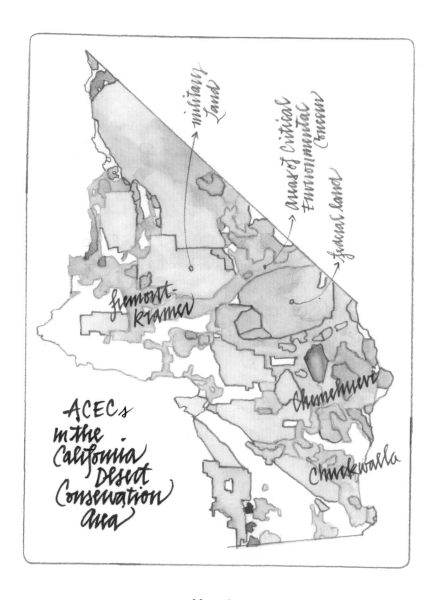

military land

Areas of Critical Environmental Concern

general land

Fremont-Kramer

Chemehuevi

Chuckwalla

ACECs in the California Desert Conservation Area

Map 08.10

## 08.10 INSIDE AN EMERGING DESIGNATION
*Areas of critical environmental concern*

In addition to the 5 million acres of land in the DRECP's conservation area that are already protected through wilderness designation or as wilderness study areas or national monuments, the DRECP plans to secure 4.2 million acres of land designated as areas of critical environmental concern (ACEC), California Desert National Conservation Lands, or other wildlife allocations.[41] ACECs are protected from development by something called a development cap. This contrivance allows for only 1 percent development across the land, and legally forbids any means by which the land may used for solar development at some future date.[42] These areas are a different kind of wilderness, not as stringently protected and intentionally designated for human recreation, but set aside nonetheless.

*Map 08.10 Source*: Adapted from P. Satin, "The California Desert Conservation Area," Mojave Desert Land Trust, February 16, 2018.

## A Vision of Governing the West by Watershed

In a lucid, prescient moment in American history, the first director of the US Geological Survey (USGS), John Wesley Powell, in his work titled *Report on the Lands of the Arid Region of the United States, with a More Detailed Account of the Lands of Utah* (1878), laid out a plan for settling the West that was built around the realities of water in what he called America's Great Desert. Powell foresaw that the implementation of traditional state borders, as they exist in the East, would result in the "piling up of a heritage of conflict" in the West because of the simple lack of water.[43] Powell stated that cities should not exist in this landscape and that approximately only 1 to 3 percent of the land area should be developed. As an alternative, Powell proposed a system of common fenceless grazing lands (perhaps an early version of today's public lands) within semistates whose boundaries would be drawn around watersheds.[44]

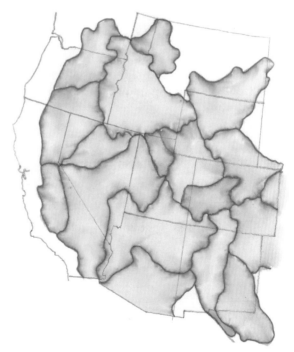

*John Wesley Powell's water map of the West, 1876*

"Heaven and earth are a bellows:
empty yet structured,
it moves,
inexhaustibly giving."
—Laotzu

what genius awaits its emergence to end
not the world of nature, the earth abides,
but to end the worlds of consumerism,
extractionism, and industrial
fundamentalism?

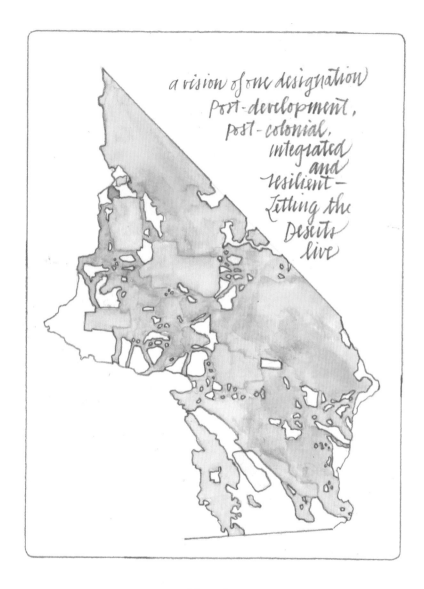

a vision of one designation
post-development,
post-colonial,
integrated
and
resilient —
letting the
Deserts
live

Map 08.11

## 08.11 A CIRCUIT COMPLETE
*The reunited desert*

Time will tell whether human agency, empowered as wisely as conceivably possible with innovative technology, Indigenous technique, and scientific specificity, can indeed reverse the forces that march so many living systems to the edge. Time will tell whether it is a false assumption that both rampant energy development and ecological sustainability can exist in this unique, twenty-two-million-acre piece of the planet. Time will tell how much time the desert needs. Time to recover. Time to transform into what it will become next.

Restoration in the desert presents many challenges that don't exist as such in mesic systems. Desert soils are of a particular structure that developed over hundreds of thousands of years, and once disturbed may never exist in that form again. Reseeding human-planted groves, a common restoration strategy, is often foiled by insects and rodents, and the process is further complicated by decreasing rainfall and by the rarity of native plants dropping their seeds.[45] Despite these challenges, creativity abounds, as do novel and traditional solutions in the stalwart community of scientists and stewards who work from a place of unending love and unfailing hope.

To reinforce the innate defenses of an ecosystem is to foster mechanics of resistance (rejecting alteration) and resilience (recovering from disturbance).[46] In conjunction with local restoration efforts, attending to a landscape-scale project to increase connectivity between essential habitats is the clearest path to bolstering what remains.[47] There are many potential causes of local extinction for isolated populations of any species, and shoring up a network of high-quality unmolested habitat blocks and extending that quality to the land that connects them may be the best strategy for developing resistance and resilience.

All the plans and all the visions of the future deserts of California as living spaces—robust with wildlife and thriving in conjunction with a postcarbon human society—are built on hope. Hope is the actionable tool that can guide the adventure when hardships threaten disaster. Hope has the power to transform reality; and then, once reality is transformed, a funny thing happens—hope is no longer needed and is replaced by gratitude. Whether gratitude manifests after a day of misfortune on the trail or after a long era of industrialization, thankfulness begins to reveal the grace of regeneration and resiliency. Having survived one thing, the mind begins to detect patterns of survivability, and abundance begins to supplant scarcity. Resources are revealed within the heart and on the land, and a matrix of reciprocation becomes a self-feeding system of being. The light of gratitude,

If I can't get to the mountain
the mountain can get to me
through the book.
Books are trails
that uncover the nature
of thought itself.

having emerged from darker moments when hope was relied on to find the path, warms the ground; and a homeostatic energy, a relationship between give and take, becomes accessible. The light of gratitude, in a last act of beauty, illuminates the shadowed heart of wilderness, presenting it as a loving place that can finally be called home. The dangerous trail becomes a familiar path. Out there, under the dusty sky and ten miles from any road, bathed in the prismatic spray of the Mojave sunset, Coyote's song of hope and gratitude bounces off the far hills. While it may seem to the cynical human ear that Coyote's joyous song is mocking or perhaps scornful of modern humanity's manic efforts to find the path before night falls, the song is offered as a knowing invitation to a new and yet ancient world that has been here the whole time.

# ACKNOWLEDGMENTS

The community responsible for making this book possible includes an enormous collection of family, friends, collectors, patrons, colleagues, bookstores, scientists, artists, citizens, collaborators, correspondents, volunteers, makers, and, ultimately, engaged readers like you. The team at Heyday who have published my books for many years now are indispensable from start to finish: Emmerich Anklam, editor; Steve Wasserman, publisher; Ashley Ingram, designer; Diane Lee, art director; Kalie Caetano, marketing and publicity director; and the rest of the team at Heyday, who provide support like a family that I am blessed to be a part of. Here I've collected a partial list of some of the professionals who have had a direct influence on the making of this book, and to whom I am forever in debt for it.

Adina Merenlender / UC Climate Stewards

Aimee Luc / Saint Joseph's Arts Society

Alice Gu / Filmmaker

Antonia Adezio / Marin Art and Garden Center

Arlene Ustin / Athenian Wilderness Experience

Beth Pratt / National Wildlife Federation

Bonnie Holman / California Wilderness Coalition

Cara Coger / Mariposa Arts Council

Chris Morrill / California Wilderness Coalition

Clifford E. Trafzer / University of California, Riverside

Cody Hanford / Mojave Desert Land Trust

David Bess / CDFW Law Enforcement Division

Dup Crosson / California Wilderness Coalition

Elizabeth McKenzie / Catamaran Literary Reader

Enich Harris / Coast Film Festival

Erin Boehme / C5 Studios Community Arts Center

Greg Sarris / Federated Indians of Graton Rancheria

Gregory Ira / California Naturalist Program

Hall Newbegin / Juniper Ridge

Jared Blumenfeld / California Environmental Protection Agency

Jared and Julia Drake / Wildbound PR

Jeff Thrope / Cold Splinters

Josh Jackson / Forgotten Lands California

Kathy Jorgensen / Borrego Arts Institute

Kelly Herbinson / Mojave Desert Land Trust

Ken and Nancy Nieland / Sandhill Crane Foundation

Kevin Connelly / Pacific Forest Trust

Kim Powers / IDEO

Laurie Wayburn / Pacific Forest Trust

Leslie Carol Roberts / Ecopoesis

Liesbet Olaerts / Sierra Nevada Alliance

Lindsie Bear / Humboldt Area Foundation

Liv O'Keefe / California Native Plant Society

Louesa Roebuck / Punk Ikebana

Magnus Toren / Henry Miller Library

Malcolm Margolin / California Institute for Community, Art, and Nature

Mats Andersson / Indigofera

Matt Decker / Premium Tattoo

Michael Connolly Miskwish / Kumeyaay Historic Preservation Council

Michael Fried / Planet Earth Arts

Michael Kauffmann / Backcountry Press

Nancy Fluharty / Sierra Foothill Conservancy

Nadia and Dominic Gill / Encompass Films

Neal Sharma / Wildlife Conservation Network

Orrin Goldsby / David Baker Architects

Sabrina Jacobs / KPFA Berkeley

Sarah Beck / Pacific Horticulture

Steve Till / Consultant biologist

Susan Burnett / Mojave Sands

Terria Smith / Heyday and *News from Native California*

Wade Crowfoot / California Natural Resources Agency

The movement to keep California's wilderness lands free from development and to end the industrialized exploitation of these lands exists within a changing story of inclusivity, accessibility, and resiliency. As the attitude of conservationism shifts from merely sequestering landscape to recognizing both the dynamic roles that tribal stewardship has played and what emergent scientific innovation can play, in terms of bolstering ecological resiliency, California relies on politically capable organizations such as CALWILD to lead the way. As a member of the board of directors of the California Wilderness Coalition (CALWILD), I am proud to witness and participate in the nuanced, courageous, and necessary sparks of activist thought that generate campaign after campaign championed by this singular organization. I encourage every one of my readers to become a member of CALWILD and to support democratic efforts to defend our precious public lands across California.

# GLOSSARY

**Allelopathy (n.), Allelopathic (adj.).** Plants that are able to generate and apply chemicals that either support or dissuade growth of other plants in the vicinity, e.g., creosote, *Larrea tridentata*.

**Alluvium.** Loose soil, sediment, or accumulated material deposited across bajadas and washes by water.

**Bajada.** The sloped feature, perhaps miles wide, that forms at the base of desert mountains, composed of alluvium and deposited by erosion.

**Biocrust.** The collection of nonvascular plants, including mosses, lichens, and blue-green algae, that form a dark-colored mat on soil surfaces across the desert.

**Detritivore.** An animal, from micro-arthropods (mites, protozoa, etc.) to the turkey vulture, that survives by feeding on dead organic matter.

**Disturbance.** A stressor that alters homeostasis within a system.

**Endemic.** Describing a species that exists only in one region, watershed, locale, or habitat.

**Endorheic.** A type of watershed that has no outlet to another body of water such as the ocean, but rather drains to some wetland feature such as a inland lake.

**Eutrophication.** The process by which an aquatic ecosystem is transformed by the accumulation of nutrients, resulting in algal blooms and oxygen depletion.

**Forb.** A flowering plant that is not a grass and generally has a nonwoody stem, e.g., Mojave sunflower, *Eriophyllum mohavense*.

**Genotype (n.), genotypic (adj.).** Referring to the complete set of genetic information within an individual. The phenotype is the expression of that genetic information in the organism's physiology or behavior.

**Halophyte (n.), halophytic (adj.).** A plant species that is adapted to live in high-salt environments, e.g., desert holly, *Atriplex hymenelytra*.

**Heliophyte (n.), heliophytic (adj.).** A plant species that is adapted to live in full sunlight, e.g., desert fan palm, *Washingtonia filifera*.

**Keystone species.** The species within an ecosystem that has a disproportionate influence on other species or processes within that ecosystem.

**Lacustrine.** One of five types of wet-lands. Lacustrine wetlands include lakes. Marine wetlands are exposed to the open ocean. Estuarine wetlands are near the ocean and contain a mix of salt and fresh water. Riverine wetlands involve flowing water. Palustrine wetlands are inland and characterized by emergent vegetation.

**Monotypic.** Term relating either to taxonomy, referring to a genus that has only one species, or to landscape ecology, referring to a grove or copse of trees that contains only one species of shrub or tree.

**Orogeny.** The process of tectonic geology that forms a mountain range.

**Parent material.** The geological substrate from which erosional processes produce soil.

**Phreatophyte (n.), phreatophytic (adj.).** Deep-rooted plants that are able to tap water deep beneath the surface in what is called the phreatic zone, where the weight of the earth from above is great enough to generate flow of the groundwater, e.g., desert fan palm, *Washingtonia filifera*.

**Pluvial lake.** An intermittent lake in a landlocked basin, formed by rainfall.

**Playa.** The flat beds of fine-grained sediment that form at the lowest parts of a basin; often plant-free and the location where seasonal lakes may form.

**Psammophyte (n.), psammophytic (adj.).** Plants that are adapted to grow in sandy or loose soils.

**Refugia.** Relict habitat that remains extant despite regime change in an ecosystem.

**Regime.** Any normalized pattern that exists as a rhythm of influence on an ecosystem.

**Relict.** A species population seen in the fossil record that was more widespread in previous eras and that remains extant today in small populations in a reduced range (may also refer to ecosystem refugia).

**Resilience.** The capacity of a system, individual, or community to respond and absorb disturbance while it maintains its original character and does not acquiesce to disturbance.

**Restoration.** Managing a habitat for resiliency based on historical integrity, whether passive (removing pollution to encourage native recruitment) or active (altering the landscape and repairing ecological functionality).

**Thermophyte (n.), thermophytic (adj.).** A plant species that survives and thrives in very high temperatures, e.g., panic grasses, *Panicum* spp.

**Trophism (n.), trophic (adj.).** The dynamic of how predators and herbivory affect species populations in an ecosystem, as described by a food chain or a food web.

**Watershed.** A geographical entity between ridgelines that defines drainage in a basin area.

**Watt.** A unit of electricity used to measure the power being used at one moment in time. A megawatt (MW) is one million watts.

**Xeric (adj.).** Denoting dry or exceptionally dry conditions in a habitat or environment. A mesic environment is one with a moderate amount of moisture. A hydric environment is one saturated by water.

# NOTES

Internet sources were accessed in 2022.

## INTRODUCTION

1. W. H. McNab, D. T. Cleland, J. A. Freeouf, J. E. Keys, G. J. Nowacki, and C. A. Carpenter, "Ecological Subregions: Sections and Subsections of the Conterminous United States [1:3,500,000]," cartography by A. M. Sloan, General Technical Report WO-76 (Washington, DC: US Department of Agriculture, Forest Service, 2007), https://doi.org/10.2737/WO-GTR-76B.

2. "National Conservation Lands of the California Desert," Bureau of Land Management, https://www.blm.gov/programs/national-conservation-lands/national -conservation-lands-of-the-california-desert.

3. "Desert Renewable Energy Conservation Plan," California Energy Commission, https://www.energy.ca.gov/programs-and-topics/programs/desert-renewable -energy-conservation-plan.

4. "Threatened and Endangered Species," California Department Fish and Wildlife (CDFW), https://wildlife.ca.gov/Conservation/CESA.

5. "Species of Special Concern," CDFW, https://wildlife.ca.gov/Conservation/SSC.

## 01. THE DIRE AND THE SUBLIME

1. US Geological Survey (USGS), "Deserts: Geology and Resources," https://pubs .usgs.gov/gip/7000004/report.pdf.

2. USDA Forest Service ECOMAP Team, "United States Forest Service Ecological Subregions of the U.S.A." (Washington, DC: USDA, Forest Service, 2007), https:// databasin.org/datasets/662c543156c14313b87d9b99b7a78221.

3. M. Lanza, "11,000 Feet over Death Valley," *The Big Outside*, October 18, 2020, https://thebigoutside.com/11000-feet-over-death-valley-hiking-telescope-peak.

4. California Department Fish and Game, "California Climate Based on the Köppen Classification System," as printed in the *Atlas of the Biodiversity of California*, 2003.

5. J. Sawyer, T. Keeler-Wolf, and J. Evens, *A Manual of California Vegetation*, 2nd ed. (Sacramento: California Native Plant Society, 1995).

6. R. H. Webb, L. F. Fenstermaker, J. S. Heaton, D. L. Hughston, E. V. Macdonald, and D. M. Miller, eds., *The Mojave Desert: Ecosystem Processes and Sustainability* (Reno: University of Nevada Press, 2009).

7. P. W. Rundel, R. J. Gustafson, and M. E. Kauffmann, *California Desert Plants* (Kneeland, CA: Backcountry Press, 2022), 90.

8. D. L. Hartmann, *Global Physical Climatology*, 2nd ed. (Amsterdam: Elsevier, 2016), 165–76.

9. R. B. Cowles, *Desert Journal: A Naturalist Reflects on Arid California* (Berkeley: University of California Press, 1977), 16–21.

10. "North American Deserts," faculty website, University of Nevada, Las Vegas, http://landau.faculty.unlv.edu//northamericandeserts.htm.

11. National Oceanic and Atmospheric Administration, "What Is EDDI?" NOAA, 2022, https://psl.noaa.gov/eddi.

12. B. L. Ingram and F. Malamud-Roam, *The West without Water: What Past Floods, Droughts, and Other Climatic Clues Tell Us about Tomorrow* (Berkeley: University of California Press, 2013), 121–29.

13. P. W. Rundel and A. C. Gibson, *Ecological Communities and Processes in a Mojave Desert Ecosystem: Rock Valley, Nevada* (Cambridge, UK: Cambridge University Press, 1996).

14. C. S. Crawford, *Biology of Desert Invertebrates* (Berlin: Springer, 1981).

15. C. J. Fridrich, R. A. Thompson, J. L. Slate, M. E. Berry, and M. N. Machette, "Geologic Map of the Southern Funeral Mountains Including Nearby Groundwater Discharge Sites in Death Valley National Park, California and Nevada," Scientific Investigations Map 3151, 2012, https://doi.org/10.3133/sim3151.

16. R. Aalbu, "An Analysis of the Coleoptera of Mitchell Caverns, San Bernardino County, California," *National Speleological Bulletin 51*, no. 1 (1989): 1–10, https://web.archive.org/web/20210103192945/https://caves.org/pub/journal/NSS_Bulletin_volume_51.shtml.

17. R. F. Butler, *Paleomagnetism: Magnetic Domains to Geologic Terranes* (Oxford: Blackwell, 1992), 205.

18. B. C. Burchfiel, D. S. Cowan, and G. A. Davis, "Tectonic Overview of the Cordilleran Orogen in the Western United States," in *The Cordilleran Orogen: Coterminous U.S.* (Boulder, CO: Geologic Society of America, 1992), https://doi.org/10.1130/DNAG-GNA-G3.

19. California Department of Fish and Wildlife, "Desert Bighorn Sheep Facts," https://wildlife.ca.gov/conservation/mammals/bighorn-sheep/desert.

20. USGS, "National Atlas of the United States," 2002, https://www.usgs.gov/publications/national-atlas-united-states-maps.

21. USGS, "What Kind of Movement Has Occurred along the Fault?" 2016, https://pubs.usgs.gov/gip/earthq3/move.html.

22. G. A. Davis and B. C. Burchfiel, "Garlock Fault: An Intracontinental Transform Structure, Southern California," *GSA Bulletin 84*, no. 4 (1973): 1407–22, https://doi.org/10.1130/0016-7606(1973)84<1407:GFAITS>2.0.CO;2.

23. USGS, "Weathering and Erosion in Desert Environments," USGS Western Region Geology and Geophysics Science Center, 2009, http://pubs.usgs.gov/of/2004/1007/erosion.html.

24. J. Belnap, R. H. Webb, M. E. Miller, D. M. Miller, L. A. DeFalco, P. A. Medica, M. L. Brooks, T. C. Esque, and D. Bedford, "Monitoring Ecosystem Quality and Function in Arid Setting of the Mojave Desert." USGS Scientific Report 2009-5064, http://pubs.usgs.gov/sir/2008/5064.

25. B. F. Hicks, "Prehistoric Development and Dispersal of the Desert Fan Palm," *Principes* 33, no. 1 (1989): 33–39, https://palms.org/wp-content/uploads/2016/05/vol33n1p33-39.pdf.

26. C. A. Schroeder, "Prehistoric Avocados in California," *California Avocado Society Yearbook* 52 (1968): 29–34, http://avocadosource.com/CAS_Yearbooks/CAS_52_1968/CAS_1968_PG_029-034.pdf.

27. Map adapted from K. L. Cole, K. Ironside, J. Eischleid, G. Garfin, P. B. Duffy, and C. Toney, "Past and Ongoing Shifts in Joshua Tree Distribution Support Future Modeled Range Contraction," *Ecological Applications* 21, no. 1 (2011): 137–49, https://doi.org/10.1890/09-1800.1.

28. Personal conversation with M. C. Miskwish (author of *Maay Uuyow: Kumeyaay Cosmology*), summer 2022.

## 02. EVERY SACRED DROP

1. "Chapter 1: Introduction, Scope, and Future Directions," in *California's Groundwater Update 2013: A Compilation of Enhanced Content for California Water Plan*, State of California Natural Resources Agency, Department of Water Resources, 2015, https://data.cnra.ca.gov/dataset/california-water-plan-groundwater-update-2013.

2. T. Woodward and J. Curran, "2022–2023 Engineer's Report on Water Supply and Replenishment Assessment," Coachella Valley Water District, 2022, http://cvwd.org/ArchiveCenter/ViewFile/Item/978.

3. E. Rode, "What Do Colorado River Cuts Mean for California's Imperial, Coachella Valleys?" *Desert Sun*, August 16, 2022, https://www.desertsun.com/story/news/2022/08/16/colorado-river-imperial-valley-coachella-valley-drought-impacts/10334232002.

4. California Department of Water Resources, "Chapter 9. Options for Meeting Future Water Needs in Eastern Sierra and Colorado River—Colorado River Hydrologic Region," in California Water Plan, Bulletin 160-98, 1998, https://nrm.dfg.ca.gov/FileHandler.ashx?DocumentID=8763.

5. National Park Service, "Mojave National Preserve," https://www.nps.gov/moja/learn/nature/springs-main.htm.

6. J. F. LaBounty and J. E. Deacon, "*Cyprinodon milleri*, a New Species of Pupfish (Family Cyprinodontidae) from Death Valley, California," *Copeia 1972*, no. 4 (*1972*): 769–80, https://doi.org/10.2307/1442734.

7. R. J. Naiman, S. D. Gerking, and T. D. Ratcliff, "Thermal Environment of a Death Valley Pupfish," *Copeia 1973*, no. 2 (*1973*): 366–69, https://doi.org /10.2307/1442988.

8. K. V. Brix and M. Grosell, "Characterization of Na(+) Uptake in the Endangered Desert Pupfish, *Cyprinodon macularius* (Baird and Girard)," *Conservation Physiology 1*, no. 1 (*2013*): cot005, https://doi.org/10.1093/conphys/cot005.

9. M. T. Roberts, "Stratigraphy and Depositional Environments of the Crystal Spring Formation, Southern Death Valley Region, California," *Special Report: Geologic Features—Death Valley, California* (Sacramento: California Division of Mines and Geology, *1976*).

10. "Places We Protect: Amargosa Project," Nature Conservancy, https://www.nature .org/en-us/get-involved/how-to-help/places-we-protect/amargosa-river.

11. "Water-Data Report 2007: 10251300 Amargosa River at Tecopa, CA," USGS, https://wdr.water.usgs.gov/wy2007/pdfs/10251300.2007.pdf.

12. "Conservation Areas," Lower Colorado River Multi-Species Conservation Program, https://www.lcrmscp.gov/activities/conservation_areas.

13. A. Hager, "Tribes in the Colorado River Basin Say They're 'in the Dark' as States Discuss Water Conservation," KUNC, August 5, 2022, https://www.kunc.org/environ ment/2022-08-05/tribes-in-the-colorado-river-basin-say-theyre-in-the-dark-as-states -discuss-water-conservation.

14. "Map of Tribes in the Colorado River Basin," University of Montana, Center for Natural Resources & Environmental Policy, http://www.naturalresourcespolicy.org /images/col-river-basin/map-tribes-crb.jpg.

15. "Lower Colorado Water Supply Report: River Operations," Bureau of Reclamation, accessed August 29, 2022, https://www.usbr.gov/lc/region/g4000/weekly.pdf.

16. "Chapter 11: South Lahontan Hydrologic Region Groundwater," in *California's Groundwater Update 2013: A Compilation of Enhanced Content for California Water Plan*, State of California Natural Resources Agency, Department of Water Resources, *2015*, https://data.cnra.ca.gov/dataset/california-water-plan-groundwater-update-2013.

17. B. M. Pavlik, *The California Deserts: An Ecological Rediscovery* (Berkeley: University of California Press, 2008). 272.

18. Mono Basin Ecosystem Study Committee et al., *The Mono Basin Ecosystem: Effects of Changing Lake Level* (Washington, DC: National Academy Press, *1987*).

19. "Mission and History," Mono Lake Committee, https://www.monolake.org /whatwedo/aboutus/missionandhistory.

20. T. Tierney, *Geology of the Mono Basin* (Lee Vining, CA: Kutsavi Press/Mono Lake Committee, *1995*), 45–46.

21. L. V. Benson, S. P. Lund, J. W. Burdett., M. Kashgarian, T. P. Rose, J. P. Smoot, and M. Schwartz, "Correlation of Late-Pleistocene Lake-Level Oscillations in Mono Lake, California, with North Atlantic Climate Events," *Quaternary Research* 49, no. 1 (1998): 1–10.

22. M. C. Reheis, "Dust Deposition Downwind of Owens (Dry) Lake, 1991–1994: Preliminary Findings," *Journal of Geophysical Research: Atmospheres* 102, no. D22 (1997): 25999–26008, https://doi.org/10.1029/97JD01967.

23. A. Steinwand and R. Harrington, "Simulation of Water Table Fluctuations at Permanent Monitoring Sites to Evaluate Groundwater Pumping," Inyo County Water Department, February 25, 2003, https://www.inyowater.org/wp-content/uploads/2012/12/SteinHarr_Water_Table_Simulation_2003.pdf.

24. J. M. Smith and M. E. Mather, "Beaver Dams Maintain Fish Biodiversity by Increasing Habitat Heterogeneity throughout a Low-Gradient Stream Network," *Freshwater Biology* 58, no. 7 (2013): 1523–38, https://doi.org/10.1111/fwb.12153.

25. "F.A.Q.," Salton Sea Authority, https://saltonsea.com/about/faq/#.

26. P. Fuller and M. Neilson, "*Bairdiella icistia*," NAS - Nonindigenous Aquatic Species, USGS, 2014, revised 2018, https://nas.er.usgs.gov/queries/factsheet.aspx?SpeciesID=947.

27. P. Fuller and M. Neilson, "*Cynoscion xanthulus*," NAS - Nonindigenous Aquatic Species, USGS, 2014, revised 2019, https://nas.er.usgs.gov/queries/factsheet.aspx?SpeciesID=952.

28. R. Riedel, "Trends of Abundance of Salton Sea Fish: A Reversible Collapse or a Permanent Condition?" *Natural Resources* 7, no. 10 (2016), https://doi.org/10.4236/nr.2016.710045.

29. "Desert Pupfish, Cyprinodon macularis," California Department of Fish and Wildlife, https://wildlife.ca.gov/Regions/6/Desert-Fishes/Desert-Pupfish.

30. J. Cornett, "The Only Bird in the World Known to Hibernate Does So Right Here in the Coachella Valley," *Desert Sun*, August 27, 2018, https://www.desertsun.com/story/desert-magazine/2018/08/27/palm-springs-area-home-poor-only-bird-known-hibernate/1111601002.

31. D. A. Barum, J. Elder, D. Stephens, and M. Friend, eds., "The Salton Sea," *Hydrobiologia* 473, nos. 1–3 (2002): 1–306, https://link.springer.com/journal/10750/volumes-and-issues/473-1.

32. J. Wilson, "Salton Sea: Fish and the Birds That Fed on Them Wiped Out This Winter," *Desert Sun*, February 8, 2019, https://www.desertsun.com/story/news/2019/02/08/salton-sea-california-fish-bird-die-off-winter/2818025002.

33. "Salton Sea Hydrological Modeling and Results," Imperial Irrigation District, 2018, https://www.iid.com/home/showdocument?id=17299.

34. S. Parker, "How the Salton Sea Became an Eco-Wasteland," *HowStuffWorks*, 2019, https://science.howstuffworks.com/environmental/conservation/issues/salton-sea.htm?srch_tag=cqz6gku3tzw5cm25j4k7q2mgmsnpwovm.

35. E. Anderson, "State Launches Salton Sea Restoration Effort," KPBS, February 15, 2021, https://www.kpbs.org/news/midday-edition/2021/02/15/state-launches-salton -sea-restoration-effort.

36. Pavlik, *California Deserts*, 86.

37. NOAA, "Paleoclimate Data before 2,000 Years Ago," https://www.ncei.noaa.gov /sites/default/files/2021-11/12.

38. J. Spector, "California Could Need 55GW of Long-Duration Storage to Meet Its 2045 Carbon-Free Grid Goal," *Green Tech Media*, December 9, 2022, https://www .greentechmedia.com/articles/read/california-could-need-55gw-of-long-duration- storage-to-meet-2045-carbon-free-grid-goal.

39. K. Brigham, "The Salton Sea could produce the world's greenest lithium, if new extraction technologies work," CNBC, May 4, 2022, https://www.cnbc. com/2022/05/04/the-salton-sea-could-produce-the-worlds-greenest-lithium.html.

40. P. Oamek, "Will Lithium Mining Turn California's Salton Sea into a Green Energy Sacrifice Zone?" *In These Times*, November 16, 2022, https://inthesetimes.com/article /lithium-mining-california-salton-sea-green-energy#:ft:text=The%20method%20 involves%20pumping%20mineral,can%20contaminate%20local%20water%20basins.

## 03. THE LIVING NETWORK

1. Millennium Ecosystem Assessment, United Nations, 2005, https://www.millennium assessment.org/en/index.html.

2. D. C. Housman, H. H. Powers, A. D. Collins, and J. Belnap, "Carbon and Nitrogen Fixation Differ between Successional Stages of Biological Crusts in the Colorado Pla- teau and Chihuahuan Desert," *Journal of Arid Environments* 66, no. 4 (2006): 620–34, https://doi.org/10.1016/j.jaridenv.2005.11.014.

3. J. Belnap and S. D. Warren, "Patton's Tracks in the Mojave Desert, USA: An Eco- logical Legacy," *Arid Land Research and Management* 16, no. 3 (2002): 245–58, https:// doi.org/10.1080/153249802760284793.

4. M. L. Cody, "Slow-Motion Population Dynamics in Mojave Desert Perennial Plants," *Journal of Vegetation Science* 11, no. 3 (2000): 351–58, https://doi .org/10.2307/3236627.

5. P. Rundel and A. Gibson, *Ecological Communities and Processes in a Mojave Desert Eco- system: Rock Valley, Nevada* (Cambridge, UK: Cambridge University Press, 1996).

6. K. Schmidt-Nielsen, *Animal Physiology: Adaptation and Environment*, 5th ed. (Cam- bridge, UK: Cambridge University Press, 1997).

7. L. E. Green, A. Porras-Alfaro, and R. L. Sinsabaugh, "Translocation of Nitrogen and Carbon Integrates Biotic Crust and Grass Production in Desert Grassland," *Journal of Ecology* 96, no. 5 (2008): 1076–85, https://doi.org/10.1111/j.1365-2745.2008.01388.x.

8. L. R. Walker, D. B. Thompson, and F. H. Landau, "Experimental Manipulations of Fertile Islands and Nurse Plant Effects in the Mojave Desert," *Western North American Naturalist* 61, no. 1 (2001): 25–35, https://www.jstor.org/stable/41717073.

9. H. E. Weatherly, S. F. Zitzer, J. S. Coleman, and J. A. Arnone, "*In Situ* Litter Decomposition and Litter Quality in a Mojave Desert Ecosystem: Effects of $CO_2$ and Interannual Climate Variability," *Global Climate Biology* 9, no. 8 (2003): 1223–33, https://doi.org/10.1046/j.1365-2486.2003.00653.x.

10. J. Ehleringer, "Annuals and Perennials of Warm Deserts," in *Physiological Ecology of North American Plant Communities*, edited by B. F. Chabot and H. A. Mooney, 162–80. (New York: Chapman and Hall, 1985).

11. D. Grayson, "The Extinct Ice Age Mammals of North America," video lecture series, University of Washington, 2016, https://anthropology.washington.edu/news/2016/06/16/don-graysons-university-faculty-lecture.

12. E. P. Hamerlynch, J. R. McAuliffe, E. V. McDonald, and S. D. Smith, "Ecological Responses of Two Mojave Desert Shrubs to Soil Horizon Development and Soil Water Dynamics," *Ecology* 83, no. 3 (2002): 768–79, https://doi.org/10.1890/0012-9658 (2002)083[0768:EROTMD]2.0.CO;2.

13. R. L. Reynolds, J. C. Yount, M. Reheis, H. Goldstein, P. Chavez Jr., R. Fulton, J. Whitney, C. Fuller, and R. M. Forester, "Dust Emission from Wet and Dry Playas in the Mojave Desert," *Earth Surface Processes and Landforms* 32, no. 12 (2007): 1811–27, https://doi.org/10.1002/esp.1515.

14. M. W. Skinner and B. M. Pavlik, *California Native Plant Society's Inventory of Rare and Endangered Vascular Plants of California* (Sacramento: California Native Plant Society, 1994).

15. R. S. Thompson and K. H. Anderson, "Biomes of Western North America at 18,000, 6000 and 0 14C yr BP Reconstructed from Pollen and Packrat Midden Data," *Journal of Biogeography* 27, no. 3 (2000): 555–84, https://doi.org/10.1046/j.1365-2699 .2000.00427.x.

16. R. F. Daubenmire, "Merriam's Life Zones of North America," *Quarterly Review of Biology* 13, no. 3 (1938): 327–32, https://doi.org/10.1086/394564.

17. Adapted from T. Keeler-Wolf, "Mojave Desert Vegetation," in *Atlas of Biodiversity of California* (Sacramento: California Department of Fish and Game, 2003), 66.

18. W. Willner, "What Is an Alliance?" *Vegetation Classification and Survey* 1 (2020): 139–44, https://doi.org/10.3897/VCS/2020/56372.

19. J. Sawyer, T. Keeler-Wolf, and J. Evens, *A Manual of California Vegetation*, 2nd ed. (Sacramento: California Native Plant Society, 2009), www.cnps.org/vegetation/manual -of-california-vegetation; vegetation.cnps.org.

20. W. H. McNab, D. T. Cleland, J. A. Freeouf, J. E. Keys Jr., G. J. Nowacki, and C. A. Carpenter, *Description of Ecological Subregions: Sections of the Conterminous United States*, Report WO-76B (Washington, DC: US Department of Agriculture, Forest Service, 2007), https://doi.org/10.2737/WO-GTR-76B.

21. D. T. Cleland, J. A. Freeouf, J. E. Keys Jr., G. J. Nowacki, C. A. Carpenter, and W. H. McNab, "Ecological Subregions: Sections and Subsections for the Conterminous United States," Report WO-76D, cartography by A. M. Sloan (Washington, DC: US Department of Agriculture, Forest Service, 2007), https://doi.org/10.2737/WO-GTR -76D.

22. K. A. Thomas, T. Keeler-Wolf, J. Franklin, and P. Stine, *Mojave Desert Ecosystem Program: Central Mojave Vegetation Database* (Sacramento: US Geological Survey [USGS], Western Ecological Research Center, and Southwest Biological Science Center, 2004), https://pubs.er.usgs.gov/publication/70200877.

23. A. Schoenherr and J. Burk, "Colorado Desert Vegetation," in *Terrestrial Vegetation of California*, 3rd ed., edited by M. G. Barbour, T. Keeler-Wolf, and A. Schoenherr, 657–76 (Berkeley: University of California Press, 2007).

24. R. A. Minnich, *California's Fading Flowers: Lost Legacy and Biological Invasions* (Berkeley: University of California Press, 2008).

25. R. J. Vogl and L. T. McHargue, "Vegetation of California Fan Palm Oases on the San Andreas Fault," *Ecology* 47, no. 4 (1966): 532–40, https://doi.org/10.2307/1933929.

26. B. Hicks, "Prehistoric Development and Dispersal of the Desert Fan Palm," *Principes* 33, no. 1 (1989): 33–39, https://palms.org/resources/palms-journal.

27. J. W. Cornett, "The Desert Fan Palm—Not a Relict," in *Mojave Desert Quarterly Research Center Third Annual Symposium Proceedings*, edited by C. A. Warren and J. S. Schneider (San Bernardino, CA: San Bernardino County Museum Association, 1989), https://nrm.dfg.ca.gov/FileHandler.ashx?DocumentID=7684.

28. J. W. Cornett, T. Glenn, and J. Stewart, "The Largest Desert Fan Palm Oases," *Principes* 30, no. 2 (1986): 82–84, https://palms.org/resources/palms-journal.

29. O. Pellmyr and K. A. Segraves, "Pollinator Divergence within an Obligate Mutualism: Two Yucca Moth Species (Lepidoptera; Prodoxidae: *Tegeticula*) on the Joshua Tree (*Yucca brevifolia*; Agavaceae)," *Annals of the Entomological Society of America* 96, no. 6 (2003): 716–22, https://doi.org/10.1603/0013-8746(2003)096[0716:PDWAOM]2.0.CO;2.

30. S. B. St. Clair and J. Hoines, "Reproductive Ecology and Stand Structure of Joshua Tree Forests across Climate Gradients of the Mojave Desert," *PLoS ONE* 13, no. 2 (2018): e0193248, https://doi.org/10.1371/journal.pone.0193248.

31. K. L. Cole, K. Ironside, J. Eischeid, G. Garfin, P. B. Duffy, and C. Toney, "Past and Ongoing Shifts in Joshua Tree Distribution Support Future Modeled Range Contraction," *Ecological Applications* 21, no. 1 (2011): 137–49, https://doi.org/10.1890/09 -1800.1.

32. D. Tirmenstein, "Artemisia tridentata subsp. tridentata," in Fire Effects Information System, USDA, Forest Service, Rocky Mountain Research Station, Fire Sciences Laboratory, 1999, https://www.fs.usda.gov/database/feis/plants/shrub/arttrit/all.html.

33. L. M. Shultz, "Artemisia tridentata subsp. wyomingensis," Jepson eFlora, Jepson Herbarium, 2012, https://ucjeps.berkeley.edu/eflora/eflora_display.php?tid=5799.

34. H. N. Mozingo, *Shrubs of the Great Basin* (Reno: University of Nevada Press, *1986*), *64*.

35. E. Muldavin and F. J. Triepke, "North American Pinyon–Juniper Woodlands: Ecological Composition, Dynamics, and Future Trends," in *Encyclopedia of the World's Biomes*, edited by M. I. Goldstein and D. A. DellaSala (Amsterdam: Elsevier, *2019*), *516–31*, https://doi .org/*10.1016*/B*978-0-12-409548-9.12113*-X.

36. S. Schwinning and M. M. Hooten, "Mojave Desert Root Systems," in *The Mojave Desert: Ecosystem Processes and Sustainability*, edited by R. H. Webb, L. F. Fenstermaker, J. S. Heaton, D. L. Hughson., E. V. McDonald, and D. M. Miller (Reno: University of Nevada Press, *2009*).

37. A. K. Marshall and K. Anna, "Larrea tridentata," in Fire Effects Information System, USDA, Forest Service, Rocky Mountain Research Station, Fire Sciences Laboratory, *1995*, https://www.fs.usda.gov/database/feis/plants/shrub/lartri/all.html.

38. D. R. Muhs, N. Lancaster, and G. L. Skipp, "A Complex Origin for the Kelso Dunes, Mojave National Preserve, California, USA: A Case Study Using a Simple Geochemical Method with Global Applications," *Geomorphology 276* (*2017*): *222–43*, https://doi.org/*10.1016*/j.geomorph.*2016.10.002*.

39. Thomas et al., *Mojave Desert Ecosystem Program*.

## 04. BIG DESERT PARCELS OF FEDERAL AND STATE LAND

1. W. Berry, "The Unsettling of America," in *The World Ending Fire* (Berkeley: Counterpoint Press, *2017*), *77*.

2. J. A. MacMahon, "North American Deserts: Their Floral and Faunal Components," in *Arid Land Ecosystems: Structure, Functioning and Management*, vol. *1*, edited by D. W. Goodall and R. A. Perry, *21–82* (Cambridge, UK: Cambridge University Press).

3. E. Abbey, *Desert Solitaire* (New York: Ballantine, *1968*).

4. L. Lindsay and P. Remeika, *Geology of Anza-Borrego: Edge of Creation* (Chula Vista, CA: Sunbelt Publications, *1993*).

5. G. Bouvier, "Jerry Schad Shows Me Anza Borrego Desert's Carrizo Badlands," *San Diego Reader*, March *15*, *2007*, https://www.sandiegoreader.com/news/*2007*/mar/*15* /nothing-not-there-and-nothing.

6. "Castle Mountains National Monument," National Park Service, *2016*, https://www .nps.gov/camo/learn/upload/CAMO-site-bulletin-*11*Feb*2016*-final-*2*.pdf.

7. L. Wright and M. Miller, "Chapter *46*: Death Valley National Park, Eastern California and Southwestern Nevada," in *Geology of National Parks*, *5*th ed., edited by A. G. Harris, E. Tuttle, and S. D. Tuttle, *610–37* (Dubuque, IA: Kendall/Hunt Publishing).

8. "Joshua Tree National Park: Geologic Formations," National Park Service, October *2*, *2017*, https://www.nps.gov/jotr/learn/nature/geologicformations.htm.

9. A. A. Colville and G. A. Novak, "Kaersutite Megacrysts and Associated Crystal Inclusions from the Cima Volcanic Field, San Bernardino County, California," *Lithos* 27, no. 2 (1991): 107–14, https://doi.org/10.1016/0024-4937(91)90023-E .

10. D. V. Prose, "Map Showing Areas of Visible Land Disturbances Caused by Two Military Training Operations in the Mojave Desert, California," USGS, Miscellaneous Field Studies Map 1855, https://doi.org/10.3133/mf1855.

11. M. B. Snell, *Unlikely Ally: How the Military Fights Climate Change and Protects the Environment* (Berkeley: Heyday, 2018), 99–128.

12. A. K. Rogers, "Peoples and Rock Art of the Coso Region," Maturango Museum, March 31, 2016, https://maturango.org/wp-content/uploads/2016/04/RockArt2016 SpecialLectures.pdf.

13. L. Ozawa, "Fort Irwin Working to Ensure Reliable Electrical Power at NTC," US Army, March 7, 2016, https://www.army.mil/article/163658/fort_irwin_working_to _ensure_reliable_electrical_power_at_ntc.

14. M. Collins, *Carrying the Fire: An Astronaut's Journeys* (New York: Cooper Square Press, 1974).

## 05. OF SAGEBRUSH AND SOLITUDE

1. M. K. Anderson, *Tending the Wild: Native American Knowledge and the Management of California's Natural Resources* (Berkeley: University of California Press, 2005), 3–4.

2. D. Eargle, *Native California: An Introductory Guide to the Original Peoples from Earliest to Modern Times* (San Francisco: Trees Company Press, 2008), 271.

3. C. J. Lortie, E. Gruber, A. Filazzola, T. Noble, and M. Westphal, "The Groot Effect: Plant Facilitation and Desert Shrub Regrowth Following Extensive Damage," *Ecology and Evolution* 8, no. 1 (2017): 706–15, https://doi.org/10.1002/ece3.3671.

4. J. W. Cornett, "Why Do Roadrunners Disappear from the Desert Each Winter? This Ecologist Has a Guess," *Desert Magazine*, https://www.desertsun.com/story /desert-magazine/2018/12/03/california-desert-roadrunners-disappear-each-winter -heres-why/2195865002.

5. "Northern Leopard Frog—*Lithobates pipiens*," California Herps, https://california herps.com/frogs/pages/l.pipiens.html.

6. "Death Valley—Geology," National Park Service, updated January 9, 2022, https:// www.nps.gov/deva/learn/nature/geology.htm#.

7. R. Thomas, *Mono Lake Deer Herd Plan*, prepared for the US Forest Service, California Department of Fish and Game, and Bureau of Land Management, 1986, https:// nrm.dfg.ca.gov/FileHandler.ashx/DocumentID=149699.

8. S. Justham, "Restoration Work in Granite Mountains Wilderness," Student Conservation Association, https://www.thesca.org/connect/blog/restoration-work-granite -mountains-wilderness.

9. L. MacNair, *Final Land Management Plan for Indian Joe Springs Ecological Reserve, Inyo County, California*, California Department of Fish and Wildlife, April 2018, file:///C:/Users/Owner/Downloads/IJSER%20LMP%204-2018%20FINAL.pdf.

10. C. Nelson, C. A. Hall Jr., and W. Ernst, "Geologic History of the White-Inyo Range," in *Natural History of the White-Inyo Range, Eastern California*, edited by C. A. Hall Jr., 22–41 (Berkeley: University of California Press, 1991).

11. "ACTION ALERT: Protect Conglomerate Mesa!" California Wilderness Coalition, August 23, 2021, https://www.calwild.org/action-alert-conglomerate-mesa-scoping-august-2021.

12. "Manly Peak," *Summit Post*, https://www.summitpost.org/manly-peak/998154.

13. Friends of the Inyo, *Eastern Sierra Wilderness Guide*, https://friendsoftheinyo.org/wp-content/uploads/2008/01/FOI_WildGuide_final.pdf.

14. "Surprise Canyon Wild & Scenic River," California Wilderness Coalition, https://www.calwild.org/portfolio/fact-sheet-surprise-canyon-wild-scenic-river.

15. "Fossil Preservation—The Nature of Fossil Preservation," National Center for Science Education, September 25, 2008, https://ncse.ngo/fossil-preservation.

16. M. Taylor, "Precambrian Mollusc-Like Fossils from Inyo County, California," *Science* 153, no. 3732 (1966): 198–201, https://doi.org/10.1126/science.153.3732.198.

17. C. Millar and W. Woolfenden, "Sierra Nevada Forests: Where Did They Come From? Where Are They Going? What Does It Mean?" *Transactions of the North American Wildlife and Natural Resources Conference* 64 (1999): 206–36, https://www.fs.usda.gov/treesearch/pubs/24289.

18. P. W. Rundel, R. J. Gustafson, and M. E. Kauffmann, *California Desert Plants: Ecology and Diversity* (Kneeland, CA: Backcountry Press, 2022), 240.

19. M. Davis, "Alerce (Fitzroya Cupressoides) Tree from Chile May Be the Oldest in the World or on Earth," *Science Times*, June 8, 2022, https://www.sciencetimes.com/articles/38098/20220608/alerce-fitzroya-cupressoides-tree-chile-oldest-world-earth-report.htm.

## 06. OF RESILIENCE AND FRAGILITY

1. "Mojave Indian Fact Sheet," Native Languages of the Americas, 1998, http://www.bigorrin.org/mojave_kids.htm.

2. R. McCord, "Fossil History and Evolution of the Gopher Tortoises (genus *Gopherus*)," in *The Sonoran Desert Tortoise: Natural History, Biology, and Conservation*, edited by T. R. Van Devender, 52–66 (Tucson: University of Arizona Press, 2002).

3. B. C. Bolster, ed., *Terrestrial Mammal Species of Special Concern in California*, draft final report prepared by P. V. Brylski, P. W. Collins, E. D. Pierson, W. E. Rainey and T. E. Kucera (Sacramento: California Department of Fish and Game, 1998), https://nrm.dfg.ca.gov/FileHandler.ashx?DocumentID=84523.

4. P. Schoffstall, *Mojave Desert Dictionary* (Barstow, CA: Mojave River Valley Museum, 2010).

5. Congress.gov. "S.32 – 115th Congress (2017-2018): California Desert Protection and Recreation Act of 2018," Section 101.a.70, US Government Publishing Office. Senate Report 115-421, December 6, 2018, https://www.congress.gov/bill/115th-congress/senate-bill/32, https://www.govinfo.gov/content/pkg/CRPT-115srpt421/html/CRPT-115srpt421.htm.

6. P. Stone, "Preliminary Geologic Map of the Black Mountain Area Northeast of Victorville, San Bernardino County, California," US Geological Survey, 2006, https://pubs.usgs.gov/of/2006/1347.

7. K. Penrod, P. Beier, E. Garding, and C. Cabañero, *A Linkage Network for the California Deserts*, produced for the Bureau of Land Management and the Wildlands Conservancy (Fair Oaks, CA: Science and Collaboration for Connected Wildlands, and Flagstaff: Northern Arizona University, 2012), http://www.scwildlands.org/reports/ALinkageNetworkForTheCaliforniaDeserts.pdf.

8. G. C. Dunne, "Geology and Structural Evolution of Old Dad Mountain, Mojave Desert, California," *GSA Bulletin 88* no. 6 (1977): 737-48, https://doi.org/10.1130/0016-7606(1977)88<737:GASEOO>2.0.CO;2.

9. G. Wuether, *California's Wilderness Areas: The Complete Guide*, vol. 2, *The Deserts* (Englewood, CO: Westcliffe, 1998), 175.

10. "Cleghorn Lakes Wilderness," Bureau of Land Management, Barstow Field Office, http://npshistory.com/brochures/blm/ca/cleghorn-lakes-wilderness-2008.pdf.

11. K. A. Howard, K.J.W. McCaffrey, J. L. Wooden, D. A. Foster, and S. E. Shaw, "Jurassic Thrusting of Precambrian Basement over Paleozoic Cover in the Clipper Mountains, Southeastern California," in *Jurassic Magmatism and Tectonics of the North American Cordillera*, edited by D. M. Miller and C. Busby (Boulder, CO: Geological Society of America, 1995), https://doi.org/10.1130/SPE299-p375.

12. A. Gilreath and W. Hildebrandt, "Prehistoric Use of the Coso Volcanic Field," *Contributions of the University of California Archaeological Research Facility 56* (1997): 37, https://escholarship.org/uc/item/51d4w31p.

13. "Smoke Tree," Calscape Taxon report, https://www.calflora.org/app/taxon?crn=6928.

14. "El Paso Mountains Fact Sheet," California Wilderness Coalition, https://www.calwild.org/portfolio/fact-sheet-el-paso-mountains-wilderness.

15. Wuether, *California's Wilderness Areas*, 97.

16. C. A. Ross and F. F. Sabins Jr., "Permian Fusulinids from El Paso Mountains, California," *Journal of Paleontology* 40, no. 1 (1966): 155-61, http://www.jstor.org/stable/1301781.

17. L. D. McFadden, S. G. Wells, W. J. Brown, and Y. Enzel, "Soil Genesis on Beach Ridges of Pluvial Lake Mojave: Implications for Holocene Lacustrine and Eolian Events in the Mojave Desert, Southern California," *CATENA* 19, no. 1: 77-97, https://doi.org/10.1016/0341-8162(92)90018-7.

*18.* J. G. Goodwin, "Lead and Zinc in California," *California Journal of Mines and Geology* 53, nos. 3 and 4 (1957): 644–57, https://catalog.hathitrust.org/Record/000055794.

*19.* R. Lohoefener, *USFS Revised Recovery Plan for the Mojave Population of the Desert Tortoise* (Gopherus agassizii), US Fish and Wildlife Service, 2011, https://ecos.fws .gov/docs/recovery_plan/RRP%20for%20the%20Mojave%20Desert%20Tortoise%20-%20 May%202011_1.pdf.

*20.* K. Kochanski, J. Pershken, and K. Brent, "Deformation in the Paleozoic Stratigraphy of the Piute Mountains in the Mojave Desert Region," MIT Department of Earth, Atmosphere and Planetary Science, May 12, 2014, https://doi.org/10.13140 /RG.2.1.1527.8806.

*21.* "Sheep Hole Mountain Trail," AllTrails, https://www.alltrails.com/explore/trail/us /california/sheep-hole-mountain.

## 07. OF THE REMOTE AND THE RUGGED

*1.* A. A. Schoenherr and J. H. Burk, "Colorado Desert Vegetation," in *Terrestrial Vegetation of California*, 3rd ed., edited by M. Barbour, 657–82 (Berkeley: University of California Press, 2007).

*2.* "Level III and IV Ecoregions of the Continental United States," US Environmental Protection Agency, 2013, https://www.epa.gov/eco-research/level-iii-and-iv -ecoregions-continental-united-states.

*3.* P. Welch, "Cal Fire, Fire Resource and Assessment Program (FRAP), Center for Integrated Spatial Research (CISR)," in *Ecosystems of California*, edited by H. Mooney, E. Zavaleta, and M. Chapin, 837 (Berkeley: University of California Press, 2016).

*4.* "Ecological Sections of California," USDA map, printed in J. Sawyer, T. Keeler-Wolf, and J. Evens, *A Manual of California Vegetation*, 2nd ed. (Sacramento: California Native Plant Society, 2009), inside cover.

*5.* K. R. Beaman, D. D. Beck, and B. M. McGurty, "The Beaded Lizard (*Heloderma horridum*) and Gila Monster (*Heloderma suspectum*): A Bibliography of the Family Helodermatidae," *Smithsonian Herpetological Information Service 136*, 2006, https://www .researchgate.net/publication/241815106_The_Beaded_Lizard_Heloderma_horridum _and_Gila_Monster_Heloderma_suspectum_A_Bibliography_of_the_Family _Helodermatidae.

*6.* J. H. Knapp and M. T. Heizler, "Thermal History of Crystalline Nappes of the Maria Fold and Thrust Belt, West Central Arizona," *Journal of Geophysical Research: Solid Earth 95*, no. B12 (1990): 20049–73, https://doi.org/10.1029/JB095iB12p20049.

*7.* D. Kaspereit, M. Mann, S. Sanyal, B. Rickard, W. Osborn, and J. Hulen, "Updated Conceptual Model and Reserve Estimate for the Salton Sea Geothermal Field, Imperial Valley, California," *GRC Transactions 40* (2016), https://www.researchgate.net/figure /Location-and-tectonic-map-of-the-Salton-Trough-ST-and-its-high-temperature -geothermal_fig1_311766462.

8. "The Chuckwalla Bench, Like Nowhere Else on Earth," Mojave Desert Land Trust, March 19, 2018, https://mojavedesertlandtrust.medium.com/the-chuckwalla-bench-like-nowhere-else-on-earth-d8709b1676ra.

9. K. Clark, D. Brown, and G. M. Harris, "Evaluation of Pronghorn Antelope Habitat in Southeastern California," Proceedings of the 25th Biennial Pronghorn Antelope Workshop, Santa Ana Pueblo, New Mexico, 2012, https://www.researchgate.net/publication/327845502_Evaluation_of_pronghorn_antelope_habitat_in_Southeastern_California.

10. A. Bykerk-Kauffman, "Neogene Sedimentation, Volcanism, and Faulting in the Eastern Coyote Mountains, Salton Trough, Southern California," in *Field Excursions in Southern California: Field Guides to the 2016 GSA Cordilleran Section Meeting*, edited by B. Kraatz, J. S. Lackey, and J. E. Fryxell (Boulder, CO: Geological Society of America, 2017), https://doi.org/10.1130/2017.0045(03).

11. "Peninsula Banded Gecko—*Coleonyx switaki switaki*," Californiaherps.com, https://californiaherps.com/lizards/pages/c.switaki.html.

12. "Important Bird Areas: Imperial National Wildlife Refuge," Audubon Society, https://www.audubon.org/important-bird-areas/imperial-national-wildlife-refuge.

13. R. Powell and K. Watts, "Mineral Resource Potential of the Chuckwalla Mountains Wilderness Study Area (CDCA-348), Riverside County, California," US Geological Survey (USGS), Open-File Report 84-674, 1984, https://doi.org/10.3133/ofr84674.

14. C. W. Epps, V. C. Bleich, J. D. Wehausen, and S. G. Torres, "Status of Bighorn Sheep in California," *Desert Bighorn Council Transactions* 47 (2003): 20–35, https://www.researchgate.net/publication/237571660_Status_of_bighorn_sheep_in_California.

15. Animal Welfare Institute, *Overview of the Management of Wild Horses and Burros*, report presented to the National Academy of Sciences Committee to Review the Management of Wild Horses and Burros, October 2012, https://awionline.org/sites/default/files/uploads/documents/FinalWildHorseandBurroReportWithStateMaps10-26-12.pdf.

16. J. Cornett, "What's Happening to California's Hummingbirds? Rising Temperatures Threaten Their Source of Food," *Desert Magazine*, October 1, 2018, https://www.desertsun.com/story/desert-magazine/2018/10/01/californias-hummingbirds-trouble-heres-how-you-can-help/1488118002.

17. D. Morion, J. Kilburn, and A. Griscom, "Mineral Resources of the Mecca Hills Wilderness Study Area, Riverside County, California," USGS, Bulletin 1710-C, 1988, https://doi.org/10.3133/b1710C.

18. J. Cornett, "You Can Find This Tiny Flower Anywhere," *Desert Sun*, February 17, 2017, https://www.desertsun.com/story/life/home-garden/james-cornett/2017/02/17/can-find-tiny-flower-anywhere/97907966.

19. M. O. Woodburne and D. P. Whistler, "An Early Miocene Oreodont (Merychyinae, Mammalia) from the Orocopia Mountains, Southern California," *Journal of Paleontology* 47, no. 5 (1973): 908–12, https://www.jstor.org/stable/1303071.

20. "Parkinsonia," Calscape, https://calscape.org/loc-california/Parkinsonia(all) /vw-list/np-1.

21. D. S. Bell and T. Herskovits, "A Newly Discovered Large and Significant Population of *Castela emoryi* (Emory's Crucifixion Thorn, Simaroubaceae) in California," *Aliso* 31, no. 1 (2013): 43–47, https://doi.org/10.5642/aliso.20133101.07.

22. K. Penrod, P. Beier, E. Garding, and C. Cabañero, *A Linkage Network for the California Deserts*, produced for the Bureau of Land Management and the Wildlands Conservancy (Fair Oaks, CA: Science and Collaboration for Connected Wildlands, and Flagstaff: Northern Arizona University, 2012), http://www.scwildlands.org/reports/ ALinkageNetworkForTheCaliforniaDeserts.pdf.

23. J. Rebman and M. Simpson, *Checklist of the Vascular Plants of San Diego County*, 4th ed. (San Diego: San Diego Natural History Museum and San Diego State University, 2006).

24. J. I. Mead, T. R. Van Devender, and K. L. Cole, "Late Quaternary Small Mammals from Sonoran Desert Packrat Middens, Arizona and California," *Journal of Mammalogy* 64, no. 1 (1983): 173–80, https://doi.org/10.2307/1380775.

25. R. B. Bury and P. S. Corn, "Have Desert Tortoises Undergone a Long-Term Decline in Abundance?" *Wildlife Society Bulletin* 23, no. 1 (1995): 41–47, https://www .jstor.org/stable/3783192.

## 08. PHILOSOPHIES OF WHAT COMES NEXT

1. "2022 Scoping Plan Documents," California Air Resources Board, 2022, https:// ww2.arb.ca.gov/our-work/programs/ab-32-climate-change-scoping-to plan/2022 -scoping-plan-documents.

2. H. Martinez, "An Evening with the Writers of the Clean Air Act: Insight into the 'Golden Age' of Environmental Law," Columbia Climate School, October 24, 2014, https://news.climate.columbia.edu/2014/10/24/an-evening-with-the-writers-of-the -clean-air-act-insight-into-the-golden-age-of-environmental-law.

3. R. Seager and G. A. Vecchi, "Greenhouse Warming and the 21st Century Hydroclimate of Southwestern North America," *Proceedings of the National Academy of Sciences* 107, no. 50 (2010): 21277–82, https://doi.org/10.1073/pnas.0910856107.

4. S. D. Smith, T. N. Charlet, L. F. Fenstermaker, and B. A. Newingham, "Effects of Global Change on Mojave Desert Ecosystems," in *The Mojave Desert: Ecosystem Processes and Sustainability*, edited by R. H. Webb, L. F. Fenstermaker, J. S. Heaton, D. L. Hughson, E. V. McDonald, and D. M. Miller, 31–56 (Reno: University of Nevada, 2009).

5. National Park Service, "Joshua Trees," https://www.nps.gov/jotr/learn/nature /jtrees.htm.

6. M. L. Brooks, R. A. Minnich, and J. R. Matchett, "Southeastern Deserts Bioregion," in *Fire in California's Ecosystems*, edited by J. W. van Wagtendonk, N. G. Sugihara, S. L. Stephens, A. E. Thode, K. E. Shaffer, and J. A. Fites-Kaufman, 391–414 (Berkeley: University of California Press, 2006).

7. K. M. Van de Water and H. D. Safford, "A Summary of Fire Frequency Estimates for California Vegetation before Euro-American Settlement," *Fire Ecology* 7 (2011): 26–58, https://doi.org/10.4996/fireecology.0703026.

8. R. J. Vogl and L. T. McHargue, "Vegetation of California Fan Palm Oases on the San Andreas Fault," *Ecology* 47, no. 4 (1966): 532–40, https://doi.org/10.2307/1933929.

9. "Dome Fire," National Park Service, https://www.nps.gov/moja/learn/nature/dome-fire.htm.

10. D. E. Busch and S. D. Smith, "Mechanisms Associated with Decline of Woody Species in Riparian Ecosystems of the Southwestern U.S.," *Ecological Monographs* 65, no. 3 (1995): 347–70, https://doi.org/10.2307/2937064.

11. Diagram based on J. C. Stella and J. Bendix, "Multiple Stressors in Riparian Ecosystems," in *Multiple Stressors in River Ecosystems: Status, Impacts and Prospects for the Future*, edited by S. Sabater, A. Elosegi, and R. Ludwig, 81–110 (Amsterdam: Elsevier, 2019), doi.org/10.1016/B978-0-12-811713-2.00005-4.

12. D. J. Germano, G. B. Rathbun, L. R. Saslaw, B. L. Cypher, E. L. Cypher, and L. M. Vredenburgh, "The San Joaquin Desert of California: Ecologically Misunderstood and Overlooked," *Natural Areas Journal* 31, no. 2 (2011): 138–47, https://doi.org/10.3375/043.031.0206.

13. C. J. Lortie, A. Filazzola, R. Kelsey, A. K. Hart, and H. S. Butterfield, "Better Late Than Never: A Synthesis of Strategic Land Retirement and Restoration in California," *Ecosphere* 9, no. 8 (2018), https://doi.org/10.1002/ecs2.2367.

14. J. Laudon and K. Belitz, "Texture and Depositional History of Late Pleistocene-Holocene Alluvium in the Central Part of the Western San Joaquin Valley, California," *Environmental & Engineering Geoscience* 28, no. 1 (1991): 73–88, https://doi.org/10.2113/gseegeosci.xxviii.1.73.

15. "Drainage," California Department of Water, Westlands Water District, https://wwd.ca.gov/resource-management/drainage.

16. T. R. Karl, J. M. Melillo, and T. C. Peterson, eds., *Global Climate Impacts on the United States* (New York: Cambridge University Press, 2009).

17. "Vegetation Distribution Shifts," California Office of Environmental Health Hazard Assessment, 2019, https://oehha.ca.gov/epic/impacts-biological-systems/vegetation-distribution-shifts.

18. K. S. Catania, "The Wall in Focus," *UVM Today*, May 28, 2019, https://www.uvm.edu/news/story/wall-focus.

19. E. Barclay and S. Frostenson, "The Ecological Disaster That Is Trump's Border Wall: A Visual Guide," *Vox*, February 5, 2019, https://www.vox.com/energy-and-environment/2017/4/10/14471304/trump-border-wall-animals.

20. J. Wilson, "These Environmentalists and Outdoors Lovers Support a Border Wall with Mexico," *Desert Sun*, March 15, 2019, https://www.desertsun.com/story/news/environment/2019/03/15/california-environmentalists-support-mexican-border-wall-wildlife-compromise/3105047002.

21. S. Scauzillo, "Victorville-to-Vegas Rail Project Threatens Mountain Lions and Other Animals, Senators Say," *San Gabriel Valley Tribune*, November 5, 2021, https://www.dailybulletin.com/2021/11/05/victorville-to-vegas-rail-project-threatens-mountain-lions-and-other-animals-senators-say.

22. "Science Confirms Cadiz Water Project Would Harm the Largest Spring in Mojave Trails National Monument," National Parks Conservation Association, press release, 2019, https://www.npca.org/articles/1810-science-confirms-cadiz-water-project-would-harm-the-largest-spring-in.

23. L. Beckett, "Joshua Tree's Popularity Is Ruining Life for Longtime Residents: 'You Can't See the Stars Any More,'" *The Guardian*, September 15, 2022, https://www.theguardian.com/us-news/2022/sep/15/joshua-tree-housing-real-estate-gentrification.

24. C. Clarke, "Letter from the Desert: Is Joshua Tree Over?" *Letters from the Desert*, May 4, 2021, https://lettersfromthedesert.substack.com/p/letter-from-the-desert-is-joshua.

25. D. Collins, "Vehicle Collisions with Wildlife Cost California $1 Billion in the Last 5 Years," *Outdoor Life*, November 16, 2021, https://www.outdoorlife.com/conservation/wildlife-vehicle-collisions-in-california.

26. L. Fitzpatrick, "World's Largest Wildlife Crossing Begins Construction in Los Angeles," *Daily Bruin*, July 17, 2022, https://dailybruin.com/2022/07/17/worlds-largest-wildlife-crossing-begins-construction-in-los-angeles.

27. P. Brennan, "Desert Damage: The Dark Side of Solar Power?" Phys.org, March 30, 2009, https://phys.org/news/2009-03-dark-side-solar-power.html.

28. "California Avoids Rolling Blackouts Despite Record Power Demand, but the Brutal Heat Wave Continues," *CBS News*, September 7, 2022, https://www.cbsnews.com/news/california-rolling-blackouts-avoided-record-electricity-demand.

29. "FACT SHEET: President Biden Signs Executive Order Catalyzing America's Clean Energy Economy through Federal Sustainability," The White House, December 08, 2021, https://www.whitehouse.gov/briefing-room/statements-releases/2021/12/08/fact-sheet-president-biden-signs-executive-order-catalyzing-americas-clean-energy-economy-through-federal-sustainability.

30. A. Fisher, "US Authorities Approve 500 MW Solar Project in California Desert," *PV Magazine*, July 19, 2022, https://www.pv-magazine.com/2022/07/19/us-authorities-approve-500-mw-solar-project-in-california-desert.

31. "The Desert Renewable Energy Conservation Plan," Center for Biological Diversity, https://www.biologicaldiversity.org/campaigns/drecp/index.html.

32. "California Solar Energy Statistics and Data," California Energy Commission, https://ww2.energy.ca.gov/almanac/renewables_data/solar/index_cms.php.

33. "Imperial Valley Geothermal Area," Office of Energy Efficiency and Renewable Energy, https://www.energy.gov/eere/geothermal/imperial-valley-geothermal-area.

34. J. M. Randall, S. S. Parker, J. Moore, B. Cohen, L. Crane, B. Christian, D. Cameron, J. B. Mackenzie, K. Klausmeyer, and S. Morrison, Mojave Desert Ecoregional Assessment (San Francisco: Nature Conservancy, 2010), https://www.science forconservation.org/products/mojave-desert-ecoregional-assessment; "Mojave Desert Conservation Value - The Nature Conservancy," https://drecp.databasin.org/datasets /cf4a92f18a2b4a7a8285e09a1b813636/.

35. Protected Areas Database of the United States (PAD-US), US Geological Survey, https://www.arcgis.com/home/item.html.

36. "Open Data," California Natural Resources Agency, 30×30 California, https:// www.californianature.ca.gov/pages/30x30.

37. K. A. Moore and J. M. André, "Rare Plant Diversity in the California Deserts: Priorities for Research and Conservation," *Fremontia* 42, no. 1 (2014): 9–14, https:// cnps.org/wp-content/uploads/2018/03/FremontiaV42.1.pdf.

38. G. Lebuhn, *Field Guide to the Common Bees of California* (Berkeley: University of California Press, 2013), 2.

39. T. Edwards, C. R. Schwalbe, D. E. Swann, and C. S. Goldberg, "Implications of Anthropogenic Landscape Change on Inter-Population Movements of the Desert Tortoise," *Conservation Genetics* 5, no. 4 (2004): 485–99, https://doi.org/10.1023 /B:COGE.0000041031.58192.7c.

40. L. J. Allison and A. M. McLuckie, "Population Trends in Mojave Desert Tortoises (*Gopherus agassizii*)," *Herpetological Conservation and Biology* 13, no. 2 (2018): 433–52, https://www.researchgate.net/publication/327540133_Population_trends_in_Mojave _desert_tortoises_Gopherus_agassizii.

41. "Conservation Designations," Desert Renewable Energy Conservation Plan, https:// www.energy.ca.gov/sites/default/files/2019-12/DRECP_Conservation_Fact_Sheet_ada.pdf.

42. A. L. Fesnock, "Desert Renewable Energy Conservation Plan Update," Mojave Ground Squirrel TAC Meeting, March 5, 2014, https://nrm.dfg.ca.gov/FileHandler .ashx?DocumentID=154659&inline.

43. G. Pitzer, "150 years after John Wesley Powell Ventured down the Colorado River, How Should We Assess His Legacy in the West?" Water Education Foundation, May 23, 2019, https://www.watereducation.org/western-water/150-years-after-john-wesley -powell-ventured-down-colorado-river-how-should-we-assess.

44. M. Reisner, *Cadillac Desert: The American West and Its Disappearing Water* (New York: Penguin, 1986. Revised and updated, 1993), 45.

45. L. A. DeFalco, T. C. Esque, J. M. Kane, and M. B. Nicklas, "Seed Banks in a Degraded Desert Shrubland: Influence on Soil Surface Condition and Harvester Ant Activity on Seed Abundance," *Journal of Arid Environments* 73, no. 10 (2009): 885–93, https://doi.org/10.1016/j.jaridenv.2009.04.017.

46. L. H. Gunderson and C. S. Holling, *Panarchy: Understanding Transformations in Human and Natural Systems* (Washington, DC: Island Press, 2002).

47. K. Penrod, P. Beier, E. Garding, and C. Cabañero, *A Linkage Network for the California Deserts*, produced for the Bureau of Land Management and the Wildlands Conservancy (Fair Oaks, CA: Science and Collaboration for Connected Wildlands, and Flagstaff: Northern Arizona University, 2012), http://www.scwildlands.org/reports /ALinkageNetworkForTheCaliforniaDeserts.pdf.

# SELECTED BIBLIOGRAPHY

The following is a selection of supplemental works, without which *The Deserts of California* would not exist.

Anderson, M. K. *2005. Tending the Wild: Native American Knowledge and the Management of California's Natural Resources*. Berkeley: University of California Press.

Bakker, E., and G. Slack. *1971. An Island Called California: An Ecological Introduction to Its Natural Communities*. Berkeley: University of California Press.

Baldwin, B. G., D. H. Goldman, D. J. Keil, R. Patterson, T. J. Rosatti, and D. H. Wilken, eds. *2012. The Jepson Manual: Vascular Plants of California*. 2nd ed. Berkeley: University of California Press. (The Jepson eFlora, the Jepson Herbarium, University of California, Berkeley, https://ucjeps.berkeley.edu/eflora.)

Barbour, M. G., T. Keeler-Wolf, and A. A. Schoenherr. *2007. Terrestrial Vegetation of California*. 3rd ed. Berkeley: University of California Press.

Barbour, M. G., and J. Major, eds. *1977. Terrestrial Vegetation in California*. Hoboken, NJ: Wiley.

Barbour, M. G., B. Pavlik, F. Drysdale, and S. Lindstrom. *1993. California's Changing Landscapes: Diversity and Conservation of California Vegetation*. Sacramento: California Native Plant Society.

Beck, W. A., and Y. D. Haase. *1974. Historical Atlas of California*. Norman: University of Oklahoma Press.

Behrensmeyer, A. K., J. D. Damuth, W. A. DiMichele, R. Potts, H.-D. Dues, and S. L. Wing. *1992. Terrestrial Ecosystems through Time: Evolutionary Paleoecology of Terrestrial Plants and Animals*. Chicago: University of Chicago Press.

Beidleman, R. G. *2006. California's Frontier Naturalists*. Berkeley: University of California Press.

Berry, W. *2017. The World-Ending Fire*. Berkeley: Counterpoint Press.

Blakey, R. C., and W. D. Ranney. *2018. Ancient Landscapes of Western North America*. Cham, Switzerland: Springer.

California Department of Fish and Game. *2005. California Wildlife: Conservation Challenges: California's Wildlife Action Plan.* Edited by D. Bunn, A. Mummert, M. Hoshovsky, K. Gilardi, and S. Shanks. Davis, CA: UC Davis Wildlife Health Center.

California Department of Fish and Wildlife. *2015. California State Wildlife Action Plan, 2015 Update: A Conservation Legacy for Californians.* Edited by A. G. Gonzales and J. Hoshi. https://www.wildlife.ca.gov/SWAP/Final.

California Interagency Wildlife Task Group. *2005. Habitat Classification Rules: California Wildlife Habitat Relationships System.* California Department of Fish and Game. https://nrm.dfg.ca.gov/FileHandler.ashx?DocumentID=65851&inline.

Carle, D. *2004. Introduction to Water in California.* California Natural History Guides. Berkeley: University of California Press.

Carle, D. *2008. Introduction to Fire in California.* California Natural History Guides. Berkeley: University of California Press.

Carle, D. *2010. Introduction to Earth, Soil, and Land in California.* California Natural History Guides. Berkeley: University of California Press.

Caruthers, W. *1951. Loafing along Death Valley Trails: A Personal Narrative of People and Places.* Ontario, CA: Death Valley Publishing.

Childs, C. *2000. The Secret Knowledge of Water: Discovering the Essence of the American Desert.* New York: Back Bay Books.

Cunningham, L. *2010. A State of Change: Forgotten Landscapes of California.* Berkeley, CA: Heyday.

Darlington, D. *1996. The Mojave: A Portrait of the Definitive American Desert.* New York: Henry Holt.

Dole, J., and B. Rose. *1996. Shrubs and Trees of the Southern California Deserts.* North Hills, CA: Footloose Press.

Durrenberger, R. W., and R. B. Johnson. *1976. California: Patterns on the Land.* California Council for Geographic Education. Palo Alto, CA: Mayfield.

Ehrenreich, B. *2020. Desert Notebooks: A Road Map for the End of Time*. Berkeley, CA: Counterpoint Press.

Faber, P. M., ed. *1997. California's Wild Gardens: A Guide to Favorite Botanical Sites*. Berkeley: University of California Press.

Farmer, J. *2017. Trees in Paradise: The Botanical Conquest of California*. Berkeley, CA: Heyday.

Forest Climate Action Team. *2018. California Forest Carbon Plan: Managing Our Forest Landscapes in a Changing Climate*. Sacramento. https://resources.ca.gov/wp-content /uploads/2018/05/California-Forest-Carbon-Plan-Final-Draft-for-Public-Release -May-2018.pdf.

Fradkin, P. L. *1995. The Seven States of California: A Natural and Human History*. Berkeley: University of California Press.

Gudde, E. G. *1949. California Place Names: The Origin and Etymology of Current Geographical Names*. Berkeley: University of California Press.

Hilty, J. A., A. T. H. Keeley, W. Z. Lidicker, and A. M. Merenlander. *2019. Corridor Ecology: Linking Landscapes for Biodiversity Conservation and Climate Adaptation*. 2nd ed. Washington, DC: Island Press.

Holing, D. *1988. California Wild Lands: A Guide to the Nature Conservancy Preserves*. San Francisco: Chronicle Books.

Holland, V. L., and D. J. Keil. *1987. California Vegetation*. San Luis Obispo: El Corral, California Polytechnic State University.

Hornbeck, D., and P. S. Kane. *1983. California Patterns: A Geographical and Historical Atlas*. Palo Alto, CA: Mayfield.

Hunt, C. *1975. Death Valley: Geology, Ecology, Archaeology*. Berkeley: University of California Press.

Ingram, B. L., and F. Malamud-Roam. *2013. The West without Water: What Past Floods, Droughts, and Other Climatic Cues Tell Us about Tomorrow*. Berkeley: University of California Press.

Irwin, S. *1991. California's Eastern Sierra: A Visitor's Guide*. Los Olivos, CA: Cachuma Press.

Jaeger, E. C. *1940. Desert Wild Flowers*. Stanford, CA: Stanford University Press.

Jenks, M. A. *2011. Plant Nomenclature*. West Lafayette, IN: Department of Horticulture and Landscape Architecture, Purdue University.

Jensen, H. A. *1947. A System for Classifying Vegetation in California*. Sacramento: California Department of Fish and Game.

Johnson, P. C. *1970. Pictorial History of California*. New York: Bonanza.

Kauffman, E. *2003. Atlas of the Biodiversity of California*. Sacramento: State of California, Resources Agency, Department of Fish and Game.

Kauffmann, M. E. *2013. Conifers of the Pacific Slope: A Field Guide to the Conifers of California, Oregon, and Washington*. Kneeland, OR: Backcountry Press.

Kimmerer, R. W. *2013. Braiding Sweetgrass: Indigenous Wisdom, Scientific Knowledge, and the Teachings of Plants*. Minneapolis, MN: Milkweed Editions.

Leopold, A. S. *1985. Wild California: Vanishing Lands, Vanishing Wildlife*. Berkeley: University of California Press.

Lightner, J. *2011. San Diego County Native Plants*. 3rd ed. San Diego: San Diego Flora.

Lindsay, L., and D. Lindsay. *2017. The Anza-Borrego Desert Region: A Guide to the State Park and Adjacent Areas of the Western Colorado Desert*. 6th ed. Berkeley, CA: Wilderness Press.

MacArthur, R. H., and E. O. Wilson. *1967. The Theory of Island Biogeography*. Princeton, NJ: Princeton University Press.

Mayer, K. E., and W. F. Laudenslayer Jr., eds. *1988. A Guide to Wildlife Habitats in California*. Sacramento: California Department of Forestry and Fire Protection. (Updated online as California Department of Fish and Wildlife, "Wildlife Habitats—California Wildlife Habitat Relationships System," https://www.wildlife.ca.gov/Data/CWHR /Wildlife-Habitats.)

McKinney, J., and C. Rae. *1994. Walking the East Mojave: A Visitor's Guide to Mojave National Park.* New York: HarperCollins.

McPhee, J. *1993. Assembling California.* New York: Farrar, Straus and Giroux.

Messinger, L., et al., eds. *2009. Habitats Alive! An Ecological Guide to California's Diverse Habitats.* Cal Alive! Exploring Biodiversity Teachers Resource Guide. El Cerrito: California Institute for Biodiversity, and Claremont, CA: Rancho Santa Ana Botanic Garden.

Miller, C. S., and R. S. Hyslop. *1983. California: The Geography of Diversity.* Mountain View, CA: Mayfield.

Mooney, H., E. Zavaleta, and M. C. Chapin, eds. *2016. Ecosystems of California.* Oakland: University of California Press. http://www.jstor.org/stable/10.1525/j.ctv1xxzp6.

Munz, P. A., and D. D. Keck. *1959. A California Flora.* Berkeley: University of California Press.

Ornduff, R., P. M. Faber, and T. Keeler-Wolf. *2003. Introduction to California Plant Life.* California Natural History Guides. Berkeley: University of California Press.

Pavlik, B. M. *2008. The California Deserts: An Ecological Rediscovery.* Berkeley: University of California Press.

Peterson, B. *1993. California: Vanishing Habitats and Wildlife.* Wilsonville, OR: Beautiful America.

Petrides, G. A., and O. Petrides. *1998. Western Trees.* Peterson Field Guide. New York: Houghton Mifflin.

Phillips, S. J., P. W. Comus, M. A. Dimmitt, and L. M. Brewer, eds. *2015. A Natural History of the Sonoran Desert.* 2nd ed. Berkeley: University of California Press.

Reisner, M. *1986. Cadillac Desert: The American West and Its Disappearing Water.* New York: Penguin.

Rundel, P. W., R. J. Gustafson, and M. E. Kauffmann. *2022. California Desert Plants: Ecology and Diversity.* Kneeland, OR: Backcountry Press.

Sawyer, J. O., T. Keeler-Wolf, and J. Evens. 2009. *A Manual of California Vegetation*. 2nd ed. Sacramento: California Native Plant Society. https://www.cnps.org/vegetation/manual-of-california-vegetation; vegetation.cnps.org.

Schoenherr, A. A. 1992. *A Natural History of California*. Berkeley: University of California Press.

Schoffstall, P. 2010. *Mojave Desert Dictionary*. Barstow, CA: Mojave River Valley Museum.

Schonewald-Cox, C. M., S. M. Chambers, B. MacBryde, and W. L. Thomas, eds. 1983. *Genetics and Conservation: A Reference for Managing Wild Animal and Plant Populations*. Menlo Park, CA: Benjamin/Cummings.

Spencer, W. D., P. Beier, K. Penrod, K. Winters, C. Paulman, H. Rustigian-Romsos, J. Strittholt, M. Parisi, and A. Pettler. 2010. *California Essential Habitat Connectivity Project: A Strategy for Conserving a Connected California*. Prepared for the California Department of Transportation, California Department of Fish and Game, and Federal Highways Administration. https://wildlife.ca.gov/Conservation/Planning/Connectivity/CEHC.

Trafzer, C. E. 2015. *A Chemehuevi Song: The Resilience of a Southern Paiute Tribe*. Seattle: University of Washington Press.

Walker, L. R., and F. H. Landau. 2018. *A Natural History of the Mojave Desert*. Tucson: University of Arizona.

Wallace, D. R. 2011. *Chuckwalla Land: The Riddle of California's Desert*. Berkeley: University of California Press.

Wheat, F. 1999. *California Desert Miracle: The Fight for Desert Parks and Wilderness*. San Diego: Sunbelt.

Wuerthner, G. 1998. *California's Wilderness Areas*, vol. 2., *The Deserts*. Englewood, CA: Westcliffe.

Zwinger, A. H. 1989. *The Mysterious Lands*. New York: Truman Talley Book/Plume.

# ABOUT THE AUTHOR

Obi Kaufmann is the author and illustrator of many best-selling and award-winning books, including *The California Field Atlas*, *The State of Water: Understanding California's Most Important Resource*, *The Forests of California*, and *The Coasts of California*. Obi will be wrapping up his Field Atlas series with *The State of Fire: Understanding How, Where, and Why California Burns*. On a constant speaking tour, Obi can be found regularly addressing issues of conservation and resilience to a wide range of groups and communities across California and beyond. Obi hosts the *Place and Purpose* podcast with Greg Sarris, which can be found at www.placeandpurpose.live, and posts regularly on Instagram @coyotethunder. His speaking tour dates are available at www.californiafieldatlas.com, and his essays are posted at www.coyoteandthunder.com.